INDIAN ODYSSEY

For Kay
My dearest friend
of many years
Chas Kuhrman

INDIAN ODYSSEY

Char Rutman

MCP - Maitland - FL

Mill City Press, Inc.
2301 Lucien Way #415
Maitland, FL 32751
407·339·4217
www.millcitypublishing.com

ISBN-13: 978-1-63505-369-2
LCCN: 2016915272

Printed in the United States of America

DEDICATION

I dedicate this book to my grandchildren:

Ashley

Justin

Kaitlin

Brianna

Lauren

Michael

Phoebe

To you, my darlings, whom I love. This was written in India when you were very young, You hardly knew me because I lived so far away and came back to visit only briefly. Never think for a moment that you were ever far from my heart and soul. You are my legacy. I am so proud of all of you. I hope this book will help you to know and understand your paternal grandmother and see her in a kindly light. I too lived, dreamed, hoped, and loved. May God bless you and give you beautiful lives, full of love and peace.

PROLOGUE

She sat still, gazing out of the porthole of the plane flying at 37,000 feet. She saw nothing really of the sky brightening in the east with the first rays of the sun, nor the light cloud covering of the earth below. A flight attendant asked if she wanted breakfast. Turning, she smiled and shook her head.

Her journey had begun. Or had it begun last winter when another plane had taken her to the land she loved and yearned for, the land which gave her joy and peace? It was autumn now, and she was on her way once again to that same land to make it her home. Where was she going to live in that country, that foreign, exotic landmass called India? She didn't know. What was she going to do there? People had asked her. She had no answers.

Two large overweight pieces of luggage in the underbelly of the 747, a heavy carry-on bag in the bin over her head, and herself. What was left of herself, that is, after months of divesting a familiar, comfortable way of life that no longer had meaning. It necessitated leaving behind a family of sons, daughters-in-laws and grandchildren. Also the few close, really close friends who knew her, loved her, cared about her and what happened to her. These were the treasures she held in her heart and could take with her wherever she went. They were not weights; only precious, jewel-like feathers sparkling in her otherwise bruised and damaged soul.

A darkness held her in its grip, a deep physical exhaustion, a mental shut-down, an emotional chaos. Her mind could not perceive beyond the moment. She moved, spoke, reacted normally to outside stimuli, but her inner self had no life, no feeling, no pulse. There was no pain, no joy, no anticipation, just a sea of emptiness.

There was a history, of course, that had brought her to this point in time, but she wasn't thinking now, nor remembering. Her mind was a blank and her actions automatic. She had traveled enough to know what was expected of a passenger changing planes in an international hub, so she went through the motions of following signs and arrows, eventually going through another security screen and finding her flight number on a monitor showing the gate and time of departure.

Perhaps it was for her own good that she was asked to change seats so that another passenger could sit with his friend. She was forced to deal with a man in the adjoining seat, alternately drinking heavily and snoring loudly. In his wakeful moments, he began to get overly friendly. She had to pull away from him often as he proceeded to stroke her bare arm and several times took her arm to hold her hand in his.. She was annoyed to a certain extent, but never feeling threatened, she did not complain to the flight attendants. He was a silly, obnoxious individual who insisted on calling her 'Darling'. Having to be constantly on her guard against this man's advances, kept her mind alert for nine hours, which helped her upon landing to function normally while going through immigration.

It was very hot and she began to perspire long before her luggage came along the moving trolley. Foolishly she decided against using a luggage cart and with the strap of her shoulder bag sliding down one arm, she pulled three pieces of luggage, one piggy-backed on another and constantly falling off, out of the terminal. No one came to help her. She was met by a sea of faces, hands and arms waving placards with names of people and various tours. She dragged her suitcases out as far as a curb, beyond the semi-circle of dark faces and dark hair. Dropping her belongings, she stood silently, patiently, watching, waiting, waiting, waiting…..

CHAPTER ONE
FIRST LOVES

After five long years of yearning, praying and hoping, she finally made it to the altar. Well, not to an altar, to a Justice of the Peace. Bran would never marry her before a priest, he had told her. Never would he agree to have his children raised as Catholic.

Catherine had fallen in love with this man in 1954. She was an RN at her home hospital working in the Operating Room as a scrub and circulating nurse. Bran was an MD in anesthesia training. Ancker Hospital was one of four hospitals on his rotation. At the outset he seemed arrogant and distant. She disliked him and felt insulted the way he looked condescendingly at the nurses. 'Who does he think he is?' she thought.

Eventually, as each took their respective turns on the surgical and anesthesia calls, they began to see more of each other, especially if they had an entire weekend where they had to work together. Conversation sprung up naturally and she soon discovered this man had more to him than an MD. She had found most doctors boring people, who knew nothing but medicine, which dominated their conversation.

This man, Brandon Forrest, talked about music, classical music. They discussed opera, and she corrected him a couple of times because she knew more of opera than he did. He laughed at her, not believing her, but the following day he would apologize. Obviously, he had researched and found that she was correct after all.

Catherine was finding this man exciting. That he was extremely intelligent was very obvious. He talked about the books he had read; deep philosophical treatises. He also spoke of wanting to travel and see the world; that in itself a great mind expanding experience. Little by little she started to fall in love. She was 22 and the time was ripe. No one to that date had ever interested her or excited her. She had had only a couple boy friends in the past few years, none she would ever consider seriously, and didn't even enjoy going out with them. But it was what was expected of her.

"How else are you going to find a man to marry?" her exasperated mother would ask.

Her parents were gregarious, her mother more so than her father. They had so many friends and were always planning parties or evenings out with them at least once a week. Her mother and father loved each other; she could always see that. Each came first with the other. Then Grandma Tanner, who came next in their concern because she lived with them, and at first, demanded absolute respect and obedience. Then in her later years, became totally dependent on them. The house was next in priority for Catherine's mother. She had her duties specifically outlined for each day and kept to them no matter what else occurred. That was the fashion of the day. It seemed to Catherine and her sister, Cindy, that the two of them came in fourth on their mother's list, although in all honesty, their mother would never have believed that or recognized that is how her daughters felt growing up.

"Get your nose out of that book," her mother would say to Catherine. "Get outside and play. Do something!"

Catherine loved to read and never seemed to be allowed enough time for it. She was also an incurable romantic, and made up love stories, acting them out in the quiet of the night, carrying on imaginary conversations with the beloved. She would also act out, in her imagination, the heroine of the story she was reading at the time, always adding her own dialogue and becoming that person. Hugging her pillow as her lover, she would fall asleep.

As a child and into young adulthood, Catherine was timid and extremely shy, so it was in this imaginary world where she lived that she felt like a real person, an interesting person, and a person someone wanted to know and eventually love passionately and forever.

At the age of eight, she became entranced by the sound of music. Her Aunt Agnes played piano and organ. Catherine wanted a piano, and her Grandmother Tanner bought one for her. She studied with her aunt for one year never realizing that she couldn't read notes. She had a great memory that fooled everyone. It wasn't until she studied at the Conservatory with the Sisters of St. Joseph that she began reading music. At this time she was forced into periodic recitals. She hated them. She was afraid of being in the spotlight, and always felt extremely nervous and upset, and consequently never did well at them. Her aunt decided she needed better training and suggested, after three years at the Conservatory, that she study with Professor Hinderer.

By this time, Catherine was almost ready for high school. She had discovered she had a voice, a beautiful clear soprano voice. She wanted to sing. She wanted to stop the piano and pursue voice training.

"No," said her mother. "You have talent as a pianist. You will continue to study the piano."

"But, Mom, listen to my voice. I love singing."

"Singers are a dime a dozen. Just keep up your piano."

Catherine practiced an hour and a half every day, but never progressed. She knew what her mother did not, that her talent was in her voice. The more she sang, accompanying herself to some degree, the more glorious the voice became. Catherine would sit on the back steps at night and sing, listening to the beautiful sounds returning to her. It gave her joy.

Angela, Catherine's cousin and elder by eight years, was singing, studying voice, and beginning to have major roles on the stage in St. Paul's Civic Opera Company. Mother would take Catherine to the performances at the Auditorium, and all Catherine thought was, "I could do that. I have a better voice than Angie." But Mother was adamant.

"Angie is the singer. You're the pianist," her mother would say.

Angie even was able to go to Juilliard one summer. She came back feeling that she didn't have the talent to be a professional. Mother's resolve not to give Catherine voice lessons was strengthened. "See, singers are a dime a dozen."

After seven years of piano study, Catherine was finally allowed to quit. She hated the piano by that time, practiced very little, and her mother must have realized it was a waste of money giving her more lessons. But she was not allowed to study voice. That was an absolute, "No." Catherine felt crushed when her mother advised the mother of Catherine's friend, Pat Hoolihan, to send her daughter to a well-known singer/coach in St. Paul. Pat had a good, strong, clear soprano voice, but Catherine knew her own to be as good, if not better than Pat's, although at the time, Catherine's voice was in the mezzo range, rather than soprano.

Pat used to say, "Cathy, I'll sing. You accompany me." Pat never knew how much that hurt Catherine, because Catherine wanted to sing, needed to sing, and was bursting with a gift as yet unrecognized by anyone but herself.

Perhaps because her parents were products of the depression years, they continually pressured Catherine to take courses in high school that would prepare her for the world. Her father didn't believe in college for girls, so what was she to do? It also became increasingly evident to her parents that Catherine would be a spinster, an 'old maid'. She was not vivacious. She was not interested in dating. "Why aren't you more like your sister?" her mother would ask. "Why can't you just go out and have a good time? You don't have to marry him. Just go out," she would say in exasperation.

Catherine didn't care to spend an evening with someone she felt no attraction for and end up having to 'neck' with him. Cindy, on the other hand, was six years her junior and dated anyone with pants. Her hormones were raging and she became pregnant at the age of 18 and had to get married.

What was open to Catherine career-wise? Her parents wanted to send her to business school to learn typing, shorthand and bookkeeping. Catherine cringed at the thought. "It was good enough for your mother. It is good enough for you," her father would tell her. "You have to have something to sustain yourself through life. How else are you going to live?" And before Cindy got pregnant, "We don't worry about your sister. She'll get married and have a man to take care of her. We worry about you. You will have no one. You have got to make a living for yourself."

Catherine was only a teenager when those words were spoken to her. Already her parents had given up on her and thought she had no potential for a full life. What options were open to her? Teaching? Not only wouldn't her father send her to college, she was so shy and scared of people, she knew that was not the career for her. What she really wanted to do was study English Literature and write, and of course, study voice. Her parents said, "No" to that again because they thought she would not find a job to support herself with that kind of background.

Her parents did not see the value of a college education. Her mother had been taken out of high school by her mother after only six weeks, and sent to business school so that she could begin earning money and bring it home. Catherine's father had finished high school and had taken an evening course in accounting at the age of 30. So both parents felt a high school education was a great accomplishment and certainly sufficient for any girl.

Nursing was the last option open to Catherine. She hated science. She loved the arts. But nursing was all that was open to her, and she had enough self-knowledge to realize that perhaps while she was helping people, sick people, she would learn confidence in her training and come out of the shell of timidity that had built up around her all those years.

"Nursing?" her father cried incredulously. "No, absolutely not. You'll be washing floors and bedpans for the rest of your life." Obviously her father was not knowledgeable regarding the modern duties of a nurse. He finally allowed her to work vacations as a nurses' aide during two years of high school, but insisted that she spend the summer after graduation in a business office. She did as she was told, but having no business skills, could only do the boring work of filing

Catherine entered the three year nursing program at Ancker Hospital in the fall of 1949. The Sisters of St. Joseph's Academy, where she had gone to high school, were incensed that she did not enroll at their hospital. But Catherine had had twelve years of schooling under those nuns, and felt it was enough. She was of German descent and those of Irish descent were always favored before her. She was sensitive and extremely hurt by many incidents particularly in high school, where she was passed over, especially in Glee Club, in favor of someone with less talent, but was of Irish descent.

When Catherine started looking for a school of nursing, she found one in St. Cloud, not far from the Twin Cities, run by the Benedictine Sisters. She had her transcript sent there, but was refused entry. That was a shock because although her grades were not excellent, she was a good average student and should not have had difficulty being accepted. Her parents drove her to St. Cloud to have an interview with the sister in charge of admissions.

"We do not want your daughter in our school," Sister said, very sternly.

"But why?" asked Catherine's mother.

"She is not cut out to be a nurse. She would have a nervous breakdown within six months."

"A nervous breakdown? But that's just not so. She has been a nurses' aide for two summers and loves the work. She is an average student."

"You would be wasting your money." Sister replied.

"We are willing to take that chance."

"Mrs. Tanner, we do not want your daughter in our school."

Angela was dating a doctor who advised her, "Catherine, apply at Ancker. It is a city-county hospital, and you will never get better training anywhere." It was good advice. Catherine applied, but when she asked for another transcript of her grades to be sent to Ancker, the nuns were indignant.

"Secretaries get paid for this service. We already sent a transcript to another school of nursing. How many times are we supposed to do this?"

Mother sent a note with one dollar. "Please send Catherine's transcript to Ancker Hospital School of Nursing. Enclosed is one dollar for secretarial fee."

Catherine was accepted with no questions. When she had her interview with the Director of Nursing, she asked, "Was there any problem with my grades?"

"No, not at all, Miss Tanner. You are an average student and should do well here. We do not accept D's as passing marks, but I see no problem for you."

"Thank you."

Catherine now knew she had been black-listed by the Josephites to the Benedictines. She felt bitter at the injustice, but determined she would do well at Ancker and become the best nurse she could be. Catherine was unaware at this time that she had been blessed. It was the very best place for training. The experience she attained there stood her in good stead wherever she went in the future. She cared for knife wounds, gunshot wounds, mutilating accident cases, victims of beatings, as well as the normal medical, surgical, obstetrical and gynecological, geriatrics, pediatrics, and communicable diseases. She cared for wards of twenty to forty men or women in one morning. There was also a psychiatric department with barred and locked rooms for the seriously ill cases. Ancker Hospital was a TB sanitarium as well. Lung resections were performed several times a week. This became Catherine's specialty. She loved the operating room and enjoyed, most of all, chest and abdominal surgery.

Catherine came out of her shell of intense shyness, but in the end, after three years of training, she wound up in the operating room where all her patients were asleep. She found she was more comfortable working in close relationship with only a few nurses. Her dealings with temperamental surgeons became challenging at times, but because she knew her field and was confident of her expertise, she didn't take verbal abuse from any of them.

What a delightful change then when she met and became friends with Dr. Brandon Forrest. But from the very beginning she noticed how he hated Catholics. He would look out of one of the operating theater windows at the beautiful Cathedral of St. Paul on the highest point of the city and remark, "Someone should bomb that place." And she, as a Catholic, felt very sad. Why the hatred? Then he professed to be an agnostic, who believed in no organized religion. She learned much later that he was Jewish, and although he did not follow the tenets of his faith, he keenly felt his Jewish heritage and had a great animosity toward Christians after the holocaust of World War II in Germany and occupied countries.

No one took a stand for the Jews and especially the Pope, Pius XII, did nothing, and said nothing, to condemn the evil that spread throughout Europe, destroying six million Jews in the death camps. So his was a valid disdain, even hatred, for all things that stood for Christian honor and integrity.

Despite the way he spoke against her faith, Catherine was drawn to him and started to fall in love with him. However, he never said or did anything to encourage her. He actually asked another surgical nurse to go on a date with him, but she was seriously dating someone else and turned him down.

Catherine and Bran had talked about Figaro, the opera character in THE MARRIAGE OF FIGARO and THE BARBER OF SEVILLE, and when the Metropolitan Opera Company came to Minneapolis on tour and offered the former, Catherie bought tickets for it and sent him one anonymously.

She was so excited to be having a sort of date with him, enjoying an opera they had shared views about, and now to be seeing and hearing it together. Catherine dressed carefully, hoping to look especially nice because he had never seen her in anything but surgical scrubs, caps and masks. She waited until it was nearly curtain time, then found her way to her seat, only to find another man sitting in the seat that was to have been Bran's. He had given the ticket to a friend of his. Catherine did her best to enjoy the opera, but the evening was ruined and she was heartbroken.

The following day at the hospital, she saw him working, but said nothing regarding the opera ticket. He finally brought up the subject himself.

"You know," he said, "Someone sent me an opera ticket for last night."

"Really?" she replied. "And why didn't you go?"

"How did you know I didn't go?"

She just looked at him and shook her head.

"You know that young man that sat next to you?"

"What about him?"

"He said you didn't talk to him."

"Why should I? I didn't know him."

"Well, I'm sorry. I didn't know what to do. I figured you had sent it, but I owed this fellow a favor and I thought he'd enjoy going."

"Fine. I hope he did. I paid a lot of money for that ticket. It was a very good seat."

This incident alone should have been a warning sign to her, but she was very inexperienced in the mating game. What pulled her heart strings the most was the way he put children to sleep. He had a very good rapport with them and while he had them entranced by his stories, they drifted off to sleep without any fright or panic. That was probably the one thing that convinced her that this was a man to have children with.

But he finished his tour of duty at Ancker without ever asking her out. She left with another OR nurse to work and live in San Francisco. While there, she received her first communication from him. He was in the army and stationed at Fort Sam Houston, about to be shipped overseas. He was lonely, and decided to correspond. She finally received mail from Munich, where he was stationed for two years. At first he was excited to be traveling to Europe and looked forward eagerly to viewing a part of the world he had only read about. Soon came his disillusionment and in the two years he was there, only five letters arrived.

In the meantime, Catherine found work at Mt. Zion, a private Jewish hospital in San Francisco. She and her friend, Shanna, had a lovely third floor apartment on the top of Russian Hill. They earned very little, as the pay scale for nurses was very low at that time. But Catherine managed to rent a piano and began voice lessons with Hans Froehlic, a Viennese voice coach. He gave her two lessons a week, and called her whenever he had a cancellation so she could have another lesson for free. This gave her great joy. She was at last studying voice and enjoying it. However, Mr. Froehlich was a coach primarily, and he didn't give her the basics that she needed, but she was unaware of it at the time. Just to be singing, learning repertoire, and singing in other languages besides English was a great experience.

After a couple of months, a classmate of Shanna's who was already living in San Francisco, moved into their apartment. And Catherine's friend, Ellie, from St. Paul, came to San Francisco. Shanna and her classmate became roommates, and Catherine and Ellie found another apartment in North Beach which was cheaper than the one on Russian Hill, and it was on the ground floor and very close to a bus line. They could see Alcatraz from their living room window.

Through Shanna's friend, Catherine had met a very nice young man by the name of Ed. He was a merchant marine sailor and was out of port most of the time. However, when he was in San Francisco, he would take Catherine to all the best restaurants, and introduced her to many seafood delicacies. On her meager salary, paying for rent and voice lessons, there was never money left over for dining out. This was a great treat for her and she enjoyed his company. After dinner they would take taxis to bars, and sometimes stay for the floor show if there was one. He treated Catherine with the greatest respect, and seemed eager only for her company. Never once did he so much as hold her hand or show affection until one night he kissed her. It was so unexpected; he apologized profusely and it never happened again. This man was not a homosexual. Catherine was aware that he frequented houses of prostitution. He told her he didn't believe in permanent relationships because of the type of work he did, at sea most of the time. So he was careful not to involve Catherine's heart and she respected him as he did her. It was a comfortable arrangement, and it broadened Catherine's life in San Francisco.

After only nine months in California, Catherine was persuaded by Ellie to return to Minnesota and enroll at the University. Catherine realized the wisdom of this, but she loved San Francisco and shed tears upon leaving. She promised herself to come back one day, but she never returned as a resident. Of course this interrupted her voice study with Hans Froehlich, but they were to continue their friendship for many years until his death in Vienna in 1991.

At the University, Catherine enrolled as a freshman, an English Literature major and Voice minor. She went back to work full time night duty at Ancker Hospital and lived at home with her parents. It was a grueling schedule. After work she had to change buses in downtown St. Paul and ride for one and one half hours before getting to the University. Often she fell asleep and awoke far past her stop and would have to walk back. She was required to carry a full load of 15 credits, so her study load plus 8 hours of work at the hospital gave her little time for study and sleep.

Then her parents learned she was an English major instead of Nursing.

"What do you think you are doing?" her father yelled. "We thought you were getting a degree in nursing."

"No, I want to study English and music. I am tired of nursing. I don't like the work anymore."

"That is stupid. Get your nursing degree."

"No, I don't want any more science. I hate science."

"Then quit school and get back to work."

"I am working."

"Well, we aren't going to help you anymore. You will pay board and room here."

Catherine did not quit school. She gave up her position at Ancker and took a very low paying one at the University Blood Bank. She moved out of her parent's home and found a one room efficiency apartment with a fellow music student, Laurie Peters.

About this time Catherine fell in love again. Eddie was a violinist and a music student. Catherine hadn't heard from Brandon in almost a year. And here was this young, talented boy, four years her junior and very immature. But she became extremely attracted to him, and he to her apparently. A relationship developed, but it did not last. He liked the opposite sex and there seemed to be no end of them in his life.

Her parents played a role in this also. As much as they wanted her to date and find a man to marry, they despised Eddie because he was a musician. They were rude to him when Catherine brought him home, barely speaking to him and wearing faces of extreme disapproval.

"What are you doing wasting your time with him?" her father asked her. "He's a lousy musician, a hop-head. He'll never amount to anything. And he's too young for you."

Her mother came to her room one evening, and got into bed with her

"Are you sleeping with him, Catherine?" she asked.

"Of course not, Mother."

"I'm glad to hear it because once you have sex, you can't live without it. You'll become a street walker."

Catherine was 24 years old then and her mother had no right to ask her such a personal question, let alone tell her such an absolute fabrication. Could her mother actually have believed that? The implication was, of course, that Catherine would never marry and be fulfilled in that way.

But of course Catherine was having sex with Eddie, not very good sex because first of all, it was her first experience and her hymen was so tight, he was afraid of hurting her. After many frustrating sessions together, he slid his finger into her vagina and gently broke and spread the hymen. She bled and it hurt, but she was grateful to him for his consideration and gentleness. She was on fire for him always, but could never reach an orgasm. She had many feelings of guilt and fear of pregnancy as well because no protection was ever used. Finally, he labeled her 'Frigid' and moved on to someone else. Her heart was broken because she really loved this boy.

Just for the record, Eddie was no 'hop-head'. He was a fine musician, a wonderful violinist and became a concert master of the Metropolitan Opera Company Orchestra in New York.

This period at the University was difficult for Catherine. She had little money and the expenses of voice lessons were high. She tried for a scholarship, and her audition was excellent. Her father told her he'd show her how to fill out the application. She trusted him and although she had some reservation, he assured her this was how she should answer the questions. She was denied the scholarship due to 'lack of financial need.'

She was flabbergasted. She lived in one room with a roommate. She had no money. She ate no breakfast or lunch. Cookies and fruit juice at the blood bank sustained her until she was off duty and stopped for one hamburger on the way home in the evening. Catherine lost so much weight that her ribs were visible through her skin. When she sang, her whole body shook. Her voice teacher became alarmed. He said, "Catherine, your voice is bigger than your frame. You have to do something."

What a fantastic teacher she had found in Mr. Roy Schuessler. He was head of the music department and normally took only voice majors as his students. Catherine did not have him the first two quarters of school. She had a woman teacher who sang with her and Catherine felt she was learning nothing from her. At her final exam, singing in front of all the voice teachers in the department, she forgot her words, and was sure she had failed the exam. Instead she was given an A. Frustrated, Catherine went to see Mr. Schuessler.

"Mr. Schuessler, I don't understand why I was given an A. I don't deserve it. I don't feel I learned anything this quarter from my teacher. She sings with me all the time, and I don't know what I'm supposed to be learning. And I flubbed my exam."

"Well," he said, "You stumbled over words, but you have a beautiful voice. Do you want to study with me?"

"Yes, yes, I really want to, but I'm only a voice minor."

"That's all right. I will take you."

For Catherine this began the most rewarding time of her life. She studied with Roy Schuessler that spring quarter. He was as pleased as she was with her progress and at the end of the quarter, he asked her to continue with the lessons over the summer. She was delighted.

"Catherine," he said, "You have a fine natural voice, but I think that over the years, you have acquired some habits that are inhibiting you from your full potential. I would like to try something with your voice over the summer. Will you trust me?"

"Of course. What are you going to do?"

"All summer I want you to sing as you would as a little girl, very breathy, and soft. It won't sound good to you, but the results will be astounding."

During that entire summer she sang as he instructed her, and learned breath control she never knew existed. One day he told her to open and sing naturally the vocal exercises he recommended. She was amazed. Her whole top had opened up to this pure high soprano she had never heard before. He was as delighted as she.

"There," he said, "That's it. That's it. That is what was missing. I knew it was there, but you covered it up so well with the natural ability you had. But just listen to what you have now. You have the rich tones of a mezzo, but also the brilliance of a lyric soprano. Your range is great. I want you to audition for the Met this fall."

"For the Met? Really? Do you think that I am that good?"

"Yes, Catherine. You have the voice. Now we will work on what you will sing for the audition."

Finally, she had to quit her other studies at the University. Her health was suffering from lack of food and lack of sleep. She could go on no longer without serious effects, and Mr. Schuessler agreed to take her as a private student.

Her parents were delighted that she quit. "It's good that you came to your senses. Now you can go back to work at Ancker and make money again. And it's all right if you want to do this singing as a side line."

Catherine moved back home and again went to work in the operating room.

When the auditions came up, Mr. Schuessler told her, "Don't emote on the stage. Your voice will do it all. I'm one of the judges, but I'll not be able to judge you."

This was a regional audition including five states and Canada. It was held at Northrup Auditorium, which was a big barn of a place with poor acoustics. Catherine sang an aria from

CAVALLERIA RUSTICANA and felt that it went very well. Afterwards, back stage, a woman judge approached her.

"Miss", she said, "I am not supposed to be talking to you or any of the contestants, but I must tell you that I was very impressed with your voice. However, you need to show some expression if you are selected to go to finals."

Before the end of the day, Charlotte was informed that she was a finalist and was to sing for Kurt Adler of the Met. She did not contact Mr. Schuessler for she assumed he was aware of the outcome. Also, she didn't think to inform him of what the woman had advised her regarding her lack of expression. He had told her to let her voice do it all, and that is what she planned to do.

The following day she repeated the aria she had sung from CAVALLERIA RUSTICANA and Kurt Adler asked her to sing another. She chose 'Dove Sono' from Mozart's, THE MARRIAGE OF FIGARO. Catherine was one of eleven finalists out of almost two hundred singers. She did not place first, second, nor third. The coloratura who won first place approached Catherine afterwards.

"You were the one I was afraid of," she said. "You have a gorgeous voice." And she went on to win the national competition as well.

Catherine's critique from Kurt Adler was that her voice was small and that she had no stage presence. Roy Schuessler was angry. "What does he mean by "small" voice? You have a big voice, but in that barn it got lost. He is used to hearing Wagnerian singers. And I'm sorry, Catherine. It was my fault telling you not to worry about stage presence. I wish you had called after that judge talked to you back stage. I could have worked with you before you sang for Adler."

"It's all right, Mr. Schuessler. I was thrilled to have had the experience. I am happy that I went as far as I did."

"Catherine, your age is against you. You should have started studying earlier. What I would suggest is that you go to New

York and sing wherever you can. There are countless opportunities there and you need to get experience. You have the voice. Go, do something with it."

She thought about this exciting possibility. She would be able to find a position as a nurse in New Your City, but it would be scary going alone and always looking for places to sing. Did she have the personality for this? She was still shy to a great extent. Would she have what it took to be assertive in the 'Big Apple'?

When she talked to her mother about it, her mother laughed at her.

"You in New York? That's ridiculous. You remember what Angie said after being at Juilliard. Singers are a dime a dozen."

"But, Mother, Mr. Schuessler told me to do this."

"I don't believe it."

"You think I'm lying?" she asked incredulously. "Then call him and ask him yourself."

The following day her mother told her she had spoken to Schuessler.

"He never said that he thought you should go to New York. He said you had a nice voice and there were no guarantees. Just forget all this nonsense and concentrate on your nursing. You have to make a living."

The auditions had ended her voice study with Roy Schuessler, and she acquiesced to her parents' wishes. She believed they had her best interests at heart, and perhaps they were afraid for her, knowing her lack of assertiveness. She sang for herself and for many of her friends' weddings.

CHAPTER TWO
BRANDON

Catherine decided one day to find out what had become of Brandon Forrest. He had to be out of the Army now and living in Duluth. She made plans to take a bus there, check into a hotel and call him. When she asked her father to take her to the bus station, he said, "Absolutely not. I'll not be a party to your making a fool of yourself. You haven't heard from him in a year. He doesn't want you."

Determined to follow her own instincts, she took a taxi to the bus station, and went to Duluth. Over and over she read the letters he had sent her, all five of them, to give her the courage to follow through with this plan of hers.

At the hotel she called the operating room at St. Luke's Hospital to get his phone number. She was put on hold and they never came back. No matter what she did, she could not break the connection. Finally she hung up and waited. Then she remembered his mother's name was Levine, and found it in the phone book. She chose one of them and dialed. She was nervous and shaking by this time. But wonder of wonders, he answered the phone.

"How are you, Brandon?"

"Who is this?"

"Catherine."

"Catherine? Catherine, who?"

She nearly hung up. She was mortified.

"You don't remember me, Brandon?"

"Catherine Tanner?"

"Yes."

"Long time, no see. What are you doing here?"

"Oh, it has to do with a New Year's resolution. I had to come to Duluth, so I thought I'd call and see if you had returned from the army."

"Well, can I see you? Are you free for dinner tonight?"

"Yes."

"Where are you?"

"At the Hotel Duluth."

"I'll pick you up at 6:00 then. OK?"

"OK. I'll be ready."

He picked her up and they went to dinner. Afterwards they saw a movie. He brought her back to the hotel, but dropped her at the entrance. He did not kiss her. The following morning she found her way on foot to a Catholic church as it was a Sunday. When she returned, the phone was ringing.

"Hello?"

"Where have you been? I've been calling you for over an hour."

"I went to church."

"Oh!" (Pause) "Do you feel better now?"

"I feel fine."

"Are you busy this afternoon?"

"No."

"Can I pick you up around 2:00?"

"That would be nice. See you then."

He drove her all over Duluth, showing her the sights of the lovely port city. Duluth was built on hills at the western tip of Lake Superior. It was a city of hills, not unlike San Francisco, but a small town, a homey sort of town. Many fine mansions graced Duluth because at one time there were more millionaires per capita than anywhere else in the United States. Forestry, mining and railroads were the big industries at one time due to the lush virgin forests of the north woods and the rich iron ore from the open pit mines of the Mesabi and Cayuna ranges.

Catherine was delighted with the spectacular views of the harbor along the skyline drive above the city. At the opening of the canal into the Duluth harbor was a lift bridge, the only one of its kind in the United States. Cars and buses traveled over it to reach Minnesota Point, known as 'Park Point'. It was a narrow spit of land forming a natural barrier between the lake and the bay. Park Point was all sand, but many houses were built there, most on slabs with no basements, and the property was expensive. The US Coast Guard was stationed on the bay side and there were numerous marinas filled with sailboats and motor boats. The season was short for boating, but Duluthians made the most of their summers.

In the years to come, the city cultivated the tourist trade by developing the area around the lift bridge and naming it, 'Canal Park'. An excellent marine museum stood beside the Lake Superior Engineering Building. A restaurant known as 'Grandma's' catered to the young and old alike with hundreds of antiques hanging from the ceiling and adorning the walls in a very rustic atmosphere. Grandma's became world famous for the marathon races that were held every spring. The starting line was at the town of Two Harbors, 26 miles up the North Shore and ending at Grandma's. Despite its attractive location, no more industries filled the vacancy left by the depleted forests and the stripped mines of top grade ore. There was still some forestry, but not to the extent it once was, and the ore mined now was made into taconite pellets.

When the St. Lawrence Seaway opened, Duluth became the western-most port for the shipping of grain to all parts of the world. Her harbor was filled during the summer and autumn seasons. Often there were ocean-going vessels anchored outside the canal awaiting berthing places at the grain terminals. It was always thrilling to hear a vessel touting its signal to the bridge, the bridge answering back, and an acknowledgment again from the ship. The bridge then rose to allow the vessel to enter the canal. Many tourists and Duluthians alike flocked to the canal to watch as ships entered and left the Duluth harbor. It was an exciting event each time.

Lake Superior was as large as an inland sea and great storms pounded its shores. Many ships have been lost on her, the most famous being the *Edmund Fitzgerald,* which turned over and broke in half, all hands lost. In the winter the lake froze over and all shipping was at a standstill until the Coast Guard cut paths through the ice in the spring. The lake was a great equalizer. Its water was extremely cold, too cold for swimming, so it became a natural air-conditioner for the residents of the city during the hot summer months. The opposite was true in the winter. As cold as the water was, the frigid air that arrived via the 'Canadian Clipper' was colder still, and when it hit the lake, the lake steamed–a fantastic sight every early winter. Winds off the lake kept the city warmer during this time. This phenomenon often resulted in twenty degree differences between the lake shore to the top and over the hill.

After a day of sight-seeing, Catherine and Brandon enjoyed another dinner and a movie. She finally admitted that she had made a New Year's resolution to find out about him, and had come to Duluth only for that purpose. A few kisses were exchanged and he dropped her at the hotel. She left the following morning pleased that the weekend had gone so well.

The next week she wrote to thank him for the hospitality shown to her and he wrote asking why he hadn't heard from her yet. Their letters had crossed in the mail. He wrote too that he planned to be in St. Paul the following month on his way back from Chicago where he was to take his oral boards in anesthesia. The Met was in town again and he bought tickets for them to see *Eugene Onegin.* Her parents were out of town, but she invited him to stay at her home anyway. He never made advances to her and remained the perfect gentleman. The evening was a disappointment. Neither of them enjoyed the opera, and he had even bought her the record album of the opera.

They talked a lot and it was decided that she give up her job at Ancker, move to Duluth and work at St. Mary's Hospital. He didn't want her at St. Luke's where he worked. She would get an apartment and they would date and get to know one another.

She had no problem getting a position in surgery at St. Mary's. Her experience in the field was extensive, and no operating room would turn down her application. Leaving Ancker was to be for the last time, she decided. All her co-workers knew she was now going to Duluth to be near Dr. Forrest. They gave her a great send-off. How many had they given her? Quite a few!

Having obtained the position at St. Mary's, she proceeded to go to Duluth over a weekend to find an apartment. Brandon insisted she stay at his home, which proved disastrous

First, she developed German measles, and Bran insisted she stay in bed and had his mother bring her meals on a tray. That evening he came to her room to talk.

"Cathy, we know what we want. Why wait? Let's get married now."

"What? But I came here so we could get better acquainted."

"We already know each other. Why waste time? Tomorrow call St. Mary's and tell them you don't want the job. We'll get an apartment at Mt. Royal and live there."

"Bran, are you sure about this?"

"Yes. Just call St. Mary's tomorrow. You can't work after we are married."

When she awoke the next morning, the house was silent. She went down to the kitchen. Mrs. Levine was not there. She was nowhere in the house. Catherine did not feel right about fixing anything to eat, so she waited for her hostess to return. It was Monday and she was able to phone the hospital and find the employment office open. She thanked them for the position they had given her in surgery, but told them a 'change of plans' necessitated her withdrawing from the position. They expressed their regret.

Mrs. Levine never returned. Catherine sat all day in the house. She never ate, but waited for Bran to get home from work. She waited and waited. It got dark and still no one came. Finally around 8:00 PM Bran arrived.

"Where is everyone? Why are you so late?" she asked.

"You have to leave," he said.

"What do you mean?"

"You can't stay in Duluth. You have to go back to St. Paul."

"I don't understand."

"My mother is at my sister's house. The family is very upset. They don't want me to marry you. You are a Catholic."

"But your brother is married to a gentile."

"She isn't Catholic. No, I cannot marry you. It's all off. I can't do this to my family, to my mother. She has been at Evelyn's all day crying."

"Bran, this is your life. You are 36 years old, for God's sake. You can't make your own decision about this?"

"I have made it. You have to go back to St. Paul."

It was too late to take a bus, so she told him to take her to the YWCA. When she arrived, there had been a call to find out if she was staying there. She called her parents and learned they had not called, so she knew that his family was checking to see if she had left. She asked her dad to pick her up at the bus station the next day.

It was raining the following morning when she boarded the bus. Her tears mingled with the rain as she sat dejectedly for the 4 hour ride. What was she to do now? Go back to Ancker? How could she? Everyone knew she had gone to Duluth because she was in love with Dr. Forrest. How could she face them and tell them he didn't want her? God! She'd have to find employment elsewhere. But she couldn't face that now. All she could do was feel the pain of rejection and a broken heart.

"What happened?" her father asked. "Did you find an apartment?"

"No, no apartment. We were going to get married."

"Get married?" he said incredulously.

"Well, that was Sunday night. He told me to call St. Mary's and cancel my job, so I did yesterday morning."

"Then, what?"

"He changed his mind, or his family changed it for him. He's a Jew and they don't want him to marry a Catholic, even though I told him I'd marry him in a civil ceremony."

"You'd give up your religion?"

"Well, for the time being. I think he would have come around eventually and allowed me to practice my faith."

"This is crazy, Catherine. What do you want with a man who doesn't respect you enough to care about your feelings, your beliefs?"

"Well, it's all moot. He doesn't want me. He sent me home. Now I have no job, and I can't go back to Ancker."

"Catherine," her mother said, "Call St. Mary's. They called you this morning."

"I don't understand. I withdrew from that position."

"Well, it wouldn't hurt to see what they want. Call them."

"OK."

St. Mary's asked Catherine to please reconsider and take the position as operating room nurse. They needed her. She immediately took this as a sign that God wanted her to go back to Duluth.

"Very well. I accept. I will come for orientation and I will need to find an apartment."

"We have lists of apartments near the hospital that are available."

So Catherine went back to Duluth, and found a furnished apartment two blocks down the hill from St. Mary's. Her parents moved her things up and she settled in and began work in the operating room. About a week later she called St. Luke's Operating Room. She asked for Dr. Forrest.

"Hello."

"Hello, Brandon."

"Oh, hello. Where are you?"

"Here in Duluth."

"Oh, NO! I told everyone you left."

"I did leave, but you don't have to tell anyone I returned. St. Mary's called me in St. Paul and asked me to reconsider working here and since I didn't have another job, I took this one."

"Oh, where are you staying?"

She gave him the address. "It's only two blocks from the hospital, so it's very convenient, especially when I'm 'on call'.

"Look, Bran. I just thought I'd let you know that I am in town. You don't have to see me."

That afternoon he came to her apartment with a small TV. "I feel responsible for you," he said.

"You're not responsible for me. I couldn't go back to Ancker. They knew I was coming here because of you. I had no job and St. Mary's wanted me, so here I am. Thank you for the TV, but that wasn't necessary."

"I want you to have one."

That was the beginning of nine months of waiting. He'd call and he'd stop by the apartment. They finally became intimate, but Catherine wondered if it would ever lead anywhere. He told her not to mention his name at St. Mary's. No one was to know that they knew each other. Not only did he not want his family to know she was in town and he was seeing her, but he wanted none of his co-workers to know either. Occasionally when she would be in his car, he would recognize someone driving in the opposite direction, and he would tell her to duck down below the dashboard so no one would see her. After about two months, he surprised her by taking her to his brother Everett's house. Everett and Tyne had some idea she was in town because his mother would call there looking for him and they hadn't seen him. One day when she was visiting at Everett's with Bran, his mother and step-father stopped by. Catherine hid in the basement for over an hour. This kind of subterfuge went on for nine months. Not only that, but often she didn't hear from him for many days. She would call Tyne and find out that he had been there, but obviously he wasn't anxious to be with her.

Catherine had expected Bran one Friday evening. He never called to say he wasn't coming. He just never showed up. The next morning he was pounding at her door at 7:00. His sister had arranged for him to meet a Jewish girl from Minneapolis. The family had decided to introduce him to one of their own if he wanted to get married. He could not say, "No" to his family, so he went out with his sister and her husband and another couple who had brought the young woman to Duluth. They had dinner, and Bran had to pick up the tab. That did not make him happy.

All the sign posts were there, but Catherine ignored them. She was in love, and foolishly thought she could change him. He never once told her he loved her. He never once said she was pretty, or attractive, and certainly he never told her she was beautiful.

Brandon had not passed his oral board exams in Chicago, so he planned to take them again the following spring in Arizona. Bran could not decide whether or not to marry. He never asked Catherine to be his wife. He discussed it with his brother and then decided he probably should marry because his mother no longer wanted the responsibility of making his meals, doing his laundry and cleaning his room. She told him it was time he found an apartment and moved out.

"So," he told her one evening, "We may as well get married. My mother wants me out of the house and I have to take my orals in April, so we could get married before then and go to Arizona on our honeymoon and at the same time, I can take my board exams. What do you think?"

"Yes," she said, "But what about your family?"

"I won't tell them. Just Ev and Tyne. But no church wedding. I won't sign my kids away as Catholics and I can't handle some big wedding. It must be private. Not your parents here either."

"That's no problem. They wouldn't come if I'm being married in a civil ceremony."

"You'd better give notice at St. Mary's. Doctors' wives do not work. But you can't tell anyone who you are marrying. I don't want anyone to know. They would tease me at St. Luke's. I can't handle that."

"All right."

Catherine wrote to her parents and her father replied, "Are you sure you want to marry this man? He seems not to care about your feelings and beliefs. You are making all the concessions. You are giving up your religion for him. How can you do that? And does he really want to be married? He may feel like a bird in a cage and someday want his freedom."

She gave notice at the hospital, and told them she was getting married. They wanted to know to whom, but she did not tell them, only that she was being married in a civil ceremony. Another OR nurse was getting married around the same time. The staff gave her a party with gifts. Catherine got nothing because it was against Catholic belief to shower anyone who was marrying out of the Church.

Catherine had no engagement ring because Brandon didn't believe in diamonds and wouldn't even think of buying one for her. Catherine went shopping for wedding bands and chose both one for herself and one for Bran. She bought them and had them engraved with the date of their wedding.

She also shopped for a wedding dress, but of course it couldn't be a real wedding gown. She did find a lovely brown lace on beige which looked beautiful on her. She already had her fine china and sterling, but had to buy pots, pans, everyday dishes and linens enough to start her home.

Just a week before they were married, they went to apply for a license. When it appeared in the Duluth newspaper, his mother saw it. That is how she learned of her son's plans.

"What are my friends going to say?" she asked him.

"I don't care what your friends say," he told her. "I don't want to discuss it."

It was the 21st of March, a chilly night. Everett, Tyne and Marlene, their teenage daughter, accompanied Brandon and Catherine to a Justice of the Peace out on the highway in Hermantown, a township of Duluth. Catherine had made the appointment and had no idea where they were going. When they drove up to the address, they found a Quonset hut, a sad and sorry looking home. Catherine walked through mud with her beautiful new shoes to get to the door. She had no flowers, not even a corsage. The ceremony was basic, brief and lasted only three minutes. All parties signed the papers and it was done. Brandon never even kissed his bride.

In the car on the way to a restaurant, Catherine started to cry. It was nothing like she had dreamed about all of her years growing up. There was no romance and certainly no beauty. When he saw Catherine crying, Bran told her, "The ceremony means nothing. It is the life afterwards that counts."

Marlene told her parents later that no way would she ever get married like that. She wanted a real wedding when her time came. They took a few photos at the restaurant and then after dinner went to a motel on the lake shore.

Catherine had made those reservations also because Bran was too embarrassed to do so. She dressed in an expensive filmy white nightgown and negligee and waited eagerly for him to comment on her appearance. He never told her how beautiful she looked. His greatest concern was the dryness of the motel and spent the whole night soaking towels to give moisture to the room.

In the morning she went back to her apartment and he went to his mother's house. He refused to stay with her in that apartment because it wasn't good enough for a doctor. When he saw their names on the door, he made her take them off. He wanted no one to think that he lived there.

Catherine had announcements printed and sent to all the relatives on his side as well as hers, and to friends of hers and her parents as well. For many years, she had given showers and had been in eight weddings, mostly as maid-of-honor. It was her turn to receive, but she got nothing. Even those friends who were not Catholic conveniently ignored the announcement. Her parents were deluged by phone calls from their friends. "Why didn't you stop this?" they asked. "You should not have allowed her to be married out of the Church." Her Aunt Agnes took it upon herself to call all the out-of-town relatives and caution them not to send Catherine gifts. However, the St. Louis relations loved Catherine and they sent her a beautiful tablecloth. A couple others on her side sent token gifts

Bran's step-brother had a furniture store in Superior, Wisconsin. He gave them letters of introduction to wholesale furniture houses in Minneapolis.

Just a week after they were married, they drove to the Twin Cities, stayed at Catherine's parent's home and went to look for furniture. They had no place to live in Duluth yet, and Bran told her on the way down, "Look, this is the only time I'm coming down here. We have to get all the furniture this weekend. And don't think you are going to change furniture every year. This is going to last us a lifetime, so be sure you know what you want."

It proved to be a most stressful weekend for Catherine. She had no idea in what price range she was to choose from. Bran had never told her his financial status or wage scale. She had no idea how much money he had. She did know that he seemed to think "blond" furniture was the style to buy. But she knew that "blond" was a fashion of the time and it would become outdated. She insisted on a natural wood and Bran went along with this decision. It wasn't too difficult to choose all the case furniture. But when it came to the stuffed furniture, it was another matter. Catherine had no idea what colors or fabrics to choose, but Bran was insistent that she make a choice. She saw nothing she liked and the saleswoman got angry with her.

"Why don't you like this sofa? It is $1000."

"I'm sorry, but I don't like it."

Bran was angry with her also and she was in tears. "I'm not coming down here again, I told you," he warned her. "I hate it down here. So make up your mind."

Finally, he called Byron, who gave him the name of another wholesale house. There Catherine found styles that she liked and ordered the specific pieces in good fabrics that she thought would complete their living room.

The next thing they had to do was to find an apartment to accommodate all the furniture they had bought. They rented an upstairs duplex, and lived there for nine months until they bought a house.

The honeymoon was a three day affair. Catherine had chosen a lovely hotel in Scottsdale, and anticipated a romantic interlude of at least a week. Bran was all consumed with his exams, which took up two whole mornings. They went sightseeing in the afternoons in their rental car. After the exams, Bran wanted to return home immediately so that he could find out if he had passed his boards. The honeymoon was nothing like Catherine had anticipated. There was no romance, only the constant worry over exams. She needed to be held, cherished, and loved. There was none of that. Bran had insisted on twin beds. They had sex, but when Catherine asked for it more than once a day, he told her he was too old. He was 37, she 27.

CHAPTER THREE
SUNIL

It had been four years since Catherine had been to India. She had not been able to leave her mother for longer than a weekend, so a month long visit to a country across the world was not an option. Mother was 94 and although she lived alone in her apartment, she was dependent on Catherine. Every day except Sunday, a hot meal was delivered to her so that she didn't have to cook and she would have a balanced diet. Catherine knew that the service of Meals on Wheels did not deliver the tastiest of food, so she found another service near her home that prepared meals for the elderly. The only problem was that she had to pick it up and take it to her mother every day. However, this forced her to see her mother and check up on how she was faring. Catherine also did shopping for her, and took her to various doctor and dental appointments as well as to the beauty shop every week. Catherine did not feel burdened. It was simply something she had to do, and she did it willingly.

There was another responsibility that she had also. A friend, Helen, was elderly and lived alone in her apartment. Helen had no family, but a third cousin, who was attentive to her, but couldn't take on the full responsibility of her. Catherine was one of four friends who helped Helen in her last years. She bathed her twice a week and took her to her doctor appointments. Helen was always invited to the Forrest home on holidays. Catherine loved Helen and didn't want her to be alone. Helen was always afraid of Catherine's trips to India. She could never understand why she wanted to go there. One day Helen fell in her apartment, injured her leg and had to be hospitalized. After that she was taken to a nursing home to recover, but developed heart failure and died. Lovingly, she left each of her friends a sum of money.

Catherine put her share in the bank and planned to use it for a future trip to India. When her sister, Cindy, retired in the spring of 1996, she asked Catherine what she could do to help her. Immediately, Catherine said, "Come, take care of Mother so that I can go to India." Cindy agreed.

Cindy wanted to take Mother to Oregon so she wouldn't have to stay in Duluth for a whole month, but Catherine thought it would be too hard on Mother to travel again. Plans were set then for Cindy to fly to Duluth and Catherine would go to India in January of the New Year.

One day in December, Cousin Joe called Catherine. In the course of their conversation, Joe made a statement that startled her.

"Your mother is really looking forward to her trip."

"Trip? What trip are you talking about, Joe?"

"To Cindy's. When I called her on her birthday, she told me she was going to Portland while you are in India."

"Really? Well, this is the first I've heard about it."

"Do you mean that this is all her imagination?"

"No, I don't think so. I think plans have been made behind my back, because I don't approve of her traveling at her age. She is so fragile, Joe. The last time she returned from Portland, I was afraid for her. She was gray with fatigue and it took her a month to recover."

Catherine was deeply upset that her sister would pull this subterfuge on her. During her next phone conversation with Cindy, she brought up the subject.

"I understand," she said, "from Joe Angeletti, that you are taking our mother to Oregon when I go to India. When did you plan to tell me? Or weren't you going to?"

"Oh, Catherine, I didn't know how to tell you. I knew you'd be mad. But I can't come for a whole month to Duluth. I have no one to take care of my dog. And the last time I talked to Bran, he said I couldn't bring Mac to Duluth. He didn't want my dog in your house."

"Of course not. Even though our Topaz is gone, Mac would smell her scent all over the house, and leave his scent as well. I can't have that. But why didn't you tell me about Mother, and why didn't she say something to me?"

"I told her not to because we were afraid of how you would react."

"Well, I have to tell you, it is a slap in the face to hear it from a cousin I hardly ever hear from, instead of from my mother and my sister."

"I'm sorry. I just didn't know how to tell you. But I will come and get her, and I will also bring her back. I plan to have wheelchairs at all the airports, so she shouldn't be too tired. And traveling with me, she won't have any worry about changing planes. It will be entirely my responsibility."

"OK, if that is what you want, Cindy. You and she made the decision, so you handle it. I just wish you had let me in on the plans so I didn't have to play the fool when Joe called."

"I'm sorry."

"Yes, well, it's all decided then. When are you coming?"

Cindy gave her the details of her forthcoming trip to Duluth prior to Christmas, and the times and dates of her return from Oregon with their mother. Catherine thought it significant that she was returning Mother two days after Catherine's return. Obviously, Cindy didn't plan to have Mother any longer than was necessary.

The plans were in motion. Sunil had faxed Catherine with the final outline of her tour, and she was at last satisfied. Christmas had to be dealt with before she could even think of India. The entire family was coming and there was so much preparation she had to make. She looked forward to their holiday, however, and always it was wonderful having the whole family together. Every Christmas Catherine spent hundreds of dollars on her children and grandchildren. This year was no exception. She probably spent more than ever before but Christmas Eve of 1996 was a memorable one, and she had no regrets. Let Bran rant and rave afterward when the bills started to come in. She didn't care. This was her family, and she wanted to make the occasion very special.

Another celebration was scheduled between Christmas and New Years. That was the annual Gilbert and Sullivan party which Catherine always hosted. It was a 'pot luck' supper, and she never told anyone what to bring. There was always more than enough food and plenty of wine and spirits. The house was gaily decorated for the holidays and with all her friends of some thirty years or more, she looked forward to this occasion. Bran never joined the party. But it didn't matter, because her friends understood. They loved coming to her house and after all the good food and drink, there was music; Christmas carols and of course, Gilbert and Sullivan. But this party was held only a few days before Catherine was about to leave for India. By the time the celebrations were over and she had dismantled the tree and put away all the decorations, she was exhausted.

When at last the trip was upon her, she no longer wanted to go. She seemed to be going through all the motions of packing, but there was no anticipation as there had been in years before. What was the matter? She didn't stop to analyze it. The holidays had been wonderful, but she was in deep depression. Probably she had been so before the holidays and the let down in the aftermath was now taking hold.

She thought about India, and couldn't get excited. "I will go," she said to herself. "I will go to India, but it will be my last trip there. I will then come home and wait for my mother to die and Bran to die, and then, please, God, let me die. I have nothing left to live for. There is no joy left in my life. I am only existing, and I don't want to live anymore. I am old, ugly and fat. My diabetes is out of control and I couldn't care less. I want to die." It was with that attitude that she packed her bags and left Duluth on January 6, 1997. She flew to Minneapolis and then to Amsterdam. After a few hours, she boarded her plane for Delhi.

It was a nine hour flight from Europe to India, and already she had been traveling for almost twelve hours.

As she waited in line for her turn in Customs and Immigration, she watched to see which line was moving the fastest, but all seemed to be going about the same speed, which was SLOW. She dragged her carry-on bag along and had her passport and entry card in hand. The officers at the desks were all business; looking at the passports, then at the passenger, stamping the passports and motioning for them to move on. No one smiled. No one talked. When her turn came, she moved up to the desk and presented her passport and card. The officer took one look at her, and with a big smile, said, "Oh, madam, you don't look at all tired. You look HAPPY!" Catherie was flabbergasted. But immediately she responded, "Of course I'm happy. I'm back in India."

Her mind and body didn't know it, but her spirit did, and there must have been something in her eyes or her demeanor that betrayed her innermost feelings that not even she was aware of. After retrieving her luggage and stacking it on a baggage trolley, she rolled out of the terminal to a sea of faces. Sunil found her, called to her, and pointed to where he would meet her. Finally, in the Ambassador car driven by a member of his office staff, she relaxed. She was in India, with her Indian son, about to take on a journey that had been planned and arranged, so all she had to do was to follow the itinerary and just enjoy.

Of course, the start of this tour couldn't begin until a proper greeting was given to Sunil's mother and wife. They drove to Chittaranjan Park, which is a Bengali neighborhood, and where Sunil's father had built a house. Papa had died almost a year ago and left the house to Sunil except for the one large room in the back, which had been Papa's. He left that for Tapa, Sunil's unmarried sister.

It was almost two o'clock in the morning when they arrived at the heavily locked house. A padlock was on the outer gate, for which Sunil had the key. Then they knocked and waited for the door to be opened from the inside. Mama opened for them and they went inside. It was terribly late and Catherine always felt badly arriving at such an hour and disturbing the household. She found both Mama and Tapa sleeping in the living room, which was something new, as they had always before had their bed in the dining room. Catherine quickly set her purse down and went to embrace them.

"I'm so very sorry to hear about Papa," she told them. And both Mama and Tapa started to cry. They just nodded and said nothing, just cried. Mama understood some English, and probably could speak some also, but she never tried. Tapa was fluent in English, but now she said nothing to Catherine. Sunil came in with the luggage and motioned for her to come upstairs. When she was able to extricate herself, she bid them goodnight and followed Sunil to his quarters above.

Sunil opened the roof door and went to his and Mita's quarters. There he knocked loudly for her to wake up and open the doubly locked door to their room. She opened, and looked out at Catherine with sleep-blurred eyes.

"Hello, Mom," she said. "Come in."

"Mita, darling, it's so good to see you. How are you?"

"I'm fine. Are you hungry?"

"No, Darling. I had food on the plane."

Sunil put Catherine's luggage down and out of the way. He picked up his son from the bed, and said, "Goodnight. See you in the morning then." Mita double-locked the door behind him, and waited for Catherine to get undressed and ready for bed.

Mita arose every morning at 5:30 to make breakfast, get Piku ready for school, wash clothes and hang them on the line outside, start vegetables for dinner, shower and dress for work and be out of the house by 8:30. She worked very hard and took it all in her stride. This is the way of life for most Indian women.

Catherine was tired, but not sleepy, and Mita wanted to talk. They lay in bed together and Mita started to unburden herself. The situation was becoming intolerable for her.

"Mom," she started, "ever since Papa died, it is bad here. You see I have my own kitchen now. Mama and Tapa eat separate."

"Why? What happened, Mita?"

"Papa left house to Sunil. Just his room he left for Tapa. When Papa died, everyone very sad. Sunil asked Sujeet and family to come live here. And then, Deepa and her husband with Sonu came. All slept downstairs, women with women, men with men."

"What?" Catherine cried incredulously. "Do you mean you didn't sleep with your husband?"

Mita gave a little laugh. "No, Mom."

"But that's crazy"

"Then I told Sunil, Piku and I come upstairs. I told him he could stay with family, but Piku and I go upstairs. Sunil came with us. Then Tapa got angry. She is angry because Papa left house to Sunil. She doesn't talk to me and tells the neighbors stories about me. Now they don't talk to me."

"My, God, Mita. This is terrible."

"I told Sunil I cook up here, not with Tapa and Mama. Tapa threw Sujeet out of house."

"Why?

"I don't know. She got angry at him. So Sunil bought him a house."

"Mita, this is incredible."

"Yes, Mom, and she won't let him come back even to visit Mama. She got mad at Deepa too, and threw them out."

"But, Mita, Papa left the house to Sunil. Why is Tapa doing all the deciding? Why doesn't Sunil put a stop to all this?"

"I don't know, Mom."

"What does Mama say?"

"Mama is very weak. She listens to Tapa. She won't listen to Sunil anymore."

"Sunil used to be Mama's favorite. He told me that years ago. Tapa is poisoning her mind against her other children."

"Yes, Mom. Mama cries all the time. She thinks only Tapa cares about her. No one is welcome here, Mom. My family cannot come. I must go to them when I want to see them."

"Oh, darling, I'm so sorry. This is so hard for you, and not good for your son. I must speak to Sunil. This cannot go on."

"But, Mom, Tapa tried to commit suicide."

"What? How?"

"She tried to hang herself in the dining room."

"Who stopped her?"

"Sunil and Sujeet were here."

"I see. That's very interesting."

"Mom, do you know the last time you were here?"

"Yes, four years ago."

"Mom, Sunil and I wanted you here. Tapa and Mama did not want you."

"Oh, Mita, I knew something was going on. I felt it as soon as I arrived. Sunil and Deepa took me to that awful house for the night. When Deepa picked me up the next morning, and brought me here, I felt so unwelcome. She left me in the living room and went to the back and closed the door. I could hear loud voices arguing. When Sunil came downstairs, I told him to take me to a hotel. He refused. Then I think he told you to fix me breakfast and I didn't want that. I just wanted to leave."

"Yes, Mom. He told me to make you breakfast and I had no time. I had to go to work. But I wanted you here, Mom. Both Sunil and I wanted you."

"Then I remember Papa coming out from the back and said he didn't know I was there. I told him I was going to a hotel, but he insisted that I stay five days. I was so uncomfortable. Then Tapa came in and told me that the family was upset because of some trouble of Sunil's at the office. She said Sunil told Deepa to explain it to the family, and that's what all the upset was about. That it had nothing to do with me."

"No, Mom. They didn't want you, but Papa said you must stay. Mom, I made all your food. They didn't do anything for you."

"Oh, Mita. I'm so sorry.

"No, Mom. We wanted you."

"Then I got sick. I got chilled in that boarding house where I stayed that first night. I remember coughing and coughing and running a fever. And then, Sonu and Piku got my cold and you had to have a doctor for Piku. I was here for ten days, not five. I wanted Sunil to send me by train to Trivandrum, because there was an Indian Airlines strike. He refused because he said it would take too many hours and I was not well enough. Finally, Tapa, you and Sunil put me on a train for Bombay. Do you remember?"

"Yes, Mom."

"Darling, we have to get some sleep now. We'll talk about this more tomorrow."

With that the two women drifted off, to be awakened by the alarm at 5:30. Another busy day began for Mita.

"Mom, today Sunil has car for us. We will go to change your money, then Sunil will go to work and you and me go to pick up Piku at his school. It's a very good school, Mom. Best in Delhi. It is Christian Brother's school, St. Columba's."

"St. Columba's?" Catherine gaped at Mita, then gave her a big smile.

"Mita, that was the name of the school I went to, kindergarten through eighth grade."

"We were so lucky to get Piku in there, Mom. He is so shy and they only take so many children from other parts of Delhi. They want children mostly from that area."

"I see. It is also Catholic, not Hindu."

"Most boys are Catholic."

"Of course. Only a small percentage then is open to boys of another religion. You are happy then with the school? Is Piku doing well?"

"Oh, yes, Mom. He is doing very well. And school is very good."

"Good. I'm anxious to see it. It will be fun to surprise Piku and pick him up."

Piku was Udayan's baby name. He was a bright little five year old, just three months younger than Catherine's oldest grandchild. Piku had the huge dark brown eyes and long lashes of his mama, but he mostly resembled his father. He was shy of Catherine and never spoke out loud, whispering to his parents whenever he wanted to say something.

Later that morning the Ambassador car came to Sunil's house and the three of them left for the American Express office so that Catherine could exchange her traveler's checks into rupees. After that the car was totally Catherine's and Mita's. They drove first to Connaught Place where Catherine wanted to shop. She wanted to buy Mita a sari, but nothing seemed to appeal to Mita, and Catherine finally bought a lovely black sari for herself. Then she found a sandalwood elephant for a friend back home who had an elephant collection.

At last it was time to go to Piku's school. It was a large complex, and dominated by a huge cathedral. Mita asked Catherine if she would like to go in. Catherine readily said, "Yes."

It was a Wednesday, and every week on that day in Duluth, Catherine visited a small chapel at St. Mary's Star of The Sea. It was an Adoration Chapel, where the Blessed Sacrament was exposed 24 hours a day. When Mita and Catherine entered the cathedral, Catherine noticed immediately that there was Exposition of the Sacrament, and she felt very blessed that she was able to spend time on this day with the Lord. After kneeling and praying for a while, she tried to explain to Mita, first about the meaning of the exposition and then how every Wednesday she prayed before the Sacrament, but somehow she knew she wasn't getting through to her. There was too much of a culture and religious gap.

Leaving the cathedral, they proceeded to a gate and entered the grounds of the school. A few men were standing talking, and Mita went up to one who apparently was the driver for Piku's bus. She explained that we would be taking him home with us. As their conversation continued, Catheine watched as crowds of little boys exited the school buildings. All were in uniform, and as she scanned them, they all looked alike to her. Suddenly, she looked down, and there was Piku standing in front of her, looking up at her. She hugged him and then Mita joined them and they left for home in the Ambassador.

That evening, Mita told Catherine that Deepa was downstairs waiting to talk to her. Catherine eagerly went down to see and greet her. They embraced and soon Mita brought them tea.

"Deepa," Catherine said, "Mita and I are going to the fair this evening. Wouldn't you like to come with us?"

"Oh, yes. I'd like to go. When are you going?"

"Soon. I just want to change into a sari. Mita has given me one of hers and I'm anxious to wear it."

They drank their tea, then Catherine excused herself.

"Deepa, I'll just be a few minutes. Please wait."

"Oh, yes, Mom. I will wait."

Catherine climbed the stairs to Mita and Sunil's room. Mita was getting dressed. "Deepa is coming with us. I asked her to wait."

"OK, Mom. Here let me help you. You wear your saris too short. They must cover your feet."

"But, Mita, I don't want to step on it and pull it out of my waist."

"You won't, Mom. See, that is much better," she said, as she stood a short distance away and looked at her appraisingly. After putting on the appropriate jewelry, Catherine took her leave of Mita and went downstairs.

As she entered the living room, she saw that Deepa was not there. She heard talking in the back, so she followed the sound and came upon Mama and Tapa looking at photos.

"Oh, Mom, you look beautiful," Tapa said.

"Thank you, but where is Deepa?"

"Deepa? She went home. She had things to do."

"Tapa, she did not have 'things to do'. She was waiting for me to get dressed."

Tapa looked guilty and at first didn't know how to answer, then she said,

"Ask Sunil." At that moment Catherine heard him come in the front door. She went to meet him.

"Sunil, where is Deepa?"

"She had a pain in her arm, so I took her home."

"Sunil, that simply is not true. We were going to the fair together and she was waiting for me to get dressed. She wouldn't have left without telling me. Now, what happened here while I was upstairs?"

"Tapa was angry to find her here, and Deepa left so there wouldn't be any trouble."

"Sunil, this is simply inexcusable. We'll talk about this later."

Mita, Sunil, Piku and Catherine left the house and walked to the tent where the fair was to be held, only to find out there was no fair. It was a meeting of sorts, and certainly nothing of interest to the four of them. They continued to walk then and proceeded to the temple where Sunil and Mita made preparations for the anniversary of Papa's death.

"Sunil, I want to talk about what happened this evening. What right has Tapa to tell Deepa to leave YOUR house?

"She doesn't have the right, but she gets angry and everyone is upset. Deepa left so there wouldn't be an argument."

"Sunil, it is YOUR house. Why don't you tell Tapa it is none of her business who comes to the house? She has the back room that was Papa's. She can keep anyone out of there that she wants, but the rest of the house is yours. Why don't you stand up to her?"

"Mom, do you know what she tried to do?"

"Oh, do you the mean the suicide thing?"

"Mita told you?"

"Yes, she told me."

"I don't know what to do. She could try it again."

"Sunil, what exactly did she do?"

"She tried to hang herself."

"Ah huh. And who was home at the time?"

"Me and my brother."

"Sunil that was a power-play. She is very smart. She had no intention of killing herself. If she did, she would have done it when no one was there. Believe me, if she ever threatens to do so again, just tell her to go ahead but wait until no one is home. I guarantee she won't do it. She's far too intelligent. No, Sunil, this was a power-play and you fell for it."

"But what can I do? Sell the house and split the money. I think that is the only way."

"Sunil, that is crazy. Papa left you the house. Act as he would have done. Put Tapa in her place. If you can't do it alone, ask your brother to stand with you and both of you tell her to behave herself. Do you think this is good for your mother?"

"Catherine, she cries all the time."

"Of course. Tapa is poisoning her mind against all of you. Tapa refuses to get married. She is lonely and jealous of her siblings, although I'm sure she wouldn't admit it. She is ill-tempered, mean-spirited, and a wretch of a woman. Mita tells me she doesn't do anything to help Mama. When she comes home from school, all she does is sit in the puja room. Mama does the cooking and the cleaning, and Tapa makes it sound like she is Cinderella, a servant. In fact, last night she told me that she pays the rent and all the bills here."

"That's not so, Mom. I pay all the bills."

"She also told me that when Sujeet and Deepa were here, they paid for nothing and she had to take care of all the bills."

"No, both Sujeet and Deepa paid me rent, Catherine, and I pay all the household expenses."

Mita joined the conversation. "Mom, Tapa is a good actor. She puts on a 'crying' act when she wants something. The other night, she was crying because Sonu was using Papa's quilt to sleep in."

"Oh, my God, I don't believe it. She always loved Sonu."

"Not any more, Mom. Ever since Deepa was living here, she has turned her back on Sonu as well as Deepa."

"Poor Sonu. I'm sure he can't understand what has happened. Tapa has always taken such care of him since he was a baby. More than his own mother has. So, what happened about the quilt?"

"I told her, 'fine'," said Sunil. "I gave Sonu ours and Piku and I used Papa's."

"This is insanity, Sunil. You have to do something. You are head of the household. This is your duty. Set her straight. Lay down rules for her. She cannot be allowed to take over. All of you are suffering because of this. Put your house in order, Sunil. You owe it to your whole family. When I come back on the 16th, I want to see a big change here."

"OK, Mom. I'll do it."

Back at the house, Catherine hugged Mama 'good-bye' and nodded to Tapa, not trusting herself to speak. She was totally disgusted with her.

The following morning, Catherine said 'good-bye' to Mita and kissed Piku. She had to be at the rail station very early. Mita gave her some breakfast, and Catherine told Sunil she needed to stop at Deepa's house on the way. It was very dark when the Ambassador car pulled up and Sunil put Catherine's luggage in the trunk. Mita stood by the car with tears in her eyes. Catherine felt so sorry for her. She had a very hard life, not only physically, but emotionally.

"Mom," Mita told her last night, "If I'd known before marriage that there was Sonu in this house, I would not have agreed to this marriage."

Catherine didn't understand this, but let Mita talk on. "Mom, I have a little house that my parents left me. Sunil and Piku and I could go live there. Tapa can have this. I don't want anything to do with her. That is why I made my own kitchen upstairs. Mama is weak and believes anything Tapa tells her. Tapa doesn't do anything for Mama. I would take her with me. Sunil and I would take care of her."

Catherine didn't have great hopes that anything would be better when she returned. But she had to say 'good-bye' to Deepa. Sunil went ahead and pounded on her door. Finally she came out. There was no light, but Deepa and Catherine embraced.

"I'm so sorry for what happened last night, Deepa. Tapa should not have thrown you out. But there was no fair, after all. It was some kind of meeting. We just walked and went to the temple. Deepa, take care of yourself. I'll see you when I come back on the 16th." They embraced once more and the car drove away to the rail station.

CHAPTER FOUR

SAWAI MADHOPUR

Leaving Delhi early in the morning, the train bore south into the state of Rajasthan on its eastern exposure. Luckily Catherine was seated with a lovely couple from Bristol, England, which helped to pass the five-hour journey to Sawai Madhopur. They were also going to Ranthambore for the chance of seeing a tiger, but their accommodations were not in the same hotel, so the chances of seeing them again were slight.

Upon arrival, Catherine was met and escorted to her lodge in the town of Sawai Madhopur. She went immediately to the dining hall because she felt her blood sugar was low. In a half hour she was to leave for her first tour of the Ranthambore Park.

Ready with camera, she eagerly waited for the canter, a high open-top bus, to pick her up in front of the lodge. The hotel/lodge was set back some distance from the road with a long driveway. Catherine assumed the canter would come in to load its passengers. But this afternoon, she was the only one, and she became worried when the canter did not arrive on time. She noticed that the manager of the lodge walked out to the road, and when he returned, he seemed shocked to see her there.

"Madam, are you waiting for the canter?" he asked.

"Yes," she answered.

"But, Madam, I thought there was no one, and I told the canter to go on."

"You did what?" she asked, incredulously.

"I told the canter that no one was here."

"Was I supposed to wait out on the road?"

"No, no. The canter always comes in. I didn't know that you were going."

"Fine," she replied, angrily. "I only had three chances to go to the park, and now I have only two."

"Please, madam, I will see what I can do. I am sorry."

With that, Catherine stalked off to her room, dismayed and angry. Obviously the canter would not return for her, so she was stuck in the lodge for the afternoon. She decided to write about this in her journal, when a knock came on her door. When she opened it, there stood the manager and a small, wiry man dressed all in black leather.

"Come, Madam," said the little man. "I will take you to your canter."

"But, how?"

"On my scooter."

Her eyes opened wide in shock. "On your scooter?"

"Yes, come, Madam."

Catherine gulped, and thought, "What the hell!" And making an instant decision, she grabbed her camera, locked her door, and followed the little man outside. There it was, a scooter. She had never been on one in her life. Catherine straddled it behind the little man and placed both arms about his waist, hanging on for dear life. He gunned the engine and they took off very fast, down the driveway and out onto the road. At frightening speed they flew across the tarmac, passing numerous cars, buses, scooters, and camels.

"Do you have any children, Madam?" he asked.

"Yes," she yelled back, because the noise of the scooter made it difficult to hear. "I have four sons."

"Four sons?" He almost did a wheelie, he was so excited. "You are very lucky, Madam."

"I know, but it would have been nice to have a daughter."

"You want a daughter, Madam?"

"No, no," she answered quickly. Catherine was sure that if she had answered in the positive, he would have found one for her. Suddenly, she found herself smiling and laughing. She hadn't laughed in such a long time. "If my boys could see me now," she thought and grinned to herself. "And here I am, racing down this road on the back of a scooter and wearing no helmet! My boys would shake their heads and have a fit. But I am having fun!"

After some time they pulled up at what Catherine learned was the Booking Station. There stood her canter, waiting for her. It was filled, and everyone was watching as they came to a stop beside the canter. All of the people aboard started applauding as she arrived. The little man jumped off the scooter and didn't turn to help her. He just strode off into the station. Catherine started to lift her right leg to get off, just as she had gotten on, but her leg would not cooperate. It would not bend backward, and she had no one to help her. She knew everyone was watching her, and she felt awkward and foolish. Since the leg would not bend backward, she brought it foreword and over the seat. In this position, she could very well land on her backside in a disgraceful pratt-fall, but luckily, she managed the difficult execution and walked away from the scooter with her dignity in place.

She then proceeded to climb into the canter and found only one vacant seat. In only a few minutes, the canter took off for the park. There was a young man, a naturalist, who spoke to the group, informing them of the wildlife they were about to see. Of course everyone wanted to see a tiger. That was the main reason for coming to Ranthambore, as it was noted for its tiger population. Only two days previously, there had been a good sighting of a kill, and the visitors had ample time for photos and just watching the magnificent animal.

The canter ride was lovely; the driver drove slowly along the trail and the naturalist was interesting and informative. They stopped many times along the way as he pointed out different species of animals and birds, and a few times, stopped in order to enjoy a beautiful landscape panorama. It was warm and comfortable on top of the canter, but as the sun started setting, it became chilly. Catherine had worn a sleeveless blouse and she started to feel the cold. It was a long drive back into Sawai Madhopur, and she could hardly wait until they came to her hotel.

At some point on the way back, the young naturalist came over to her and told her that a jeep was a better mode of transportation in the park. He said he'd be in the hotel around 8 o'clock and to see him then about a jeep, that he would "fix" it with her agent. Some people said it was better to have a jeep, others said it didn't matter. Catherine heard that there were only ten jeeps allowed in the park and there was some kind of listing as to what agents and guides were to get them.

Arriving at her hotel, she got off the canter and proceeded to her room, where she freshened up, put on a sweater and went to the dining hall. The food was good there, but the restaurant looked seedy. Tablecloths were dirty and for the three days Catherine was there, they were never changed. After enjoying her meal, she went back to her room and completely forgot that the naturalist was coming at 8 PM. She was exhausted and looked at the bed. First of all, she requested tea and toast for 6 AM because she needed to eat after taking insulin. Her shower was miserable due to no hot water, but she managed and then got into bed, which was another problem. There was a bottom sheet, but no top sheet. Only blankets and quilts. "Oh, well," she decided, "This is a park and one must know how to 'rough' it." But she kept wondering how many had slept under those same blankets and quilts. Then she fell asleep and it didn't matter.

Her alarm woke her, and she went to take another shower, deciding it was OK to sleep with someone else's blanket on her, but she needn't live with the feel of it. This time she let the water run a long time, and finally it became warm enough to shower.

Afterwards, she dressed carefully, layering as much as she could to get enough warmth. She knew it was going to be cold on that canter before the sun arose, and it was to pick her up at 6:30. She wore her wig as she had the day before, wondering if everyone could tell it was a wig with the wind blowing it helter-skelter. But then she decided she didn't care if anyone knew. She knew no one and was out to impress no one. This was her holiday and for the first time in years, she was enjoying herself.

At the appointed time, Catherine was in front of the hotel waiting with three other people for the canter. The manager gave each of them heavy wool blankets. She was so glad of that when the canter started off. The cold was bitter, the wind making it more so, as they rode in the open. Coming from a cold climate meant nothing to Catherine. This was deep, chilling to the bone, cold. She covered her face as much as she could, only her forehead and eyes exposed. Her glasses kept the wind from her eyes, and she hunkered down in her seat to wrap herself with every inch of that very welcome blanket.

This time there was another naturalist, but she found that he wasn't as attentive as the one she had had the day before. They followed a different trail also, but saw many animals and the terrain was interesting. At one point, they made a comfort stop and came upon two jeep-loads of tourists. There was the naturalist from the day before. She said, "Hello" to him, and he nodded in recognition.

The "comfort stop" was just a building out in the park. Those who needed to, walked to the back to relieve themselves. Catherine refrained from doing so. But as the canter drove off, she saw the young man she had spoken to, peeing against the side of the building. It struck her as funny, although she had seen many men in India relieving themselves in like manner. When nature called, one took care of it the best he could and no one was shocked or sensitive about it.

No tiger was seen that morning and only one chance was left for her, the afternoon excursion. That turned out to be a very trying experience. At the Booking Station, the canter picked up a load of Indian teenage students. They were loud and talkative and never quieted down throughout the entire ride. The naturalist talked to them most of the time and paid no attention to the other tourists. The trail they took seemed to be far away from any other in the park. Very little wildlife was seen, and if there had been any, Catherine was sure that all the noise of the passengers would have frightened them away. Also, the driver was going at top speed and many tree branches struck the passengers about the head and face. Catherine had to keep watch and had to duck many times so as not to get hit. It was disaster as far as Catherine was concerned. She was angry and disappointed, and was happy to return to the hotel.

That evening there was a knock on her door, and when she opened it, there was a young, very dark, handsome Indian standing there.

"Mrs. Forrest?"

"Yes."

"My name is Rakesh. I'm a friend of Sunil. He asked me to look in on you and see if you were all right. I have a group here that I'm escorting."

"Hello, Rakesh. I'm very glad to meet you. I am fine, but I am wondering if there is any chance that I could get another visit to the park. The one I had this afternoon was quite awful."

"I don't know. When are you leaving?"

"Tomorrow afternoon train."

"My clients have hired a jeep and there is room for one more, but I would need to ask them if it would be OK to include you. But then, you would have to come back early in order to get your train."

"Well, that is kind of you. See what you can do, and if not, it is no problem."

"I will let you know." With that he left and Catherine held out hope for one more chance to see a tiger. However, after dinner, the manager came to tell her that her friend had called and said that his clients did not favor having someone else with them.

The next morning the manager suggested that since she had so much time before the train, she should hire a jeep and go to see the Ranthambore fort. Catherine felt this was an excellent idea, and she asked him to arrange it for her. Before leaving for the fort, she packed and dressed for the train journey, and vacated her room.

The distance to the fort was almost as far as the park and they drove along the same road. At one point, instead of continuing into the park through an archway, the jeep pulled to a stop and parked. From there, Catherine looked up and saw the fort, 800 ft. up on a towering hill. It was then she realized that they would have to climb and she had shoes with small heels for traveling, certainly not for climbing. It was stupid of her not to think of that beforehand. She made the best of it and bravely followed her driver/guide up the side of the hill, climbing step after step. He took her at a slow pace and she was grateful. The steps were shallow and wide, but she had to watch her step just the same. Her guide told her this was the entrance that was used for elephants. At several stages, they looked out at the splendid panorama of the valley. Her guide even pointed out crocodiles on the banks of a distant lake. Catherine's eyes were not that fine, and even looking through the telescopic lens on her camera, she couldn't spy them. There were four massive gates with evidence of long ago battles, and temples to Shiva and Ganesh. A magnificent chatri dominated the summit where centuries ago audiences were held by the ruling king. It was a fine experience and Catherine was happy that she had had the opportunity to see this famous fort.

Arriving back at her hotel, she had just time enough to use the facilities and sign out. Her agent arrived and told her that he would take her to the train station, but her ticket was wait-listed.

"What do you mean? I thought it was all arranged from Delhi."

"Well, no, Ma'am. But we will get it confirmed at the station. Please come."

Saying good-bye to the manager, she stepped into the waiting car with her agent. There were many people waiting for the train, and the agent told her to sit by the rail with her luggage and he would see to her ticket. Actually, she never saw her ticket in his hand. What she did see was an exchange of money between her agent and another young man. The two of them seemed to be searching the crowd, then the second man moved away. The train arrived and people were boarding. Still no ticket. What was going on? Then suddenly she espied the second agent talking to a gentleman, who gave him his ticket in exchange for a hand full of rupees. Catherine's agent ran up to her and said the ticket was confirmed and told her to follow him onto the train.

"Just a minute," she said. "That isn't my ticket."

"Yes, it is."

"It is all grungy and I saw your friend give that man some money. You bribed the man for his ticket."

"It is all taken care of. Please, just follow me."

Her luggage was being carried aboard, so she followed it and her agent, shaking her head at the machinations. Her seat was on the aisle next to a large Indian family. They looked at her with dismay, and she knew she was not wanted there. Her agent told her that was her seat and she was to wait there for the conductor.When he arrived, he took her ticket, and looking at it, said, "Twenty rupees."

"Twenty rupees. What for?"

"For the confirmation."

She shook her head again, and delved into her purse for the money. What was this anyway? The train started and the Indian family kept looking at her as an intruder. She didn't know where else to go. Across the aisle there were single seats facing each other, whereas on her side the benches held four or five. Suddenly, the man across the aisle spoke to her.

"Would you like to exchange seats with me?"

"Oh, yes. That would be very good of you." And they made the switch. The family seemed pleased as the man apparently was part of the group. And Catherine felt more comfortable having a seat to herself. Looking back on the train station incident made her want to laugh again.

It was a two hour journey to Jaipur. She slept most of the way, the windows too dark and dirty to see out, and another passenger across from her apparently not interested in conversation. Arriving in Jaipur station, she watched as the other passengers grabbed their belongings and scurried out of the train. Her luggage was cumbersome and the largest piece had been stowed above her head. Finally, when there was a lull of people exiting, she grabbed the overhead piece and pulling it down, nearly beaned herself. Catherine had two carry-on bags as well as her purse, so she was hoping someone would come into the car to help her. However no one showed, so she pushed the heavy bag with her foot and got as far as the door. Luckily some gentleman saw her difficulty and reached up, taking her suitcase out of the train. She thanked him, then stood in place looking for the agent who was to meet her.

Many wallas wanted to take her luggage for her into the station, but she shook her head. Taxi drivers also accosted her, hoping to be hired. But Catherine stood her ground and waited. She was becoming more and more impatient, wondering where the agent was who was supposed to meet her and take her to her hotel. After nearly half an hour, she spied a young man coming to her.

"Mrs. Forrest?"

"Yes."

"I was waiting for you in the station. Why didn't you come in?"

"Because I had too much luggage and I expected you to find me here."

"I'm sorry. Please come."

The agent signaled a walla to take her bags and they went off to his car and driver, who then drove them to her hotel. She was to stay there only one night and was to take the following evening flight to Udaipur.

After registering her name and passport number, Catherine was welcomed by a woman who obviously worked at the hotel as a public relations person. She told Catherine of a barbecue buffet dinner followed by folk dancing and a puppet show. The cost was Rs. 500, so Catherine reserved a place for herself.

Her room on the 5th floor faced the pool and there was a nice view of the garden. She showered, washed and set her hair and got out the sari that Mita had given her. It was navy blue and she had a blouse to go with it. She planned to feel elegant when she went off to dinner. But the entire evening was a disappointment. The food was just fair and the folk dancing was pathetic. Three women doing tricks of walking on glasses and carrying things on their heads as they danced. It was very gimmicky. Catherine waited eagerly for the puppet show to begin, because Rajasthan is known for its puppets and puppet shows. She had seen a very good one at the Jai Mahal Palace Hotel back in 1988.

There were several rows of puppets on the floor in front of a puppet stage, all very colorfully attired. The puppeteer came out and began working the strings. He used only two puppets and there was no story line, just silly actions, which were repetitive also. Catherine wondered when he was going to use some of the lovely puppets on the floor. He never did, as they were only on display for sale. Catherine was disgusted and left as soon as she was able to get away.

The next morning she enjoyed a breakfast of south Indian food, then looked for the beauty salon, where she hoped to buy much needed hair spray. When she found it, it was closed for the Hindu kite festival. Catherine was told she had to check out by noon, so she packed her things and sat out near the pool. She had a book with her, but couldn't get interested in it. Finally, she took out her camera and photographed a variety of birds.

She noticed at some point that there was a meeting going on in the hotel. There were men in suits milling around on the ground floor. Then she saw a man coming toward her. It was a long way from the hotel, so she assumed it was someone from the front desk. However, it was a young man from the meeting.

"I saw you out here taking photographs of the hotel, so I wanted to come and talk to you," he said.

"How very nice of you. But I am not photographing the hotel. There are birds that keep flying there in a flock and they are green."

"Oh, those are parrots. Are you staying here at the hotel?"

"I was here only one night. Now I am waiting for the evening flight to Udaipur."

"You are going to Udaipur?"

"Yes."

"That is my home. Have you been there before?"

"No, but I've wanted to visit there for a long time."

"Where are you staying?"

"At the Lake Palace."

"Ah, yes. I live just behind the City Palace. I am going home tomorrow, so maybe we will meet again."

"That would be very nice."

"Now I have to get back to my meeting."

"Thank you for coming to talk to me. I enjoyed meeting you."

There was an arcade that she had visited the day before, and promised the shopkeepers that she would be back. So she decided to see if possibly there could be anything that she would like to buy. The men recognized her immediately and all wanted her to come into their shops. With so much time to kill, she obliged.

In the Kashmiri shop, Catherine told the owners that she already had rugs and papier mache that she had purchased some years back in Kashmir. When one of the men took out a shawl and started to remove his ring, she laughed.

"Don't do that. I know that is a pashmina shawl. I am not going to buy."

The man smiled and stopped, but said, "Won't you have some Kashmiri tea?"

"Oh, yes. I'd really like a cup of tea. Thank you."

She chatted with the shopkeepers, drank the delicious tea, then moved on down the arcade and talked with the others. At some point, all the lights went out. Catherine was told that there was a power outage every day at that time and the hotel would not give them auxiliary lighting, so they had to sit in the dark until 5 PM. It was hardly good for business.

At a jewelry shop she stopped to talk with the young man who was the owner. He told her that he came from a joint family and that his grandfather gave him the money to open this shop. His family home was a large farm in Sawai Madhopur. He was so delighted that Catherine had stopped that he invited her to his house in Jaipur. It didn't seem to matter that she was not interested in buying anything. With a flashlight he showed her pictures of another lady tourist who had visited him. However, Catherine declined his invitation as there was not enough time before she had to leave the hotel.

Her agent arrived at the appointed time and they drove to the nearby airport. There he saw to her check-in and baggage, said good-by and left. She was soon airborne and looking forward to her stay in the romantic city of Udaipur.

CHAPTER FIVE

UDAIPUR - CITY OF LAKES

After what seemed an entire day wasted in the hotel in Jaipur, she left via Indian Airlines on a late flight to her next destination, Udaipur. For many years she had wanted to see this city, the city with the beautiful man-made Lake Pichola, and stay at the renowned Lake Palace Hotel set on an island in the middle of the lake. The man sitting next to her in the plane carried on a companionable conversation, and before he deplaned in Jodhpur, he gave her his business card. He owned a company in Bombay and told her if she ever needed anything, to be sure to call him. It seemed Catherine was always meeting people like this in India.

Now the plane had landed and she made her way to the terminal. Several people held placards and one held the name, "Mrs. Catherine". She knew that it was for her, that they had her name backwards. She introduced herself to the young man holding the card and he ushered her to a waiting room and asked how many suitcases she had. She told him and he went to find them. When he returned with the luggage, he placed her in an Ambassador car with a driver.

"I have other people I have to see to," he said. "Please, I will see you at the Lake Palace."

"OK," she said, but she was not happy at being left. It was silly, but she felt that the other people were obviously more important than she. The taxi took off and she was surprised that the airfield was so far from the city. It was dark, and the lights from on-coming cars were blinding. Then she noticed the hills surrounding the area.

"Oh," she commented to the driver, "I didn't know there were mountains in this area. No wonder the airport is so far from the city." But the driver made no response. Perhaps he did not understand English. They drove for many miles, finally entering the city of narrow streets and well lighted shops. Once in the city itself, it wasn't far to the boat landing of the Lake Palace. There she encountered the man who had met her at the airport. He was seeing to the other people in his charge. Then he placed her luggage aboard the ferry and told her to get aboard.

The Palace was lit up and not far from the mainland. The boat ride over was lovely and she eagerly stepped off onto the famous landmark hotel. After registering, she was told she would be met by her guide the next morning at 9:00. Then she followed a bellhop through the lobby and a beautiful candlelit area of lily ponds. She wondered just where he was leading her as they wound up and down and around. Finally he opened a door and led her into a spacious suite. She could hardly believe it. How was it that she was given this magnificent room? That Sunil had arranged it she had no doubt. It must be costing a lot of money, but she really didn't care. It was included with the tour price and she couldn't care less what the price was. It was sumptuous, and what fun it was to be pampered this way!

When she was alone at last, she opened the drapes across the long wall and was stunned by the view across from her. It looked like another palace, also lit up. There was a small enclosed balcony jutting out from the side of her room and hanging above the water. It was only big enough for a small table and two chairs. It was round, and the walls were of stone with tiny holes and windows. The view from here was of the mainland and she could see some of what she was to learn was the City Palace. Her room was twin bedded and had a sitting area. There was also a dressing room and a huge tiled bathroom. She was so excited but also very hungry, so she left her lovely room and hurried down to the restaurant.

As she entered, the Maitre'd met her at the doorway.

"Are you alone?" he asked.

"Yes."

He looked dismayed as he quickly glanced about the room. She followed suit and saw many tables empty and only a few diners. He turned back to her. "Could you wait in the bar, please? I will clear a table for you."

"Yes," she answered, and left, but didn't understand why he wasn't able to seat her when there were so many empty tables. Granted they were large, but so what? She was used to eating alone, and at this point she didn't care how big the table was. Her blood sugar was low. She could tell by the signs; her hands were beginning to shake and her lower lip was getting numb. She needed food very soon.

After a fifteen minute wait in the bar, she was angry and upset. She quickly returned to her room and ordered room service, which arrived in a very short time. The food was delicious and she ate everything on her tray. After all, it was past 10:00 and she was starved. She placed the empty tray outside her room and decided to call home. She simply had to share this with someone.

Bran was home having his breakfast. He wouldn't stop eating long enough to talk to her. She could hear his chewing on the other end of the line. He was eating his cereal. Snap, crackle, pop! He wasn't interested in her description of her suite. He asked her how she was, and told her the weather was cold and snowy in Duluth. With disappointment she hung up the receiver. What did she expect anyway? She should know by this time that her husband couldn't care less about such things. There was never anything beautiful or exciting that she could share with him.

She decided then to put through a call to her sister, Cindy, and her mother. It was early in Portland and Mother was still asleep, but Cindy was delighted to hear from her. Catherine described her hotel and her suite and got the excited response from her sister that she had been hoping for. Cindy told her that Mother was doing well and enjoying herself. Catherine was relieved to hear this. After the call, she took her shower and chose one of the beds and dropped off to sleep, first making sure that she set her alarm for an early rising.

The next morning she arose and ordered breakfast in her room. She had no desire for a repeat of last night's rejection in the restaurant. After opening the door to her balcony she realized there was a chill in the air, so she took out her Kashmiri shawl and wrapped it Indian style around her shoulders and proceeded to the lobby to wait for her guide.

There was a group of Americans also expecting their guide. They arrived together on the same launch. Catherinee's guide was short of stature, balding, with a short beard of black and white hair. He spotted her immediately and approached her.

"Mrs. Catherine?" he asked.

"Yes," she replied, smiling.

"Please wait one moment." And he hurried away to Reception with papers in his hand. He appeared to be very busy and preoccupied, but Catherine stood and waited patiently for him to finish his business. As he walked away from her, she noticed that his left foot turned in and seemed to drag at the toe. Her nurses training kicked in and she wondered if he had had polio or if it was a birth defect. He returned shortly from the restaurant/bar area and with a smile told her his name was Aadi, and they could go now.

During the short ride on the launch, he turned to her.

"We have met before," he said

"No. I have never been to Udaipur."

"But surely we met somewhere, no?"

"No, we have never met."

"I was supposed to take a group today, but it was canceled," he told her. "And then I was given you. Are you sure we have never met?"

"I am sure," she told him.

"I feel that we have," he said again.

On the mainland a car was waiting to take them to the City Palace which was only three minutes away. When they arrived the gates were still closed, so the driver parked the car and as they waited, her guide gave his shoes to a shoe-shine boy who begged for the job. She thought it was most kind of her guide to give this boy a chance to earn a few rupees. It was probably his first customer of the day.

When the palace grounds opened, Aadi led her to the outer courtyard and pointed out the exquisite architecture of white carved marble, beautiful arches and cupolas, and filigreed balconies. He showed her where best to take her photographs, and then they entered the palace itself.

As they climbed a narrow and winding stairway, Catherine was amazed at how steep the steps were. Coming to the top at last, they met the American group that she had seen at the hotel. They were all clustered about one of the men, who had collapsed and was propped against a wall. He was pale and sweating. Their guide was very concerned and a woman, obviously the man's wife, was crying.

Catherine turned to Aadi. "He should be seen by a doctor. He may be having a heart attack."

The man was helped to stand and walk to a bank of steps where he could sit and rest more comfortably. Aadi conferred with the other guide and then came to Catherine.

"The guide must take his client to a doctor, but he cannot leave his group unattended. Would it be all right if I take them with you until he returns?"

"But of course. Please tell the guide to do what he has to do."

Aadi went back and spoke to the guide and then told the group that Catherine had kindly agreed to let them join her. They thanked her, and the tour proceeded. Catherine was entranced by this palace, now a museum. She was especially interested in the mirror work, the stain glass and the mosaics. Aadi was an excellent guide and pointed out many things she would have not noticed, such as the particular way some of the frescos were painted. Before they had completed the tour of the palace, the other guide returned.

He reported that the doctor had diagnosed the condition as fatigue and too much spicy food. The gentleman was resting at the hotel. Catherine was relieved to hear it was nothing more serious.

On their way out of the palace, Catherine questioned Aadi as to the advisability of going to Eklingji, and Nagda, where they were scheduled to go next.

"Not go to Eklingji?" he asked incredulously.

"Well, some friends of mine were here a couple months back and told me that the trip to Eklingji was a waste of time, that there was nothing there."

He laughed and shook his head. "If you do not like Eklingji, I will take you somewhere else. But I assure you it is very good."

"OK," she said, and they started back to where the car was parked.

"You seem to enjoy your work, Aadi."

"Yes, I like it very much."

"Do you work for International Tours and Travel?"

"Yes, but I am free lance, so I work for many companies."

"Are you a city guide only?"

"Oh no. I can go all over India."

"Then you have very extensive knowledge."

He didn't reply to that.

"Are you married? Do you live here in Udaipur?"

"No, I am not married. I live in Udaipur with my parents."

"I see. Well, I asked about International Tours and Travel because my Indian son works for that company."

"Your Indian son?"

So she told him about her history as a travel agent and how she had met Sunil and had become his American mom. Her experience escorting a group to India always made good story-telling and she could see that her guide enjoyed hearing about it.

After explaining that she was a registered nurse and the knowledge came in very handy when some of her clients became ill. He told her about a friend of his in Udaipur, who was in his 50's and had heart trouble. The doctors in Udaipur did surgery on his heart, but it was not successful and the man then went to Jaipur, where he soon died.

"He was just ten years older than me," he told her.

"So," she thought, "he is in his 40's, this man, this guide." Somehow she thought he was older, but when she looked at his skin, she understood that his gray hair and baldness was premature, and that he really was still a young man.

It was about 30 km from Udaipur to Eklingji and the road wound through the mountains, the Aravalli Hills, which surrounded Udaipur and formed a natural defense. Aadi sat in front with the driver and told her about Eklingji, a 16th century Shiva temple complex. When they arrived, Aadi led her toward the temple, stopping briefly to buy a garland of golden marigolds, which he brought into the temple as a gift. As they stopped in front of the idol, Aadi knelt and with great respect touched his head to the floor. Catherine was very impressed. She had visited many temples in India with an assortment of guides, but none had ever shown such reverence. She guessed rightly that he was a Brahmin. He sat back on the large rug facing the idol, and invited her to join him. After placing her hands in an Indian greeting and bowing to the idol, she sat down next to him. He pointed out that the idol was of black marble and was four-faced. He told her this was the private temple of the Maharana and that a member of the royal family visited here once every week. A priest of the temple approached them and gave sweets to Aadi, which he shared with Catherine. When they stood, the priest blessed each of them with a dab of oil on the forehead. Catherine began to feel a strange kinship with this man, this guide. She was a spiritual person herself, and she felt this to be a very sacred moment here in this Hindu temple. Outside was a large statue of Nandi, the bull and mount of Shiva.

As they made their way out of the temple area, Aadi met friends of his, with whom he spoke for several minutes in Hindi. Then he led her to a small shop and ordered tea for the two of them.

"I wonder," he began. "Would you like to have a picnic?"

"Oh, yes," she replied.

"It would be very simple food. Not hotel fare."

"I don't care. I'd love to have a picnic."

"My friends are here and they are going to join us, if that is all right?"

"Yes, of course. Where will we have the picnic?"

"I will show you. It is near Nagda, where we go now."

Before leaving the town, Aadi bought food from a shop. It was wrapped in newspaper. Catherine wondered about eating food from street shops, but she wisely trusted that her guide would not purchase anything that was not safe for them to eat.

A short drive brought them to Nagda, which was out in the countryside, and the temples there were in ruins. But Aadi pointed out the beautiful carved figures in the 10th century temple. After giving her time to take photos, he led her across a large field.

"Where are we going?" she asked.

"Over there, by those trees," he said, as he pointed. "We will have our picnic there."

Catherine noticed there was a wall, spreading left and right with no apparent opening of any kind. As they approached, the wall looked formidable to her. It was at least six feet high, and she wondered how they were going to get over it. Aadi laughed and said, "Come, I show you."

Just there were perpendicular stones protruding from the wall. Aadi led the way, and gave her his hand. The steps were steep, but she attained the top of the wall, with Aadi at her side. Looking down the other side, however, she realized she had a problem. There were no stepping stones on that side. How was she to get down without breaking a leg? Aadi jumped and held up his hand to her.

"I can't," she said. "I'll break my neck!"

"No you won't. It isn't that far. Come."

"I don't know how I'm going to do this, but take my camera." She handed it down to him, and saw him smiling encouragingly.

"Come, you will be all right."

She looked around and tried to figure out how to do this. She was a big, obese woman, and here she was standing on top of this wall, about a foot in width, with a six foot jump in front of her. Catherine thought if she could first just sit on the wall, perhaps she could slide down, and the jump wouldn't be so high. But how to get into a sitting position? First of all, she was wearing a skirt, and secondly, her knees no longer bent the way they used to. She had arthritis in both of them. There was no easy way to do this, but she decided to give a little jump to land on her butt on the top of the wall. That in itself was quite a feat, but she did it. Luckily she didn't think of how silly she looked, or she probably wouldn't have tried it at all. Actually, she didn't think about it very long. She just did it, and for a few seconds, she nearly lost her balance as she landed on the wall. Aadi looked dismayed, but thankfully he didn't laugh. She did though, and then grabbed his hand while sliding and jumping the last few feet to the ground, nearly knocking him over. She was a heavy-weight and next to him, felt like a big oaf.

The driver was already there and watching all this with a big grin on his face. She probably should have felt like a fool, but she didn't. It was an adventure, and despite the way she must have looked to those two Indian men, she was having a wonderful time. But then she had to pee and wondered what she was going to do.

"I have to make a nature call," she told Aadi.

"Just go over there by those trees," he told her.

She grabbed her purse and found her way up a short hill and squatted as best she could behind the leafy doorway. In the meantime, Aadi and the driver were piling rocks around the area where they had come over the wall. Aadi was preparing it for his friends. For a while he was afraid they wouldn't show up, but he didn't tell her that just then.

Then they did come, on scooters, and had no trouble executing the ascent and descent of the wall. They all sat around on the grass. Aadi motioned for Catherine to sit on a log. Again, she made an ass of herself by losing her balance and nearly rolling off. But she laughed and recovered without further mishap.

Aadi's friends spoke only Hindi, but she felt comfortable in their presence. The newspapers were spread out and the hot food was uncovered. It was all deep fried and tasted wonderful to her, even the chilies. Aadi mentioned that you could tell how hot the chilies were by the sweat on his head. Catherine noticed many beads of sweat, but she could see how much he was enjoying the food. Then she spied the dessert and recognized it from having tasted it in Belgaum.

"Oh," she said. "Til ladu!"

"Yes," Aadi replied, a big smile on his face. The others also seemed pleased that she knew the name of the sweet, and encouraged her to eat more and more of it.

"No, thank you," she said. I am a diabetic and I have to watch my sugar intake." Aadi translated this to his friends and they smiled at her, but didn't offer any more sweets.

After the picnic, they cleared away the paper and wrapped and took what was left of the food. Then everyone left, Aadi, driver and Catherine bringing up the rear. This time she had no problem climbing the wall, and instead of going all the way to the top, she sat on it and swung her legs over and facilitated the steps on the opposite side with ease.

Catherine was smiling, and turned to Aadi.

"Thank you so much for the picnic, Aadi. It was so much fun."

"You enjoyed it, then?"

"Oh, yes. Very much. And I liked the food. It was very good."

"It was very simple food."

"But it was hot and delicious. I really enjoyed this whole day."

"It isn't over yet. You still have to visit a beautiful garden."

When they were back in Udaipur, Aadi had the driver stop at a shop selling miniature paintings. This is the custom, to take clients to shops where it is hoped they will buy and the guide and driver both get commissions on anything the client spends. Well, Catherine had no intention of buying miniatures, even though she found them lovely. She dutifully looked at the paintings on paper, cloth and bone. Finally, she found Aadi and told him she wanted to leave.

The next and last stop was to the lovely garden, Saheli ki Bari or 'Garden of the Maids of Honor', which dated from the early 18th century, and whose fountains are fed from nearby lake, Fateh Sagar. Here, Aadi took Catherine to the lotus pond, around which are four elephant fountains. Again he showed her the best place to take her photos, and wanted to photograph her with her camera.

"Oh no", she laughed. "I take horrible pictures."

"But this is proof that you were here."

"I don't need proof. I know that I am here. I will always remember Udaipur. I certainly don't need a photo of me. It would be a waste of film because I would end up throwing it away."

"Why do you say that? You are a beautiful woman." She laughed again. "No, Aadi, I am not beautiful. And you are the only person who has ever called me that."

"But, I don't understand. You are beautiful. Why do you think that you are not?"

"My mirror tells me so, Aadi. I have a very heavy figure, and no one likes to see a big woman."

"Is that how Americans look at you?"

"Of course. Everyone, and I'm sure in most western and eastern cultures, people prefer to see nicely shaped bodies, not overweight ones."

"But I don't think that. I think you are a beautiful lady."

"Thank you, Aadi. That is very kind of you."

As they exited the inner garden area, Aadi excused himself and asked her to please wait. She stood and watched him hurry across a grassy parkland and figured he probably had to make a nature call. Once again her trained eyes noticed his leg and foot and she wondered what had caused them to turn in. He returned after a few minutes and they proceeded to the Lake Palace boat landing.

He walked her down to the boat, and she turned to thank him.

"Aadi, it was a beautiful day. I had such a lovely time. Thank you so very much."

"This is the end of your tour with me," he said, "but I wonder.... Would you like to see the lights of the city tonight?"

"The lights of the city? Why, yes. I'd like that. How?"

"I will pick you up, but I'm afraid not in a car, in my scooter."

Catherine nearly choked, but held back her giggles.

"Your scooter? Sure, fine. But do you really want to do this?"

"Yes," he said.

"What time should I be ready?"

"Please to meet me here at 7."

"All right. See you then." With that she turned and boarded the launch. This was crazy, she thought. Was this a date? She supposed so, but not the usual kind. But what fun! A new adventure! This day had been full of adventure already. Why not another? Certainly she would not have this opportunity if she were not traveling alone.

Now in her suite, she went through her clothes to decide what she was going to wear that evening. But the first thing she had to do was find the beauty shop and buy some hair spray. She had forgotten to pack it and her hair was not holding shape. Especially if she was going to be riding on the scooter, her hair needed something to hold it in place.

She found the beauty shop on the main floor just near the pool. The beautician sold her two cans of spray. They were small compared to what she had at home. When she used them in her bathroom, however, she nearly choked on the fumes. They were extremely strong, and she had to hold her breath while spraying some distance from her head.

At last she was ready. She chose a dress that she felt she looked particularly well in. It had no waist to speak of and hung loosely. The fabric was soft and had silvery patterns on a lovely blue background. She didn't go to eat because it was too early, but she wore her fanny pack and took money along in case they stopped for dinner. She didn't want him to pay for her. At just 7:00, she boarded the boat and went to the mainland.

He was not there waiting for her, but that didn't bother her. She was on time, so she just stood looking out over the lake at the lights of the Palace. She heard the phone ring in the boat house, and soon the hotel security officer came to her with a message.

"Mr. Aadi will be just a few minutes. Please will you wait?"

"Yes, of course."

After twenty or thirty minutes, he arrived on his scooter. He first went into the boat house and conferred with security, then came out to meet her.

"I'm sorry. Someone came to my house just as I was about to come. I could not leave."

"That's all right. It is a beautiful night, and I enjoyed watching the lake."

"Come," he said. "I show you how to sit on scooter. See, like this." He showed her how to sit sideways back of him, placing her feet on a small step. Then he asked her to wait until he started the motor, after which she sat behind him as he had instructed. Instead of wrapping her arms about him as she did the scooter man in Sawai Madhapur, she held on to each side of his sweater. For some reason she felt shy of him.

"Please, ma'am," he said, "Do not hold my sweater." She let go, but placed her hands on his waist, and they took off. He drove slowly, especially over the speed bumps, of which there seemed to be many. The only thing that bothered her was the iron rod behind his seat, into which her leg kept pushing. It was very painful, but she would have died before she admitted it to him. She tried shifting her weight, but found it difficult because of the hills they were traversing up and down in the Old City.

"See, how beautiful," he said as they drove past brightly lighted shops along the narrow, crowded streets. "Have you seen *Octopussy*?"

"No, I'm not a James Bond fan. Why?"

"This is where they were filming. Here in this street and over in the Lake Palace. They were in Udaipur for three months."

"Really! Well, I will have to see the movie when I get home."

"Are you familiar with 'The Jewel and the Crown'?"

"Oh, yes," she said enthusiastically. "I have the entire set of video tapes. It is a special favorite of mine."

"This is where they filmed Hari Kumar's apartment."

"Oh, my gosh! Where?"

"Here in this area."

They stopped at the bottom of a small incline, and got off the scooter.

"Come, please come," he said. "We walk from here."

"They walked for a short way up the street, which then went downhill. He pointed out old houses and hotels to her, all painted white, some with blue trim.

"See, how beautiful," he said. "You could stay here, or you could stay at my house."

"At your house?"

"Yes, or you could stay separate. All these houses are very old and have been modernized. We live a very simple life here."

They came to the bottom of the hill and entered what appeared to be a house of some kind. The doors were wide open, and led into a courtyard but it was quite dimly lit. She noticed a few chairs on one side upon entering. Aadi spoke to someone there at the entrance, then motioned for her to follow. He started up a stairwell, and she went after him, panting with the exertion. Why did all the steps in India have to be so high? At the top, he turned, walked a short way, and started up another staircase. And again another staircase until they came to the roof.

Here, not only was she out of breath, but breathless with the sight in front of her. The Lake Palace Hotel was there, all aglow on the water. She could see the other Palace, which she viewed from her hotel window, off in the distance. She gasped in awe, and Aadi smiled at her and told her to turn around. There on the hill was the City Palace, also lit with diffused lighting. And all the houses were twinkling on this side of the lake and on the opposite. Not one house obstructed the view from another. It was a virtual fairyland.

"Oh, Aadi. This is magical! It is so beautiful!"

He pointed to a particular light shining on the hill and told her that it was a temple. Just then a young man came up to them. Aadi introduced him as his friend, Jannu, who owned this house. Jannu asked if they would like tea, and Aadi said yes, but no sugar for her because she was a diabetic. They sat at one of the small marble tables and Aadi told her about the house.

"This is a guest house. It is very special. No groups come here, just a few guests who appreciate living in an Indian home, sharing their food and living simply as they do. It is far better to stay here than in the Lake Palace. Every room is different and in simple Indian style, but Jannu has put modern bathrooms in each room. You could see one, but they are all filled at the moment by Americans. Jannu's family lives here, and the guests eat with them."

The tea was brought to them and Jannu joined them for a while with his niece in his arms. Aadi played with the little girl, teasing her and making her laugh by pretending to fall on the floor.

"My father had diabetes," Jannu told Catherine. "Now he takes no more medicine. He is completely cured."

"Do you mean that he is controlled by his diet, then?"

"Oh, no. He doesn't have to watch his diet at all. He eats whatever he wants."

"But how is that possible? Are you sure he is or was a diabetic?"

"Oh, yes. But he went to a doctor of Ayurvedic medicine and was cured."

"Ayurvedic medicine? I've never heard of that. And I am a registered nurse."

"Well," explained Jannu, "It is all natural medicine. No drugs of any kind. You must find out about it. It is very popular here in India."

"Yes, I will do that. Thank you."

After they finished their tea, they left Jannu and his lovely home and walked back to the scooter. Catherine had no idea where they went from there, but it appeared they followed a route to another lake, and then they just rode around the city. At one point they stopped at a house that was away from the crowded houses of the Old City. Aadi told her to come and they went up to the door. Aadi knocked and they were ushered into a room and told to wait. A woman spoke to him in Hindi and then Aadi led the way out.

"My friend is an artist. I wanted you to meet him, but we disturbed. He was taking food. Come, we go."

By this time, Catherine was very used to the scooter, even getting on and off. But her leg against the iron bar still hurt. They drove around again and suddenly there were bright lights just behind them. As Aadi stopped the scooter, the truck behind them also came to a halt. Two boys jumped out and yelled a greeting to Aadi.

"Where are we?" Catherime asked him.

"At my uncle's. Come, please come."

The boys led the way, and Catherine and Aadi followed. In the house were a man, the uncle, a woman, obviously the auntie, and two daughters. Aadi and Catherine were invited to sit in the drawing room and the uncle asked Catherine if she would like anything to drink.

"What kind of drink?" she asked.

"Whiskey," he said, as he poured one for himself.

"No, thank you," she said, but looked at Aadi. "Unless you......?"

He just shook his head.

The three of them talked about many things; India, patterns of migration, the Indus Valley, Sanskrit being the father or basis of many languages, also Muslims and the Koran. It was obvious to Catherine that the uncle had no love for the Muslims and mistrusted them. He insisted they practiced the only religion that preached hatred, so their beliefs had to be false. Catherine had no love for the Arabs either, having been married to a Jew for almost 40 years.

At last, the women called everyone to come eat. Catherine was given a place next to the uncle. She scanned the table and noticed there was a large spoon at each plate. She then knew that the spoons were set out of courtesy for her. If she picked one up, they would all follow suit. This was not their custom. As food was served on her plate, she immediately used her hand instead of the spoon.

"Oh, good," sighed the uncle, as he noticed her taking food in her hand. "Now we can eat." The family seemed relieved and Aadi pleased. He told all of them that she was a travel agent. This was information she had given him that morning, but she noticed that he didn't mention that it was a past occupation and no longer valid. Obviously, he wanted them to think this was no real 'date', but a professional courtesy.

The family spoke Hindi the majority of the time, and Catherine felt entirely comfortable. Occasionally Aadi would translate. At one point, he wanted her to taste a particular food.

"This is made of five herbs. You will never see it or taste it anywhere but in Rajasthan. It is desert food." And Catherine enjoyed it so much she had two helpings of it.

After dinner, the four adult children sat around the table with Aadi and Catherine. They were playing a game of pretending to light cigarettes, smoke, and flick ashes. All were laughing, and really laughed hard when Catherine joined in by coughing and fanning away the imaginary smoke.

Later Aadi pointed out framed paintings on the wall, which he told her were works by Auntie. One of the daughters was also an artist.

The evening had been lovely and the food delicious. Catherine and Aadi thanked them, and off they went again on the scooter. Now that she felt she knew Aadi better, she held on to him more securely.

"When is your birthday?" he asked her.

"Oh, I just had one," she said.

"When?" he asked again.

"January 3rd," she replied. "When is your birthday?"

"15 October," he told her. "I wonder….."

"Yes?"

"You don't leave Udaipur until late tomorrow. Wouldn't you like to go somewhere else? You don't want to sit in the hotel the whole day, do you?"

"Where could I go?"

"To Ranakpur. It is a Jain temple, very beautiful."

"Is it far?"

"Yes, it would take the entire day."

"But, would I be back in time to catch my flight to Delhi?"

"Oh, yes."

"How much will it cost?"

"Fifteen hundred rupees, about $60 American."

"Can I pay by credit card?"

"Yes, I'm sure that can be arranged."

She wasn't worried about the money, only that she would have enough cash.

"Yes, I'd like to go," she told him.

"There is only one thing," he said. "You must check out early because we won't be back when you have to leave your room. Can you do that before we leave?"

"Yes, of course. What time will we be going?"

"9 o'clock."

"Fine. I'll be ready," she told him.

Then they were at the boat landing. They got off the scooter and Aadi walked with her to the boat. He gave her the traditional Indian greeting of 'namaste', hands folded together and a small bow of the head.

"Oh, Aadi, thank you for an absolutely wonderful evening. I just loved every minute." And she impulsively put her arms around him and gave him a hug, then turned and boarded the boat and didn't look back.

Rising at 5:30 AM, Catherine packed her luggage, took her shower and dressed for the day. She went to the coffee shop overlooking the lake and ordered breakfast. Seated by a window, she looked for and found the house where Aadi had taken her the night before. Earlier she had realized that the last role of film in her camera had not engaged and therefore all the photos she had taken the day before at the City Palace, Nagda, the picnic and at the Saheli ki Bari garden, and inside photos of the Lake Palace were lost. She was dismayed, but there was nothing she could do, but retake photos of the Lake Palace, which she did while waiting for Aadi. She had checked out and her bags were safely stored in the lobby of the hotel.

Once again she encountered the American group. They too were waiting in the lobby for their escort. One couple admired her Kashmiri scarf, which again felt good in the cool morning air. The man who had been ill assured Catherine that he was well, that he had slept the entire day and night and felt perfectly fine. He and others thanked her again for allowing them to join her on the City Palace tour. One woman, who seemed to be traveling alone kept telling her what a fine looking man Aadi was. This same woman had mentioned this to her the day before also. Catherine had no answering comment. She supposed the woman was right, but she had not been thinking of him in that respect. He was a fine escort, very intelligent, and certainly a knowledgeable guide.

Aadi arrived at 9 AM as arranged and made sure that she had checked out and that her bags were in safe keeping. They took the launch over to the mainland, where Aadi had a short conversation with the security officer. Then they proceeded to the small parking lot where once again Aadi had his scooter. Next to it stood a tour bus and the Americans were about to enter it. Some saw the scooter and gaped as Catherine jumped on the back. She had her camera case, her hand bag and a large carryon which contained her medications, including insulin. All these she slung over her left shoulder and held on with her left arm. With her right arm she encircled Aadi and told him she was ready. As they took off, she started to laugh.

"Why are you laughing?" he asked.

"The look on those Americans' faces," she said. "They are so jealous."

"Jealous? Why?"

"Because I am having the fun of riding on a scooter, and they have to get on a bus."

CHAPTER SIX
UDAIPUR-RANAKPUR

They rode down Lake Palace Road and stopped in front of the Rajasthan Tours office. The Ambassador car and driver they had used the day before were there awaiting them.

"Just go to the car, please," Aadi told her. "I just come."

She did as he indicated, while he went to park his scooter. Very shortly he returned with a bundle of gray sticks in his hand. He placed them on the floor of the front seat and got into the back with her. She was happy about that because it was going to be a long drive and it was easier to converse if they sat together. She did not ask him what the sticks were for. They settled in for the long drive through the beautiful Aravalli hills.

"Tell me, Ma'am, how do you compare your country with India?"

"I don't compare the two. It is impossible."

"What do you think of the poverty?"

"Poverty is but one part of India and I accept it as I accept all of India. I come here and absorb all the sights, the smells, the sounds, and let India become a part of me. I don't judge her. I wouldn't dream of wanting to change her. I accept her just as she is. I love her, and I love her people."

After a while he began to tell her about the Jain temples of Ranakpur, which they were on their way to visit. He explained in great detail the history of the Jains and their basic beliefs. She was fascinated and listened to him with an attentive ear. He was extremely knowledgeable, and obviously well educated.

Aadi kept calling her, "Ma'am:" until finally she spoke up. "Don't you think you know me well enough now so that you can call me by my first name?"

"Catherine?" he asked.

"Yes", she replied.

"Good morning, Catherine," he said quickly and perfectly. "Are you French?"

"Gosh, no. I'm of German and Czech descent. Why?"

"When I saw the tour order, your name was Mrs. Catherine."

"Oh, yes. At the airport they found me with Mrs. Catherine on the card. It is confusing sometimes because I have two first names. I usually have to spell the last name for people, even in the States, because it is hard for people to think of Forrest as a surname."

They were driving through lowlands, farming areas. Aadi pointed out ancient waterwheels drawn by oxen. One in particular looked very picturesque.

"Oh," she said, "Could I get a photo of that?"

"Yes, of course." He told the driver to stop, and he and Catherine walked over the field to the well. There were several children there and they were excited that a stranger, a foreigner had stopped to take a picture. Catherine started to snap a photo, and nothing happened. She checked the number of photos she had taken and there were only eleven. Surely this roll was a 36 exposure. Aadi took the camera from her, and tried to wind it back and make it work. It would not, and she felt so sad, thinking somehow she had pushed some unknown lever and made the camera inoperable. With a sigh, she turned to go back to the car.

"One moment," he said. "Let us see what is wrong." Very patiently he went over everything, but could not make it work. So, they went back to the car and drove on. Aadi still had the camera in his hands, and suddenly he realized what the problem was.

"It is out of film. There are only twelve exposures on the roll."

"Twelve?" she asked incredulously, "But that's crazy. I was sure that I brought only the 36 exposure film."

"See? Only twelve", he said as he took the film out of the camera.

"Oh, how stupid of me! But now that I think of it, I bought packages of what I thought were three 36 exposures at a special price. I'll bet one of the rolls in those packages had only 12 and I didn't notice. I will have to check all the other rolls before using them, so I don't make this mistake again. Now I have lost the chance to take a photo of that lovely waterwheel."

"No, we will stop there on our way back. Don't worry."

Then he was telling her his ideas on how to modernize a farming community by instructing and working with one village, and in turn they would help another village and so on. It seemed so simple, but of course India is not simple. Everything in this country was complicated. But how wonderful it would be if just one idea could be implemented. Who knows where it would lead?

The two hour drive went quickly, and suddenly, in the distance, they glimpsed the snowy white temples nestled in the arms of the Aravalli Hills. Just before coming to them, Aadi spoke to the driver in Hindi. The car pulled up, and stopped on the left side of the road. Aadi got out of the car and climbed a small embankment. Catherine could see a half-built structure on the top. She saw that he was looking or searching for something. But he came back to the car and spoke again to the driver. They drove slowly and stopped once again at the direction of Aadi. He espied someone in the field, proceeded to take the bundle of sticks from the front seat and gave them to him. And once more they were on their way to the temples.

"What was that all about?" she asked.

He smiled at her and said, "It is a surprise for the way back."

"Great, I love surprises," she smiled back at him.

At last they arrived at Ranakpur. She needed to find a toilet and Aadi showed her where to go. A servant went into the cubicle for a few minutes and she assumed that he did something to clean it. When she came out, the servant was standing just outside, and she was somewhat embarrassed that he would be waiting so close. Was he going to clean the facility after her? It was very basic and she had to squat, but it served the purpose.

She found Aadi and they proceeded to remove their shoes, climb the steps, and enter the temple. It was magnificent and Catherine gazed about her in awe. Most of it was pristine white marble, although Aadi told her some of it was sandstone. The carvings were exquisite and intricate. More than 1400 pillars, no two carved alike. It was breathtaking.

They moved to the center of the temple and Aadi knelt down in front of the image of Chamukha (four-faced), and touched his head to the floor in great respect. Catherine gave a "Namaste" and slight bow. Then they began a tour of the great temple, walking along the side and finding niche upon niche of Jain saints. Aadi told her that each was named and had its own symbol to identify it. They walked slowly, but it was difficult to absorb it all. They were in the main temple, which is dedicated to the Jain 'revealer of truth', Adinath.

Catherine was carrying her camera with the telephoto lens, but had forgotten the flash attachment in the car.

"Give it to me," Aadi told her, indicating the camera. She did and he examined it and began to change the settings. Soon he was taking photos of the pillars, and lying on his back, took photos of the ceiling and intricate carvings in the dome. He told her where to stand to give the photo depth and a sense of its greatness. Obviously he was a fine photographer along with his many other talents.

They came once again to the center where a Jain priest placed oil on their foreheads. This was not her faith, but Catherine felt blessed, and as in the temple at Eklingji, she felt a bonding with her guide.

"Would you like to walk around again?" Aadi asked her.

"Oh, yes," she answered. He led her to one side and they walked slowly around once more. At one point Catherine, not thinking, raised her right arm and placed her hand on Aadi's back. He responded in kind, but she immediately realized what she had done and removed her hand. He followed suit. Afterwards she understood that she was acknowledging a sharing of something beautiful, but it was too intimate a gesture. He was her guide, after all, not her companion.

When they left the temple and were putting on their shoes, Aadi noticed a group of men on the steps. They apparently knew Aadi and they began to converse in Hindi. One of the men asked Aadi to take their photo, as Aadi still wore Catherine's camera about his neck.

"This is not mine," he told the man. "It belongs to my client."

"Please, take their photo, Aadi," she said. "I will send you the picture."

"Then, please," the man said, "send the negative also so that each of us can have a photo."

"Yes, of course, I will do that."

After that, Catherine saw an immense tree of deep pink bougainvillea and asked Aadi to take a photo of it.

"You stand in front of it," he told her.

"Oh, I will spoil the picture," she said. Her blouse was orange and she knew the colors would clash, but he insisted, so she stood while he snapped two photos of her. Then he led her to the large mess hall where long trencher tables were set with thalis and katoris. They removed their shoes again.

"Do you have a napkin?" Aadi asked her.

She dug in her purse and gave him a Kleenex. "Is this OK?"

"Perfect," he said. "Come." She followed him to a table where their driver was already waiting. Aadi wiped one of the thalis and all the katoris. They were clean, but had water left on them. He was making sure that her utensils were dry, so that the water would not harm her. She felt very grateful and protected by this man.

They sat and waited a short time until a man came with a pail of dal, which he ladled into one of the katoris. Next came vegetables and poori. Everything was piping hot and delicious. They came with seconds and even thirds, but Catherine could only eat the first helping. It was filling and wonderful. They ate with their hands and afterwards, Aadi showed her where to wash her hand at a common sink.

Fully satisfied, they left the hall, retrieved their shoes, and went to their car. "Thank you, Aadi," Catherine said, with great feeling. "It was wonderful! I'm so glad you suggested I come here. I would not want to have missed this for anything." He just smiled at her, and she felt warm and happy to have had this experience.

As they drove off, it was only a short distance when they came upon three Ambassador cars ahead of them. Aadi spoke to their driver, and he overtook the three cars and passed them.

"Those are all the Big Guns," he said. "The men at the temple."

"What do you mean? Big Guns?"

"They are all important men in the tourist business."

"So that is how you knew them."

"Yes."

Before long, they were at the point along the road where they had stopped earlier with the sticks. The driver slowed and parked the car on the opposite side of the road from the embankment.

"Come," Aadi instructed her. As she exited the car and started across the road, the three Ambassador cars pulled up behind their car and parked. All the 'Big Guns' got out and proceeded to follow Aadi up the embankment.

"What the hell is going on?" Catherine wondered. She hung back and one of the men walked with her.

"Is this your first trip to India?" he asked her.

"No, my sixth," she told him.

"Your sixth?" He lit up like a Christmas tree and told a few of the others. They looked at her with new eyes, eyes of approval and delight, happy that she liked their country so much. The one man did not follow Aadi and the others farther up onto another hill. He stayed behind with her, giving her his business card and telling her that they were on an inspection tour of hotels and guest houses in Rajasthan, rating and accrediting them. Among the eight men, one was owner of Rajasthan Tours, one head of the Taj Hotels, one owner and manager of Heritage Hotels and another from the Government of India Tourist Office. They were indeed 'Big Guns,' but what were they doing here at this place? She still had no idea.

The men were there no longer than fifteen minutes, and afterwards Aadi looked at Catherine with shining eyes. He was obviously very happy.

"What was that all about?" she asked him. "What is this place?"

"It is my property with a partner. We are building a restaurant here. See?" He indicated a partially built structure. "Come, I show you."

She followed him and he showed her the inside of the structure, and an adjacent building which he told her was to be the kitchen.

"We are using only materials from this area; the stone, marble, and no cement. Already we have planted hundreds of trees. This will be an ecological guest house. We are planning to have many separate houses all run on solar energy with none disturbing the trees."

"That's fantastic," she cried, joining him in his enthusiasm. "How much land do you own?"

"Come, I show you," he said, as he led her to the top of another hill, the same place he had taken the 'Big Guns.' "See," he said, pointing, "To the top of that hill, down to that river below and over beyond where the men are working." Two men, one of which was the one who had come to the car on their way to Ranakpur, were digging up a piece of ground.

"It's lovely, Aadi. Really, it is a beautiful spot, so peaceful. The men? What were they doing here?"

"I invited them to come and see this. They were very interested to see what we have done here."

Suddenly, Aadi turned to Catherine, and clasped her in his arms. He held her so tightly, his arms very strong.

"Thank you," he said.

"For what?" she asked, stunned.

"You decided to come to Ranakpur today. I didn't know that these men would be here. Because of you, I met them and they came here to the site. It was very important that they saw this, and it is all because of you."

"Aadi, this had nothing to do with me."

"Oh, yes, it was because of you." He was still holding her tightly.

"Aadi, you are a good man. God loves you, and He used me to bless you. It is God you must thank, not me."

"I still thank you. I want to show you everything."

She was getting concerned, and wondered just what he meant. Was this a come-on? Everything?

"Everything? I don't think so," she told him.

He hesitated a moment, then said, "I mean all of India."

She felt sheepish then, and pulled away from him. She had totally misunderstood him.

"All of India? I'd really like that."

He still had her camera about his neck, and he smiled at her. "Stand there," he told her, indicating a background of lovely trees. "I want to take your picture."

"Oh, not again. Aadi, I take terrible pictures. Please don't."

"But you are beautiful."

"Aadi, I am not beautiful."

"I just take this photo, and you will see how beautiful you are. Please."

So she posed once more and he snapped another photo of her.

"Now tell me," she said to him, "What were those sticks you left here on the way to Ranakpur?"

He gave her a big smile. "They are cuttings from my olive trees in my garden at home. Olive trees are not indigenous to India. I imported them from Greece." She was very impressed and smiled back at him.

"Come, please come. I would like you to help me to plant them."

Catherine was absolutely delighted. "Really? I'd love to do that."

He led the way back down the hill to the area where the two servants were tilling the soil. Aadi showed her just how to hold and plant each cutting at an angle. Catherine knelt in the dirt, and started to dig with both her hands. Oh, the joy of it! Kneeling in the rich Indian soil, planting olive trees. Talk about adventure! This day was certainly an adventure, a surprise, an extraordinary experience, one to be remembered for a lifetime

After a while, he joined her and planted beside her. Then she left him to reach for her camera, now on the small porch area of the servants' hut nearby. She took two photos of him, one with his head and eyes down, intent on the work he was doing. The second with his attention on her and a big grin on his face. It was obvious that he loved this kind of work, and when she questioned him about it, he told her that he had a big garden at home in Udaipur.

When the planting was finished, the servants made tea for Aadi, Catherine and their driver. Then it was time to leave and they drove off, once more enjoying the lovely scenery of the Aravalli Hills. Coming down out of the hills and once more in the farmland, both Aadi and Catherine noticed the waterwheel where they had stopped before. Aadi told the driver to stop, and with her camera in his hand, he opened the door.

"I just come," he said, and walked across the road and into the field. He went alone to photograph the scene she wanted to capture on film. She felt grateful, because she was feeling tired and a bit warm, and it was comforting to have someone do this for her. And then the children appeared. They looked in the open door, all smiles. She opened her purse and found small rupee coins and gave them to the children. There were big smiles of delight.

Catherine made it a habit of never giving to beggars. But these children were not begging. They were only interested in seeing a foreigner and trying to talk to her. Therefore it gave her pleasure to give them some small token that would make them happy. Aadi seemed to take quite a long time, but when he returned they were off once again.

At some point, Catherine told Aadi about her meditation practice. He wanted to know all about it. She tried to explain 'Centering prayer' to him.

"I think silence is very important," he told her. And then to her great surprise he told her his beliefs in God.

"I believe there is only one God," he told her. "The idols of the Hindus are mere reminders of the one God, the universal God. All of us worship Him in our own way."

"Oh, yes. I believe that too. Only one God, but we worship him as Christ, Shiva……"

"Allah, Buddha, etc,"

"Each according to his or her own customs and heritage. I had no idea that Hindus believed in this way."

Catherine felt another bond had just been drawn between them. She took out some photos of her family and showed them to Aadi. Then she removed her itinerary and showed that to him, which he seemed to be more interested in. After a while, as they sat in comfortable silence, her left hand on the seat between them, he covered it with his. Catherine did not move away. She felt it was a fitting ending to a day of shared beauty and spiritual awareness. There was a rightness to it, a kinship, a natural progression from the temple at Ranakpur to the planting of the olive cuttings, to the sharing of their beliefs in God. His hand was warm and she enjoyed the closeness, not once thinking anything physical or sexual, just enjoying the contact of another sensitive human being who had shared this very special day with her.

"You enjoy travel, don't you?" she asked him.

"Oh, yes," he told her. "I've been to Europe."

"Really! Where in Europe?"

"All over."

She was impressed. There seemed to be no end to the dimension of this man.

"Aadi, you must give me your address so that I can send you that photograph of the 'Big Guns'."

"Of course. Do you have something I can write on?"

She found a small tablet in her purse, and gave it to him with a pen. She watched as he printed his name and almost gasped as he wrote his last name, Abhimani.

"Aadi Abhimani," she said aloud. "What a beautiful name!"

He smiled at her. "Do you like it?"

"Very much. It is musical."

"Catherine, will you write to me? We can exchange ideas about our countries, and I would like to know any ideas you might have that would make our guest house and restaurant a success."

"Yes, of course. I will give the site a great deal of thought and send you whatever I can come up with."

Off to their right, the hills in the distance seemed to take on a particular shape. "Look," Catherine said to Aadi, "Doesn't that look like a camel with his hump?"

"I see a woman lying down, and that is her breast."

Catherine laughed. "Isn't that just like a man?"

"But look, don't you see? Her head and then her breasts."

"Yes, yes, I see," she agreed, still chuckling.

Coming into Udaipur, Aadi let go of her hand, and they were back in the real world again. The magic was over. After stopping at the Rajasthan Tour office so that she could pay for her tour to Ranakpur, they arrived at the boat landing for the Lake Palace and he went with her to the hotel.

"Is there somewhere I can wash up?" she asked him when they were in the lobby.

"Yes, down there," he pointed out to her.

She found the ladies room and proceeded to relieve herself then wash her face and hands.

When they met again in the lounge area, he seemed concerned.

"Is everything all right?" he asked.

"Yes," she assured him with a smile. "Everything is just fine now."

"Come, just come," he said.

"Where?" she asked.

"Your boat ride."

"But do I have time for that?"

"Oh, yes. There is time."

"OK then. I love boat rides." She followed him to the entrance and the boat that was loading up with hotel guests. She started to follow the guests, but he called to her.

"No, Catherine. Here, this boat." It was a private boat, with only the boatman and Aadi. She looked at him in surprise.

"Oh, you did this. I was supposed to go on the hotel launch."

"No, you paid for it." But she didn't believe him. Another lovely treat, and again her heart swelled in gratitude to this man who was so very kind to her.

They motored away from the hotel and went into the lake toward Aadi's friend's home. He was holding her camera again and as it needed more film, he changed the roll for her.

"Is it caught on the spool?" she asked. "I lost one roll with all the photos of the City Palace because it didn't catch."

He smiled at her. "Yes, it has caught." And he proceeded then to photograph the lovely houses facing the lake in the golden light of the late afternoon sun. As they motored by his friend's house, she saw his friend on the roof.

"Look, your friend is there," she pointed.

Aadi told the boatman to stop. He called, "Jannu, Jannu," and they both waved as his friend saw them and recognized them. The boat made a large circle and started back toward the palace.

"I love water," she told him.

"So do I," he said, smiling at her.

"What a lovely smile he has," she thought to herself. "His eyes light up and sparkle like diamonds in a night sky."

Catherine thought wrongly that they were returning to the Lake Palace. Instead, they circled around it and headed for the other palace on the lake, the Jag Mandir. Aadi told her that it was not used as a hotel, but only for special parties. There were cupolas and a dome and stone elephants facing the lake. They disembarked and walked into a huge courtyard

"You can see the mogul influence here," she said to Aadi.

"Oh, no," he corrected her. "This is pure Hindu."

She felt like an idiot. "I'm sorry," she said.

"No, no, that is all right," he assured her. "Come, please come," he said as he led her to some steps and they climbed to another small courtyard between two cupolas. He still wore her camera, and took photos of the palace for her. Then they climbed into one of the cupolas and enjoyed the view from their vantage point.

"Stay here," he told her, and ran down the steps, across the courtyard and up into the opposite cupola. "I want to take your picture from here," he told her.

"All right," she said, and turned to face him and the camera. Afterwards they both went down their respective staircases and met in the center of the small courtyard. It was a very private spot, and not a soul was about. Suddenly, he flung her camera over his left shoulder and grabbed her in his arms. He began kissing her neck, her hair, her face, her forehead and her eyes. She was stunned, but she did not resist. Finally he placed his mouth on hers and kissed her soundly, placing his tongue inside her open and willing mouth.

My God but he had strong arms! She never remembered being held that tightly in all of her life. The embrace was exactly like the one on the hill at the site, but this time he had gone further. She froze suddenly, realizing that she hadn't been kissed on the mouth for twenty years. What was going on? She felt such a bond with this man, but not a sexual attraction. What was it anyway? She was very confused, and after taking her mouth from his, she held him as he held her, and she spoke softly.

"Aadi, oh, Aadi."

Catherine couldn't figure out why this man had kissed her. If he had wanted sex there certainly was no place nor time for it. The palace was an open area and the launch from the Lake Palace Hotel was just landing, people coming ashore. They broke their embrace and he led the way down the steps.

"Please tip the boatman," he told her.

She groaned. "More tips! I am so sick of tipping everywhere I go," she said.

"Isn't there tipping in your country?" he asked.

"Yes, yes of course. I'm not thinking clearly just now," she told him. Actually, she was shaking inside. She was totally confused and didn't know how to handle it. And of course she tipped the boatman after asking Aadi what amount to give him.

"Whatever you like," he told her, which was no help at all.

They boarded the boat which then circled around the back of the palace, then turned in toward the Lake Palace. After arriving at the hotel, Aadi suggested they go to the coffee shop for tea. They were ushered to a table for two; she sitting with her back to the door, and he facing the entrance.

He ordered tea for them, and sat looking at her.

"Did I offend you?" he asked.

"No, of course not. It's just that I have not been kissed by another man in twenty years. I am very confused."

He looked at her, smiled and pursed his lips in a silent kiss to her across the table. In response, she let her tongue slide over her lips.

"I don't understand all this," she told him.

"I feel affection for you. I felt your eyes communicating with mine. Don't you feel affection for me also?"

"What is he talking about?" she thought to herself. "How do I answer him?"

"Yes," she finally told him. "I feel a bond between us. But this is all a fairyland, this wonderful city. It is magical."

"No, it is not magic," he said. "Magic is not real. This is very real."

God, how was she supposed to answer that? And then they were interrupted by a young man coming to their table. Aadi greeted him and told her this was his partner in the guest house at Ranakpur. He excitedly told his partner about the boon of meeting the 'Big Guns' and showing them the property. He told him they wanted to know what they could do to help them with this project. But Catherine noticed Aadi's partner did not seem as excited about the chance meeting as Aadi was. He soon left them and she found she was still shaking and confused.

"You know, Aadi," she said, "I don't know what has happened to me. I always know my own mind, but now I'm so confused."

"I wanted to buy you a gift," he said, "but there was no time."

"A gift? A gift for me? Aadi, do you do this with all your clients? Do you take them to your uncle's house for dinner? Do you take them to see the lights of the city? Do you take them to your friend's home? Do you take them on private boat rides?"

With each question, he shook his head in the negative.

"Aadi, I simply don't understand. I have so many mixed feelings. You know, my friends always say that they know exactly where they are with me because I always speak my mind and tell them how I feel and how I think. At this moment, I don't know how I think or feel."

And then she went on to tell him of her mother who always said what she thought other people wanted to hear. She went on and on, not knowing how to stop, all an indication of how distraught she was.

"I'm sorry. I didn't mean to go on like that. Aadi, I wish I could stay here. I don't want to leave. It is so beautiful, so peaceful, and I am so confused right now, but my tour has been planned and I have to leave."

It was time to go. She paid the bill and they left the coffee shop. In the lobby was her escort to take her to the airport. He wanted to leave immediately as her luggage was aboard the launch. But Aadi had gone somewhere in the hotel, and she insisted on waiting for him. He was only gone a few minutes, so the three of them boarded the boat and left for the mainland. There was no further opportunity for them to speak privately. The driver that had been with them for the two days was there waiting for them, and after the luggage was packed in the trunk, the escort got into the front seat with the driver and Aadi got into the back with her. They only had a short way to drive before stopping to let Aadi get out. It was already dark, and just before he got out of the car, she gripped his hand in hers and gave it a squeeze.

"Have a good journey," he told her, and backed away from the car.

The Ambassador was already moving, but she looked back and saw him standing there in the twilight watching as the car pulled farther and farther away. The escort was talking to her, but she wasn't paying attention. Suddenly she felt bereft. Totally alone and for the first time in years, lonely. She wanted to run back to this man, but knew that she was being utterly foolish and besotted. It wasn't as though she desired him physically, sexually, just this terrible need to be with him, sharing more beautiful moments such as they had shared these past two days.

Finally she turned her attention to the escort. He was telling her that the driver told him that she ate with her hand just like an Indian. At the airport, she tipped the driver and walked away. Looking back at his smiling face, she felt like running back and giving him a hug, but she restrained herself and thought that he would probably be very embarrassed, so she just waved good-bye and went to the airline check-in counter. She was now on her way back to Delhi and full of joy, but sad also at leaving this wonderful magical city of Udaipur, and a lovely man who had been so kind to her.

CHAPTER SEVEN
KANYA KUMARI

Catherine was on a high when she reached Delhi. She could hardly wait to tell Sunil of the wonderful time she had had in Ranthambore and of course in Udaipur. However, she in no way wanted him to know of the personal aspect of what had transpired between herself and Aadi.

Mita quickly prepared food for her as she had eaten nothing since noon and she needed to raise her blood sugar level. Then as she related the scooter incident in Sawai Madhopur, Sunil and Mita laughed hysterically. Sunil related an experience he had had with one very large client who wanted a ride on his scooter.

"Mom," he said, "she sat behind me and stretched out her legs. When I tried to start, the scooter tipped backward with her weight." They all laughed again. It felt so good to Catherine. It was a great release.

"Now I must tell you about Udaipur. What a wonderful, exciting time I had there. I had a great guide, very intelligent and knowledgeable."

"Who was he?"

"Aadi Abhimani."

"What does he look like? I don't know that name."

"Well, he is about your age, grey hair, beard and balding."

"Is he dark like me?"

"Dark like you? What do you mean?"

"His skin. Is he dark?"

"I don't know. He is Indian. I don't think of light and dark. Anyway, I must tell you that we went to Ranakpur to see the Jain temples. And there we met eight men. Aadi called them, 'big guns of the travel industry'. It was just by chance and Aadi had my camera and took a picture of them. I'll send you one when I get it developed. I promised to send one to the men also."

"Do you remember their names?"

"Oh, heavens, no. But they were heads of Taj Hotels, Heritage Hotels, Government of India Tourist Office, and so on. I can't remember all. But it was very impressive. They were delighted to learn that this was my sixth trip to India, not just my first. I let them know how much I love this country."

"Mom, I'd really like to have one of those photos."

"Of course. I'll send it."

Then Catherine went on to tell of her experience at Nagda, relating the incident of the wall. All three of them roared again with laughter. Piku slept through all the hilarity.

"Mom," Sunil laughed, "I wish I had a picture of you on that wall."

"Never mind. It was embarrassing enough without having a permanent record of it. Tell me, Sunil, what is happening here? Has the situation changed?"

"Yes, I think it is better. I told Tapa that I was going to sell the house, and she got scared."

"Mita, do you think things have changed?"

"No. They are still the same."

"But, Mita," said Sunil, "They are better, don't you agree?"

"No."

"Oh, Sunil, I told you to get your house in order before I came back here. Obviously, you have not done anything. You must put down the law to Tapa. You can't allow her to run all your lives. It isn't fair to you, to Mita, and believe me, it is not good for your mama."

"All right. I will do it."

With that, they all retired. Sunil took Piku in his arms and went downstairs. Mita turned off the lights, but Catherine was keyed up and sleep would not come. Over and over thoughts came of Aadi, and she felt a longing for him so deep that it totally surprised her. It wasn't sexual, but a desire to communicate, to share beauty as they had done in Udaipur. This was so foreign to her, and her need was very strong. Suddenly, Catherine had an inspiration. She would write to him and invite him to join her in Goa. Writing is what she always did best, and how better to find out just what this was all about. Was he serious, or was it just a moment in time that meant nothing at all? She had to find out because her emotions were doing flip-flops. As the hours sped onward toward dawn, Catherine composed the letter in her mind. She had to be very careful, because she didn't want to give him the wrong impression. There was no way that she intended to have an affair with this man.

Mita's alarm went off and the two of them got up and dressed for the day. Catherine was taking an early morning flight to Trivandrum, so Sunil, Mita and Piku took her to the airport in a car from Sunil's office. She thanked them, told Sunil once again to get his house in order, then entered the terminal building.

The flight was four hours long, but Catherine loved flying and it was enjoyable. Her proposed letter was still on her mind, as well as all the experiences she had had in Udaipur. She felt a warmth and joy enfold her that she hadn't known for years.

Arriving in Trivandrum, her agent met her, and although he spoke English, it was very difficult to understand him. There in the state of Kerala, the local language is Malayalam, and hearing it, Catherine thought it sounded like they were speaking with marbles in their mouths. The accented English had a similar effect on her ears.

They drove around Trivandrum, whose original name was Thiruvananthapuram, but Catherine saw little to interest her in this city. Sixteen kilometers south was Kovalam Beach, where Catherine was to stay. The hotel was not new, but had newer additions, and was located on the beach. Catherine was delighted with her room, which had a balcony overlooking the Arabian Sea. The water was some 20 feet below her window, and she loved hearing it crash against the rocks.

The first thing she did after getting settled, was to take her pen and start the letter that had been occupying her thoughts since the night before. She had composed it over and over again so often, that the words came easily to her mind and to paper.

She told him how much she had enjoyed Udaipur and meeting him. She wondered if he would be interested in joining her in Goa, and gave him the name 'Taj Village' where she would be staying and the dates. She told him that he would have to come on his own and stay separate, and that he was not to expect anything. She had only sunshine and relaxation to offer, as well as conversation between friends. Also, she made it clear that he was under no obligation to answer. If he was unable to come for business or personal reasons, it would be all right. He would owe her no explanation. If that were the case, she would assume that was the way it was meant to be. She signed her name and took it to the desk the following morning. They told her it would be posted and would probably arrive in Udaipur in two days' time.

The letter was hardly in the box in front of the hotel, when Catherine started sending ESP messages to Aadi. "Please come. Please come. Please come." It never occurred to her that she could just as well have picked up the phone and talked to him. She had his phone number as well as his address. But instinctively she probably realized it was safer this way and her words on paper would not oblige him in any way. He could read it and decide without having to acknowledge it. She also knew that he had a job coming up after 10 days. He told her he would be leaving Udaipur then. So perhaps he would be busy and unable to come even if he wished to do so. But she also knew that he worked free-lance and thought that if he really wanted to join her, he would somehow arrange it. Well, all she could do now was wait.

Catherine had, for a long time, wanted to travel to the tip of India, to Cape Comorin, or as it is known, Kanya Kumari, where the three oceans meet; the Arabian Sea, the Bay of Bengal and the Indian Ocean. From Trivandrum it was but a half day journey. Her guide picked her up and they proceeded south along the coast of Kerala. They stopped at the lovely old, 17th century wooden palace, Padmanabhapuram, the former home of the Maharajas of Travancore. The museum was well worth the visit also. Arriving at Kanya Kumari around noon, Catherine asked her guide to locate a good restaurant. Having found one, she invited their driver to join them and they enjoyed a very fine south Indian thali lunch. Afterwards they had to wait until the tourist business opened again, having shut down over the lunch period. When they were able, they walked through the colorful, busy streets with vendors on all sides. At the water's edge, many devout Hindus were bathing in the sacred waters. Besides bathing in the Ganges and at Varanasi, bathing in these waters completes the lifelong pilgrimage of Hindus. There is a temple on a small island not far from land, where it is said that Pavarti prayed for Shiva to fall in love with her, and when this proved unsuccessful, she dedicated herself to remaining a virgin. A ferry takes tourists and devotees alike to another, larger island, upon which is built the Temple of the Rock, where the Swami Vivakanada meditated before traveling to the West to enlighten people with Hinduism.

The following day was one of rest. Catherine decided to take advantage of the lovely beach, although she was not one to sunbathe. There were numerous beach chairs and umbrellas out on the sand. By giving her room number to an attendant, she was given a towel, which she spread over her lounge chair. For long hours, she sat there gazing at the sea, moving her umbrella occasionally as the sun traveled south and west.

In the afternoon, once again back in her room, she decided to do some spiritual reading. Since arriving in India, she had not done her Centering and she did not feel like doing it then either.

Opening her Benedictine prayers, she began to read. Suddenly, tears started flowing and she got up to go out on her balcony.

The sun was on its last journey into the west. The sea was golden, and she listened as the surf crashed against the rocks below her. She looked up into a cloudless, bright sky, and spoke to God.

"Why, why am I constantly coming back to India? What is the attraction? Why do I have to come back?"

It was as if a curtain was pulled aside. She saw no vision nor heard a voice. But in her heart and soul, she knew God was speaking to her.

YOU HAVE BEEN FAITHFUL TO ME ALL OF YOUR LIFE. INDIA IS MY SPECIAL GIFT TO YOU. THIS IS WHERE YOUR HEART SINGS AND YOUR SPIRIT SOARS. YOU DO NOT NEED ALL YOUR POSSESSIONS. COME HERE, LIVE A SIMPLE LIFE AND BE HAPPY. I HAVE BEEN CALLING YOU FOR A LONG TIME.

The tears flowed down her cheeks and she wondered why she hadn't known this until now. She probably had not been ready for it. Now, the floodgates opened and she sobbed. All of the pain and anguish of a lifetime started to surface. She had kept it bottled inside her for so long. When was the last time she had cried? She couldn't remember. But now, now everything was coming and she didn't know how to stop. All the needs and yearnings of the past many years broke forth, and she felt alive for the first time. Yes, she felt the pain, but also release, and deep sorrow that perhaps she had not been fulfilled as a woman.

Of course she had given birth and had known the joy and fulfillment of that, but she had missed out on a loving relationship, a mutual sharing with a man she loved and who loved her in return. That she had been denied. And because of the trauma she had experienced in her marriage, she no longer loved the man she married 37 years ago. He treated her with such disrespect, such emotional cruelty, that she had deliberately submerged all her feelings. She loathed his touch now and permitted it only because she felt it was her duty.

The weeping finally subsided and her most consuming desire was to share this wondrous experience with someone. That someone, she realized immediately, was Aadi. Why? She barely knew the man, and yet they had shared beauty and something deep, a spirituality that bonded them. At least this is how she felt, and prayed that he would come to Goa.

The next day found her traveling with a driver/guide north to the city of Cochin. They stopped along the way visiting Kottayam, where two Syrian Christian churches were well known, Valia Palli and Cheria Palli. Her driver pointed out various rubber trees, which she was beginning to recognize after her previous trip to Kanya Kumari. Also, pepper vines. She had no idea that pepper grew on vines, and asked about white pepper, and if it grew the same way. He told her that the white pepper grew inside the black. She was astounded. This was lush, fertile country and Catherine enjoyed the entire drive north.

At Cochin she found her hotel to be very seedy. It was dingy and dark, and the carpet in her room was filthy. The restaurant was good, however. The menu was totally south Indian, and she readily ordered from it. The waiters had different ideas, knowing that she was a foreigner. They assumed she would prefer western food, and each time she entered the restaurant, they advised her to choose the buffet. She would shake her head and order a la carte. At breakfast, she decided to have a paratha, but when they brought it, it was without pickle.

"Where is the pickle?" she asked.

"You want pickle, Madam?"

"Yes. It is included on the menu."

The stunned waiter walked away and quickly brought her pickle, then watched as she took some on her plate and proceeded to eat it with her paratha."

At dinner she ordered 'rasam', which is a spicy tomato soup. The chef ran out and said, "Madam, madam, this is not tomato soup." The usual tomato soup was cream of tomato, and it was always very good, but she wanted the rasam.

"I know. Please bring me the rasam."

"But, Madam, it is very spicy."

"Yes, I know. Please bring it to me."

They did, and again watched as she ate it with much pleasure. She couldn't believe it the following day when another chef came out with the same concern.

"Madam, madam, this is not tomato soup."

"I know. I had it yesterday. Please bring it to me."

Her guide around Cochin was a young woman whose name was Suzanne. With a name like that she obviously was Christian. She told Catherine that at present her family was arranging a marriage for her to an Indian boy in the United States.

Here Catherine was taken to Jew Street, where Cochin's Jewish population lived. However, there were only 18 Jews left in the town, most having immigrated to Israel in order to find mates. A lovely old man was standing on the street, watching as Catherine and Suzanne walked toward him.

"Shalom," Catherine said to the man.

His eyes opened wide and he smiled. "Are you Jewish?" he asked.

"No, but my husband is," she told him.

He turned to Suzanne. "Be sure to show her everything," he said.

Before entering the famous synagogue, Catherine noticed symbols on the walls and windows along the street; the Hindu 'swastica' beside the Star of David. Truly this was the one place on earth were Jews were treated kindly, without persecution and accepted into the community.

The Mattancherri Synagogue was beautifully decorated with blue and white Chinese tiles on the floor, and a bevy of Belgian crystal chandeliers hanging from the ceiling. She learned that the tabernacle held ancient scrolls of Mosaic Law. Among its many treasures, a copper plate grant from the Rajas allowing the Jews to call Cochin their home.

A short distance from the synagogue was the spice market. Suzanne brought her to one shop where they enjoyed a cup of spiced tea, and Catherine bought a small sample of the spice combination.

They visited St. Francis Church, originally Roman Catholic, which became Protestant under the Dutch rule and Anglican with the British Raj. Then a visit to the Dutch Palace, where they enjoyed another cup of tea and went off again to the shore to see the Chinese fishing nets.

The backwater cruise they took the following day was not at all what Catherine expected. For some reason she had envisioned narrow waterways, gliding under a ceiling of overhanging trees. But the backwaters were wide canals leading from the ocean. As they sailed along, Suzanne pointed out one island after another, but it was disappointing to Catherinem.

She left the next day for Goa, only the flight was delayed by two hours. Her driver, Agnelo Fernandez, was waiting for her at the airport and they took off immediately for the long trip to Belqaum.

CHAPTER EIGHT
BELGAUM, GOA, MUMBAI

Having left the airport at 4:30, they found the roads good in Goa, but dusty and poor in Karnataka. They wound through the mountains and at the border with Karnataka, a toll had to be paid and papers of driver inspected. Catherine wondered how long it would take to get to Belgaum, but she was enjoying the night as the moon and stars were bright in the sky.

After five hours, they drove into the city of Belgaum. Agnelo asked directions several times of people and drivers on the streets. Catherine told him the address was off Dr. Ambedkar Road. Even in the dark, she thought she would recognize the area. Driving along, nothing looked familiar and she had no phone number. When she was in Delhi, she had tried calling the number she had for Belgaum, but it had been changed. Sunil told her to write a note to Ramu, which she hurriedly did, then he had sent it via courier.

Now, the city seemed so big and Catherine wondered if it was going to be impossible to find the house. But suddenly there was the statue of Dr. Ambedkar and she knew where she was. She told Agnelo that it was on the right side of the road and there was a Muslim cemetery behind their house. They found the cemetery, then Catherine found the road which went off the main artery and meandered down to Ramu and Asha's house.

She jumped out of the car and went to their door. The screen was open and the family was inside.

"Hi, I'm here."

"Charu," Ramu exclaimed. "We were worried about you."

"My plane was late coming into Goa, but here I am."

"Good, good." Ramu came outside.

"This is my driver, Agnelo. He will return for me on Wednesday."

Ramu and Agnelo spoke, then Agnelo brought her bags into the house and left.

"You are coming from Bombay?"

"Oh, no. I was down south. Trivandrum, Kanya Kumari, and Cochin. My plane was two hours late leaving Cochin, and Agnelo, the poor boy, was waiting all that time for me in Goa."

Catherine embraced Asha and Preema and Vimala, as all three stood with smiles on their faces. She felt at home and comfortable to be with these wonderful people once again.

"Come, see your room," Ramu said. "We have made changes since you were here last."

She followed Ramu up the stairs and Preema and Vimala carried her bags. There at the top of the stairs, only a few steps up from Asha and Ramu's room, was a large new area. One room on the right had been made into Ramu's office and sitting room. Next to it was a large tiled bathroom, and across the hall a lovely bedroom. It had windows overlooking the garden on the side and also in the back. Catherine was delighted with her accommodations.

Of course Preema had dinner ready for her and she was grateful to be enjoying her wonderful food once again. Asha and Ramu reminisced with her about their trip to the United States a year and a half ago. Seventeen days they had spent with Catherine in Duluth.

The Shenoys had flown to England and visited their daughter, who had just had her first child. Then they came to America where their older son lived in Maryland. Ajit rented a van and took his family along with his parents to Niagara Falls and visited Washington D.C. on the 4th of July. Ramu thought his son could drive them to Minnesota and that Catherine would drive them back. He had no idea of the distance between the east coast and the Midwest.

"That's not possible, Papa," Ajit told him. "You will have to fly."

They flew into Duluth and were greeted warmly by Catherine. She couldn't believe they were actually there. So many years had passed since she had first met them in England, and ten years of correspondence before she ever saw them again in India. Then there were many visits to their home when she came to India. How she had yearned for them to come to her country, and finally they had come.

When Catherine had heard from Ramu of their proposed visit, she started cooking Indian food and storing it in her deep freeze. She knew that, for the most part, they were vegetarian, but she had prepared chicken dishes as well, just in case they would enjoy non-veg.

The only meal she had trouble with was breakfast, because she didn't know how to make dosas or any other south Indian food. Finally, Ramu got tired of her fare and told Asha to show her how to make 'Oopmah', or as Asha called it, 'Karnataka Opittu', made with cream of wheat, or Indian 'sooji'. After tasting that spicy dish, Catherine decided she would never eat cream of wheat the western way again.

Asha showed her how to make several kinds of dosas and gave her more recipes, such as sambar and idli. They had a wonderful time in Catherine's large kitchen and they wished only that Preema could have been with them.

Asha and Ramu were devotees of Ganesh, the elephant headed god. Catherine set up a shrine with a large picture of Ganesh and a small idol of him in their room. They were so pleased that they were able to worship and told her they felt it was just like home. Everyday Catherine went to her garden and picked a daylily for Asha to place before the shrine.

After several days, Catherine took them, along with her mother, who had met them also on the same trip to England, to the Twin Cities. After all, they had come from so far, they also had to see the capital of Minnesota and more of the beautiful state where she lived. In the Cities, they stayed at a motel and were able to meet two of Catherine's sons, who lived in the area. She took them on a boat ride on the Mississippi River, to a Somerfest concert at Orchestra Hall, on a tour of the State Capitol and a visit to the Minnesota Museum of History. Included in the tour was a drive through the beautiful lake district of Minneapolis and a visit to the famous Minnehaha Falls. Asha remarked over and over how clean it was. Ramu made another observation.

"Where are all the people? All I see are cars. There are no people on the street."

It was difficult to find restaurants where they could get the food they could eat. There were so many fast food places, but try to find somewhere that served vegetarian. Catherine took them to one Indian restaurant, but they didn't care for the food, or the attitude of the owners.

"Catherine," Asha said, "Your rice is very good. This is not cooked right. Let's go back to your house."

And when they asked for finger bowls because they had eaten with their hands, the management told them, "Our customers don't eat with their hands." They did however find them bowls, but they were large serving bowls, and Catherine was indignant, feeling that her guests had been insulted.

They drove back to Duluth, where she also took them on a day trip to the iron range to see the large open-pit mines. Of course there were many sights around Duluth and the weather held beautifully for them. They took a boat cruise on Lake Superior and most of all they enjoyed the rose garden. Catherine took many photos of them and consequently sent them several copies of each one. It was a most memorable visit and one that Catherine would never forget.

Now she was once more a guest in their home, but she felt more like their sister. Asha even told her, "I lost my sister and now I have you."

They spent many hours talking and reminiscing. And every afternoon, they would take a nap. Catherine didn't always sleep, but prayed and wrote in her journal. Sleep was difficult at night, because she went over and over in her mind what Aadi had said to her and she could still feel his arms about her. She carried on one-sided conversations with him until she thought she would go mad. She prayed that he would come to Goa so they could talk, and one morning she awoke with the certitude that he was coming. From then on, she couldn't wait to get back to Goa.

Just after she arrived in Belgaum, Ramu had a different idea.

"I thought we would get in the car and drive to Ankola to visit Sadhana and Dinu, then drive up to Bombay."

Catherine was dismayed. This would have spoiled all her plans. "Ramu," she replied, "I only want to visit with you. I've been traveling since I got to India, and I thought we would just be together here."

"Don't you want to go to Ankola?"

"Yes, but some other time. I have all my reservations made for the rest of my trip. I only want to be with the two of you and enjoy the quiet here."

"See, I told you," said Asha to Ramu. "There is no use driving all that distance to Ankola. She just came from Goa. It is better to stay here."

So it was settled. They stayed home and Preema cooked different dishes for her every day. Vimala called her, 'Auntie', and her smiling face was always there wanting to serve her. She washed her clothes, cleaned her room and brought her water or tea or anything else she could think of to please her. Catherine felt comfortable and happy here with her Indian family of so many years. They were truly her sister and brother. It was not long before she became quite proficient in using water to cleanse herself after going to the toilet. She realized that it was far more sanitary than using toilet paper.

Wednesday arrived and she waited eagerly for Agnelo to come for her. Now she was anxious to the point of jittery. She could hardly wait to get to Goa, because she was sure that Aadi would be there, or would come soon to visit her. Agnelo was late, and she was afraid she was showing her nervousness. Of course she never said anything to Asha or Ramu about what had happened to her in Udaipur.

Catherine had told them of her desire to live in India some day and that she was anxious for that to happen. Ramu told her she could live like a Maharani with her money. She didn't want to live like that, but it was fun to think about where she might live and what she would do. Ramu was very enthusiastic about her intent to eventually 'shift' to India, but Asha said, "Catherine, you want to live in India where it is so dirty. I want to live in America where it is clean." And Catherine laughed.

Agnelo arrived, and had his girlfriend with him. He said they had come to Belgaum the night before so that he would be ready to pick her up in the morning. The luggage was stored in the car, and the girlfriend sat in the back, leaving the front available to Catherine. She said her good-byes and Asha blessed her before leaving by placing a tiki on her forehead. She was very touched and emotional as she looked back and waved to her dear, dear family, wondering when she would see them again.

The drive through the mountains in daylight was spectacular. They stopped at many places to take photos. Agnelo took a different route from the one in which he had brought her. This particular road took them only three hours and they were in Goa. Catherine couldn't figure out why he had taken the longer route the first time. But at last she was in Goa, and this being his city, Agnelo drove directly to the Hotel Taj Village.

She thanked Agnelo, gave him a generous tip, said her good-byes and went to Reception to check in. There she signed the register and filled out the passport information. She also took a quick look at the faces in the lobby.

"Were there any messages for me?" she asked.

"No, Ma'am."

Catherine was taken to her villa, which was just around the corner from the reception hall. It was an eight room cottage and she had one on the ground floor, with a lovely verandah in the back overlooking the beautiful gardens and manicured lawns. It was very private and she felt happy.

So sure she was that Aadi was coming, she hurriedly unpacked and took her shower. Dressing in a sari, she tried to relax and wait. And wait she did, hour after hour. By 5 PM, she knew that he was not coming and she began to berate herself.

"You foolish, ridiculous, old woman, Catherine! My God, you REALLY thought Aadi was coming! You could hardly wait to get here. You barely slept last night and couldn't wait to leave Belgaum. Well, here you are. If he were coming, he would be here already. Dumb! Dumb! Dumb! You misread EVERYTHING! And your wild imagination was just that! Stupid! Stupid! Stupid! You opened your heart for the first time in years, and now you are devastated. Well, it's your own fault."

The tears started flowing down her cheeks and she let them fall. She told herself it was crazy, because she had been definite about giving him the choice not to come if he couldn't or didn't want to. She also had made it plain that he owed her no explanation. Even though she felt she had prepared for this eventuality, her feelings now indicated that she had not. Looking at her phone, she willed it to ring, but it didn't.

Wiping her tears away, she freshened up and walked down the lighted pathway to the restaurant. There she was greeted and seated by a young hostess. She ordered typical Goanese food and enjoyed the highly spiced fish and vegetables. After dinner, she walked around the grounds, following the lovely paths and remembering her last visit to this place four years earlier.

Back in her room, the first thing she did was look at the phone to see if there had been any message. Her heart fell and once again the tears started. She undressed and put on her nightgown. It was a beautiful night, so she went out on her verandah and sat watching the sky and the myriad of stars. Her heart ached, but she was angry with herself.

She lay in bed unable to fall asleep. The tears kept coming and she let them fall. Despite all those 'conversations' she had had with Aadi when she was in Belgaum, this was different. She had been so wise about the situation then. Oh, she was not physically attracted. Oh, no! And whatever he might think or desire, she had been determined not to give in to anything sexual. "No," she had told herself. "I must keep faith with God and that means to keep to my vows. I am a married woman. Even if it will be difficult for me, Aadi will help me."

How utterly unrealistic she had been! He didn't want her, otherwise he would be here or he would have sent a message. This had all been in her mind. It was nothing more than wishful thinking. What a fool she was!

The next morning she made her way to the small shore café, The Caravel, and had her breakfast. It was marvelous to sit under an umbrella and look out at the sand and the sea. She knew what she was going to do. Back at her room, she changed her clothes and rubbed a sun block on her arms, face, neck and legs. Then she started off for the beach, where she walked along the water's edge, often getting her skirt soaked up to her knees. She started to pray, and as she did so, the tears fell again. For a long way she walked and prayed and wept.

"Why, God, did you bring this man into my life? Why did you awaken me after so long, only to be disappointed? I can't believe this pain that I am experiencing. I allowed so many emotions to surface after years of suppression, only to be hurt and disillusioned again. Why is this happening to me? Am I to be allowed no happiness in this life?

"Now I hold suspect that 'awakening' I had in Kovalam Beach. Were You truly speaking to me or was that another fantasy? I know You hear me and I know that You know my heart and how I feel even better than I do. You know what I need. What I don't understand is why You leave me so bereft in this beautiful spot, in this beautiful country. I thought You told me that this is the only place on earth where I will be happy, but I am so miserable right now and my heart is breaking."

For the first time in years she was lonely. She had steeled her heart against that emotion because she was always alone. But despite being alone, she had managed somehow, over the years, to keep from being lonely.

These were her thoughts as she walked along the beach. Returning, she sat by the pool in the shade of a coconut palm and fell asleep. She had lunch at the Caravel again, and ate their wonderful coconut ice cream. Afterwards, Catherine took off once again for the beach. It seemed the only place where she wanted to be, but the prayers and weeping continued. After her walk, she showered and went to the reception hall, where she watched people coming and going, willing to see the familiar face she so longed to see coming toward her. When she had told him in her letter that if it wasn't meant to be, then so be it, she would accept that. She hadn't known then how painful, how hurtful it would be to 'accept'.

Her blood sugar was keeping low, so obviously she was eating correctly, and too, the exercise of walking the beach was doing its work. She dressed in another sari and was again seated by the same hostess in the restaurant.

"Are you Indian?" she asked Catherine.

"Oh, no, I am not, but thank you for the compliment."

"Do you live in India?"

"No, I am here on holiday. Why do you ask?"

"Because you come in a sari."

"I have many saris and I enjoy wearing them."

"You look beautiful in them."

"Well, I thank you, dear. You are very kind."

Catherine got through another night, waking sometime in the middle of it and weeping. If this didn't stop, she was going to be sick. What was happening to her? Back to the beach she went the following morning and her prayers never ceased. It was her only release. And speaking to herself, she tried to come to grips with the situation.

"I have to get through this pain so that I can enjoy this beautiful spot and have good, happy memories of this, my sixth time in India. Never have I felt like this in my India. Always I have drunk in her beauty and loved her people and it has been enough for me. Now, I can't get Aadi off my mind. I would so have loved to share this place with him. He is sensitive to beauty and nature. We could have been so happy here together. That is why I am so lonely, because I am not able to share this with him. Father in Heaven, help me to stop hoping and dreaming. I still have three days left in Goa. I must find peace. I have read my psalms, my Rule of Benedict and *Too Deep For Words*. But I end up crying all the time."

Asha had told her in Belgaum that crows 'caw' when someone is coming. She had said that she had heard a crow 'caw' before Catherine arrived. Catherine sat now on her verandah and listened to the caws of many crows. But it was not meant for her. Her visitor did not arrive.

Again she awoke in the night. Her arms ached for the feel of him. Her whole body felt the need of him. Oh, God! Why is this happening?

"Father," she prayed, "If I cannot have four, nor three, nor even one day with Aadi, could I please have just 10 minutes? Surely that would be all right. No harm could come from that." Sobs came again, and it was a long time before she slept.

Aadi had told her when he had looked at her itinerary that he always stayed at the Taj Hermitage. That was up on the Fort Aguada promontory, and only a 10 minute walk, but she could not make herself investigate. She seemed to be stuck there at the Village. Perhaps she unconsciously thought if she left, he might come and not find her. However unreasonable, it held her fast.

This day she could not go to the beach. The soles of her feet were sore from the hot sand of so much walking. Once again she thought to write to him. She spent most of the day composing it, put it away, then read it over and over and put it away once more. There was always a possibility that she would regret something she wrote after she had mailed it. So, she waited.

In this letter she asked questions of him. Why had he taken her in his arms? Why had he taken her to that special place to plant the olive cuttings? Why had he held her hand? Why had he hired a private boat for her? Why had he held her again and kissed her? Why had he thrown kisses across the table at her in the coffee shop? Why had he told her he had wanted to buy her a gift? What had happened, really, between them? She wrote that she would go home and heal herself, but she had felt a bonding with him and thought that he had had a similar feeling. She also mentioned that she had had a spiritual experience in Kovalam Beach and that she had wanted to share it with him.

At dinner that evening, the hostess started a conversation with her, and the waiters, knowing that she enjoyed the spicy food, brought her several varieties of pickles to sample. She was touched by their delight in serving her.

Her hostess' name was Gitane, and she was only 17 years old. Gitane was very excited when she learned that Catherine was from America.

"Oh, you won't believe this," she told Catherine, "But I have always wanted to go to America. I told my mother this when I was just a little girl."

"Well, then someday you will come."

"I don't like it here. I hate it."

"But why?"

"There is so much gossip. I can't live my life. I go to school, but I work here. I am the only girl, and if I talk to one boy, the others are jealous. And I am getting a reputation because I am working with all boys. I just hate it."

"Could you look for another job?"

"Yes, but I want and need this experience, because I want to be in hotel management."

"I see. Well, would you be able to leave India and come to the United States?"

"Yes, I think so. I have an auntie who lives in Canada."

"Well, Gitane, how would you like to come to my city? You could go to school there and live in my home. I have a big house and there are two colleges within walking distance."

"Really? I would like that so much. But I would have to talk to my parents about it."

"Yes, of course. I will give you my address and you can write to me."

Not once did Catherine give a second's thought about what her husband would say about this. If she had thought about it, she would have known that he would be furious. But here in India, the hospitality of these people was so open, and when she had spent time with them, she began to think as they did. So she felt comfortable with this invitation, thinking how nice it would be to have a young person in the house again.

Catherine continued to feel sorry for herself and the tears kept falling. She knew for certain now that Aadi was not coming and she had to find acceptance. Every night in Goa she had awakened weeping. Now she looked at and read the letter again. It still seemed right to her.

Then, on her last day, she decided she had to call his home. She was terribly nervous, but she felt compelled to phone him. The call went through and a man answered and told her that Aadi was not in Udaipur. She thanked him and hung up. So, he must be on tour, for he certainly was not in Goa. After settling her bill at Reception and checking out, she mailed her letter there at the desk.

The Taj Village van took her to the airport, where she had difficulty because her ticket was marked, 'wait-listed'. She knew that it no longer was because Sunil had informed her that it had been since confirmed, but she couldn't get the agents at the counter to listen to her. It finally took the agent from the Taj making a great show of importance by running from one area to another to finally tell her that HE had seen to the confirmation. All they would have had to do was look in their computer. But knowing the ways of India, she simply gave the agent a good tip and she had her ticket confirmed.

In Bombay Catherine was met by Mathew Albuquerque. His smiling face was there to greet her. He flagged a taxi and took her to her hotel which was in Santa Cruz, the same area where the Albuquerques lived. She had come to Bombay with the express purpose of visiting them.

They had first met in Duluth at Catherine's church of St. Michael's. It had been the same year that Asha and Ramu had visited, but the Albuquerques had just left when the Shenoys arrived, so they never met.

Catherine had been to her church for a meeting when she looked out of the window and saw, standing in the parking lot, this Indian couple, the woman wearing a sari. Catherine ran out and started talking to them, telling them that she had often been to India. They were a lovely couple and very friendly. They were visiting their two sons who lived in Lakeside, an area in the eastern part of Duluth, but told her they lived in Bombay. While they were conversing, a car drove up and it was their older son, Mahesh. Catherine told the three of them that she was free during the day and would be happy to take them sightseeing or anywhere they would like to go, since Mahesh was working and his brother, Hilo, was in school at UMD.

That was the beginning of a lasting friendship. Catherine was invited to their house in Lakeside for lunch and again for dinner. She drove them around Duluth and showed them sights that their sons had not shown them. Catherine did not think it was a coincidence that she had been at her church on a particular evening when she met them. She felt God was at work in her life. For two years she had been unable to go to India, so God brought India to her; first by introducing her to the Albuquerques and then by bringing Asha and Ramu to Duluth. A year before that, Catherine had just happened to be at a Mass where two Indian priests had con-celebrated with Father Frank Melosovich. One of those priests had been Teresa and Mat's son, Sunder. After that Mass, Catherine had stayed to talk to those priests, asking Fr. Frank if he had told them there was a parishioner there with ties to their country. So Catherine felt there were too many coincidences to call them anything but providential.

One day, Catherine decided to have a dinner party for the Albuequerques. She invited Mahesh and his girlfriend, who was a student from Turkey, and who lived with him. Hilo asked if he could also bring a friend, and Catherine agreed.

"Teresa," she said, "I am going to cook Indian for you."

"Oh, no, Catherine, that isn't necessary. We like American food. Please do not trouble yourself."

"But I want to do this. And, Teresa, I cook Indian often in my home."

Catherine could tell that Teresa was dismayed and thinking that she didn't know how to cook Indian. She smiled to herself and thought, "You will see. And you will enjoy."

The appointed evening arrived and when they were ushered into the living room, Catherine gave them sweet lassi, which is a delicious yoghurt drink, and cauliflower pakoras, small flowerets dipped in batter then deep fried. With the pakoras, she served a yoghurt based mint-coriander chutney, or dip. Teresa immediately exclaimed that the lassi tasted 'just like home.'

The ensuing dinner was an equal success. Even the fried, puffy bread called, 'poori', turned out perfectly. Teresa told her, "Catherine, this was a lot of work."

"Only another Indian cook would know that," Catherine laughed.

"Really, we had no idea that you could cook Indian like this."

"I know, Teresa. You were afraid of what I was going to serve you."

"But this is delicious. I can't believe that an American can cook Indian food like this."

"Mom," teased Mahesh, "She cooks better than you." They all laughed and the evening was a triumph.

The Albuquerques were Goanese. They spoke the regional language of Konkani, as did the Shenoys. The Albuquerque's ancestors remained in Goa when the Portugese invaded and were Christianized and renamed. The Shenoy's ancestors fled and remained Hindus.

So now Catherine was in Bombay where the Albuquerques lived most of the year. However, they had a home in Goa, in the Anjuna area. Teresa was an author of several books relating to Goa and Bombay, and Mathew was a retired microbiologist, who had worked for a pharmaceutical company.

Now, having arrived at her hotel, an argument ensued between Mat and the driver of the taxi. He was going to charge Catherine Rs. 450, when Mat argued that the charge should be between Rs. 40 and Rs. 60. Leaving Catherine at the hotel, Mat had the driver take him to his home, but on the way, he insisted that they stop at the police station. Mat was going to report this incident. When the driver realized what was happening, he was most satisfied with the fair price that Mat was willing to give him.

That evening she dressed in a new black sari which she had purchased in Delhi with Mita. In Belgaum, Asha gave her several more saris and arranged for blouses and petticoats to be made for her. So this evening, she felt very elegant, and in the lobby, awaited Mathew to pick her up.

At the Albuquerque residence, Teresa welcomed her warmly. There she met Mat's unmarried older sister, Sunanda and Sarita,

Teresa and Mat's daughter and granddaughter and a friend of the family, Bella, from Canada. It was a lovely evening. Catherine enjoyed the food and the family.

During the evening, Teresa told Catherine she had a favor to ask.

"Of course, Teresa. What can I do for you?"

"Mahesh and Nihal are getting married, and Mahesh has asked that we send a sari. We have been invited to the wedding, of course, but we don't feel that we want to go. I told you in Duluth that we asked Nihal to be married in our church, but she refuses. We didn't ask her to become Catholic, only to be married by a priest. But she will not do this. So they plan to be married in a civil ceremony."

"I see. Well, Teresa, I know this is hurting you. It hurt my parents deeply when I married Bran before a Justice of the Peace. But two years later we were married by a priest. Perhaps something like that will happen to Mahesh and Nihal."

"We don't have much hope for that. But, Catherine, please, if you cannot do this, we want you to tell us."

"What is it, Teresa?"

"Could you take the sari back to Duluth for us?"

"Oh of course. It would be an honor for me to do so."

"I want to show it to you. My daughters and I chose it."

Teresa went into another room and brought out a handsome box and opened it. There was the lovely sari in white with red and gold embroidery. Catherine sighed with joy when she saw it.

"Oh, Teresa, Nihal will just love it, and look so beautiful in it."'

Teresa also took out a petticoat and the sari blouse and a pair of chappels, sandals with thongs.

"Do you have room for these?" Teresa asked her."

"I'll make room. But I am afraid that I cannot take the lovely box. However, I promise you that I will gift wrap it beautifully when I get to Duluth and present it to her. I will take photographs also and send them to you."

"Catherine, I have another favor to ask."

"Yes?"

"This bangle," Teresa showed her a beautiful gold bracelet studded with gems. "This," she said, "belonged to my mother. I want Nihal to have it. Would you take it to her? Or if you do not feel 'right' about it, please say, 'No.'

"Oh, Teresa, this is so very lovely. Of course I will take it to her. I will wrap this separately from the sari. This is a very great honor for me. And I feel very 'right' about it. I will carry it with me at all times. It will not go in my suitcase."

"Catherine, you accept this favor just like an Indian would, you feel honored."

"I do feel that way and also I feel honored that you see me as Indian." She then invited them to have lunch at her hotel the following day and they accepted.

Sunanda's husband, Lulu, arrived with his car and driver. They took Catherine back to her hotel on their way home. It turned out that Lulu had a sister by the name of Catherine.

That was her last day in Bombay, and she was to have checked out by noon, but Sunil had called and arranged for her to stay until 4 PM. However, she had packed and saw no reason to remain in the room since the Albuquerques were coming for lunch and she wouldn't need it any more.

But before vacating, she picked up the phone and called Sunil. He was at the airport, Mita told her. She had called to say good-bye and promised to write soon. Mita told her that Piku had been asking when 'Mum' was coming back. That pleased Catherine because he was so shy, she couldn't figure out if he liked her or not. Then, she placed a call to Udaipur. A man answered, whom Catherine was sure was Aadi's father. He was soft spoken and sounded very kind.

"Aadi is not here," he told her.

"I see. Would you please tell him the American lady called to say, 'good-bye'?"

"What is your name?"

"My name is Catherine."

"Is there a message?"

"I just called to say, 'good-bye'."

"I will tell him."

"Thank you, Mr. Abhimani." And she hung up.

Catherine and the Albuquerques enjoyed a delicious lunch of lobster in the hotel restaurant. Afterwards, Mathew and Teresa invited her to come to their home until it was time to leave for the airport. Catherine was pleased to do this because there would be many hours to kill before her plane left in the wee hours of the next morning. But before they left the hotel, there was a phone call from Sunil, so she was able to say her good-byes to him also.

At the Albuquerque's home, they opened the flat next to them and put a sheet on a bed for her to take a nap. They had the keys to the flat while the neighbors were away, and were sure that it would be OK for Catherine to use the bed and the bathroom facilities. Later, she had supper with them. Then Lulu sent his car and driver so that Mathew could take her to the airport.

Her journey in India was over. Always leaving India, she cried. This was no exception. How many tears had she shed this time?

On her way home, Catherine relived the great moments, and hugged them to herself. She still felt bereft without Aadi, and wondered if he would answer her letter.

"He will probably write after he gets the photos I will send him," she thought. "Maybe he just doesn't give a damn, and I won't hear from him at all. Maybe he will tell me to get lost, or something like that, but very kindly, of course, because he is a kind man. Whatever, I have got to get a whole new perspective because I think of him all the time."

CHAPTER NINE
A TALK WITH SONS

"You only know me as your mother," she began. "You don't know anything about ME, the child I was growing up, the young adult with dreams and visions of a bright future, the young wife and the woman she became."

It was a cold snowy night in February of 1997. The roads were extremely icy in spots and Catherine drove carefully down the freeway, passing many cars that had slid off the road and were waiting for assistance or a tow. She had left St. Paul and was on her way to her son, Russell's home, in Blaine, where she had plans to meet with all four of her sons. Randall lived at Russell's and Robert was there from Fargo, working on Russell's basement. It was a new house and Robert, having finished basements in two of his own homes, offered to do the same for Russell. Roland and Anne, who lived in Plymouth, were due to arrive at Russell's also, and all had to wait until Russell finished work and made it home.

Earlier that day, Catherine had driven out to see Russell's house. Julie, Russell's fiancée was home and the two of them sat and had a cup of tea.

"How was India, Cathy?" Julie asked.

"Oh, Julie, it was a wonderful trip. So much happened to me. That is where I belong. Someday I have to live there."

"Cathy, what do you mean, 'live' there?"

"Just that, Julie. I've been called to go there and make a life there. Not yet, of course, but eventually."

"But, Cathy, why?"

"That's where I'm happy. I'm healthier there. My spirit is renewed there."

"Cathy, you just can't do this. What about your sons?"

"Julie, what about my sons? They are adults with their own lives."

"But you have to talk to them. They don't understand why you love India so much, and they are going to be completely thrown by the news that you want to move there. And what about Bran?"

"I don't know about Bran. I haven't thought that far."

"You have to talk to your sons."

"All right, Julie. Robert is here, so it is a good time. I'll call Roland and Anne and get everyone together tonight. Is that all right with you?"

"Yes, but Russell works late."

"That's OK. I'll wait until he gets home. I won't have a better chance to talk to all four of them. I want you and Anne there also. I just wish Kerry could be here too."

So, now they were altogether, some on sofas, others on the floor, sprawled over Russell and Julie's living room. She had just opened her talk by telling them they only knew her as their mom.

"I was here at Russell's earlier today and after talking to Julie, I decided this was a good time to talk to you about India. I know none of you understand why I am so attracted to that country and I didn't either until this last trip. But in order to explain the effect India has on me, I need you to understand who I am, who I really am.

"When I was a little girl, in grade school, I was extremely shy. I know that is hard to believe of me now, but I was afraid to talk. I was so shy that if I saw someone coming down the street that I knew, I would cross the street rather than meet and have to talk with them. I hated it when my mother would send me to the store. They were not supermarkets like now.

You had to tell the clerk what you wanted and he or she would get it for you. I remember the butcher shop particularly. There were two butchers in the department. My mother always told me, "Go to Jack, not Doug." Well, I'd go and Jack would be busy, and Doug would ask me what I wanted. What was I to do? I let him wait on me, and then my mother would be angry when I got home. I was too embarrassed to tell Doug that I had to wait for Jack. Things like that upset me terribly. Randall, I know that you inherited so much of my shyness. I understand, probably better than anyone, how painful it is. I don't think you ever believed me when I told you that I too was shy as a child. But also, I was shy into my young adulthood. Always in school, I would never raise my hand if I knew the answer to a question. I would shake my head if called upon, because I couldn't open my mouth to speak. I don't know why I was so shy.

"I was very sheltered as a child. My grandmother lived with us, and she dominated the household. If my parents agreed to allow me to do something, Grandma would disapprove, and I wouldn't be able to do it. For example, I wanted a bicycle. My parents were going to buy me one, but Grandma forbade it because she had seen someone killed on one. I was never given a bike and I can't ride one to this day. I know that my grandmother loved me, but she hovered over me, smothering me. I would be playing with my dolls and as I talked to them, she would listen, so that I was unable to play comfortably by myself. I was never allowed to play outside of our fenced in yard. My friends could climb the apple trees, play in the alley, but not I. I knew nothing of sports. My parents were not sports-minded and I never learned at home how to play any kind of ball. And because I wasn't allowed to play outside of my yard, I didn't learn from the kids in my neighborhood. Consequently, I was a lame duck at school when I was required to play softball in the gym. No one wanted me on their team, and I felt deep rejection.

"Another rejection I felt was being a student at an Irish Catholic school. I was of German descent, so I was not considered as good as the Irish. Our pastor was Fr. Casey, and he told us repeatedly that if we weren't Irish, we should wish to be. I was never given a front row seat in a classroom. Always I was seated in the back while the Irish students were seated in front.

"My friends were few, and only girls of course. In those days, girls and boys barely spoke to one another. We were shy of one another, and the nuns did nothing to dispel this attitude. I went to numerous birthday parties as a kid, and my grandmother always bought me a handkerchief to give as the present. She thought it was the best gift anyone could give or receive. She was probably right, but the girls would always laugh at me when the gift was opened. "Don't you ever give anything but hankies?" they would say, and I would be mortified. My birthday, as you know, is January 3rd, and always fell during Christmas vacation. I would send out party invitations. My mother would set the table for eight or ten or for however many I had invited. Seldom did all of them come. I remember one birthday in particular. Only one girl showed up, and the two of us sat at this huge table all by ourselves. Do you have any idea what this did to a sensitive, shy little girl?

"Another thing that made me stand out as different from the others. My hair was very fine and very straight, like yours, Robert. My mother insisted that I wear braids. I hated braids. My hair was long and Mother wouldn't hear of it being cut and curled. "You look neat," she would say. But I didn't care about being 'neat'. I wanted to look pretty like the other girls. I wasn't allowed to cut my hair until I went to high school.

"Being so shy with everyone, it was no wonder that I was scared to death of boys. In high school the girls were starting to date, and by the time I was a junior, there was the Junior-Senior Prom that had to be attended. I didn't know anyone to ask and it was extremely painful when my friends were talking about the dresses they had bought and anticipating the wonderful evening they were going to have with their dates. I attended a girl's academy, so if we wanted boys to accompany us to our dances, we had to do the inviting. This was completely impossible for me to do. My cousin, Joe, who was the same age as I, and was going to a boys' military academy, fixed me up for a date once or twice. The dates were always disasters because I never found them attractive and I was required to 'neck' with them after we had gone to a movie. I hated dating and my parents shook their heads in exasperation. They could not understand me. Neither of them was like I was. It was in high school that I began to write. I was such a romantic and I read romantic stories, not trash like there is out now, but good love stories. I imagined myself as the heroine and I craved someone to love me, to understand me, to cherish me. I yearned for someone I could talk to, but of course there was no one, so I made up stories in my head and pretended I was the loved one. I pretended every night before I went to sleep. I carried on imaginary conversations, pretended I was being kissed and made love to with great passion. It was in this world of imagination where I felt like a whole person, a person people admired, a person people respected, a person people wanted to be with, a person people loved. I lived in this make-believe world until I got married at the age of 27.

"My sister, Cindy, was born six years after me. It is very strange talking with her now and recalling our childhood. She remembers hers as the most wonderful years of her life. I remember mine with deep resentment and bitterness. But Cindy and I are exact opposites. She was the happy one, the carefree one, always smiling and full of personality. She liked talking to anyone and everyone, and everyone loved her. Cindy was the daughter my parents had wanted and expected me to be. To this day, I am still trying to make my mother accept me. She probably does, but I am so used to her criticism that I expect the worst all the time. "You aren't going to do that, are you?" she said often to me, even after I was married. Also, "Shame on you." She still says that to me, when she doesn't approve of something I've done.

"Cindy doesn't remember how Grandma treated our parents. She was too little at the time. But I remember vividly. My father would take my mother out every Saturday night. That was the one time they had alone together or enjoyed their friends without Grandma sitting in. When they had friends to the house, Grandma always felt they were her company as well, and sat with them, listening to everything they said and interjecting her ideas or opinions. Every Saturday night, and I stress EVERY, I would be awakened from a sound sleep by my grandmother standing at the top of the stairs, which were just outside my room, screaming down at my parents that they were coming home too late. It would be 1:00 AM. She would yell at them for leaving her alone all that time. She would scream they had no right to be coming home at such an hour. They never corrected her. They treated her with the greatest respect. My father never told her it was none of her business when they got home. They allowed her to upset them and the entire household. Our dinners became contests of wills between Grandma and my father. Most of the time, he would leave the table too upset to finish his food.

"Because of Grandma, we never took a vacation anywhere. I remember the only time we took a cabin up north, at Woman Lake. I was five. It is so vivid to me yet. My mother took me out in the lake. Neither of my parents could swim, so we were in very shallow water. I sat down in the sand, and the water covered my head. I didn't know enough to get up, and when my mother noticed, she pulled me out and got angry with me for being so stupid. We were only at the cabin for three days because Grandma ate the wrong foods and had a gall bladder attack and we had to leave in the middle of the night to find a doctor. That was the last vacation we ever took until I was 21 and out of nurses training. My parents were afraid Grandma would get sick again, and there was no chance of our taking any vacation without her. I watched and listened as my friends took off to cabins and various other vacation spots and died inside of envy. A couple of times I was invited to go along on a day trip with a friend, but it was never allowed. They were so afraid something would happen to me.

"I studied piano because it was the first instrument I was introduced to and I fell in love with it. I wanted one and wanted to play like my Aunt Agnes so my grandmother bought me one. My aunt taught me for a year, then I studied with the nuns at the Conservatory. There it was mandatory that I take part in recitals. For three years I suffered through those awful exposures. But around that time, I became aware of the instrument that God had given me, my voice. I lost interest in the piano then, and I wanted to sing. But my mother would not allow me to quit the piano. She kept telling me and everyone else that I had talent at the piano. I don't know where she got that idea, perhaps wishful thinking, but that was not where my talent lay. It was my voice. That was what was special about me. This glorious soprano that came so naturally when I opened my mouth to sing. All through high school I begged for voice lessons. My mother said over and over to me, "Singers are a dime a dozen."

"My cousin Angie was singing, studying and performing on stage. I don't know if, in my shyness, I could have performed on stage, but I wanted to sing and I knew my voice was better than Angie's. This is one of the greatest disappointments of my life, not being given the opportunity to develop my voice at an early age, when, with the proper training, I could have gone on to become an opera singer, one of international renown. I am convinced of that.

"Randall that is why I have continually encouraged you to develop your art abilities. You have such a special gift and could do great things with it if only you would study. It would open a new world for you, one in which you would feel comfortable, with people who have similar interests. You are not too old. One is never too old for art. My voice was totally different. If you don't get the proper training early, and gain experience, no one will book a singer in later years, because the human voice is the most delicate instrument of all and will last only a couple of decades, and then it is gone forever.

"I never liked science, but I became a nurse. At that time, there was very little open for girls. Business school is what my parents wanted for me. Teaching, but that meant college, and not only was I too shy to stand before a classroom, my parents, especially my father, did not believe in college for girls. "A waste of money," he would say. "A girl gets married and then the education goes to waste." Well, that is another story, because from the time I was a teenager, my parents were sure that I would be a spinster. I didn't have the personality to 'catch' a husband. I was a dud. Who would ever want to marry me? Well, it turned out they had me pegged very well. I don't know how they could know that so early, but they also made it clear to me, at that early age, that I would have to find a job to take care of myself, because no one else ever would. So, I chose nursing, my only alternative. The fact that I wanted to go to college and study English Literature and music was entirely out of the question because my parents told me that I would never make a living out of either, and I had to prepare for my future.

"My father was against my going into nursing also, but I won out. I was not going to sit in an office all day, typing and taking shorthand like my mother did. If she felt it was all right for her, OK, but I wanted nothing to do with that kind of life.

"When I was still at St. Joseph's Academy, probably 15 or 16 years old, I got the idea of joining the convent. However, I didn't want to become a Sister of St. Joseph, like the ones who had been teaching me since Kindergarten. I wanted to become a missionary. There was an order called, "The Medical Mission Sisters". It was located in Philadelphia. I corresponded with them for some time and I had visions of someday going to India and nursing there. I had completely forgotten about that until Mary Ann reminded me of that long ago dream. My parents were adamant again. No way would they allow me to join a convent. They told me the order would never train me for nursing.

I would be given menial jobs in the convent and never allowed to become a nurse. They told me it would be OK if I joined AFTER I finished my training.

"By the time I finished training, I had a terrible hunger to become a mother. I could hardly become one in the convent. I dated here and there, but I never met anyone I wanted to spend a life with nor to have children with. Until I met Brandon Forrest. I chose him. He never chose me.

"All my life I had wanted romance. I craved it, needed it, but the choice I made for a husband and father to my children had no romance in him. I was attracted to him because of the way he put children to sleep and he was the most interesting and intelligent man I had ever met. I fell in love with him, and he told me he thought of me like a sister, and not once asked me for a date. I ran after that man for five years and he finally married me, not because he loved me or even cared about me. He told me from the beginning that his mother wanted him out of the house, and I was available so he decided to marry me. He never asked me. He never told me he loved me. We were married in a civil ceremony because he refused to be married in my church.

"I had always dreamed of walking down the aisle in a white wedding gown. Every girl does, I think. That was not to be. Not only did I not have a beautiful wedding, it was horrible. I walked through mud to enter a Quonset hut where a three minute ceremony took place. I had not even one flower, just a beautiful brown lace dress and ruined shoes. I didn't even receive a kiss at the end of that brief exchange.

"Prior to that, I worked at St. Mary's Hospital in the operating room. I was not allowed to tell anyone that I was seeing Brandon. He wanted no one to know. Of course his mother and sister were against his having anything to do with me because I was a Catholic. So, I hid. After two months in Duluth, he took me to Uncle Everett's and they kept the secret of my existence in town. I could not tell any of my friends who I was dating, not even when I was about to be married. I received no parties, no showers, and certainly no gifts. I remember one day when I was visiting at Uncle's house, Grandma Rose and Grandpa Mosey stopped in. I was shoved into the basement, my purse and coat hidden behind the sofa. I sat on the basement steps for over an hour until they left. Often I had to hide below the dash of the car if he recognized someone driving in the opposite direction.

"After marriage I was not allowed to have the friends I had made at St. Mary's. They were from my former life, I was told, and I was not to associate with them any longer. When my parents would come to visit, my husband would run out of the house and barely speak to them. They could never figure out what was wrong, but they were very uncomfortable. After they had left I was grilled as to what we had said about him.

"My wedding night was not a romantic interlude either. I made the reservation for the motel, and my new husband spent the night wetting towels to give moisture to the motel room. We had a three day honeymoon in Arizona so that he could take his oral boards in anesthesia at the same time. Then he couldn't wait to get home to see if he had passed them. The results came to his house in the mail, you see. We did not live together after we were married, either, because we had no apartment, and he refused to live in mine. It wasn't good enough.

"We went to Minneapolis to buy furniture soon after we came back from Arizona. Uncle Byron had a furniture store in Superior at the time, but it was not quality. He sent us to wholesale houses, two actually, and I had to choose all our furniture that weekend. I mean all, because my husband told me he wouldn't make another trip down to the Cities, and I had better be sure of what I chose, because he would never buy me any other for the rest of our lives. I had no idea in what price range to look. I was never told about his wage scale, or about anything financial. Also, we had no apartment, no house, so I had no idea what to buy. It was a most stressful weekend, but I chose the furniture with which you grew up and is in our home today,

"We found a duplex on 21st Avenue East and lived above our landlady. I had no friends, no contact with anyone except Auntie Tyne. Doctors' wives didn't work at that time, so I had little to occupy my time. My husband would come home at night and be angry with me because I was able to be home and he had to work. Finally I called St. Mary's and asked if they could use me during summer vacation time when they were short of help. They readily accepted my offer. When my husband came home that night and ranted again about my having such a soft life at his expense, I told him I had gotten my job back at St. Mary's. He was furious with me, and I had to call the hospital the following day and tell them I wasn't able to work after all

"During my first year of marriage I became very ill. I had been trying to get pregnant, and I ended up with a cyst on my right ovary which was removed. My doctor found I had endometriosis, which was why I was not conceiving. He told me he had cleaned me out surgically, but didn't want me to menstruate for a couple of months, so prescribed Enovid, the birth control pill, a synthetic estrogen. I was allergic to the drug and went into full blown hepatitis. I was hospitalized for forty days, during which time they did exploratory surgery because the doctors refused to believe the drug had caused the hepatitis. I was terribly ill all this time, with constant fatigue, jaundice, and intense itching. I was on complete bed rest, but could not sleep because of the itching. They did many blood tests; every day I was stuck with needles. I was given both upper and lower GI exams, and nothing pointed to the reason for my disease. After the surgery I had special nurses around the clock for three days. I was so weak that I couldn't speak a complete sentence without gasping for breath every two words. I had IV's in both arms and a tube in my belly draining bile. During my entire stay in the hospital, my husband never spent even ten minutes with me. He saw me in the morning on the way to work and maybe a couple times during surgical breaks during the day, just to poke his head in. He never saw me after work. He always went home without saying good-bye, and never once came back in the evening. I was alone. My parents didn't come, because my sister had just had a baby and she needed them. One day, my Uncle Myron stopped to see me. He was in Duluth on business. When he saw me, he must have gotten scared, because he went back to St. Paul and told my parents if they wanted to see me alive they had better go to Duluth right away. They came.

"I knew that I really had no marriage, not the kind anyway that I had always wanted and dreamed of having. I could have chosen to end it, but I opted to stay in it. There were times when my husband would not speak to me for days, the longest I remember was three weeks, but I wanted children above all other things, so I chose to put up with the emotional abuse. We went through a living hell trying to adopt. The first problem was that there was no religion in the home, and there was a state law that children had to be placed in homes of the same religion as their natural mothers. My husband decided that I should go back to my religion and then we could adopt a Catholic baby. My parents were our witnesses as we went through another ceremony. It was no celebration. I had had a cyst removed from my breast the night before, and we just stood with our coats on one Saturday afternoon in church and said our vows before a priest. My husband was angry and barely spoke to me. I remember him saying to my mother, "Well, are you happy now?" And my mother replied, "Yes." We also had a problem because we were in the medical field, and the case worker kept asking us to agree to take a baby with severe medical problems. I would cry after she had left our home, and my husband would scream and yell.

"But we finally got our beautiful son because our first case worker went back to school and mercifully we got another one who was human and understanding. I got pregnant the following month, but it was a blighted ovum and I miscarried. Then I got pregnant again and carried the fetus for thirteen weeks, at which time I went into labor, entered the hospital and lost the baby. Again I was alone. My husband spent no time with me in the hospital. I labored alone, and I aborted alone in the middle of the night. I was emotionally upset, having lost a baby. I called my husband to tell him. He came to the hospital, stood at the foot of the bed, and yelled at me. He said I should not expect to ever get pregnant again, because he would never go thought this again. I cried all the rest of the night and into the morning when I had to go to surgery for a D&C, to remove the last vestiges of my lost pregnancy. I wept for days as I remembered the tiny perfect figure of what was to have been a boy child. He was about six inches long, and I noted each of his fingers and toes. In my mind, his name was Benjamin.

"When I got pregnant with Roland I was scared to death I would lose him as I had lost the other. I worried about it every day and at times, if I felt any kind of twinge, I took an injection IM of something. I don't know what it was anymore. I was told on more than one occasion by my husband that if my child was deformed or retarded, he would divorce me, because he would not be able to live with a handicapped child. So I lived with the possibility of losing another baby and raising my children by myself.

"We had Roland and we had two more beautiful sons. My whole life centered about them. I had no marriage. It was a mockery. But I chose to stay in it. It was entirely my decision. I wanted a home with two parents for my sons. I wanted to be able to stay home and take care of them. I knew if I got a divorce, I would have to go back to work.

"But my decision to remain in a loveless relationship took its toll on me. Oh, I had all the material comforts, and I had my kids. Personally, I shut-down. From the very early years, when I would wake in the night and ask to be held and loved, I was rejected strongly by my husband who yelled that I had awakened him, to leave him alone, that he had to work the next day.

"Don't ever do that to your wives. It will crush their spirit and will kill their love for you. Always, always, be loving to them. Women need to be told often that they are loved, cherished, desired, and appreciated. Be sure you remember that always, and hold them for no reason than just to feel close. Sex is great, or can be, but a woman sometimes just wants to be held.

"So, as I said, I shut down, sexually and emotionally so that I wouldn't have to need, feel, and enjoy ever again. This was very deliberate on my part. I denied every tactile sensation that could give me pleasure and I buried my needs deeply inside of me. I place no blame on anyone for this. I had choices to make and I chose to stay in a senseless, hurtful relationship.

"I don't remember now what year it was that I saw an attorney and asked your father for a separation. Everything was so black. I was told by my husband that we are not on this earth to have fun or be happy. We are here only to procreate, to see to their welfare and education, and then we are supposed to die. I was desperate. I felt that I had no present, no future. Two of my beautiful sons were being emotionally damaged by their father. He told them night after night at the dinner table that they would be nothing but garbage hawlers, because they were stupid. He told them they could not be from his loins, indicating that they were dumb like their mother. That was another emotional abuse that I took. I was called, 'Dummy' for the first two years of my marriage. I was told that doctors should never marry nurses, because they were not their intellectual equals. Anyway, I told my husband that I wanted a separation of six months. I told him that if, after that time he had seen a psychiatrist, and promised not to abuse his little sons anymore and promised to take me on one vacation a year, I would consider ending the separation. He never forgave me for throwing him out of the house. Actually, I never threw him out. He took three weeks to find an apartment and move out.

"My parents took the side of my husband, and were angry with me. I never told them of my deep-seated unhappiness, nor of any of the problems in my home. They thought I was being foolish and jeopardizing my comfortable lifestyle. "What are you going to do? You have four sons. How are you going to raise them on your own?" You see, they were still thinking 'security'. As products of the depression, they could think no other way.

"My husband moved out, but came to the house frequently. I never forbade him seeing his sons. I remember well how angry you boys were at me for doing this to your dad. Robert, I don't know if you remember, but you told me that Dad never hit me, so what was my problem?

"I did this because I felt I had no other choice. My life was so bleak. I felt I was losing my sons, that I was losing all control of my life. I was extremely depressed, and I didn't know what else to do. I think that was the first time I felt that I wanted to end my life. I had to survive however because I had my sons and they were still very young. Randall and Russell, you were still in grade school.

"Your father returned after six months. The psychiatrist that he saw told him he had never seen Bran happier than when he was separated from me. Isn't that revealing? But he wanted and needed his sons, so he came back with the promise that he would take me somewhere every year. You see, up to this period in time, my husband told me I had no right to have a vacation. He said, over and over to me, "You wanted kids. You've got them. It is your responsibility to stay home and care for them. You have no right to jeopardize your safety, possibly getting killed in a car or a plane, and leaving your sons without a mother." I asked him, "Please, then, just take me to a motel for a weekend. Just to get away and have a little time to ourselves." He laughed at me and told me I was crazy.

"Every year my husband had a long vacation, two to three months, during which time he could be free from his work and do as he pleased. He never told me when his vacation was going to be. I would find out when he didn't get up for work at the usual time. He was afraid that I would make plans for him and his vacation was his vacation. I had no part in it.

"We started traveling then, after the separation. You are aware that we traveled the globe, to the British Isles first, then Western Europe, Israel, Greece, Morocco, China, Singapore, Thailand, and Russia, which was still the USSR at that time. Yes, my husband took me to all those places. Do you have any idea what it is like to travel with someone who wishes he were not there, but at home? With someone who hates every minute he is away? With someone who can't wait to get to the hotel and watch television, even if it's in another language? With someone who sees no beauty in anything new or old? I was determined to enjoy the opportunity of seeing and experiencing lands and cultures I had only read about. I filled my soul with all that I saw and felt. It was as if I were alone, but I determined not to feel lonely. After all, that was how my whole life had been.

"When I entertained in our beautiful home, I did so practically alone. Often my husband would dine with us, but disappear afterwards to the basement or bedroom and I would be left to entertain alone. It was embarrassing. When my opera friends would come, he always retired to the basement and never joined in the dinner, and never came upstairs to greet the people. These were my musical friends for over thirty years. My husband couldn't stand them. He called them, 'phonies'. Our last New Year's Eve, I had invited Connie and Mike for the evening and to see the New Year in. I couldn't believe it, when Bran got up from his chair at 11 PM and told them he was going to bed. Of course, our guests then left. The whole point of the evening was lost, but he saw nothing wrong with that. I felt badly because this couple has been very good to us.

"Little by little we lost all social contacts with people in the neighborhood. We would be invited to their homes and I had to tell them that my husband was 'on call' and we couldn't come. This happened so many times, they finally stopped inviting us. I had a beautiful home, I had beautiful china and sterling, everything to set a fine table, and I was a gourmet cook who loved to have people enjoy my food and hospitality. Very seldom did I feel that I could invite anyone and be comfortable with it. And by the way, I think it was significant that we had no friends among the medical field, except Uncle Bernie. And we were rarely invited to their home either. If we got together with the anesthesiologists, it was because of business, to entertain a new or possible addition to the anesthesia department.

"I found the Duluth Light Opera Company to be a wonderful opportunity to use the voice that God gave me, to meet and sing with people who also loved music, and enjoy their friendship. From the year that I joined this group, I sang in several operettas, and always had a lead role. From that exposure came my membership in Matinee Musicale, where I sang every year for membership audiences. Then I was invited to become a member of the exclusive Cecilian Society, also singing once a year for the members. My husband didn't seem to mind my singing for relatively closed audiences, but when I sang on stage in costume before the public, he was embarrassed. He would not speak to me for days until the performances were over. Many of his colleagues would tell him that they had heard me and raved about my beautiful voice. He would laugh and say, "Oh, yes, she is very proud of herself." I was humiliated. He would tell me, you see. Once I sang a particularly difficult aria for Mary Ann and Harold when we were visiting them. My husband humiliated me in front of my best friend, by laughing at me and saying, "Who do you think you are? You are no Maria Callas. What makes you think that they want to hear you sing?"

"He would often make fun of me when I sat at the piano practicing. When he retired, I quit singing because I knew he hated my voice and it would irritate him to hear me practicing. With no practice and my advancing age, my voice deteriorated, until I could no longer trust it, and I stopped altogether. I think the last public singing I did was at your wedding, Robert, and just a few more times in church, but that also, I had to give up. My voice was a part of my soul, the greatest gift except for my children. When I stopped using it, it was like an amputation. I mourned for it for a very long time. When I hear beautiful vocal music that was once a part of my repertoire, I still ache with the loss.

"It was Kay Reardon, my friend and singing buddy, who advised me one day to become a travel agent since I enjoyed travel so very much, and had acquired knowledge having traveled abroad. I thought about it, and decided I would like to do that. After becoming an agent, I went to a seminar in Minneapolis given by Air India, for travel agents to become more familiar with India. I had been corresponding with an Indian couple I had met in England with my mother in 1978. They couldn't understand why I went all over the globe, but never visited India. The seminar excited me and stirred an interest in me to see this country. I went back to my employer and told him that I wanted to put a group together and lead them on a tour of India. He thought I was crazy. "You will never get anyone to go from Duluth," he said. "I'm going to find the people," I answered, "Because there is so much there to see and it looks like a fabulous destination." "Fine," he said. "Go ahead, but I'm telling you that you won't find anyone to go." Well, I wrote to people I'd traveled with before and I advertised. I worked very hard and finally got 15 people, half from Minnesota and half from Massachusetts. In the meantime, Air India offered all the agents who had been to their seminars all over the country, the opportunity to see India at the expense of the Indian government and very low airfare on Air India.

"I went, of course, and was totally enchanted by India. I can't explain it, but I loved it from the moment I stepped foot on her soil. I didn't know why I felt this way until this last trip. Finally I had my answer after all these past years of yearning to go back there. You see, after a trip to India, six months later I would start dreaming of her, and the need to return was like that of a magnet. I wanted to see other places, such as Australia, New Zealand, Japan, but whenever I got enough money together, I had to return to India. It was as though I had no choice. I simply had to go there. Your father, of course, would never even consider going there, and now I know the answer to that also.

"Something happens to me over there. I start living again; I start enjoying life. I feel accepted there. It is as if they know I love their country and they react with respect and hospitality."

"Mom," Russell said "you know you are a tourist and they want your money."

"I thought of that, but I've watched how they treat other tourists, and it is different with me. I don't know how to explain it, but they talk to me without condescension, and they appear to enjoy being with me. I feel good with these people. They are very spiritual people, and although they are Hindus and worship differently than we do, I see God's light shining in their faces. The poorest of the poor are smiling and happy. It is a very humbling experience to see such faith in people who have hardly the minimum to sustain them.

"Before I left on this trip it had been four years since I had been to India. I couldn't go because I had the responsibility of Grandma. I was so depressed before I left, that I could hardly make myself go. Finally, I told myself that this was probably the last time I would ever go to India, and when I got back, I would wait for Grandma to die, and for your father to die and then, please God, I could die, because I didn't want to live anymore. I had nothing to live for. I was miserable. Day after day with nothing to do, just total boredom.

"I had been eating myself into a state of disease, so much sugar, and then something else to take away the sugar taste, then again finishing with sugar. Ice cream I ate by the pint and I put on a lot of weight. I didn't care. I got diabetes, which I knew I would, considering the diet I was on, and when the doctor put me on a strict diet, I paid no attention. I went from oral medication once a day, to twice a day, then insulin twice a day plus the oral meds, and still I didn't watch my food intake. The doctor didn't know how to scare me, because you see, I didn't care. I wanted to die. This was the state I was in when I left for India in January.

"The moment I set foot on Indian soil, something happened. I didn't realize it, but the immigration officer took one look at me, and gave me this bright smile. Now I had been traveling for many hours, and I was bone tired. Probably I had traveled farther than anyone else on that plane. The officer looked at me and said, "Oh, Ma'am, you don't look a bit tired. You look happy." My immediate response was, "But of course, I'm back in India." Now this officer had been stamping passports with no smile for anyone, just doing his job, checking the photo with the face in front of him, stamping the passport and seeing to the next passenger. I was the only one he spoke to, and he seemed to light up like a Christmas tree when he saw me. Now, I had no idea that I looked happy. I really didn't feel that way, but my spirit knew it, and this man saw it, even if I was unaware of it.

"In Delhi I didn't feel joyous. The situation at Sunil's was unsettling, and I felt pain for this family who was going through so many trials and conflicts. It wasn't until I got to Sawai Madhopur that I started to come really alive."

Catherine then related her experience regarding the canter and riding behind the little man on the scooter. She told them about the gentleman who left his meeting at the hotel in Jaipur to come and talk with her, and the man on the plane who gave her his business card with his assurance of help if she ever needed it.

She shared with them her arrival in Udaipur and how beautiful her hotel and suite was and how desperately she needed to share it with someone. Catherine then began telling her story of the lovely city of Udaipur. She told of her guide taking her sight-seeing and about the picnic where she climbed the six foot wall and jumped to the other side.

"Well, what can I say? It was so simple, so insignificant, but the experience filled me with so much joy. Even at my own expense, I was having fun."

Catherine then related the lovely evening she spent with her guide; riding about behind him on his scooter; seeing the lights of the city, visiting his friend's guest-home on the lake, having dinner at his uncle's, and agreeing to visit Ranakpur the following day. She told them about the car trip through the mountains to the Jain temples and the stop at her guide's property to plant olive cuttings.

"Let me tell you, that experience touched my soul as nothing else had, up to that time. I knelt in the rich, dark soil of India, and dug and planted with my bare hands. My spirit was soaring when I left Udaipur.

"I went south and stayed in a resort called Kovalam Beach. It was there that I had a spiritual experience which enlightened me as to why India is so important to me. I had a room facing west, the Arabian Sea spread out before me, the waves lapping the shore just beneath me. For some reason I was having a hard time meditating. My Centering prayer was not going well. I sat in my room this one day, doing some spiritual reading. I was restless, and I decided to walk out onto my little balcony. It was around 4 PM. I looked out at the sea, which was a lovely golden color, the sun almost to the horizon. I looked to the heavens, and prayed.

"Why, Lord," I asked. "Why do I have to come back to India all the time? What is it that brings me here? Why? Why?"

"It was just as though a curtain parted. Now, I didn't see a vision, nor did I hear a voice, but God spoke to me just that clearly. I heard Him in my soul. And what He said was, 'You have been faithful to Me all your life. India is My special gift to you. This is where your heart sings. This is where your spirit soars. You don't need all your possessions. Come, live a simple life and be happy. I've been calling you here for a long time.' And it was over.

"The tears fell from my eyes. All the hurt and disappointments of a lifetime started to surface, and I wept. I felt no bitterness, just an over- whelming sense of sadness for all the lost years. Also, joy, peace, and a sense of direction. I had this terrible need to share this with someone, but there was no one.

"In Goa, I walked the beach all day, and prayed and wept. I know that I have to live in India. When? I don't know. I haven't thought that through. I just know that India calls to me, my health is so much better there, and I feel good about myself there."

There was total silence in the room as she spoke to them. They listened to her, and she felt their love and their attempt to understand. When she finished, she asked them,

"Do you have any questions?"

"Mom," Robert began, "What was all that about asking someone to come and live at our house?"

"In Goa I met this lovely young girl. Her name is Gitane and she is only 17 years old. She was a hostess at the restaurant where I dined every night. After talking with her, I learned that she wanted very much to come to America and go to school. You have to realize that Indian hospitality is very open. Everyone is always welcome in their homes and when I am there for a while, I start thinking and acting like an Indian. It came so naturally for me to invite her to stay with me in Duluth and go to UMD or St. Scholastica."

"But, Mom, don't you know that Dad is very upset? That house is his castle. How could you invite her knowing how Dad would feel?"

"You are right, of course, Robert. I know that your father called you and that you discussed it with all your brothers. I know too that all of you agree with your dad, and that is OK. You see, I made a mistake. It was an honest mistake, because I only thought of how I could help this young woman, and I really thought it would be enjoyable and fun to have a young person in the house. But I was wrong not to have discussed it with Bran first. I realize, now that I am home again, that such an idea as this is totally impossible. When I am in India, the whole world takes on a new light, and I think positively, not negatively like I do in Duluth. I have told your father that I would rectify the situation. The first thing I need to do is write to Gitane as soon as I get home. I made a mistake. What more can I say? I'm sorry, but I am even sorrier to break this girl's heart. You see, I just received a letter from her hoping that I hadn't changed my mind because her parents had given their approval. I hope she will forgive me in time."

"Mom," said Robert, "Do you know how often you need to go to India?"

"Yes, I think I need to go every six months."

"Every six months?" Russell asked incredulously. "Wouldn't once a year be enough?"

"Well," she answered, "It may have to be only once a year. I have only my social security to travel on, and it isn't very much. A round-trip ticket is almost two thousand dollars."

"Mom," Robert said, "If your health is so much better there, and if you feel that it is necessary, then Dad should pay for your trips. He can afford it."

"Oh, no, Robert. He hates India, and he hates the thought of my going there. He would never agree to pay for my trips over there. Besides, all I hear from him is that we have no money. We can't afford to go anywhere. So it comes back to what I can save from my social security and the little money that Helen left me in her will."

"I'll talk to Dad. He can afford it. And you have to do this for yourself."

"Mom," said Roland, "Do you mean to live there some day?"

"Yes, Roland. I don't know when, but I think that is what I have to do."

"But, Mom, why so far away?" asked Russell. "Couldn't you go somewhere closer?"

"Honey, it is India that calls me. I've been all over the world almost. India is the only land that pulls me."

Randall was sitting next to her. He put his arm around her and said, "Go for it, Mom. You have been unhappy for so long. Just do it."

Anne was crying. "But how will your grandchildren get to know you if you are so far away?"

"I love all of you dearly. I love my grandchildren. But you have your own lives. Your mothers-in-law and fathers-in-law are younger than I and your dad. Your children will grow up more with them than with us. I have already accepted that fact. It was difficult to face, but I did so long ago."

"What about Dad?" Russell asked.

"I won't abandon him. There is also Grandma. I can't just up and leave. I don't know how or when this will all come about. When I first mentioned this to Julie this morning, she told me I had to speak to you because you would never understand why I have to leave you. Now you know me better, I hope, than you did before. I made so many choices that were perhaps wrong for me, but I made them in good faith. I chose to remain in a relationship that was harmful to me. It was my decision. It was my choice. I take full responsibility for my own determination.

"My greatest concern was for all of you. You cannot know how much I love you. I wanted each and every one of you so very much. I cherish you. I am so proud of you, each of you, for who you are and what you have accomplished. I think you have made wonderful choices for your mates. I couldn't have done as well choosing for you as you did for yourselves. I dearly love my daughters-in-law. Julie, you aren't yet, one of the family legally, but I think of you already as my daughter-in-law. Boys, you are so lucky to have found women who love you. Be true to them. Always remember their needs first. If you care for them, love them, do for them, you will be blessed a thousand fold. Your wife will give you so much joy and fulfillment. Just make her your whole life. You have, and will have children that you will love and care for, but remember that they will grow up and leave your home. Your wife remains with you until the end, so work on that relationship. Don't let it stagnate. Your children will be very important, but do not let them become more important than your wife. She must always come first with you.

"Robert, your wife is Lutheran. She is active in her church. It doesn't bother me that you are not practicing your Catholic faith. Go with your wife and children. Pray together. Worship together. Roland, your wife wants very much to join a church. You are both of the same faith. Join a church, and go to Mass. Be with your wife. I spent years worshipping alone. It is not good for anyone, certainly not the family. Russell, you and Julie have a lovely Catholic church not far from here. You are being married by a priest. Join the church and go to Mass. The same goes for you, Randall. All of you have been so very, very blessed by God. You can go to church and spend an hour a week thanking Him for His goodness. There will come a day when your lives aren't all that they should be. Life is not one continual glow. You will need to pray then, and how will you be able to ask God for a favor if you don't even know Him? Think about it."

"Cathy," Anne asked, "Have you told anyone else what happened to you in India? That spiritual experience?"

"Yes, I've shared it with several people."

"Did you tell your sister?"

"Yes, I told Cindy."

"What did she think?"

"Well, she just looked at me, and laughed, then sang that "do, do, do, do; do, do, do, do," from Rod Serling's TV series, *The Twilight Zone*. She is the only person that has laughed."

Robert shook his head in disgust. "It's no more than I would expect of her," he said.

"Well, Honey, she is my sister. It hurt me, but she is a skeptic. It doesn't matter what she thinks. I know what I felt and heard in my heart. And it matters to me what you, my sons think and feel."

"We believe you, Mom," said Randall. "But I wish you didn't have to go so far away."

"I will be only as far away as a telephone. It will take me longer than if I were in New York or Hawaii, but if you need me, all you have to do is pick up the phone and call. I will come to you at any time."

She stood up and her sons came to her, each hugging and kissing her. Then Julie and Anne did likewise. Her heart was so full of love for each of them, it was near to bursting. She could never remember when she had had a more meaningful conversation with her sons. It was more of a one-sided dissertation, but they had listened to her as they never had before, and had shown her great respect, understanding and compassion.

The evening had gone better than she could have dreamed. She wasn't usually adept at expressing herself orally, only in the written word, but this was different. She felt deep within her that God had guided her this night. Something was happening to her. The awakening that had begun at Kovalam Beach, had continued here in Blaine. She was convinced that God had wonderful plans for her, changes that would reshape the rest of her life.

CHAPTER TEN
ANOTHER TALK

The drive home to Duluth from St. Paul was uneventful but for the glow that had spread through Catherine, remembering her talk with her sons that weekend. Oh, how blessed she felt. All the years of emotional trauma were dissolved, first at Kovalam Beach and again after the night at Russell's. The tears started to roll down her face as she remembered her conversation with them. And ever since Kovalam she was experiencing a surfacing of pain felt long ago that had been suppressed and forgotten. So she cried now, driving down the snow cleared freeway. Her tape machine was playing old romantic tunes, and one especially touched her. It was "Plaisir d'Amour", played by Richard Clayderman. She cried out loud with a great sob, in pain and anguish.

For how many years had she ached for romance and for someone to cherish her? That this tune could affect her so deeply was an indication that she was still vulnerable, despite her age and her looks. That short interlude in Udaipur brought more tears. What was all that about? She hadn't heard from him, so obviously, it meant nothing to him. Could she have been so mistaken? Why had he held her and kissed her? Certainly there had not been time for any intimacy, so why, why did he make those advances to her? Perhaps she would never know.

Over and over she replayed the scenario of her two days in Udaipur. It had been so unexpected. She was confused at the time, but there were moments of bonding with this man. It wasn't the physical, because she felt no sexual attraction for him. It was deeper than that, a kind of spiritual kinship, a sharing of mutual interests and concerns. But the physical could not be denied either. He had held her hand. He had folded her in his arms so tightly she could still feel them. And finally, he had kissed her; her neck, her hair, her forehead, her eyes, and then fully on her mouth. It had been a complete surprise to her and she had frozen.

Then she remembered Goa, and how she had waited and waited to hear from him, and the deep disappointment when there was no visit from him and no word. How did it happen so fast? She had felt the need to share her experience at Kovalam Beach with him. And it wasn't until he didn't show up and sent no word, that she felt such desolation, a sense of deep loss. He had passed through her life in a matter of two days and one evening. That was all it would be, and she felt bereft. It was crazy. But those were her feelings that afternoon as she sped northward to her home in Duluth.

At last she was coming into her city. Spirit Mountain, the ski resort, was on her right. Always, at this point, she felt an air of expectancy. As her car climbed the last hill and topped it, the Port City appeared before her. It was a thrill to see the St. Louis River, the bay, the harbor, the Bong Bridge, and off in the distance, the Blatnik Bridge and finally the Lift Bridge and canal, and beyond them, Lake Superior. There were ships in the docks awaiting the first good thaw of spring so they could again travel the Great Lakes and on into the ocean. This view at night was spectacular with all the glowing lights, but even in daylight, it was an impressive scene. Ten minutes and she would be home. And then what? She didn't know. Somehow, God would guide her and let her know when and how to proceed.

After emptying her car of luggage, which she carried into the house, she parked the car in the garage. Bran was in the basement. She could hear the TV going. She unpacked, then tackled the kitchen. Whenever she left for the weekend, she always left a clean kitchen, nothing in the sink, nothing on the stove, and no dishes in the dishwasher. When she returned she always found a sink full of dishes, fully water-soaked and beginning to smell. That was the only thing out of place, because Bran was a 'neatnik', and never could tolerate a mess. Why he couldn't put the dishes and glasses in the dishwasher instead of piling them up in the sink, she could never understand. Evidently he heard her walking around, so he came upstairs.

"Oh, you're home," he said.

"Yes, just a few minutes ago."

"Did you see the boys?"

"Of course. We had a get-together at Russell's."

"Well, madam," he said in an accusatory voice, and shaking his finger at her, "I've made some decisions. I'm seeing an attorney and I'm going to divorce you. And I really mean it this time. You've gone too far. I won't stand for it. This is my home, and what you did, asking that girl here when you knew I wouldn't approve is the last straw. You have gone completely nuts over India. I want out of this marriage. There's nothing left of it anymore anyway."

"Fine, Brandon," she said resignedly. "Go ahead. You have been threatening me with divorce all our married life. So, go do it. I don't care anymore."

"I'm going to do it," he said angrily. "You have completely lost your senses. I can't trust you. I told Robert about what you did. He thought you were being very selfish. And that's what you are, a selfish bitch. Always thinking of yourself. You did that deliberately. You knew I wouldn't tolerate having someone in my house. And yet you went ahead and asked someone to live here. How could you believe that I would go along with that?"

"Yes, Brandon. I know that I made a mistake. I am going to write to her today and try to explain to her why I can't have her come."

"Well, I'm still going to see an attorney. I have had it with you. This India thing and your self-centeredness. All you think about is what YOU want."

"OK, Bran. Just go ahead. I won't fight you." He stalked off and went back to the basement. Catherine went to the computer room and started her letter to Gitane. She tried her very best to be kind and encouraging despite the news that she could no longer consider having another person living in her home. After rereading it several times, she printed it, addressed an envelope and placed it on the desk in the foyer, where it would remind her to take it to the post office for weighing and stamping.

Later, in the early evening, the phone rang. She answered it and it was Robert calling. "Hi, Mom, how is everything?"

"Hi, Honey. Well, everything is OK, except that your dad has told me he is going to see an attorney about a divorce."

"Oh, no! Mom, I'll talk to him."

"It's OK, Robert, it's all right. He has threatened me like this for years, ever since we were first married. He does say that he means it this time. I don't care anymore. I'm tired. Just let him do it."

"Mom, I will talk to Dad. I just wanted to tell you that I was so very impressed with your talk to us. Mom, I realized afterward that I had some of the very same traits as Dad, and I came home and talked to Kerry for three hours. Mom, for the first time in my life, I cried. I cried for an hour and a half. I realized that I had to change my life. I am so grateful to you. I just want you to know how proud I am of you. And I love you very much."

"Robert, I am overwhelmed by this. I was so proud of all of you the way you listened to me. Probably for the first time in your lives you saw me as a real person, as a woman. I am deeply touched and humbled that you felt that what I had to say was of such importance to you. I love you, Robert, so very, very much."

"Mom, would you put Dad on the phone, please?"

"OK, just a moment." She called downstairs to Bran. As he picked up the phone, she hung up and went into the living room. She turned on the TV and picked up her needlepoint. Using the remote control, she changed channel after channel and found nothing to interest her. Since her return from India, TV did not interest her. That was, in itself, a great change. For years this recreation was her only outlet; dramas in the evening, soap operas during the day. Now she didn't care. Even her needle art would not allow her to concentrate. Her mind was on her visit with her sons and back in India with the man who had held her and kissed her.

Bran came into the living room where she was sitting. "I just talked to Robert. I've never heard him talk that way before. He is very, very impressed with you. Whatever you said to the boys, it certainly made an impression. Never, never have I heard him talk about you that way. So I guess I was wrong about wanting a divorce. He told me to forget it."

"OK, fine."

"What did you say to them?"

"Nothing special. I just told them about me, about who I am. And I tried to explain why India attracts me. You see, I got my own answer to that question when I was over there this time."

"And what was that?"

She proceeded to tell him of the spiritual experience she had in Kovalam Beach. He listened and didn't laugh. He was dismayed and looked pained.

"I knew it," he said. "I knew it. You are going to that place, that pest hole to live. I had hoped that you would be here for the boys after I'm gone. You are going to abandon them, your sons, and they will have no one."

"That is not so. I would never abandon my sons. Many parents live miles away from their grown children. That doesn't mean that they have abandoned each other. Their lives have taken different courses. I will only be a phone call away from my sons. As I told them, it will take me a little longer to get to them, but I will always come if and when they need me."

"And what about me? You are going to abandon me. And what about your mother?"

"I'm not abandoning anyone, Brandon. You are my husband and my mother is old. I can't leave yet. I know that. But some day India is where I must live. I am happy there and I am healthier there. Even my doctor asks how he can get me back to India."

Bran left her then to return to the basement. The phone rang again. She picked up the receiver. "Hello?"

"Mom, this is your son, Roland."

"Hi, Honey. What can I do for you? Or do you want to talk to your dad?"

"No, I want to talk to you."

"OK. What's up?"

"I just wanted to tell you that I'm proud of you, Mom. I never heard you take responsibility for your actions before. I was so proud of you and I love you very much."

"Oh, Roland, that makes me feel so good. Robert called a little while ago and he said basically the same thing. I guess we should have had that talk a long time ago, but I'm so glad we had it now, when I had you all together. I'm sure God was blessing all of us, and I am so very grateful. It has been a very emotional few days for me. I just had a conversation with your dad also. I told him about Kovalam Beach and I think he feels very threatened."

"But you told him you weren't planning on going to India now, didn't you?"

"Yes, but ever since I started going to India, he has been afraid. I don't know of what. I don't think he knows, except maybe he senses that India is where I have to be. He is also so afraid of disease and he thinks India is a disease-ridden country, which it is, I suppose, but not to the extent that he sees it."

"Well, Mom, I love you. You have to do what is best for you. We all support you."

"Thanks, Honey. I so appreciate your call. Do you want to talk to Dad?"

"No, not this time. See you, Mom."

There were no other phone calls that night. She felt very good, but there was a deep ache in her also. She was healing. She understood that, but it would take time, and this was only the beginning.

CHAPTER ELEVEN
A PHONE CALL

It was 2:30 in the afternoon. She was just finishing a letter to Mary Ann on the computer. Her fantastic experience in St.Paul with her sons was so fresh in her mind, she needed to share it with her best friend. The phone rang in her office in the next room. She was somewhat perturbed by the interruption, but she hurriedly went to answer it.

"Hello," she said.

"May I speak to Catherine?" a man's voice answered.

"Hello." this from Bran, who picked up the phone in the basement.

"It's for me, Bran," she told him, and he hung up.

"Yes?" she answered the caller. "This is Catherine."

"How are you?" an accented voice asked, and her pulse quickened as she recognized the accent as being Indian.

"Who is this?" she almost whispered, her heart and voice full of surprise and hope.

"I'm calling from India," he said.

"Oh, God! Aadi! Aadi! It is you." Emotion choking her, she started to cry, tears falling down her cheeks.

"How are you, Catherine?" he asked again, with a special emphasis on the "how".

"I'm fine, now that I am hearing your voice. Oh, God, Aadi, I miss you," she spoke very softly.

"You miss me?" he answered, also very softly, almost in awe.

"Yes, yes, terribly. I'm crying."

"You received my fax?"

"What fax? I didn't receive any fax."

"I sent one to you at the Taj in Goa."

"But no. I didn't get it."

"Catherine, I tried calling you ten, twelve times from Jaisalmer. I couldn't get through, so I faxed you."

"But I never got it," she said in dismay. "Did you receive my letter?"

"Yes, but I couldn't come to you because of my busy schedule."

"You don't have to explain. I made that clear in the letter, you owe me no explanation."

"But it doesn't hurt to tell you why I could not come. There was a call. My father told me. I knew it was from you."

"Yes, I called from Bombay to say, 'Good-bye'. I wrote another letter from Goa. Did you get that?"

"No, no, I'm not home yet, but I know there is another letter for me. My father told me."

"Not home? Then where are you?"

"I'm in Jaipur. At the airport. I'll be home in two hours."

"Aadi, I've been thinking. How would it be if I came back to India for another tour, say during the monsoon, and…."

"Wait, I want to read your letter. Then we will talk."

"Oh, I'm sorry. I'm rushing ahead here. Sorry."

"That's all right, but Catherine, please will you call me at my home? I will be there after two hours."

"Yes, yes, of course."

"I want to talk to you after I read your letter. Will you call?"

"I will call. I promise. Aadi, thank you for calling me."

"Good-bye."

"Good-bye."

She hung up the phone and stood looking at it, not quite believing that she had just spoken to the man who had been on her mind constantly for weeks. She was shaking, and her mind was in a whirl. "My God, my God, he called me! And he wants me to call him back. Oh, God, thank you. Thank you, God. Thank you."

Her pulse, her heart was beating with excitement, anticipation, and joy filled her whole being. She went back to the computer, and in her delirious joy, wrote of the call to Mary Ann. She realized later what a mistake that was, but at the moment she had to share this happiness with someone, and why not with her best friend?

Then suddenly she asked herself, "Where am I going to call him from? I can't call from here." She started to feel panic. "Think, Catherine. Think! A neighbor? Hardly! Think! Kay? No. Marge? No. Who? Where? LISA! Yes, Lisa. Of course. She of all people will understand and help me."

She started to calculate the difference in time between Central Standard and India. Eleven and a half hours ahead in India. When should she call? First of all, she had to wait for Lisa to get home from work. This was going to be a long afternoon of waiting. She figured if it took two hours for him to get home, then he would need to sleep, so she decided to call him around 11AM his time, making it 10:30PM in Duluth.

"I have to call Lisa," she thought. "I know it will be all right, but I have to ask her."

For the rest of the afternoon, she thought of nothing but the phone call she had received and how wonderful his voice sounded to her. It was a miracle that he had called. She had been waiting for a letter; counting the days that he probably would be out on tour and when he could be expected to return. That he would answer her letter or letters, she had no doubt, if only to thank her for the photos she had sent him, but every day she had checked the mailbox only to be disappointed. Now this. This was better than any letter. To hear his voice, that beautiful soft voice asking for her. And the way he asked her how she was, was so unusual; the stress on the 'how' was very unique.

Now she was in turmoil; excited, scared, impatient, and full of wonder and anticipation. It was very difficult to concentrate on anything else, so she allowed herself this joy, this feeling so alien that it was like the first time she was attracted to a man, and that was so very long ago, she had forgotten what it felt like. But it was sweet now and wonderful, and she hugged it to herself like a warm, snuggly blanket.

At last it was 5:30 and she could call Lisa at home. Zachary answered.

"Hi, Zach. It's Catherine. How are you, darling? Listen, honey, is your mom home? Oh, not yet. Well I'll call again. Please tell her to call me if she gets home before I call her back. OK? It's urgent, Zach."

She hung up disappointed, but knew it was only a matter of time and she would hear Lisa's voice on the other end of the line. It was just so difficult waiting. What if Lisa told her she wanted no part of this? After all, Lisa was a friend of Bran also, and she may not approve of this clandestine relationship she was embarking upon. Was that what it was? Well, it was a secret, but was it a relationship? Not really. Not yet, anyway, but she was hoping that it was going to become one. Otherwise, why all the feelings that she had experienced after she had left Udaipur? Why this strong sense of having bonded with this man? Definitely there was something there, but what was it, and what exactly was happening? The phone call later tonight would give her that information.

Alternately pacing the floor and sitting at her office desk, she waited impatiently for Lisa to return her call. Then she took the photo, the one of him planting the olive cuttings at the site, that she had had enlarged and framed. There it sat on her shelf with so many other framed photos. No one had noticed this one, or the other two she had taken of him at the site and were also framed and in full view for anyone to take notice. She touched the top of his head with the tip of her index finger. She could feel the way his arms had held her there on the hill and again at the Jag Mandir. She shivered remembering how tightly he had held her. He had tremendous strength in those wonderful arms. And the kisses he gave her, on her neck, hair, eyes and mouth, and how foolishly she had broken the embrace. God, to have those arms around her again, to have another chance with him! Will it be possible?

It was 6:00 PM, She picked up the phone and again dialed Lisa's.

"Zach, is your mom home yet?"

"No," he told her. "She's meeting Kevin for supper, but she should be home in half an hour."

"OK, honey. Please tell her I need to talk to her."

"O, Lord, how can I wait? I'm going crazy." She said to herself. She wanted to shout out with joy, but it had to be kept all inside her. "Please come home, Lisa. Come home," she prayed. It was dinner time, but she couldn't think of putting food in her mouth. Bran had fixed his own supper at 4:30. He never bothered to ask who it was that had called, but he didn't hear the voice, only hers. Besides, he was never interested in her calls or anything she did, for that matter, unless it concerned the spending of money.

"It was 7:00. She dialed Lisa's once again. This time Lisa answered.

"No, Catherine, Zach didn't tell me you called. I've been with Kevin."

"That's OK, Lisa. Are you free now? I need to talk to you, and I desperately need a favor."

"Of course, Catherine. Do you want to come over?"

"Yes, Lisa. Please can I come now?"

"Of course. Come right away."

"OK, I'll be there in a few minutes. Bye." She hung up, grabbed her purse, and called down to Bran in the basement.

"I'm going to Lisa's."

"What?" he yelled. The TV was on full volume and he had to turn it down to hear her.

"I'm going to Lisa's," she told him again

"OK."

Finally she could do something besides sit and wait. She drove her car quickly, but carefully, down I-35, taking the downtown exit to Park Point. She was breathless when she entered Lisa's house, and she was warmly greeted with hugs from both her and Zach. These two were very close to her even if she didn't see them often.

Lisa was a fellow student with her in travel school back in 1986. Zach was still a baby then. Lisa had been divorced and was raising this son by herself. Her mother had disowned her because Lisa didn't believe in the religion of her parents, but her father saw her occasionally. Zach's father had drowned by accident in the Bay just after Catherine had met Lisa. And Lisa, being the age of Catherine's sons, was looked upon by Catherine, as the daughter she never had. Lisa, never having had a real mother-daughter relationship, gave her affection to this surrogate mother, and never forgot Catherine on Mother's Day. Zach was always a special little boy, and now was growing into a fine young man. Lisa had done a splendid job raising him with no help and no example to follow. Catherine loved both of them very much.

"Lisa, I have to talk to you. Privately."

"Sure, let's go in the kitchen." Lisa led the way, and Zach remained in the living room watching TV and doing his homework. The house was tiny, and Lisa had it decorated simply with antique pieces scattered here and there to give it character. It belonged to her and Zach and they were very proud of it.

They sat at the glass-topped kitchen table, and Lisa looked worriedly at her. "Catherine, what is it? What has happened?"

"Lisa, I need to call India."

"Of course, Catherine."

"I can't call from home."

"Call from here."

"Thanks, darling. I knew you would say that, but first I must tell you why. I don't want you to agree before giving you enough information for you to make an informed decision. You know Bran, and if you feel this is in some way a betrayal and it is not morally all right for you to agree to allow me to call from here, then I'll find another place."

"Catherine, it's OK. It's OK"

"Lisa, I met a man in India, in Udaipur. He has become very important to me and only after two days and one evening with him. I never expected to see or hear from him again, but he called this afternoon and asked me to call him back. He was in Jaipur and said he would be home in two hours and please would I call him."

"Catherine, I love you. Anything you need, anything, it is yours." Lisa got up, went over to Catherine and hugged her.

"It is really all right then if I call from here?"

"Of course."

"And you don't feel some moral objection to this?"

"No, Catherine. Whatever you need, I am here for you. There's the phone. Use it."

"Well, you know, it was the middle of the night over there when he called, plus another two hours for him to get home. I also thought I would give him some time to get some sleep before calling him. That would mean another couple hours to wait."

"That's OK. You are welcome to stay all night if you want. Zach and I would love that."

"Well, I don't think that would be a good idea, darling. Not tonight."

"OK, but I want you to know that whatever you want or need….."

"Yes, Lisa, I know, and you have to know you are the only one that I could come to with this request. It's crazy, you know. He was my guide, and although I didn't feel any great attraction to him physically, I felt we had bonded. And when I left Udaipur, the moment we said, 'Good-bye', I felt I'd lost something very important. I didn't sleep that night and the following day I wrote him a letter asking him if he'd like to join me in Goa. Now I knew he was due to go on tour in ten days, and he probably wouldn't be able to come, even supposing he wanted to come. I told myself that he probably wouldn't, but when he didn't show up, I was absolutely devastated. Isn't that nuts?"

"You said you were with him for two days?"

"Yes, he was my guide, but his job was finished after one day. He asked me if I wanted to see the lights of the city that evening, and of course I said I would. He picked me up on his scooter, and we went all over Udaipur and ended up at his uncle's house for dinner. Then he asked me if I would like to go to Ranakpur to see the famous Jain temples the next day. I said "Yes" to that too. We had a great time, and at one point he took me in his arms and held me so close. He was thanking me for going on this extra tour because he got to meet some important men in the travel industry whom we just happened to meet by accident in Ranakpur. Then when we got back to Udaipur, he took me on the boat ride which was included in my tour. However, I was supposed to go in the big launch from the hotel. He had arranged a private boat for the two of us. He told me I had paid for it, but I don't believe that. Anyway, the boat stopped at this island across from the Lake Palace Hotel, and he showed me the Jag Mandir Palace, which is only open for parties. It was there that he took photos with my camera, and at one point, grabbed me, held me again so tightly in his arms and started to kiss me. Lisa, I was absolutely stunned. Confused. What the hell was going on? I broke the embrace, and later he asked if he had offended me. Of course he hadn't, but Lisa, I haven't been kissed on the mouth for twenty years! Anyway, we went back to the hotel and had tea, and I was shaking. I couldn't think, and he threw a kiss across the table at me. Now, come on! Lisa, this man is young. I could be his mother. Why? Why? And what is wrong with me?"

"Catherine, you have been starved for affection for so long. Enjoy it. And so what if there is a difference in ages? He called you, so he must feel something too. Just let it happen. It's about time you had some joy in your life."

At last it was time for her to call India. She was anxious, nervous, and scared. Lisa left her to go to Zach's room and to give her privacy. She picked up the phone, checked the long series of numbers; international code, country code for India, city code of Udaipur, and finally his phone. She waited for a few seconds as the direct dialing connected across the world, and then she heard the double ring and again another double ring. A man with a very soft voice answered,

"Hello."

"Hello," she said, almost choking. "May I speak to Aadi?"

"Aadi here. How are you?" he said again in that special way.

"I'm fine, and you?"

"Fine. I've been waiting for your call."

"You were getting home so late, I thought I'd give you time to get some sleep."

"I have not been to sleep. I read your letter and then I could not sleep. I read and read and read, and waited for your call."

"I am not home. I couldn't call from there, so I came to a friend's house. I had to wait for her to get home from work and then ask her if it would be all right. I'm sorry that I made you wait."

"That's all right.

"Oh, Aadi, it's so good to hear your voice."

"Yes, it is like you are here in India with me. Catherine, what is 'bonkers'? I couldn' find it in the dictionary."

She laughed. "Oh, I'm sorry. It is a slang word meaning 'crazy'. And I think that is what has happened to me."

"Why? What do you mean?"

"Aadi, this situation. What is happening here? I wrote you all those questions. Do you have answers to them?"

"You know the answers. You know what is happening."

"Yes. But it is crazy."

"Why? Why do you say this?"

"So many reasons. So many differences between us." She pauses, afraid to go on and spell it out.

"Catherine, talk to me."

"It's difficult."

"Just talk to me. Talk to me, Catherine."

"I'm confused, feeling so many things, and it is crazy."

"Please don't think of this as all physical or sexual. It is a 'flow of expression.' There is something else here, something deeper."

"Yes, I felt that too. I thought of it as somehow spiritual, a bonding."

"Do you remember when we met? I told you I thought we had met before, like deja vue? I asked you if you felt the same."

"But I didn't, Aadi. It wasn't until the last day, after we had shared so much, that I felt a real connection with you."

"What did you think when I held your hand in the car?"

"I just felt it was a natural progression after the planting of the olive cuttings. We had shared something wonderful, I thought. It touched my soul very deeply, that experience."

"Your letter said something happened in Kovalam Beach. What was that?"

"I had a spiritual experience. I don't want to tell you over the phone. I will write you about it. But after it happened, you were the first person I thought of to share this with. If you had come to Goa, I would have."

"I wanted to come to Goa, but due to my busy schedule, I couldn't. I tried to contact you ten times from Jaisalmer, but it wouldn't go through."

"Yes, and I didn't realize how much it meant to me until you did not come and I heard nothing. But I told you in my letter that whatever you chose to do would be all right. If it wasn't to be, then it wasn't."

"Catherine, why didn't you call me?"

"I did, but you had already left on tour."

"I see. Last night you told me you missed me."

"Oh, yes, yes, I do miss you terribly. I wish we could go back in time to that moment on the island."

"Did I offend you when I kissed you?"

"Oh, no. I was just so confused. I told you later in the coffee shop that I had not kissed another man in many years. The truth is that I haven't been kissed on the mouth by any man for 20 years. I froze when you kissed me, but I wish now that I hadn't. I wish we could do that all over again."

"Catherine, close your eyes. Are they closed?"

"Yes," she almost whispered.

"Feel my arms around you. They are holding you. Do you feel them?"

"Oh, God, Aadi. Yes, yes, I feel them. You have wonderful, strong arms. I have never been held like that before."

"Now I am kissing you, kissing you, kissing you." He made kissing sounds. "Kiss me back," he said.

"Yes, yes, I am" she replied, although she was too shy to make the sounds of kissing, she was opening her mouth and imagining his open mouth on hers. She felt his tongue and his teeth touching hers, and the sweet smell of him.

"I can't hear you. I want to hear you kiss me."

"Yes," she says, now making the kissing sounds also. "I feel your beard against my face. It is so soft. I love it."

"You love my beard?"

"Oh, yes."

"You love my kisses?"

"I love your kisses. I feel your tongue on mine. Oh, how I want to be there with you."

"You are here. I am holding you. I am kissing you. When you sleep tonight, think of my arms around you, and remember the kisses I am giving you. Whenever you miss me, just think of my arms and my kissing you."

"Yes, I will do that."

"I remember the way you held me on the scooter."

"What? On the scooter? Really?"

"Yes, your arms felt good to me."

"I was shy at first and held only your sweater."

"And I told you not to hold my sweater because it wasn't strong enough to hold you if I had to stop suddenly."

"I remember."

"It felt wonderful when you expressed an embrace when you were about to leave for the hotel."

"And I worried that I had embarrassed you."

"No, I liked that. When I went to Delhi, I saw Biswas, your son. He told me you loved Udaipur."

"Yes, I told him all about Udaipur, but nothing personal."

"No, Catherine. This is just between us, just between us."

"Yes, of course. I agree."

"No one is to know about this, Catherine."

"I understand. I won't tell anyone."

"I like that. Do you want me to call you, 'Cathy'?"

"I want you to call me whatever you want to call me."

"Catherine, do you have somewhere I can fax you?"

"Yes, it is a travel agency, and you can't be too personal, but here is the number." She gave him the number at Portown Travel. "Do you have a fax number?"

"Yes, here it is, and it is very private. Very private. You can say anything." He gave her the number.

"Aadi, I want you to have this phone number also, of my friend, in case you need to call me. Oh, and there is another letter on its way to you."

"You sent me another letter?"

"Yes, with the photos from Ranakpur."

"Did you send me the photos I took of you?"

"I sent one. The one you took of me at the Jag Mandir."

"But the others, I want those too."

"Oh, no. They were awful. I told you I took terrible pictures, but you kept insisting on taking them. I can't send them. But the ones I took of you at the site are great and I sent those. And I enclosed some ideas I had for your restaurant and guest house. Please don't be offended. I was so dictatorial. I just felt strongly about a few things, but I wish I hadn't said so much. I'm sorry."

"It will be all right. Catherine, I will fax you tonight. I have to go out on tour again on 5 March. Thank you for calling me."

"Oh, Aadi. It was wonderful talking to you. Thank you."

"Remember, I am holding you, and I am sending you my kisses."

"And I send you mine."

"Good-bye."

"Good-bye."

She hung up, and a warm glow filled her soul and spirit. Her whole body was shaking, trembling with a thrill of happiness and joy. Never in her whole life had she felt this way. It was everything she had always thought it could be. Could this be happening to her? Oh, how wonderful it felt.

"Thank you, God," she prayed. "Thank you. Thank you, God."

She stood for a moment hugging herself, feeling his arms about her, his kisses still wet on her mouth. She passed her tongue over her lips as though tasting him, and a shiver went through her. She went into Zach's room and found that Lisa was sound asleep. Touching her arm, she called to her softly.

Startled, Lisa jumped up with a sharp intake of breath.

"Oh, I'm sorry. I didn't mean to scare you."

Lisa gave her a big smile. "It's OK, it's OK." She got out of bed and the two of them went into the kitchen.

"How did it go?" Lisa asked.

"Oh, Lisa, Lisa, it was wonderful. Oh, God, Lisa, he spoke to me as no man has ever spoken to me. He is so romantic. He held me in his arms and kissed me over and over."

"He's in love with you, Catherine."

"No, no. He can't be. I'm too old for him. And this is crazy. But it feels so good. Lisa, am I crazy?"

"No you aren't, Catherine. You haven't had anything for years. Bran has never given you love. Enjoy this. Be happy. But protect yourself."

"How do I do that? I'm already in so deep."

"Just enjoy, Catherine. You deserve it."

"Oh, look at the time! It's past midnight. This call is going to be expensive, Lisa."

"That's all right."

"Be sure you tell me as soon as you get the bill. I'll pay you in cash."

"Whatever way you want. It's OK and you can call him anytime from here."

"Thanks, Sweetheart. Oh, and he doesn't want anyone to know about this relationship. I have to keep this absolutely secret."

"Of course."

"Darling, I have to go. It's late. How am I ever going to sleep tonight?"

Lisa laughed. "I love you, Catherine."

"I love you, Lisa." They hugged and she put on her coat and boots. Giving Lisa another hug, she went out to her car. There was no traffic at that late hour. There was a spread of warmth all over her and she felt like singing. But she didn't sing anymore, so she let out a yell, screaming as loudly as she could in the confines of her tightly closed car.

"Ah..h……..h! Yes, yes, yes!!!!!"

CHAPTER TWELVE
FAXES

It was Wednesday, the day following the phone call to India. Catherine spent every Wednesday morning from 9 to 10 at the Adoration Chapel. It was a very tiny chapel, just off the street across from St. Mary's Hospital and part of St. Mary Star of The Sea Church. There were only eight chairs and a priedieu in front of the altar. The Blessed Sacrament was exposed 24 hours a day. There were two other ladies, adorers that were assigned to the same hour as she was. But visitors came and went all during the day. Adorers were given appointments to make sure that someone was always in the chapel. That was a requisite of having the Exposition of the Blessed Sacrament.

This morning Catherine was bursting with thanksgiving and joy. Her heart was full and all she could do was look at the monstrance, which held the Body of Christ, and cry. She prayed over and over words of thanksgiving for the beautiful gifting she had received from God. Just before her time was up, the two ladies arrived for the following hour. She smiled at the first to come, and the lady looked at her with dismay as she noticed her tears. But Catherine indicated they were not of sorrow, but of joy.

From the chapel, she drove the short distance to Portown Travel. Aadi had told her he would send her a fax. When she arrived she was greeted warmly by her three agent friends, Suzanne, Wendy, and Sarah. She hadn't seen them since she had returned, so they were all anxious to learn of her trip.

"Cathy!" exclaimed Suzanne, who was the first to spy her. "Come in. How was India?"

The two other agents sat up and greeted her also with joyous faces.

"Oh, it was wonderful. The best ever."

"Great! I hope you brought us pictures."

"Of course I did. But first, did a fax come in for me?"

"No," replied Wendy, as she glanced into the little room behind her. "No faxes have come in yet this morning. Do you expect one from Sunil?"

"Not from Sunil. Someone else."

"Cathy," said Suzanne, "you look absolutely radiant." And laughing she asked, "Are you pregnant?"

All of them laughed at that impossibility. "Hardly," she answered. "But you are right. I feel radiant. I am so very happy."

"Oh, oh, what happened?" asked Suzanne.

"So many things. I had such a fun time for the first time in years."

"Well," said Wendy, "Tell us."

Luckily there was little business and no customers. When the phones rang, Sarah answered them. So Catherine proceeded to tell them about the scooter ride, the picnic near Nagda where she climbed the wall and almost fell off. And she told them she had met some one very nice.

"I knew it." Suzanne nodded, grinning and shaking her finger. "I knew there was something about you that was different."

"Now just wait a minute," Catherine cautioned. "There is no future in this. It is just for —— for now."

"Tell us, Cathy. How did you meet and who is he?" asked Wendy.

"He was my guide in Udaipur, and he called me yesterday. I expect a fax from him this morning."

"Wow, Cathy!" this from Suzanne. "Do you have a picture of him?"

"Yes, of course."

Catherine opened the album she had bought for these photos, and showed them first the beautiful sights of Udaipur, then pointed to the two pictures she had of Aadi.

Suzanne gasped and said, "Wow, he looks just like Sean Connery."

"He is not that old, Suzanne. He is very young, too young for me."

"So who cares?"

"Well, it just seems strange, that's all."

"Heh, enjoy it, Cathy. I've never seen you look like this before."

"Cathy!" Wendy yelled. "A fax is coming in. I'll get it." She jumped from her chair and hurried into the back room. "Yup, it's for you. Here it is."

Catherine was so excited she could barely breathe.

"Look at her," Suzanne said to Wendy. "Just look at her glow."

"Oh come on, Suzanne," said Catherine. "It's not that evident."

"Ah, but it is. You should just see yourself. Go on, read you fax."

Catherine smiled at her friends and with her heart beating rapidly, she read the message from Aadi.

> *Dear Catherine I left Udaipur on 30th Jan. and the same day I was lucky to receive you letter. I tried to contact you on telephone and fax. I could not manage to Communicate with you due to busy schedule and that too in other part of India. I had the letter with me and thought and thought of the wonderful time we shared together. I came back here and read you another letter. It was very subtle and meaningful. I read and read ——waited for your telephone call.—I heard you around 11o'clock. It was if you were talking to me in India. You told me about the photographs and the letter you sent*

me—— I have just received this. Thank you very much for this. Your advises about the sight are always welcome. It is so nice of you . The picture of orch framed lady is so beautiful. I will be soon sending the photographs to different guests. You please use 0091-294-4555555, the fax number to say to me—— I will be Leaving for a tour on 5th of March of 97.

Please take good care.

With kiss Aadi Abhimani

After reading the fax, Catherine held all his words inside her and almost started to cry.

"Thanks, guys", she said to them. "I'll probably come by soon with an answering fax."

"Hey, Cathy. Come by anytime. It's great to see you."

Catherine left for home and as soon as she got there, she went to her office and put away the fax from Aadi. She looked at his framed photo on the shelf above her desk. He was smiling out of it at her. She smiled back. Here his picture stood, in full view of everyone, but no one noticed it. There were many photos on the two shelves, so one more seemed insignificant, but certainly not to her. She looked at it many times a day, and remembered the moments, aching to be held by him once again.

She went into the computer room and took out her personal floppy disc and started the computer. Then she began to write.

Dear Aadi;

I spent an hour at worship in chapel this AM, thanking God for his many, many blessings, especially His gift of you. I truly believe He has given us both something very special. We are connected, you & I, just as you said last night-not physically, but by something so much deeper, so personal, so deeply spiritual & emotional. I think the word is, 'Soul-mates'. I felt it coming back from Ranakpur, but I didn't realize it then. After chapel I immediately went to the travel agency & asked if a fax had come in for me. They hadn't seen me since I came back & couldn't believe how 'glowing' I was. Well, if I glowed before, since yesterday I am absolutely on fire, all due to you, of course. Anyway, no fax, but I sat around talking about India, & suddenly the fax rolled & there was your letter. How is that for a connection? No, you cannot be too personal on this line, but they will inform me if you sent a fax & I trust them not to read it. I loved talking to you last night, and yesterday afternoon too. I had forgotten the sound of your voice. It is very soft and very beautiful. Did you know that?

Anyway, I had difficulty centering in India, so I spent time in spiritual reading. This one evening, after I had sent the 1st letter to you, the sun was going down, around 4 PM, I think. I could hear the surf hitting the rocks below my balcony, the water was that beautiful golden color like the photos you took of Lake Pichola. I don't know what triggered the prayer, something in the reading, but I went out on the balcony & prayed, "Father, what is it that keeps pulling me back to India? What is it here that I can't seem to live without? Why, why am I here?" It was then that a curtain seemed to pull aside, and I saw everything so clearly. I didn't hear a voice, I saw no vision. It was just a clarity of my soul, and God said to me,

"You have been faithful to me all your life. India is my special gift to you. Here your heart sings and your soul rejoices. Come live a SIMPLE LIFE" (words from your mouth, Aadi, when we were in the old city). "You don't need all your possessions, Come here & be happy. I've been calling you here for a long time." And it was over. Tears were streaming down my face, and I kept saying,'yes, yes, yes!' and then the floodgates opened and all the emotions I had buried so deeply for so many years came rushing to the surface. I was truly alive again, and I felt everything acutely. My first thoughts were of you. I wanted to share this with you. I ached to tell you. I needed to share all of it with you. Because, you see, you played a part in it. I saw it juxtaposed to the way God used me to bless you with the meeting of the 'Big Guns'. The heart I once gave so freely was broken and trampled. At Kovalam Beach it became whole again. It is all yours if you want it. I will never give it again to anyone.

Anyway, I want you to know I would never do anything to harm your position in your family, your profession, or community. Secrecy is vital here as well as there because I don't wish to cause unnecessary hurt in my family either, which makes me think about the possibility of getting a P.O. box, not because of anyone opening my mail, but getting letters frequently from someone unknown here would bring questions. I'll see about it.

Until then feel free to write to my address. Please take care. I pray for your safety & for your well-being. I am sending this fax because you wouldn't get it via mail by 5 Mar.Please write.

Catherine

Catherine answered the phone and it was Mary Ann. She had received Catherine's letter and was furious with her.

"You are a damned fool, Catherine. A romantic idiot! Such adolescent thinking and emotions. He must realize you are desperate. What would a young man want with you? Let's face it, Catherine. You are old and you are very heavy. Just what does he want from you? This is very suspect. And now that you tell me this, I don't believe you had a spiritual experience in India. It was all your imagination working overtime. God, I'm glad I'm intelligent and a realist. This is just so childish, Catherine. I've known so many women who build their dreams on fantasy and it never works out. I could tell you of so many in the orchestra whose hearts were broken after believing in someone. This is ridiculous and you are making a fool of yourself. He doesn't care for you. How could he? In just two days? What nonsense. Catherine, all this is, I have to say is sex, sex, sex, sex"

"You are wrong, Mary Ann."

"No, I'm NOT wrong. What do you think you have that he could possibly want? Maybe your money?"

"For heaven's sake, Mary Ann! No!"

"Well, you haven't found out yet. But there will be something he wants. And it isn't YOU. I can tell you this woman…."

"Forget it, Mary Ann, I don't want to hear anymore. I have to hang up."

"No, you don't want to hear the truth. You want to go on living in you fantasy world, just like a teenager."

"Good-bye, Mary Ann."

Catherine hung up and started to cry. Suppose she was right? He was too young for her. But Aadi didn't want her money. There was something else between them, and it certainly wasn't sex. How could she say such awful things to her? And not to believe she had that experience in Kovalam Beach? Well, that was insulting. But Catherine knew that Mary Ann didn't hold for the spiritual anyway. She found God in nature and no longer went to church nor believed in a personal God. Whatever, Catherine was crushed. Mary Ann had been her best friend for fifty years. Her heart was sad, and she cried.

On Sunday Catherine called Lisa and asked if she could come to see her. She drove down to Park Point and was warmly greeted by this dear girl, whom Catherine loved.

"Hi", Lisa greeted her, with a big hug and smile.

"Hi, Darling. I've got a problem."

"What? Tell me."

"Lisa, I got a fax from Aadi the morning after I talked to him here."

"Did you? What did he say?"

"Just that he couldn't get in touch with me when he was on tour, that he thought about our time together, etc, etc, and that he was leaving on tour again on 5 March. It was very nice."

"Well, then? What's the problem?"

Catherine told her about her conversation with Mary Ann.

"What do you think, Lisa? Am I a damn fool?"

"No, you aren't, Catherine. I think you should just enjoy the wonder of whatever it is. But you must protect yourself too."

"I don't know if I know how to do that. I am already too involved emotionally."

"Then just enjoy the happiness, Catherine. You deserve it. You have been a saint living with Bran all these years."

"Well, I'm no saint, Lisa. But I've never been unfaithful either, despite all the emotional abuse."

After talking to Lisa, Catherine felt better, but decided she would send another fax to Aadi. Perhaps she had gone overboard on the long one she had sent him on Thursday. Besides she wanted to send him the P.O. Box number that she had just rented, so that he would feel free to write her while on tour. The fax she sent him was as follows

3 March

P.O. Box 3174
Duluth, MN 55803
USA

I have been thinking that I have been leading with my heart and leaving my mind some 6000 miles or more behind. At great risk I have laid bare my soul. Please know that if you are uncomfortable, if I have raced ahead into territory I should not have entered, I will retreat, for it is still difficult for me to understand your attraction to me. I am a foreigner, a Christian, a woman old enough to be your mother and obese, {a term on my medical records, but nevertheless, valid}. I was trying to explain that on the phone, and not doing a good job because it is hard sometimes not only to face the truth, but to put it into words. Have I allowed my romantic emotions to override my good sense? Is my imagination running wild? You did mention wanting to correspond re our countries, customs, etc. A mutual learning experience. If you want to back-track to that kind of a relationship, it is OK. I really don't know how you are feeling. Perhaps I will understand better after receiving a letter from you, which I hope is already in the mail. But I have to know your thoughts and feelings because I am so afraid I am just being an old fool, trying to recapture a youth that has long past. I will not self-destruct. I am much stronger than that. I just need to know.

C

That same day, she wrote Mary Ann a short note telling her that she was right, that indeed she was a fool, and that she had done some soul-searching after their conversation. Indeed, what would anyone want with an old, obese woman, especially a young man? She told her that she had faxed Aadi and ended it all. It was a lie of course, but she couldn't tolerate her knowing anything more, nor berating her again. However, Catherine started worrying about what Aadi was thinking. Was he disgusted? Could he understand where she was coming from? Well, she would have to wait. She hoped a letter was on its way. If not, there was only one day left before he left on tour. Would he send a fax?

India was a half day ahead and as Catherine figured the time difference, she realized that it was still 3 March in Duluth, but already 4 March in Udaipur. Over and over she told herself, 'Patience, patience, patience.'

The following day there was no call from Portown Travel and she didn't want to bother them by calling. So she busied herself cleaning her office, and writing in her journal. That writing was daily now, because she wanted to remember everything that happened between Aadi and her. Bran mentioned that there had been a call that morning, but when he answered they had hung up. Catherine wondered and felt it well could have been Aadi. She couldn't call him now because it was now the middle of the night in India.

On the 5th she called Portown in the middle of the morning and they told her there was a fax and it had come in the day before.

> *Thank you very much for your fax which I anticipated. I will leave for Delhi just after 6 – 7 hours. Please relax. You did nothing wrong. I won't make a big bill like last time. Please call me earliest. Aadi*

Catherine was sick when she read it because if she had received it when it had come in, she would have called him and heard his voice again. Now it was too late. He was already in Delhi. But she prayed, 'God bless that wonderful man.' He had found nothing upsetting with her long fax and had told her to relax. That made her heart swell, and joy filled her heart once more.

CHAPTER THIRTEEN

DIRECTIONS AND A DECISION

Life seemed to go on as usual for several days. One decision Catherine did make was to get herself a spiritual director. She felt the need and acted on it immediately. Although she knew of several persons who were excellent, she decided to call Meridith Schifsky. Meridith had introduced her to Centering Prayer and she felt comfortable with her. She called for an appointment and Meridith was able to see her on Saturday, the 8th of March. The most convenient place to meet for both of them was McCabe Renewal Center, which was next door to Catherine's house. She had asked for a two-hour session, but Meridith told her the usual was one hour and at the most, one and a half hours was enough to work through. But Catherine was right, the session lasted two hours and she felt it well worth the $25 per hour.

They were in a small intimate room on the second floor that Catherine had been in many times for Centering. Meridith lit a candle and proceeded to read a prayer. Catherine opened with telling her of her experience in Kovalam Beach, calling it her 'awakening'. She told her about the talk with her sons, the disaster of her marriage, some of the disappointment of her youth, but mostly how she had been faithful to God.

"I knew He was always there for me, always, always He was there being faithful to me."

She also told of her death of spirit. "I had suppressed my desires and needs. I was, or had been, waiting for death."

She related her experience of meeting Aadi and how they were now communicating. "I feel no guilt about him. I truly feel he is a gift from God."

"Catherine," Meredith said, "Now you must pray and ask God how He wants you to go? What path are you to follow? Where is He leading you?"

"I'm having difficulty focusing."

"You are that way because of all the junk that is surfacing after all these years."

She told her that she cried often in the night and that she knew it was part of the catharsis. Catherine promised to call Meridith when she felt she needed her again. And they both knew that she would.

The following day, she went to an Oblate meeting at St. Scholastica. She had been going to these meetings and had a great desire to become a Benedictine Oblate, which was a lay person who has a prayer life, and who wishes to follow the Rule of Benedict. The monastery gives one about a year to start living as one, then is formally brought into the community during an oblation ceremony. Catherine had not reached that point in time yet.

God, how she missed Aadi. She kept waiting for the letter she knew was coming, but there was no access to the post office on Sunday. She had an idea and decided to call Lisa and run it by her.

"Lisa, you and Zach are going to Mexico soon. Would it be all right if I had a key to your house so that I could call Aadi?"

"Of course, Catherine," Lisa agreed immediately. "I'll have one made or you can have Zach's."

"Oh, Lisa, you don't know how I appreciate this."

"No problem. I'm happy for you, and whatever I can do for you, you know that I will do it. I love you, Catherine."

"I love you too, Darling." Catherine wanted to cry.

She had another thought that weekend and wanted so much to share it with Aadi. Whenever she got to India to live, she would like to have a puja room, combining a Hindu shrine and a Christian shrine, so that Aadi and she could worship together. She wondered what he would think of that.

There was no letter the following day either, and the ache went all the way to her toes. She realized for the first time, perhaps, that it wasn't even sexual. Well, at least that wasn't the greatest part. She ached to see him, to be in his presence, to talk with him. That was her greatest need. It hurt so badly that she wanted to weep, even scream. And she felt disconnected because she couldn't reach him. Catherine decided that when he came back from his tour, they were going to have to talk about arranging to converse at least once a week.

All the emotion she felt surfacing since Kovalam Beach, was continuing. It was not diminishing, but seemed to be growing stronger. This was very unsettling to her. She was not sure, but it felt like a whole new experience to her, one that had not been encountered up to this time in her life. She had to deal with it somehow. It probably would give her great strength once she got through it. She was not only aching for Aadi. She was remembering the pain of her marriage, the lost years, the pain of being always alone, the pain of never feeling the love and companionship of her mate. And too there was the pain of emotional abuse, always there since she married Brandon and continuing to this day. She cried, she wept, and she sobbed.

Not that it was going to help, but she found her emotions controlling her, and she just let it come. Catherine had purchased a Sergio Lub bracelet in copper, silver and brass for Aadi. She was, at first, going to wait until she saw him again, then decided to mail it to him. With it, she enclosed a short note.

Dear Aadi–Just a small token of my deep love and respect

Please wear it and think of me. C

She wondered if she wasn't asking or saying too much. Catherine decided that she had to stop doubting this man. She knew he cared for her, so why was she questioning the relationship? She supposed that he had her photo with him. He must be thinking of her in his free moments. She had too many free moments and couldn't stop thinking about him. But she needed to have something in her hand to read and read. Finally, she couldn't stand it, she had to write to him.

Dear Aadi,

I didn't call you before you left because I didn't get the fax in time. The travel agency did not call me. I happened to go there and they said something had come in the day before and it was in an envelope posted to their board with my name on it. When I read it, I realized you had already left on tour. Your fax machine does not print the date and time of transmission. Would you put that info on your next fax so that I know when you sent it, please? Also, it might help if you want me to call, or if it is urgent, to put at the top of the page, "PLEASE CALL CATHERINE, 724-7722, ASAP." Maybe they will read that far & call me. They are nice ladies and we are friends, but they are very busy, so I can't fault them for not bothering to call me. You must know I would have called had I known you wanted me to do so. The phone bill is of no consequence to me. I need to hear your voice and I need to talk to you.

What would you say to my phoning once a week when you are home? Would that be OK? Because I do feel disconnected. I have been expecting a letter from you also ——-nothing has come. I too would enjoy holding something in my hand and *reading, reading, reading. It would help too if you told me, not only when you are leaving Udaipur, but when you are expected home. A small package went out in the mail today. Not much is made in the US anymore, but this was. I hope you like it.*

But Aadi, I don't know how you are feeling... not yet I don't. I keep waiting and hoping to hear from you. Won't you please share some of your life, your thoughts, and your dreams with me? I would never pry, but I want to know you, and I can't if you don't communicate. I'm sure it is difficult to do so in English instead of in your home language, but I don't care. I'll understand. Please write to me. Everyone here expects me to go to India again this fall. I haven't heard from you re this. Do you still want me to come? If so, when? If not, I need to make other arrangements.....to visit Belgaum, Delhi, etc. But come I will, because I need it for my health and my spirit. All my sons support me in this.

One more thing. My friend's name is Lisa. She lives with her 14 year old son. They love me as family and would do anything for me. I have given Lisa your name, address, phone, and fax in an envelope, in the event something would happen to me here and you would have no way of knowing otherwise. I hope that is OK. And one more thing. You don't need to put that new address with the

> *P.O. Box on the fax. I rented the box so you could write to me there in complete privacy. Catherine*

After this an acceptance came. She would not hear from Aadi until he got back from his tour. At least she was not nervous anymore and having anxiety attacks. Catherine attributed this to prayer. She kept asking for faith, faith in Him to handle everything for her. He had put Aadi in her life for some purpose. She didn't know what that was yet, but she thought they were destined for more of their lives touching.

She was becoming more and more dissatisfied with her present life style. Catherine was anxious to get on with living and move to India. However, Russell's wedding was set less than two months ahead. She would wait for that and then see if she could make the break with Bran. This was definitely no life. But there was her mother to consider also. Catherine decided she needed to pray more, so that she would know what He wanted her to do.

In her prayers she asked for hope as well as love and faith in Him. She also realized that she needed to place more faith in Aadi. Even though he hadn't written, she had to assume that he still felt as he did two weeks previously, when they had talked. Certainly the faxes she had received from him were supportive of that. She knew how vulnerable she was and how low her self-esteem had become after years of abuse. Although her strength of purpose had gotten her through the empty years, suddenly now she was a needy woman and a lonely woman. Of course that brutal verbal attack from Mary Ann had done nothing for her. What it had done was make her doubt herself and Aadi.

She wrote to Ramu asking his advice about sending him the $5000 from her CD that she had received from Helen White. With that in place in an Indian bank, the interest it would accrue would allow her to purchase property there. And then she went to see her mother.

"Mom, I have something I must discuss with you."

"What?" she asked worriedly.'

"Mom, I am going to get a divorce."

"A divorce? Why?"

"Because I have no life. I haven't had one for many years. My husband doesn't love me."

"Oh, he does too."

"Mom, he does not. He never did. He married me because his mother was throwing him out of the house. He told me that before we got married."

"I don't believe it."

"Well, it's true."

"But, will he give you any money?"

"Of course. It is the law. I will get half of everything."

"Oh, well that's OK then. But what about me?"

"Mom, I'm not divorcing you. But I have to tell you that after the divorce, I am going to live in India."

"You are?" she cried incredulously. "Well then, I suppose I'll have to go and live with Cindy."

"Would that be difficult for you? Moving away from here that is?"

"No, I like it in Portland. I can live with Cindy. She'll take care of me."

"Well, I'm sure she will, but I haven't spoken to Cindy yet. You are the first person that I've told about my decision to divorce. I don't want anyone to know yet because I haven't told Bran and I want to wait until after the wedding.

"Yes. You should wait until the wedding is over."

"I don't want anything to spoil Russell's day."

"What about your house?"

"Well, you know, Mom, I've been clinging to that house. It was my dream house. I had so much to do with the plans before we built. It was I who talked the Benedictines out of that property. I raised all my boys there. It was the only thing I had to hold on to. I loved that house and Bran always told me that the way I spent money, we would not be able to afford to live there much longer. I wanted to cry thinking about when I would have to give it up. Now, Mom, it doesn't make any difference. We will have to sell and split the proceeds. And do you know what?"

"What?"

"I don't want that house anymore. I don't care about it. All I want is to start a new life, a life with some purpose."

"Have you been so unhappy?"

"Oh, Mom. I never let on, I never told you how terribly unhappy I've been for years. I've had no companion. I've been alone. We don't eat together anymore. We don't sleep together. And we never talk. He isn't interested in anything I have to say, unless it concerns money. And he only talks to me when the bills come in. In fact, he doesn't talk, he screams at me. I'm tired of it all."

"That bastard! Here I thought he loved you. He was giving you a good life. He always treated me well."

"Well, materially, he gave me a good life, Mama, and he gave me my boys, but I gave them to him also. But, I never had the love that you and Daddy enjoyed. I've craved that all my life."

"I'm sorry."

"Me too, but now I'm going to do something about it."

After the talk with her mother, Catherine realized that she had come a long way in her thinking and in her emotional state. Now she began to envision a house in India; all on one floor, surrounded on three sides by gardens, with water on the fourth. She had no idea yet what she would do there, but Catherine had always wanted to write, and she thought that India would be the place for her to start. Whatever, it made her very happy just to think about living there. The next thing she did was to call Robert, and tell him of her plans.

"Well, Mom, if that is what you have to do, then you have to do it."

"Thanks, honey."

"It should be fairly cut and dried. You will just split everything in half. It should take about a week to get everything settled."

"Really? That quick?"

"I don't expect that Dad will contest. He certainly won't want to cheat you. The biggest problem will be getting rid of all the household goods."

"I will take care of all that, Robert. I plan to divide all the personal items among you boys. There is a lot of it, especially the things that have been passed down through generations. But that will be my job, and I'll handle it."

"Mom, I want to warn you not to invest money in India."

"Why? Ramu told me I can get very good interest there. Much better than here."

"Mom, if something happens to you, we wouldn't be able to get it out. Besides, Kerry has been investing for people here and getting them 15-18% interest on their money which is great."

"If she can do the same for me, then I will leave it here."

"Just be careful, Mom. Check out the banks in India, before you put any money over there."

"OK, Robert. Thank you for your advice."

It was now the 20th of March and Catherine noted that although she had had some anxiety the day before, she had controlled it with prayer. She left for the post office, at her usual time to check her box. After so many disappointing visits there, she opened the box with very little hope. But, there it was. There was a letter from Aadi. She took it out and held it to her breast. She put it in her purse, unopened, and drove home. She couldn't open it right away, needing to feel that it was actually there, there in her hand. She waited for two hours, just savoring the joy of having heard from him. And then, carefully, so as not to tear any part of the envelope, she slit it open and began to read.

Dear Catherine,

It was wonderful to talk you on the phone. I wished you were here and talking to me. I have seen you in the lobby of Lake Palace and I felt dejavue.....and the same I asked you. I don't know what did you feel? I was very much touched, when you allowed me to guide the group. I felt your' great concern regarding gentleman who fell ill during his visit to the City Palace Udaipur. I also felt your eyes communicating with me all the time. I felt wonderful when you expressed an embrace when you were about to leave for the hotel—-the only night.

It was so good of you for coming to Ranakpur. I met the guests which I did'not know to happen. I enjoyed seeing you planting glowing. I *the olive cuttings. Your history is not important to me. I feel delighted to know that you started expressing your feelings which you suppressed for years. It was enchanting to know that you are glowing. I did see you glowing while looking at me, have seen you glowing but shy when I put you in my arms, I felt you glowing and vibrant when I folded you in me, and I have seen you glowing and sweet when I kissed you Please don't consider this all just physical but this is flow of expressions. You are sweet and beutiful lady and I expressed the same to you. Please smile.'*

I missed coming to Goa owing to my busy schedule, but I thought and remembered the time which we passed together on all these days. I did kiss you many times in these days.

I will let you know the right dates in September for your visit to India. Please wait for some days.

I did phone you at home, but you were not on the phone. I faxed you a brief note, but I could not listen your sweet voice.

I will be not at home till 18th. I will miss to talk to you. I will fax you whenever it is possible during my trip.

many many kisses.....Aadi

CHAPTER FOURTEEN
PAINTING AND TOUCHING

It was the 21st of March, her 38th wedding anniversary. Bran had forgotten, obviously, for he had said nothing to her. "I don't care," she told herself. "It is over."

She hugged herself, remembering the phone call she had placed to India the night before. It had been around 11 AM in Udaipur, and Aadi's father answered the phone. Catherine could hear Aadi running to answer when his father called him. It was so very good to hear his voice. Always he asked how she was in that special way of his.

"I tried to call you last night," he told her. "But I hung up when you didn't answer."

"Oh, I knew that was you. I was told that there had been 'a hang up'."

"I called you before, before I left on tour."

"Oh, Aadi, I knew about that too, especially after I got your fax. I figured you had tried to reach me. I'm so sorry that I wasn't home."

"Catherine, it would be better if you call me at night here. Because in the morning, I could be away from home."

"Of course. I can do that. Lisa has given me the key to her house, and that will be better too, for me."

Actually, her rates would be much higher, but she would be freer to talk when she was alone in the house. They went over ground that they had spoken of before. So many reminiscences of her time in Udaipur. Then he began to kiss her, over and over and over.

"Kiss me back," he told her. "I want to hear you kiss me." And she did, but not as volubly as he. She wondered how he could be so demonstrative in his home. Surely it wasn't that private because she could hear much background noise. But if he felt comfortable, there was no reason for her to be concerned.

"If I had come to Goa, do you think we would have become intimate?"

"I don't know. I don't think I was ready for it then, but maybe, because I missed you so."

"I think we would have."

"I received your letter today. It was wonderful to read your words."

"You liked it?"

"Oh, yes! But you know, I didn't open it for two hours."

"Why?"

"Because I just wanted to feel the joy of having it first."

"I see. When you write to me, please, I would like to see your hand writing."

"Oh, OK. I will write like that from now on."

"We should not talk long now."

"I will call you tomorrow, tonight for you. OK?"

"Yes," he said. "Call me tonight."

So it was morning in Duluth. Catherine had just shopped for her mother and brought lunch to her. Now she was free to drive to Lisa's. Her anticipation was great and a feeling of warmth filled her, knowing that soon she would be talking to him again.

This time, he answered the phone. His voice was ever so soft.

"How are you?"

"Fine," she answered. Were you asleep?"

"No, I was waiting for your call."

"Tell me about your house, Aadi."

"It is a very small house. And there is a garden."

"Your parents live there. Do you have brothers and sisters?"

"A sister. She is married and lives nearby. Her little girl lives with us."

"I see."

"What are you wearing?"

"Wearing? Well, just a T-shirt and jeans. Why?"

"I am imagining how you look."

"What are you wearing? Pajamas?"

"My birthday suit."

"What?" she said, not thinking she heard him correctly.

"My birthday suit."

"Oh!" she said, suddenly shy. "Of course, it must be very warm there now."

"Yes, and the moon is full and shining in my window."

"I wish I could be with you."

"You are with me. I'm holding you and kissing you." And over and over again he made kissing noises. Suddenly, she started to giggle.

"You're laughing at me?" he asked, incredulously.

"Oh, no. I'm just happy. How could you think I was laughing at you?"

"Kiss me back," he told her.

"Oh, yes, yes, yes."

"Can you feel me holding you?"

"Yes," she whispered. "I feel your whole body next to mine."

"Tell me," he said.

"I am standing close to you. You are kissing me and I feel our bodies touching, all the way to our toes. You have the most wonderful arms."

"What are you feeling?"

"I am feeling wonderful."

"What are you feeling about me?"

"I feel your strength. I feel your gentleness. Yes, I feel you touching me all over."

"Yes, and what else?"

"I feel your hardness," she said very quietly.

"Ah, yes! You feel that. That is what I want you to feel. Take off your shirt."

"You want me to undress?"

"Yes, first your shirt….now your pants. I want to see you. I would like to have one of those gadgets so that I could see you over the phone,"

"You've got to be kidding! That kind of thing is not private. There is no way I would ever do that."

"I would like that. I want to see you….all of you."

Catherine was shaking all over, and more than ever she ached to be there with him. Surely they had talked another hour.

The following day, she had her hair done, and while under the dryer, she made a list of things she wanted to discuss with him. Somehow, the minutes always sped by and they got so wrapped up in each other, they didn't get much conversation going. For certain, she wanted to apologize for laughing the day before when he was kissing her. She wanted no misunderstanding between them.

He answered after only two rings. Obviously he had anticipated her call.

"How are you?" Again that special way of asking.

"Fine, now that I'm talking to you"

"Very fine."

"Aadi, I need to tell you how worried I was about yesterday, when we talked."

"Why? What happened?"

"You thought that I was laughing at you. Aadi, I don't know if I made myself clear when I tried to explain. I think it is easy to misunderstand each other when there is such a cultural difference and then the physical distance. We can't see how the other person is reacting. Aadi, I would never, never laugh at you. I would never hurt you. My joy was bubbling up inside me when you were kissing me and it just exploded."

"Relax, I understood. I thought no more about it."

"Good. Now tell me more about your garden. What do you grow?"

"Fruit trees, some vegetables, roses and other flowers."

"Tell me about you, Aadi."

"What do you want to know?"

"Anything. Everything. Do you like to read?"

"Oh, yes. I have many books on nature, gardening, biographies, and philosophy. I have a degree in English Literature."

"You have? Aadi, you know that I am an RN, but after some years I went back to school and my major was English Lit. I can't believe this coincidence! What about music? What kind do you like?"

"Classical."

"Me too. Who is your favorite composer?"

"Classical Indian music."

"Oh, of course. I don't know anything about Indian music. But western classic music is my favorite. What else about you?"

"I speak fluent Spanish and French."

"Oh, my God!"

"What?"

"Aadi, I can't speak either of those languages, but I studied two years of Spanish in high school, and when I went back to college, I studied French."

"You can't speak them at all?"

"No, I only know a few words here and there. But I sang in five languages, so I know the pronunciation."

"What are you wearing?"

"A white shirt, blue jeans and my neck scarf. Lisa turned down the heat and I'm chilly."

"I will wrap you in my arms and then you will be warm. Can you feel me?"

"Yes, I feel warmer already. You know, Aadi, I am so jealous of your clients."

"Why?"

"Because they are with you and I can't be."

"I'll quit work."

"What did you say?"

"If you're jealous, I just won't work."

"Oh, Aadi, you are joking, of course, but it was so sweet of you to say that. And oh, how I wish you were here."

"I am kissing you, and I am touching you. Do you feel my hands on your body?"

"Yes. I love your hands. I love your kisses and your beard is so soft."

"I had difficulty falling asleep last night."

"Why, Aadi?"

"Because I kept thinking and thinking about you."

"I have the same problem. I want so much to be with you. You know, I've been thinking. When we finally are together, I want to create a beautiful mood, with candles, and incense, and soft music. Would you like that?"

"Oh, yes, I would like that very much. Catherine, I will fax you on Monday."

All that day she was smiling. 'Glowing' would probably be a better word. She felt warm and loved and extremely happy. The next day was Sunday and she couldn't stay away from Lisa's. She let herself in and went to the phone.

"Hello, how are you?"

"I had to call, Aadi. I just had to make use of this time. Lisa and Zach are in Mexico for a week, so I have the house to myself."

"Good, then you can speak very open."

"Yes. I am totally alone except for the cat." She laughed. "I don't like cats, but this one is OK."

"Catherine, this is the festival of Holi. Do you know about it?"

"Oh, the colors!"

"Yes. I want to paint you."

"Really? You want to paint me?"

"Yes. I am painting your face red. Now your hair and back, orange. Your neck I am painting blue." There was a short silence. "Catherine, what is below your neck?"

Catherine grinned and wanted to laugh. "Aadi, you know what is below my neck."

"I know the word in Hindi, but I don't know it in English."

"Oh, yes you do. I can't believe you don't know the word. Come on!"

"No, you must tell me. What is below your neck?"

"So what color do you want to paint my breasts, Aadi?"

"Gold!" The answer came so fast, this time she laughed. "So are you going to paint the rest of me?"

"Yes." He finished painting her, then, "Will you paint me?"

"I'd love to," she answered, and proceeded from his head down his body. She painted his waist to his thighs gold and finished with his legs and feet.

"You missed something."

"No, I didn't. I'm sure I got all of you." She started to squirm because she knew what he was asking for, but she played dumb.

"Catherine, you forgot something very important."

"I'm sure I didn't."

"Catherine, you skipped part of me."

Then, very nonchalantly, she asked, "Oh, your penis and scrotum?"

"Yes."

"I thought I covered that with the gold from waist to thighs. But OK, I paint your penis and scrotum blue."

"I like that. I am touching your breasts."

"I love that. Oh, God, Aadi, you make me feel so good."

"I want you to feel wonderful."

"You are wonderful, Aadi."

"I am very ordinary. I am just, Aadi."

"No, you are very special, Aadi." There was silence on the line. Her hand was shaking as she held the phone and tears streamed down her face.

"Let me touch you more. And I am kissing you, kissing your breasts."

"Aadi, did you have a hard time falling asleep last night?"

"Yes, it was a long time before I slept."

"Aadi, don't you take care of yourself?" He was very quiet and it was apparent to her that he didn't know how to answer. "I do," she finally told him.

"What do you do?"

"I touch myself and think of you."

"I do the same," he admitted.

"Every morning I wake and make love to you."

"What time is that?"

"Five o'clock. Why?"

"Then I will make love to you at that time."

"Oh, yes, please. Then it will really be good for us both."

Catherine tried over and over again to fax Aadi the following day, but it wouldn't go through. She was very frustrated. And nothing came from him either, and she feared something had gone wrong with his machine. The next best thing was to write to him.

Dear Aadi,

I so very much enjoyed talking to you these past three days. Each day was better than the last. Don't you agree? I have been bubbling and bubbling over the painting. That was wonderful!!! I'm so glad you thought for us to do it. It amazes me how shy you are. You always lead me right to the brink and then expect me to say the word or words for you. I'm not sure if it's shyness on your part, is it?? Or are you worrying I would be offended if you spoke first, or are you enjoying hearing me voice the words? Whatever, it certainly has succeeded in breaking down any barriers between us. I am enjoying all of it. You are so much fun to be with. You had me going for a while with that video phone business. I love your sense of humor. You give me joy and fill me with such happiness. You are so romantic, Aadi. We are truly soul mates, don't you feel that? I loved your telling me about the full moon – its light shining through your window. And I'm so glad you agree to setting the mood for our first encounter with candles, incense and soft music. It will be very beautiful. If you see beauty in my eyes that is my soul shining with God's love. In Eklingji, and on the hillside at the site I told you God loved you and was blessing you with the encounter with the guests. Don't ever tell me again that you are 'ordinary'. I can't imagine where you are coming from when you say that.

You seem to have infinite patience and accept what cannot be changed. Your love of nature and your work in the soil makes you one with the earth and God's creation. You are humble, self-less, and unmaterialistic and have great courage. You are intelligent, knowledgeable and idealistic. You appreciate the natural beauty of a garden, a work of art, a piece of music–all of which enriches your soul. You enjoy and love life–I see that in your romantic, loving and sensuous nature. The latter is most attractive to another person who recognizes those earthy attributes in herself. Oh, you are unique, Aadi. I've never known anyone to compare with you. C

Then when she went back to Portown the next day, the fax did go through.

Hi—

I loved the Holi painting yesterday. The only problem–it was very difficult getting it off in the shower this morning–the orange on my back that is. I couldn't reach! Also that gold on my...... what was that word? The one you couldn't remember? Oh, yes–BREASTS. Well, the gold paint must have been made with some substance other than the other colors, because that was hard to get off. I've never had so much fun

She placed her mouth on the page and left an imprint of her lips. Then a fax came for her with the explanation of why the fax was not working.

I tried last night but could not send fax due to the festival of Holi. I think same happened. Thanks for the purification ring. I just received this evening —— is it to purify me!!

It was wonderful to talk to you. I hope to have the new apparatus, so that I could see all that. I have also received your letter, few days before. Please let me know if you need something from India. I have posted a book of R.K.Narayam. He is a very good fiction writer. He is from Mysore.

With many kisses

Aadi

This morning she brought a two pound box of Russell Stover chocolates for her friends at Portown Travel. They were so good to her, calling her when a fax came in and putting up with her numerous calls to them. Then of course, she had to call him again. Every day was better than the last.

"Catherine, tell me where you are."

"In Lisa's kitchen. It is a very small house. I will take pictures and send them to you."

"I want pictures of you."

"Well, I've told you that I take very poor pictures."

"I want some of you. Now, tell me what are you wearing?"

"Pink shirt, jeans."

"Is it cold in the house? Because I want you to take off some clothes."

"It is warmer today. I'll manage. What do you want me to take off?"

"Your pants."

"All right." Still holding the receiver, she wriggled out of her jeans and panties. "OK."

"I have my fingers on your clitoris. And now in your vagina. What other word to you have for vagina?"

"I don't know. I call it, 'vagina'. I want to play with you too."

"Take my penis. Stroke my penis. Catherine, what color is your hair?"

"Aadi, you know the color of my hair."

"No, no, I mean.....down there."

"Oh.....gray. Did you have trouble going to sleep last night?"

"Yes, I was very excited."

"Didn't you take care of yourself?"

"No, I waited for you....five o'clock, when I knew you were making love to me."

"Oh, Aadi. I am crying. I am so touched. So happy."

"I want to do the same today, but sooner, when you go to bed."

"At night. OK."

"And again in the morning, when you wake up. Promise me."

"Of course I promise. I'll go to bed at 9 PM here and then wake at 5 AM. We will make love twice in a day. That will feel wonderful. And you will find relief."

"Catherine, tell me where you like to be touched."

"I like you to kiss my breasts. I like it when you touch my clitoris. I love your hands all over me."

"What positions do you like?"

"I feel best when you come from behind me."

"I am kissing your clitoris. Do you like that?"

"Oh, yes. Let me kiss you too."

"You want to kiss my penis?"

"Yes, I want to take you and stroke you and taste you."

"Tell me what you were thinking when you were here in Udaipur."

"Well, golly, I think I've told you everything I can remember. I certainly didn't feel about you the way I do now. We had only two days. But I knew that I had lost something when we had to say 'good-bye'. I felt awful. Aadi, would you like me to send you my thoughts about that time? I have them all in my journal."

"Yes, I'd like to read."

"All right. I'll copy what I wrote and send it to you."

"What was the perfume you used in Udaipur?"

"PARIS, by Yves St. Laurant. Did you like it?"

"Yes. I liked it very much. I remember smelling you when I kissed you. Catherine, I am worried."

"About what?"

"The money you are spending calling me every day."

"It's expensive, yes. But I need to hear your voice. I am getting addicted to this."

But this was Holy Week and Catherine had to start thinking of Easter, when her family would be coming home. She needed to shop for groceries and get her house in order. How she was going to do all that when thinking constantly of Aadi, she didn't know. But she felt she could call him one more day before waiting until after the holiday.

"Hi!"

"How are you?"

"I'm fine. And you?"

"Fantastic."

"Aadi, this will have to be my last call for a while because of the Easter Holiday. My family will be coming home and I'm going to be too busy to come down here to Lisa's. Do you understand?"

"Of course. We must fax and write more. It will take the place of the calls and be much cheaper."

"I'm not sure that faxes and letters will be as good as talking, but we can try that."

"Did you make love to me last night and this morning?"

"Aadi, I have to tell you. Last night I was at choir practice."

"At nine o'clock?"

"No, no. Wait! I watched the time and ran out of practice before it was over so that I could be home and in bed by nine."

"What happened?"

"Oh, God, Aadi. I got home, undressed and got into bed. I opened my legs for you. I felt you there, but I was so relaxed, I fell asleep. Aadi, I'm so sorry. I had to tell you."

"That's all right. You were tired. But I was there."

"I knew that you had been there. My spirit knew it too because when I woke up at two in the morning, I was all wet down there–not only my vagina, but the whole area."

"I found you sleeping on your belly. I entered you, the way you like it–from behind. You raised your hips to me, and I put my penis into you and made love to you."

Softly, and with much emotion, she told him, "Aadi, I love you so.! Would you do something for me before we hang up?"

"What do you want, Catherine?"

"I want to make love to you–to go down on you, and I'd like you to have an orgasm over the phone. I don't want you to be frustrated after our conversations. I want you to be relaxed so you can go to sleep for a change."

So quietly that she could barely hear him, he answered, "For you I will do it. What are you wearing today?"

"My pink shirt and jeans."

"I like your pink shirt. Take it off."

"Ok, it's off."

"What color is your bra?"

"White." But he didn't ask her to remove it.

"Now take off your pants.....Did you also remove your underpants?"

"Yes, I am naked from the waist down except for my sox."

They kissed and fondled each other and then he told her, "I have an erection. I want to enter you, from the back. How does it feel?"

"Oh God, Aadi, this is killing me. I am in the kitchen, and I need to lie down. Oh, oh, God!! Aadi, I want you in my mouth."

"Here, take it, take it, take it."

"Guide my head, darling. I am tasting you, sucking you. My tongue is on the head. Do you like it? How is it?"

"Fantastic. Oh, I'm going to come. Oh!"

"Go deeper, deeper. Let me take all of you. That's it. Come, darling. Come."

"It's over now."

"Is your hand all sticky?"

Laughing, he said, "Yes."

"Let me take it. I am sucking each finger, and now I am licking your palm."

"Thank you. I am all clean now."

"Thank you for letting me do this to you. It made me very happy."

"I want to do it to you too."

"I don't think it would work. Not until we are really together."

"You could lie on the table, or the floor."

She laughed. "The table is glass and it is in front of a window. The floor is out also. It is full of cat hair. But I have to tell you something."

"What?"

"The cat! She must have sensed something going on here."

"Why? What do you mean?"

"She was lying at my feet, rolling and squirming and purring and rubbing herself all over."

"Could you use the bed?"

"I'd have to use the cordless phone, but it doesn't seem right to use Lisa's bed. I have to think about that."

CHAPTER FIFTEEN

AN END AND A BEGINNING

With Easter over and the family gone, Catherine had the extra clean-up that was always there after a big holiday. That finished, her mind turned once again to Aadi, if he ever was apart from her. She was also thinking of her divorce. She had decided that she wouldn't wait until after Russell's wedding. There was too much to do and little time to do it. Although her plans were still in the formative stage, more and more she was thinking not to make two trips to India; the first, only a tour of Rajasthan with Aadi, the second, to move to India. It was expensive to travel back and forth. It made more sense to start divorce proceedings immediately, get all her affairs in order and leave permanently for India the first of September.

Robert and his family had not come to Duluth for Easter, so she had called him the week before and asked him to recommend a divorce attorney. He was very professional, and did not question her, only told her he would get back to her with a name. Robert's office was in Fargo, but his main office was in Duluth. He called his boss, who gave him a recommendation, and he got back to her with the name of Jack Setterlund. She called Setterlund's office and made an appointment for 15 April, but didn't tell Bran about her decision.

Catherine prayed every day for God to guide her regarding the right, or best time to tell Bran. She knew he was paranoid about receiving bad news in March, so she held off. She knew he would be shocked and hurt, but this was something that had to be done, and she was determined to go through with it. After her decision was made, she had no second thoughts, only a feeling of relief and great freedom. The following months were not going to be easy, but she felt God would see her through this challenging period.

There was no fax from Aadi, as he had promised, but she was not in any anxiety. The intimacy they had shared had succeeded in healing that deep ache within her, but, even so, she missed him very much. He was a part of her now; a part of her being, her soul. She loved him as she had loved no other man. And she ached to be with him. Now that her family duties had subsided, she took this opportunity to write to him.

She put together photos of her beautiful city along with post cards depicting surrounding areas. She enclosed no photos of herself however, because there were none that she felt were good enough. She told him of her decision to divorce and to sell her house and divide everything. She wanted him to know about the house she envisioned having in India, of buying property and building. She asked him if he would help her to design a simple house, for she wanted nothing elaborate. Among the photos were pictures of her stained glass work. She told him she was hoping to continue this work in India if at all possible.

The next day Catherine sent the following fax.

> *Hello! How are you? I'm missing our talks every day. How about you? Yesterday I mailed some photos, post cards and a letter. I'm sorry, but it doesn't take the place of hearing your voice. Lisa gave me her key to keep, since she works during the day and that is the time we talk. When summer vacation starts for her son, (sometime in June), our timing might change a little. We'll have to see. I loved the intimacy we shared especially last Thursday. I hold the memory in my mind and heart all the time. How do you feel? Please, before*

> *you go out again, let me know in time so we can talk again. And remember this agency is closed Sat & Sun. You thought you'd leave on the 7th–so if that holds, I'll call you on Friday. OK? Another thing–we go on Daylight Saving Time 6 Apr–so instead of 11 ½ hrs ahead–you will be 10 ½ hrs ahead of me. Waiting to hear from you. I was going to put a drop of my perfume on the letter I mailed, but I forgot. C*

Once again she imprinted her lips on the fax and sent it off. There was none coming in for her, and when she checked the following day, she was again disappointed. Her mind started turning cartwheels and she got scared.

"Why hasn't he faxed me? I get so worried and scared when I don't talk to him or hear from him. Why am I so vulnerable? I trust him. I just need to have more patience, but it's difficult when I miss him so much. I must have faith in God who placed him in my life for a purpose. And I must have faith in Aadi and our relationship. It is possible that he left Udaipur suddenly and has had no chance to fax me. I wonder if he will answer the phone when I call him on Friday? He hasn't let me down once, and has always been supportive, so why am I worrying?"

Paranoia was setting in and her thinking was negative. It was understandable after many years of low self-esteem. When had she last been told of her worth? It was never anything positive that she received. She lived constantly with put-downs. No wonder she questioned herself now. And no wonder too that she couldn't quite believe in this new relationship, no matter how well and right it felt.

At Lisa's on Friday, she nervously picked up the cordless phone and dialed his home. He answered and sounded good, although a bit sleepy.

"How are you?"

"Oh, Aadi, I've missed you so."

"I've been busy. I worked in the garden and I had a group for four days."

"Aadi are we OK?"

"Yes."

"I've been very anxious. I have been concerned and scared and I am so vulnerable."

"Relax, everything is OK."

"I have a cordless phone, and I brought towels, so I can lie down in Lisa's bed."

"Good. What are you wearing?"

And so it began again, always with the question of what she was wearing. This day she removed all her clothes, and lying on Lisa's bed, made love with Aadi as she never had before. He reminded her before ending the conversation, that he would be going out again on April 7, but told her he would fax her before then.

She had been praying steadily about telling Bran about the divorce. Too many people already knew and she knew the time had to be soon. Then it happened, the answer to her prayer. Bran came into the kitchen and started to talk to her. That in itself, a surprise. They hardly spoke to one another these days.

"Paul Gregg called me."

"Oh? What did he want?" Paul was a former associate of Bran's in the anesthesia department.

"Some woman is retiring from the department, and he asked if you and I would come to the party."

"What did you say?"

"I told him he knows that I don't do that sort of thing. But he insisted I ask you if you wanted to go. But you know I'm not going."

"When is it?"

"April 15th."

And there it was. Her answer and it all came out very smoothly.

"Well, we can't go on that day anyway."

"Oh? Why not?"

"Because we have an appointment on that day."

"An appointment? What kind of an appointment?"

"To see an attorney about a divorce."

"Oh! A divorce! I see." With that he went over to a chair and sat down. She took a chair across the room from him.

"When did you decide all this?"

"Just recently. I called Robert and asked him to recommend someone and he called back after checking with Francis. I made the appointment and then wondered how to tell you."

"Robert knew?"

"He's a professional and he is our son. He will not take sides. But I wanted to hire someone good so I had to ask his advice."

"You are going to India, I suppose? Don't you think you need to see someone?"

"What do you mean?"

"A psychiatrist. This is not normal."

"I don't need a psychiatrist. And I'm not getting a divorce because I have to go to India. But that is a big part of it."

"I knew it, I knew it. That damn India! I knew you would leave me for it."

"Bran, you know we haven't had a marriage for years. There is no communication between us. There hasn't been anything for so long. I can't live like this anymore. It is ruining my health. I am miserable here."

"Oh, you're miserable, are you? Well, Missus, who has it better than you? Which of your friends do you envy?"

"I don't envy anyone, Bran. This has to do with me, no one else."

"You have the best house in the neighborhood. Who has it better than you?"

"Yes, I have a lovely, beautiful house. But I am not happy. That can't be a surprise to you. And just recently you told me you wanted a divorce, remember?"

"I was just talking."

"Well, you threatened me with divorce more than once over the years, so you haven't been that happy either."

"I thought you never wanted to leave this house. Now you are giving it up to go to India?"

"No, I'm giving up a way of life that is killing me."

"Oh, so now I'm killing you, am I?"

"This is no life for you either, Bran. Be honest. You know it isn't."

"I'm content here. This is my home. What more is there?"

"So much more. There is more to life than a house. There is more to life than having money."

"Oh, yeah? Well, how would you know? You've had everything you ever wanted all your life."

"I've had all the material things, yes. I am grateful to you for all of that. But my spirit, my health, my mind, my heart. They have had no nourishment in our relationship. We don't speak to each other. You only talk nicely to me when you need sex. We don't sleep together...."

"You moved into the basement bedroom. I knew that was the end when that happened."

"I've been down there a long time already. We don't eat together either."

"Because you don't cook for me. And you eat all that Indian garbage

"No, because you are used to eating according to the times when Topaz wanted to eat. You shared all your meals with her. I don't resent that. She was your pet and she adored you. But I can't eat McDonald's and 4 PM is too early for me to eat dinner."

"You were jealous of a dog?"

"Hardly! I just mentioned her to make a point."

"Don't you love me anymore?"

"No, Brandon. I haven't loved you for years. That died long ago. But you never loved me."

"I did in my own way."

"Yes, maybe, but it wasn't enough for me."

"Well, we're going to have to sell this house."

"Yes, I realize that."

"I thought we'd live in it for the rest of our lives."

"Brandon, you've been telling me for years that we were going to have to sell and live in an apartment because it cost too much to live here."

"Oh, no. It's cheaper to live here. I thought you never wanted to leave here."

"That's true, I didn't. It was the only thing I had to hang on to. But I don't care anymore. My life is more important than a house."

"Who is this attorney?"

"His name is Jack Setterlund. I know nothing about him."

"Well, I'll have to get an attorney too so you won't cheat me."

"Bran, I have no intention of cheating you. We'll split everything in half, just as the law prescribes."

"Yeah? Well, we'll see. But it would be cheaper if we both used the same attorney."

"That's your decision. I think you should accompany me on the 15th however. Then you can do as you like."

"I'm going to talk to Robert."

"Yes, do that, but don't put our son in the middle. It isn't fair."

"Is this fair?"

"This is our problem, and we must handle it. Robert and none of the other boys should be brought into it."

"Are you sure you shouldn't see a psychiatrist?"

"Brandon, people see a psychiatrist when they have a problem or are unhappy. I don't have a problem with this. And I am not unhappy having made this decision. It is the right one, even though you can't, or won't see it that way. I know that I've shocked you and probably hurt you, but I simply cannot and will not go on like this, waiting for death. I have years ahead of me and I can still be useful and productive.

"Just a few weeks ago I learned a former classmate of mine had died. We used to be close friends when we were in High

School. She died in England. Anyway, I realized that I can't afford to wait. If I want to live in India, I have to make the break now. What more can I tell you?"

Brandon sat there in stunned silence. She left him then, to think and ponder and worry by himself. She knew, without a doubt, that the first thing that he would worry about was the money. After the initial shock, it would be the money and how it would be distributed that he would be interested in the most.

Catherine then put in a call to Russell. She had to tell him that this would not interfere with his wedding, and that she would do everything she could to keep things running smoothly and that his father and she would sit together, be together, as if nothing were going on. She told him not to worry, but knew that he was deeply troubled and sad.

On the 7th of April, Portown called her.

"There's a fax for you, Cathy."

"OK, thanks. I'll be right down."

> *It was wonderful to talk with you last night. In some parts of North India there is cyclonic rains and the temperature is lower then when you were here. I will be leaving Udaipur on the evening of the 7th of April. I am sorry that I did not fax you earlier. It was so thrilling to think, to feel, and to share all wonderful moments with you. I do ask you to utter some of the names because I feel good to listen from you and also I feel your participation. It is good to talk on the phone, I like it and you like it. But it costs a lot of money. It will be good that if we fax and write letters often and think all that, just think about it. You may use this money for some better cause. I am leaving early in the morning to Kumbahlgarh fort and then to the temples of Ranakpur with the clients. You did not*

see Kumbalgarh. It is also beutiful. You will like it when you visit Udaipur with me. Aadi

She was excited to receive such a beautiful fax and read it over and over that day and evening. The next day she went for a massage next door to Sr. Teri. It was difficult getting an appointment because Teri was so booked up with regular customers, but she called Catherine when she had a cancellation. When she returned she checked her messages and heard from Portown Travel again. They never left more than a 'Please call us' on the line. And then a second message; she heard a voice coming on. It was Aadi, saying 'India'. She nearly went through the floor. That's all he said before hanging up. She listened to his beautiful voice again, then went to Portown as fast as she possibly could. There was another fax from him.

Dear Catherine,

Received your letter with photographs and cards. India is wonderful country. Foreigners cannot buy property in India. Please don't sale your property instantly. Visit India and choose, then feel it and decide. Take your own time.

I have seen artists doing stain glass work like you do. Today is New Year as per Hindu callander. I wish you a very happy New Year. You do very beutiful stain glass work. Photographs are wonderful.

How is your blood pressure? Please take care.

I have to leave on 9th instead of 7^{t} .Aadi Very Important

She decided to phone him immediately, so drove to Lisa's. It was later than usual, but she needed to talk to him. Picking up the cordless phone, she went into the bedroom and closed the door. This time she did not take all her clothes off, but they made love and she felt good. She told him not to worry about her coming to India, but was shocked to find out that she could not buy property. She told him that she and Ramu had talked about her investing when she was in Belgaum and he never mentioned that fact. But they spoke of all that before the lovemaking. They were in the throes of passion when she heard something.

"Oh, my God!"

"What happened?"

"There's someone in the house. It must be Zach. Wait a minute."

She straightened herself and opened the door just a crack, and saw Zach standing there in the hallway. "Had he heard anything?" she wondered.

"Hi, Zach. I'm on the phone. I'll be out in a second."

She closed the door again and went back to the phone.

"Aadi, it's OK. Thank God I wasn't naked."

"Catherine, I still have an erection."

"Oh, Aadi, I'm sorry, but I can't talk with the boy here. Just know that I'm holding you, caressing you, and yes, kissing, kissing, kissing you. I have to go."

"Catherine, can I call you at 4 tomorrow morning?"

"Yes, yes, but there is another number for the phone in my bedroom."

She gave it to him, and said 'good-bye'. Afterwards, Catherine went into the living room where Zach was watching TV. She talked to him for a little while and got the impression that he had not heard anything, having just arrived when she became aware of his presence. She would talk to Lisa about this later this evening. She drove up the north shore and parked for a while, savoring the joy she had just experienced. Then she went home and sat down to write Aadi a long letter.

Dear Aadi,

This was one fantastic day! First, the travel agency left a message on my machine, so I knew you had sent me another fax–and just after I had received one from you yesterday. Then on the answering machine I heard 'India'–your beautiful voice, and I nearly jumped out of my skin. I'm at my desk now and I keep playing the tape over so I hear you say, 'India' again and again. And then–talking to you and making love to you at Lisa's. The only thing out of cinq was Zachary coming home.

I had forgotten the time and didn't realize he was expected. It was OK though. I wasn't unclothed and I think he had just arrived so he didn't hear anything. He seemed fine when I talked with him. I called Lisa just a while ago and told her I would never be there again when Zach was coming home. She was OK with everything too, so I guess it was nothing more than a 'close call' and I just have to be more careful.

I am looking forward to your calling me at 4 AM my time tomorrow morning. I need to explain about that 555-1088 phone. It is our second line into the house and we had it for the boys when they were home, because Bran needed our line open when he was 'on call' for surgery. Anyway, we kept it–mainly for computer use. There are 4 phones on that line – one being in my bedroom. There are 6 phones on the main line. Big house, but you can understand how things could get awkward once in a while. If I ever cut you short, please understand. My sister and I often talk on the phone in my bedroom, since Oregon is 2 hours earlier than Minnesota and we like talking at night–it's cheaper and we can talk longer. What I'm getting at is–if this line rings in the middle of the night, it's either my sister or, most often, a wrong number. But during the day it is not wise to use it. Soon all this subterfuge should be over.

We are seeing an attorney 15 April to start the divorce proceedings. My husband and children all know now about the divorce and everyone is getting over the initial shock. There is no animosity. Everything seems amicable and reasonable.

I was shocked when you wrote that foreigners cannot buy property in India. I told you I had discussed this with Ramu when I was in Belgaum. He told me I could get property and build a decent (?) house for $45,000 US.

I don't know what he means by 'decent', but you know I want something very simple. But now you have me very concerned. Not only do I worry about <u>where</u> I can locate, but <u>if</u> I can. I don't want to rent. I want a place of my own. Sure, I could rent a guest room for a while, but I don't want to be a 'guest'. And then, what do I do? I didn't expect this, but I am not giving up my dream and calling to live the rest of my life in India. Somehow I am going to make it work. And I know God has called me there, so I'm going to leave it in His hands. However, we could help Him along a little. Would you make some discrete inquiries for me? And I will write Ramu and see what he has to say. I will tell him only that it has come to my *attention that foreigners cannot buy property there. And what does he suggest? I don't want to do anything illegal, but maybe there is some way to get around the red tape.*

After I left Lisa's today, I drove up the shore a way and parked the car so I could look at the lake. The blue water had ice floes on it and the big ice mass had blown out away from the shore. The sun was shining and it was quite beautiful, although the wind was still cold. I thought about our love making and I felt so good, so warm inside, and so full of joy. You fill me up, Aadi. You fill my heart with your tenderness, your kindness, and your caring. You make me feel beautiful and desirable. Your words and your touches thrill me and I ache for you to possess me.

I told you today that I never talked like this to another person. Shy? Maybe, but I think it has more to do with trust. I was shy with you at first, but you brought me out of that with your gentleness, your sweet humor and loving persistence. You make me feel good about myself, that I am someone worth knowing and caring about. I cried today when you made love to me; my emotions again so close to the surface I couldn't contain them. The joy you bring me is so deep that it is almost like pain. You excite me, you thrill me, and my skin starts to tingle, those arms of yours around me–holding me so close I can barely breathe. I ache for your kisses on my neck, my face, my hair and finally open-mouthed–touching tongues and teeth and exploring. I ache for your hands to hold my buttocks close in to you, so I can feel your penis hardening between us. I ache for your fingers caressing my breasts. When you touch them–over the phone–they push out to you, wanting more. My nipples go erect and ache for you to suck them. And I want your hands caressing my body – down the thighs and finally my perineum–finding my clitoris, stroking it with your fingers, putting your fingers in my vagina at the same time. And yes, I want you to kiss me there, to suck and lick me and make me crazy until my hips jerk and push out for you to enter me and fill me with your wonderful, throbbing, hard penis. I ache for you to pound into me–never letting up,- never stopping–never leaving me

All I really want now is just to be with you. It might get embarrassing in the car–on the road–if I can't keep my eyes and hands off you. I'm joking.- I really wouldn't do anything to embarrass you–no matter how I felt.

It is 10 PM now and I want to get into bed so that I'll be awake when you call me at 4 AM. I can't wait to hear your voice again. I love it, you know–along with everything else about you.

You will read this when you get home from your tour. I want to receive letters like this from you too. I know you will write me. They just take so long to get here. Goodnight.

C

7 AM 9 April I had to take the receiver off the phone, since he got up and started roaming around upstairs at 4 AM. Then he came down and tried to get in- door locked–to check on phone so he could use it with computer.

It's getting a bit difficult, but I can handle it. Don't worry. Since I couldn't talk to you–I did have you with me anyway and we made love and I had an orgasm. Hope you did too.

Yes, Bran had pounded on her door that morning.

"Why is this door locked?" he wanted to know. She didn't answer him, but went to unlock it. She allowed him to see the phone with the receiver off the hook.

"I want to use the computer. Why is the receiver off the hook?"

"It must have fallen off the bed after I used it."

"What's the matter, don't you want me to touch you anymore?"

"No, that is all over."

CHAPTER SIXTEEN
ANOTHER WOMAN

Now began the grueling task of sorting, dividing, and packing all her beautiful things for her boys and daughters-in-law. Catherine made lists of the things she had already promised, such as her sterling, china, and cut-glass. She had many expensive figurines by Lladro, which she needed to decide which to give to whom. There was also her jewelry; gold bracelets, earrings, necklaces, rings. Heirlooms were another challenge for her. Not only did she decide to gift her children, but her grandchildren also. On these items she gave a detailed history and requested that each be kept in trust for the child when she/he became a responsible adult.

Box upon box began to be packed and her dining room began to look like a fine china shop. The table was loaded with all the lovely things that she had treasured through the years. There were three distinct piles, one meant for Robert, another for Roland, and another for Russell. Randall was not married and he planned to live with Russell and Julie when their house was built. However, it didn't look like he might ever marry, so Catherine decided to compensate him by selling her large 2 ¼ carat diamond and giving him the proceeds. There were a few items, however, that she ear-marked for him. But the vast majority was divided three ways.

Soon the dining room could take no more boxes, and she started to place them in the kitchen area. There was also the need to go through all her clothes and Bran's. Most of them went to St. Michael's Church 'Next to New' store in downtown Duluth. Bran decided he wanted very little of his clothes and discarded beautiful suits and sport coats without a second thought. Many large plastic lawn bags were filled with clothes and taken out. There were large pantry-like shelves that had to be sorted out and the contents taken to the Food Shelf.

Of course all of this took time, days and weeks, but it was a constant chore that she had to face every day. Then there were the preparations for Russell's wedding on May 10th.She shopped for a dress that she knew she would wear only once. The two lovely gowns she wore for Robert's and Roland's weddings were still in her closet, but could not be worn for Russell's. The one she found had to be ordered specially, so that took more time. Then there was the bridal shower to attend in St. Paul on the 12th of April. While she was in the city, she finished arranging the rehearsal dinner to be held at the Sheraton-Midway Hotel. There were invitations for that event to be ordered and mailed also.

Whenever she went to the cities, Catherine stayed at Carmel and Al Wawra's house. Al was her father's first cousin and now was very elderly and in late stages of Multiple Sclerosis. Catherine loved these two people. They were very special to her. It was just like being at home at their house. She was always welcome and she always felt comfortable. Carmel and Catherine had become close friends as well as relatives over the years. And this time, Carmel made astounding observations.

"Catherine, you look different."

"I do? How?"

"Your skin is so clear, glowing."

"Really?"

"And at night, I watch you when you sleep, and your face is more at rest than I have ever seen it."

"Well, I've told you I feel good about my decision to get a divorce."

"You don't even scream anymore at drivers on the road, and you don't jump me with nasty remarks."

"Oops!"

"Well, it's true, Catherine. You can be very caustic."

"I know, and I'm sorry if I've hurt you."

"No, I'm just saying, there is something different about you."

"I'm also very much in love, Carmel. I told you about Aadi. But there is no future in it. He is too young for me."

"I don't like to see older women with young men. It isn't natural."

"Well, you see many older men with very young women."

"That's different."

"Well, all I can say is that he started all of it, and I fell in love."

"Is that why you are going to India?"

"No, I told you about my experience in Kovalam Beach. That is the reason I'm going. And I should have ended my so-called 'marriage' a long time ago."

Returning to Duluth the following day, Catherine was able to attend her Oblate meeting at St. Scholastica Monastery. It was important to her to become a Benedictine Oblate, and this was her first year of learning about it and living a life according to the Rule of St. Benedict. It gave her great peace to be among this group of spiritual, prayerful people, both men and women.

One of the women oblates who hardly knew Catherine, came up to her. "You look different," she said. Another person had recognized the change in her. This woman lived on the north shore at Two Harbors. She told Catherine that she and her daughter had a prayer house called, 'Manna House'. This intrigued Catherine and gave her the idea that someday she might have something similar when she became settled in India. Perhaps it would be a prayer house for Hindus as well as Christians. She would let God direct her if this was to be.

"Perhaps," she thought, "a house in India could be a kind of hermitage or retreat for my family. Maybe God is calling me for something more. If one of my children or grandchildren needs to get away for a while, he/she would have this house of mine in India. It is just a thought, and I need to pray about this.

"I must pray too that my feelings for Aadi are OK. There is so much sexuality surfacing in me. I know that it is all part of the larger picture of my coming to a full life, which has been denied me for so long. I truly feel love for this wonderful man, not just sexual lust."

Aadi had told her a while back that if she found the physical to be not as good when they came together as she expected it to be, that he would accept her just as a friend. But she couldn't imagine that happening. Her need and ache for him was becoming a gnawing presence, such as she could never remember having for anyone. The waiting until September was unbearable.

When she checked her box at the Post Office on Monday, there was a letter from Aadi. She took it home and opened it at her desk.

Dear Catherine,

I was in north of India, Lakhnow and around it in addition to Orchha, Khajuraho, Gwalior and Varanasi. Lakhnow is the capital of the state of Uttar Pradesh. Nawab was the courtier of muguls and he worked as Governor of the state of Avadh, then the area around Lakhnow. After the decline of muguls, Nawab became more important. Lakhnow was an important center for the revolution of 1857. The well known Indian director Satyajot Rai made a film ke Kholasi (The Chess players) on the life of the nawab, who loved intellectual persuits, dances, music......but did not understand enough the english attack on the state. There are beutiful mosques with the gardens and tombs. The stucco work is beautiful. The river Gomti adds to the beuty of the city. Advdh food is very well known for its charm. I also liked the residency, the quarter for British agent, is also very interesting. I did drop a letter from here. Orchha village, beautiful river, Gomti makes it just lovely. I like the village very much.

I have been thinking about your letters from Kovalam and Goa for all the time–I feel those wonderful moments we passed in Udaipur. I did not come to Goa, though I wanted due to my busy schedule. My nostrils feel the sweet smell of you. It is very good to know that you will be visiting India in September. I have not taken any work, the best will be right the first week of the month. in the first week of July I will go to Germany. I did not say you earlier, I have German friend for many years and I go to her during my summer holidays.

Thanks for your letter. I miss your handwriting. I love reading your hand-writing. We Hindus believe in earlier life and later life depending on the deeds. You have been taking care of your mother and husband for many years though you are not happy with them. I don't know happenings around you ——— I know your husband does not treat you well, He is a cancer patient like your mother, won't your decision to divorce will cause mental and physical injurous to your mother and the family? Please think. You are the best judge.

Today I am back after many days, to the to be orchard, the place where we had taken picnic with my relatives and friends. We are planting about 60 new fruit plants because these many died after the plantation last year.

I am listening Barbell, lepugs, doves, parrots———and writing to you am feeling talking to you———It is so lovely and beutiful.

I do think also the wonderful talk we had on the telephone, it is like cinema. I did not sleep for a long time and then slept thinking of you.

With a big kiss

Aadi

The beauty of the letter became a blur in her mind. Her only focus was on the two sentences "in the first week of July I will go to Germany. I did not say you earlier, I have German friend for many years and I go to her during my summer holidays."

"He visits HER on his summer holidays! God!!!! God!!!! God!!!!"

She was in total shock and terrible pain. The only thing she could think to do was to write him immediately. Her balloon had burst. He didn't care about her after all. What was all that romantic stuff about? Why had he pursued her if he had someone else? She had trusted him. Oh, God, how was she going to live through this? If she put it all down on paper, maybe she could find some sense in it all.

Dear Aadi,

Your letter arrived today. Thank you for telling me something about Lucknow. I've never been there. I had to go to St. Paul this past Friday. There was a bridal party for my new daughter-in-law. Everyone invited brings a gift and then a luncheon is served. I drove down after having had my annual eye exam and got there in a little more than 2 hours. I always stay with a cousin when I go there. She mentioned that I look "different", that my skin is clearer, that I look more at peace when I sleep, that I don't scream at other drivers anymore etc., so she says that whatever I am doing for myself–it must be right.

My decision to divorce was long over-due. I could no longer remain in a house with so much negative energy. Not one person who knows me has told me I am wrong to do this. Not even my sons. My mother is 93 and in good health–no cancer. She is absolutely delighted to be going to live with my sister–who has always been her favorite, the one who has always been the most like her. They have fun together. My husband has wanted to sell this house for years–I mentioned this in an earlier letter. Now he has decided to move near our sons in the Twin Cities (St. Paul/Minneapolis). He is content with this and so are the boys, so I am free to do as I please and I will have enough money to do what I want to do. And that is, to move to India, make my home there. That decision was made for me in Kovalam.

I don't know what God wants of me, but I know He has called me there. So the biggest decision I have yet to make is <u>where</u> to locate. I am very, very confused about this now and it is extremely upsetting, but somehow I'm going to have faith that it will work out for me.

You mentioned the first week of September as a good time for me to visit India. Are you also saying that <u>one</u> week is all that we can spend together?

That's OK, but I need time to find a place to live, so perhaps this is not the time we should be running around the countryside sightseeing. I don't know if you are willing to help me find a place. If not, I need to ask someone else. So please tell me how you feel. I knew we would hit some obstacles in this relationship sooner or later. And it seems a few have arisen, haven't they?

You have cautioned me, at least twice, maybe three times, about leaving my family, selling my things and moving. Are you uncomfortable with my decisions? I assure you–they have <u>nothing</u> to do with you. They would have been made even had I never met you. I will admit that your entering my life at this time was an added bonus, showing me that there was life out there, and joy. I will always be grateful to you for that. In fact, I know that I expressed something like that to you from Lisa's after a particularly intimate conversation. And if that was all that was to be, I'd accept that. Aadi I backed away a couple times–but I also was the first to start things between us by the two letters. Although you responded, I went the further. Perhaps–because I have been starved for so long and you gave me attention and hope. Forgive me for coming on like a steam roller. Our relationship did heat up very fast, and perhaps your comparison to a cinema was justified ——— an X-rated one? I am truly sorry, Aadi. I won't allow that to happen again, either on the phone or by letter.

I am not sorry that I gave you my heart. You have been kind, loving, caring, and complimentary to me. I needed all of that desperately. You supplied it a thousand fold. Again, I am so grateful. You are a beautiful, wonderful man. But you have just told me there is someone else in your life. I should have known there would be. All this time I wondered why you weren't married to a lovely Mewari girl who could warm your heart and bed and give you beautiful children. Now I understand. Some lady in Germany has your heart. You should have told me earlier. But I am not angry, just very sad. I am not sure where WE go from here, because I still feel there is such a bond between us–and not the sexual, physical one. What did you call it? A 'flow of expression'? I don't know exactly what you mean. And at this moment, I can't define what that 'bond' is because of all the emotions that are surging through me right now.

For almost two months I had so much joy, love and hope–such as never before in my life. Before that I was ready to die, never having experienced any of it. Instinctively I knew that it would not go on indefinitely, that at some point it would all end. I guess I didn't expect it to happen this quickly, but then I wasn't being realistic–just too romantic. I allowed it to happen and even for this short time, I am glad I did. I was <u>always</u> aware that you didn't love me, but you were <u>loving</u> toward me and so very good and kind. I bless you for that.

You must know that I can never have a sexual relationship with you now. To share you with someone else like that would be degrading to me. About September–what, if anything, is left between us? Aadi, please write to me. I need to hear from you, how you feel about this–what you are thinking- what I should do. C

The shock was still with her, but she felt no anger. She loved him and felt grateful to him for giving her what she had needed all her life. She felt no betrayal, just a deep, heart rending sadness. Did this change her desire to live in India? No, not at all. Catherine was as determined as ever to make her new life in India. That is where God had called her and she felt the rightness of her decision.

Pain set in the next day, and tore at her insides, but she had to continue. She had experienced pain before, but never, she thought, was it this intense. And this was the day when she and Bran would see the attorney for the first time.

The meeting went well, Catherine thought. She liked Jack Setterlund, and Bran seemed to think that Jack could represent him also. Jack agreed to that, but cautioned Bran that he was primarily Catherine's attorney, and that he would be looking out for her interests. Jack laid out the plan as to how everything would progress. The house had to be appraised and then put on the market. Catherine was to make an inventory of everything in the house that she wanted. It was all very painless to her, but she realized the agony that Bran was going through. He was very worried about how the money would be divided, particularly the IRA, but Jack told him it was a common occurrence and that it would be handled fairly.

Bran contacted Robert as soon as they returned home and talked to him at length about the meeting. Robert tried his best to remain on the sideline of the case. But Bran kept him informed everyday as to what he was thinking and the questions he had regarding the attorney, Catherine, and his money. He was becoming increasingly angry and stayed awake nights worrying about the division of the money. Every morning when Catherine came to her desk, she found pages of questions and statements regarding his thoughts. Bran also sent copies to Jack and to Robert.

Another appointment was made by Bran for a consultation with their accountant. This was another Jack, Jack Schilling, their neighbor, friend, and tax accountant. He called in another CPA and the four of them went over the assets together. Bran kept asking questions, which both accountants thought were superfluous, but tried to assure Brandon that everything that he was concerned about would work out without their handling it precisely the way he thought it should be handled.

Catherine went at her regularly appointed time to the adoration chapel. There she placed all the pain she was experiencing over to God, realizing that Aadi had someone else in his life. She asked God to help her through this, but for some reason, she seemed to be bombarded with reminders of him. At the supermarket, Catherine ran into an old acquaintance.

"Hi, Barb," she greeted her.

"Well, Catherine, what have you been up to?"

"You will probably be shocked, but I am going to India to live."

"You are? That is a surprise. Is Bran going also?"

"No, Barb. We are getting a divorce."

"Oh, I'm sorry."

"That's OK. I'm very happy to be going to India."

"My daughter's best friend is from India."

"Really? What part of India is she from?"

"Golly, I don't know. She is just a beautiful girl. Her name is Aadina."

Catherine nearly fainted. "That is a beautiful name," she told her.

The following day, Sr. Mary Charles gave Catherine a magazine to read regarding international monasticism. She particularly wanted her to see that there was a Benedictine community in Bhopal, India, where she might want to visit some time. But as Catherine read through the entire magazine, she saw, on the last page, a small picture of a man tending another man's leg. She read the article that came from the state of Tamil Nadu in the south, along the eastern coast of India and spoke of a FR. ABHIMANI.

Again and again and again, she was being reminded of Aadi. What did it all mean? What was God telling her? Her heart was heavy, but she had so many things on her mind, so many things to do, it was difficult to focus. She had sent a letter to Ramu telling him that she had heard it was not possible to buy property in India. When she did not receive an answer, she became anxious and decided to call him.

Ramu told her that he had written in answer to her letter and was surprised that she hadn't received it yet. He promised to send her a copy. However, he sounded extremely agitated to Catherine when he told her that he had been unaware, until he looked into the matter, that indeed foreigners are not allowed to buy property, and that she would have a great deal of difficulty immigrating. Ramu said it was very complicated and that she should contact Sunil, since he lived in the capital, and maybe he could find out more about it.

It seemed another hurdle to Catherine, but she wasn't daunted by this information. She then phoned Sunil, who told her not to worry, that he would see to her immigration that it would be no problem. She thought that he was being naïve, but she let it go. Sunil was very worried about the divorce and wanted to know what had happened. She promised to send him all the details.

After sending Sunil a long fax, Catherine was at loose ends. There was a lot to do around the house, but she couldn't concentrate. She needed to be somewhere else, away from the house and alone. A sudden inspiration hit her, and she knew that God was helping her. She called Sr. Laura and asked if it was possible to use the Merton Room. Sr. Laura told her to come.

Sr. Laura was a Benedictine and an avid fan of Thomas Merton. She had read almost everything he had written and had studied his life, before and after he had become a monk at the Abbey of Gethsemani in Kentucky until his accidental death in Asia during the late 1960s. She belonged to the International Society of Merton also, that met every other year somewhere in the U.S. A year before, Sr. Laura had begun a Merton Society in Duluth and Catherine, who had read many of Merton's books and was also a fan, decided to join. It was a small group and not all were regular, but Laura was given a room in the old St. Anthony Church, and interested people would meet there once a month. Sister had told them that the room would be available to anyone who needed it. All of Merton's books and cassette tapes were there, photographs of him, some of him with the Dalai Lama, magazines from the international society and news clippings. It was a comfortable room, with easy chairs, tables, and best of all, windows overlooking Lake Superior.

Catherine found it quiet and restful there. Her mind was in turmoil, and she tried to compose herself. She wept at times, prayed and meditated, and then just sat in silence, sometimes getting up and walking around, and sometimes simply gazing out at the lake. Somewhere around 5 PM, Sr. Laura came to her and asked how she was, and then invited her to share dinner with herself, Sr. Timothy and Sr. Armella. They lived in what used to be the rectory, which was attached to the church. Catherine was grateful for the invitation and readily accepted. It was a peaceful and light-hearted meal, which Catherine needed and enjoyed. When she left, Catherine was told that the Merton room would be open for her on the next day also, if she needed it.

She knew that things had gone so smoothly and beautifully up to the point of Aadi's last letter, and in her soul she had been waiting for that zinger she was sure would come. She had mentioned that to Meridith, who didn't quite believe her. But God did send her one and now she had to show her faith by patiently praying and persevering. It was very difficult, but she tried remembering when Jesus was sleeping in the boat with his apostles and a storm came upon them. Jesus quieted the storm, but all it would have taken was a leap of faith from one of the apostles. What was it Jesus said to them?

"Oh ye of little faith." So she prayed and put her faith in Jesus. God was continually testing her and she had to remember that and wait for Him to act for her, making things right again.

On Sunday she decided to call Mahesh Albuquerque. He might know of the rules in India regarding property and immigration. After going once again to the Merton Room, this time for the monthly meeting, she drove to Mahesh's home on Superior Street. It was a lovely home and the wedding was to be held there. She had delivered the gifts from his mother to Nihal as soon as she had returned from India, and had taken photos of the happy event. Now she told both of them that she was in the process of divorce and that she was planning to live in India as soon as possible.

Mahesh told her that he saw no reason why she couldn't buy property and told her of his cousins and other relatives who were Canadian citizens who had property in India. He assured her that his father would help her. They spoke of the plans for the upcoming wedding, and Catherine suggested a particular judge that they might want to officiate. He was a Catholic and was a parishioner of St. Michael's Church. Catherine thought this would ease the heartache of Mahesh's parents over the civil ceremony. She had received a letter from Teresa telling her that they planned to come for the wedding after all, because Mahesh felt so bad that they didn't want to be there. Not only were Teresa and Mathew coming, but also Sunanda and her daughter, Sarita. It was a happy time for all of them. The wedding was scheduled for late in June, so Catherine decided to put the question of property in India on a back burner and wait to talk to Mat.

After returning home, she decided to send Aadi a fax so that he would receive it just after he came home and read her letter. It was a long fax and took up two pages.

Hello–How are you? How was the tour? By now you must have received my letter dated April 14. I told you once that I always write when I'm in crisis.

Your news hit me very hard, and I can't say that I am not still in pain. This past week and a half have felt like Goa all over again. However, I believe I have gained some perspective since the 14th, and I feel an acceptance now that I didn't have before. We do need to talk–and I so wish it could be face to face.

Aadi, I have no claims on you. Our lives have touched only recently and in only one small area. Your life is <u>*your*</u> *life and is none of my business. You have to follow your own star, your own heart, your own spirit, and be the person you were meant to be. I wouldn't want you to be anything less than that; free to be your own person, free to be Aadi, the wonderful man that you are.*

Just as your life is not my business, my pain is not your problem either. I can't help the way I feel, but I will deal with it. We have a cultural difference I think, that comes into play here. And I can't say good-bye to you. Perhaps you will explain it to me. The more I can understand, the sooner I can come to terms with this. For God's sake, help me, I can't say good-bye

C

She sent the fax with prayers; her heart and mind in great agitation. Catherine had meant it when she had told him she couldn't say good-bye. He always told her to 'relax' and that is what she had to learn to do.

"God," she prayed, "He means so much to me. Don't let me muck up this relationship. My hope is Aadi's strength, wisdom, and patience. Please, God, let him understand where I'm coming from and let him help me."

CHAPTER SEVENTEEN
HELGA

Twice a week Catherine visited the beauty shop and Conny did her hair. There were many women who were regulars on Tuesday and Saturday and Catherine got to know them over the years. However, there was one lady who only came occasionally. She was a friend of Conny's and knew Catherine only slightly. Her name was Helga Ragan and all Catherine knew of her was that she liked and cooked Indian food and had been to India once. This one day Conny told Catherine, "She does readings, you know."

"Readings? What do you mean, Conny?"

"Readings. She belongs to the Spirtualist Church."

"OK, but I still don't know what you mean by 'readings'."

"She's a psychic, Catherine. She does readings."

"Really? Oh, my gosh. Is she good?"

"Oh, yes."

"Conny, what is her phone number? I want her to do me."

Suddenly, Catherine just had to do this. She went to the phone and made the appointment. Helga told her to bring a cassette. On the appointed day, Catherine found Helga's house, which was somewhat out in the country. It was a modest abode, well lived in and a happy place. Jim, Helga's husband was there and he appeared to be a very nice man. He made himself scarce when Helga got down to business.

Catherine sat at her kitchen table and Helga walked a short distance away to get into her 'altered state'. It only took a few minutes and she was back. She put the cassette into her recorder and started the machine. Then she took Catherine's hands in her own and breathed deeply. That was how it all began.

First, Helga told Catherine about herself, then about her husband, her children and again about Catherine's intended move to India, about her 'house of money' and her 'house of communication.' Catherine was amazed at how accurate Helga was. She had Brandon pegged exactly. She called him 'the one in the closet'.

"Cathy, I'm sorry, but I don't know how else to describe him. At some point, you became the strong one and he just walked into the closet and closed the door. He never shared himself with anyone; not you, not his co-workers, not with his children.......Cathy, do you have a dog? It seems that he only shared himself with a dog."

"Yes, we had a dog and Bran was extremely attached to her."

At another point, Helga said, "It feels, it feels like you are wanting to be understood. You think no one understands you. You especially want your children to understand you. And, Cathy, sometimes you don't even understand yourself.

"How many children do you have?"

"Four sons."

"They are not all married."

"Two are. The third will be married next month."

Helga placed her hands on four spots on the table. "This one over here is the most like you. He understands you best. He's not married, is he? I don't think he will be." Catherine looked at the third position on the table and knew that she spoke of Randall. Then Helga placed her hand on the fourth spot and said, "This is the one who is getting married. He just says, 'Be at my wedding. Just be at my wedding.' This one.... what does he do?"

"He sells large appliances for Wards."

"Did he go to college?"

"No."

"Well, I see him studying. He is picking up books and I see them going through his head....maybe when he is 31 or 32 he is going to be studying to do something else, and he is surprised that he is understanding it.

"This one here," she said, pointing to the second place, "He is brilliant. It's like he has a photographic memory. But he needs to be warned so that his need to succeed doesn't get him into a closet like his father. He has those same tendencies.

"This son.....I don't understand.....he is smart, but not like that one. But he is not connected, somehow. He is very different from the other three."

"He was adopted."

"Oh, now I see. But it doesn't affect him. He says, 'I got what I wanted, so I don't care.' He and his wife are very superficial. They are concerned with how they look and their social standing, but there doesn't seem to be any depth there. I'm sorry, but that is how I see them."

Catherine said very little. She just listened, amazed at how accurate the reading was. Then Helga came to the area of India and how it was affecting Catherine.

"I'm asking–show me, show me, show me.....Where does the great love for this foreign country come in? Where does this great love for India come in? Immediately I saw — I'm sure that you were there when the things were polished and beautiful because I'm seeing the Brights and the shininess of some of these places. You have been both into the elite and you have also been a servant, because I see both roles that are being shown.

"But the thing....was....It was WHERE you were in through there. I felt the joy and sometimes you feel the joy so that you want to go. Now show me Future. I am asking, 'Can you reach some of that in the future in that country?' They tell me that it will all depend on your mind-set. It feels...it feels that you will not be satisfied. You think you will not miss your children and grandchildren, but after three months there, you will be wanting to come back. I saw a sadness come. It is almost like a caving in. You need to pick yourself up and come. I see a balancing. You are not Far Eastern no more than you are Western. You are neither. You are going to share two cultures. You can go three months and then you've got to have a taste of another. It's sad, but that is what I see. You are on a journey of coming and going.

"I've asked, 'Give me a way you could have some of both.' I asked if it was an ethnic group, like in Toronto. It did not fill the bill. It was something inside yourself. It came with the way the sun shone and it came with the way the moon glowed. So you have to have some of the real thing. It's not just the spirituality. It's not just the food. It's a remembrance that you're remembering so close to the surface.

"I'm sensing there's another person there–unless that older person is here, but he looks East Indian and I think I see–and it feels like he's male. And this one has some depth. And I see someone spoon feeding you wisdom. You're going to be hurt because some are not as spiritual as you think. I'm not saying you're not going to be happy. There's a longing here, a draining. In some ways you are more spiritual. I see the rest, they come and they go. But this one spoon feeds you. I don't know if it's a one to one or a group knowledge.

"I don't see you as overly religious. I see you searching, almost hunting for spirituality. And I see you asking, 'What is the purpose? What do we gain? What are we doing? Why did I come here?' All these questions keep coming up. You're really on a search and it's a deep search. Why? Because I feel it deep. BIG search. It just feels like–sometimes–I feel you're searching so deep and you haven't found what you're really searching for. Whether it's meditation, health issues, relationships -Whoever this older man is–he has some knowledge. He teaches you how to find it inside of yourself."

And later, Helga tells her, "You wouldn't be wanting to go back there if they had hung you. No, you were happy there. Even as a servant, you worked very hard, but I see you singing.

You were happy." Near the end of the session, Helga asked her if she had any questions. Catherine could think of nothing to ask her, so Helga came out of the altered state.

A few days later, Catherine still had not heard from Aadi and she was becoming frantic with worry. She went to see Lisa and told her what had happened and what she had written and faxed. Lisa told her that she thought that she had frightened Aadi. But Catherine felt that she had angered him, and she was sick with the thought.

"My heart is breaking and I just want to cry, but I've nowhere I can go to cry. It hurts so badly. It's like Goa all over again except now that I know what a truly wonderful man he is, the pain is worse. I can't feel him beside me in bed when I go to sleep and when I wake in the middle of the night, I can't find him. I think he must have turned himself away from me deliberately, otherwise I know I'd be able to sense his presence. This hurts, oh God how this hurts! And I don't know what to do. My head tells me to give him space–to work out whatever he feels he must. My heart is screaming to call him and hear his voice. I must not do this. I must not."

This was a busy week. She had a dental appointment and another with Lynn Beechler, the real estate agent chosen to act for the sale of the house. Also, another massage by Teri, which she needed badly. Teri told her that her neck and back muscles were very tight indicating much stress. Catherine was lying on her abdomen, with her face in a kind of hoop, looking downward. The tears started to come, but she made no noise. She was surprised when Teri handed her tissues.

Then on the weekend, Roland, Anne and little Kimberly arrived. The main purpose of their visit was to choose what furniture they would like to have from the house. It was a good time for Catherine to hand over the chest of sterling to Anne. That had been a very precious possession, and it hurt somewhat giving it up, but she knew she would never need or use it again. Roland noticed something about her.

"Mom, are you all right?" he asked. "You seem so subdued."

"Yes, darling, I'm fine. I'm just going through something right now."

It was good that Roland and his little family were there, because she was so tempted to go to Lisa's and call Aadi. She talked to herself a lot.

"My heart is so heavy. I'm crying inside and sometimes outside. Aadi, Aadi, I need you so much. I need to hear your voice. I'm trying to have patience and let him have space, but I can't stand the silence. Is he angry? Disgusted? Fed up? Hurt? Disillusioned? What??? I will send him a short fax tomorrow, and then I'll call him. I can't take this anymore. I'm in terrible pain. Only he can take it away. Please, God, let everything go all right when I talk to him. I don't care about Germany. I don't care if he fucks all his clients. I miss him. I need him in my life."

This relationship meant more to her than she had realized. The situation was becoming unbearable. If she had waited and not written immediately after receiving his letter, perhaps she would not be going through this hell now. She had to learn patience.

She needed to call Lisa to ask when she would be home for lunch the next day, so as not to intrude upon her and also to have the privacy she needed for the call to India.

"I feel like my heart is in a vice and my emotions are seething beneath the surface. I even have been tempted to call him from here. Now that really would be foolish! I worry also–what if my fax doesn't go through tomorrow? Has he left on another tour? Is there a 'Dear Jane' letter already on its way here? Aadi, Aadi if you say good-bye to me, I'm going to die. I just can't take this. There was so much that we had together. Please, God, don't let me have thrown it all away. I love him so, and he gave me such joy."

Catherine drove to Portown Travel to send the fax, which went without delay, for which she was most grateful.

Aadi

Please–I haven't heard from you and I am going crazy worrying. I felt you needed some time and space to think, so I haven't called you. Are you terribly angry with me? Have I messed up everything there was between us? Forgive me, please. I can't bear this silence. I need to call you later. Please–I hope you will be there to talk with me.

C

After sending the fax, Catherine drove home because it was too early to call India. She was surprised to find a package in the mailbox addressed to her. It was from Aadi. He had sent it to her home rather than the post office. She took it to her room and carefully opened it. It was a book entitled, MAY YOU BE THE MOTHER OF A HUNDRED SONS. There was also a short note.

Dear Catherine,

It is so good to listen you, feel you and participate with you.

I am worried. India is a very different country. It is not easy. We are not what we seem.. Please decide with time. Come to India, stay here, and feel all the reflections, only think and think. You are the best judge. Take your own time. Thinking is the best way reach over any conclusion and also reach to that conclusion. I am sending you a book, I like it . It talks about women in India. I hope you will like it.

With kisses Aadi

Catherine held the book and note to her heart. She had already read the book, having bought it when it was first published. However, this copy was precious to her because it came as a gift from him. She prayed the rest of the morning that he would be home when she called and that she would say the right things to him.

She was shaking when at last she was at Lisa's and dialed the many digit number to get through to him; the international code, the country code for India, the city code for Udaipur and finally his home number. His father answered the phone.

"May I please speak to Aadi?"

"He is at home, but not in until later."

"Thank you, Mr. Abhimani." She hung up, still shaking, and sat down to wait.

An hour and three quarters later, she once again dialed and Aadi answered.

"How are you?"

"I am miserable. I've missed you."

"I only just got home from my tour."

"Please forgive me."

"For what?"

"For being a fool, an idiot."

He chose to ignore this statement and went on to talk about her trip to India.

"Aadi, your book arrived this morning. Thank you so much. I read your note and you don't have to worry about me. I'm going to take your suggestion. I'll come and live there and see how things go before deciding anything permanent. I'm not your responsibility. Please don't worry."

He never brought up the subject of Germany and neither did she. But what he did say seemed to make light of it.

"Catherine, when you come in September, I'll be entirely yours."

Although it killed her to think of him with this other woman, she decided she could never talk about it to him.

"Aadi, you sound different."

"No."

"Tell me what you are feeling, what you are thinking."

"I am thinking of you."

But she knew there was something. He seemed guarded. He had told her nothing really. Maybe he was still worrying. But she didn't want to push it. She was so grateful that they were still OK. However, she felt they were not what they had been, that he had lost some of his softness for her. But she felt that too was OK, that she could perhaps win back what had been at her instigation. They began to make love.

It had to come from her first because she had written him that she would never do this again. It was beautiful and she went home feeling comforted and full of joy once again.

Portown called her the following day and she went quickly to pick up the fax from Aadi.

> *I just did convey to think and wait and then act for important events of life. Also I expressed facts. Please do not mind my this very approach. It was wonderful to talk with you last morning, night. It was good to listen you and feel you. Unlike other years, it did rain last morning a cloudy day and cooler day. A very unusual scene. I enjoyed seeing and taking out of grape fruits, pumpkins and papaya was thrilled to touch these fruits, very gentle feeling. And the sight of plantano became sensational, very close to papaya and pumpkins. All very beautiful. Nature is so great.*
>
> *You should be very busy in organising marriage of your son. How many days it will take to complete all the rituals. In India it is notone day*

affair. It is takes more days and very very expensive affair, Please take good care.

Aadi

She so enjoyed the fax but never saw the allegory. She thought he was talking about his garden. And she felt the beauty of it. The missive itself gave her warmth.

There was another session with Meridith that day and it went well, and the hour went quickly. However, Meridith was surprised when Catherine told her she had seen a psychic. The following day, she sent Aadi a fax.

Dear Aadi,

Your beautiful fax came in yesterday. I love the way you express yourself. You are so sensitive to God's creation. The way you described the fruits of your garden touched me deeply. Please write more like that. Don't ever worry about anything you say to me. I know you always mean well for me, and I would never 'mind' anything you feel and wish to express.

This morning I made love to you. I imagined our being on the hill at the site. I felt the pungent odor of the earth; the sweet scent of grass, and felt the breath of a warm breeze over our bodies. It was very good and very beautiful. I saw you smiling and your eyes sparkling. I fold you in my arms.

C

Once again she left the imprint of her lips on the fax. She felt good until she went to see Helga. This time the reading left her with many misgivings.

"New growth! Something is happening — I don't know who or what — I want to say you've dusted off the old and something new, like spring buds is coming from within you. Camouflage has been dusted off — It's all inside of you. New growth, freshness of the new green. It's like, 'Cathy, who are you? What do I know?' It's more than meditation — that was like pouring warm water on the seeds. And the growth had not started then. It's like, 'now I have the opportunity to grow.' There's no panic now. All is in order now. 'It's OK, I can wait'. And whoever your guide is, has been trying to tell you for a long while, because I feel a peacefulness from the other world too. Because when anybody gets excited, they want to do it yesterday. And it's like that other world doesn't have a clock. Question?"

"I want to ask you about my mother, because for so many years I felt such animosity toward her, and since I returned from India this time, I don't feel this anymore."

"A calmness has come. You can let some of these things go because they no longer matter. You have grown. You look at her and see she's an old lady and in a sense has forgiven her. Now it doesn't matter. It's like — 'Have fun, Mom.' You were always looking for her approval and didn't get it. — Now to your husband. Mother and husband came from the same seed pod — You also wanted his approval for many years and then you didn't want it at all. Now it doesn't matter. You begged for it — he — and then you slammed it over there — You didn't want it at all, and now it doesn't matter. All the change has been in you — the growth in you. Mom is still the same Mom. And she can be obnoxious one day, demanding the next, soooo helpless, then so conniving the next day. She — in some other life — I see her as — either an actress or a lady of the night. I can see her standing, flinging her cape over her shoulder. Oh, I wish you could see it! She attracts the men, she likes them."

"Catherine laughed. "She likes them in this life too. She plays the helpless female and it works. Even to this day."

"And your husband can now be trying to make conversation, or is quiet, but — questioning and you are like——'Oh, I can talk to you about that.' And he's going to ask you, 'When did it go wrong?' Because it's in his head. And I want you to be honest and tell him–'the first time I had my feelings extremely hurt.' Don't go into any emotional thing. I see him puzzled. When you're the husband, you make the money. And if you make the money, you're the boss. You didn't have to be the servant. You didn't have to scrub floors. But you had to play his mind game. You had to follow — You had to serve him about the way he expected you to behave. And you didn't do that, and so he retreated. I don't know your life, but this is what they are showing me. When the children were little — it was — he was the father, 'I'm the boss'.

"And then at some point, you stood up with this big stop sign. You didn't even listen to the little things. You stopped everything. You didn't know how to defend yourself and the kids when the kids were real little. Then it was at a later date when I saw you really become the traffic manager–Stop, Stop. And some of the kids did too. You got bigger than he did.

"I'm knowing — sensing — he's mulling things over. He's looking for reasons. He can't stand it when things don't go right. It's like the little slivers of glass on the floor. He's looking for the big broken glass. He doesn't know you can cut a vein with a little sliver just as well and you get enough slivers and you can't walk. And he is still looking for the big thing. He wants to know, 'Well does she have a lover?' How does a lover come into any situation? By the little tiny things that kill feelings. You can't have two lovers at one time. You can't have that kind of emotion for two people. One has to be dying down before the next one really comes in. It has to — He thinks everything's been OK and 'I got to look for it right here.' He's looking for what happened. He is searching. He keeps asking at least once an hour. 'What happened?' He keeps looking for a big thing instead of all the little things that killed it. And what I see — for many years what happened at your house — you cried and you put on a mask. You hid many feelings. It wasn't a hatred, but it was like – 'Ah!' It's the woman who always has to carry out the garbage — a woman who doesn't get positive strokes.

"Now, question?"

"I'd like you to tell me about this man whom I met and fell in love with in India. And he gives me life and joy."

"All right, give me his age and give me his first name."

Catherine did, and then watched as Helga took deep breaths through her nose, her left hand holding Catherine's right, her eyes closed. There was some silence and then she began slowly.

"I want to say — go easy. I'm sensing everything is not quite how you think it is. Be yourself — oh, no wonder they had me talk about the husband first. Really you have been starved. This man gives you attention, but he also is playing a game. This man is not everything he appears to you as. He's quite polished. He's suave — he knows how to do these things —— I'm going to be straight out — He's trying to get something. It's like playing this game, playing this game, playing this game and when he thought you weren't watching, he takes something. He takes something and I cannot see what it is. It's going to happen in a clever way. This does not mean that you cannot enjoy this person. Of course you can. This only is saying, 'Be aware'. It's exciting and you need to feed a portion of yourself. This man knows how to make you feel good. And they're telling me down here, 'Is this going to be a permanent thing, on and on and on?' This is what your question is even if you didn't say. And the answer is, 'everything is not what it appears.' They're telling you to be careful. It's like you were unaware that he took something. I don't know what it is. Remember, people think Americans are rich."

"You think he's after my money?" she asked incredulously.

"I don't know. He takes something, but I can't see what it is. Usually if it has to do with money, they show me a coin. But I don't see it. I'm just thinking that -what if he comes with you, you bring him in and then he sets himself free like a bird? Just be aware. Think about what I'm saying. What if we put this woman who needs love, who loves this country, who finds these people absolutely beautiful. And what if he knows this, he plays this game."

"He's been telling me to slow down and to think before I make any decision."

"This man himself is telling you to be careful. And are you going to find love? I sense that there is love that's going to be there, but the last time you were here they told me not to talk about this one yet. This time they want me to tell you not to go in blind. They want you to pack the stop sign so that you can stop it at any time."

Catherine then told Helga about the beautiful letter she had recently received with the almost hidden sentences revealing his interest in a woman in Germany.

"He's telling you, 'Go slow'. I feel he's got money, but not wealthy. I feel this German woman also pays his way. For God's sake, women can play the same game. 'I'm enjoying this.' Eyes Open! But you need this love. You definitely need this love and this is OK. And what if you've been dead inside so long? You needed this one to be awakened. You —— How would you find the person who ——?"

"Do you think I'm going to find someone over there?"

"I don't think you're going to be alone. I think you will have someone. But a lot of this is a healing process. It's like, 'I've put so many bandage tapes on my hurt feelings' — you have to remove them — this is practicing again. How do we act with a man who shows us a future? How do we act with our own feelings? Because it's almost like I see them bubbling out of you and I want to say, 'Oh, oh, slow down. I want it to spread through my arms and legs.' And when you feel good about yourself–Do

I see you with someone? The answer is, 'Yes'. Are you going to go there? Yes. Are you going to have a place there? Yes. Are you going to buy a place? No. I'm looking for a deed–I can't see it. I don't think so.

"What I'm getting–I'm smelling India. I'm feeling that warm sun. I'm smelling some of that dry earth. I'm watching a beautiful sunset. I know that you've got a place because you're not sitting on a street corner. I don't know where. I don't know how. A part of you is searching."

"I'm just wondering if I have to leave all my belongings in storage permanently if I'm not going to be able to bring them to India."

"I'm looking–I see you with furniture. It's seems to be yours, but I don't know if you brought it from here. I'm seeing Delhi, Parliament, for lack of a better word, and this man who says, 'Foreigners can't buy'."

"What I've dreamed of was a house with gardens and water."

"I can find you in a place, but I don't see the water."

"Do you see a marriage?"

"I don't know if it's a marriage, Cathy, but I see you standing close to someone. I see someone with you. It feels like you're not alone. I asked if this woman was happy and immediately I saw a happy face, happy, but not giggly happy. It's like, 'I feel so appreciated.' And you're so appreciative of whoever it is, I'm getting the feelings —— I would say the answer is, 'Yes, Yes, Yes. Are you going to have a partner? And when I get a 'yes', I get a line of energy that comes from here, and it's a big yes. You're going to have someone. There's going to be someone in your life. Is it in India? I don't know."

"I'm still back on Aadi. What is his relationship with this German girl? Is it a sexual thing?"

"I don't think it's as much anymore as it was."

"Is she middle aged? Is she married? Older?"

"Hmmm. That's why I said, 'was'. I feel she's older. Now she's become a friend. It was very sexual at one time. Now it's becomes – sometimes -. It's not the relationship anymore based on sex. It started with sexual. It was like she was infatuated, and he didn't know what to do. He was younger. This guy is so polished–he's such a handsome dude. And he has — Eyes! His eyes are so expressive and this guy has these gorgeous teeth and his smile —— It's just like, WOW! He dazzles you."

"I didn't feel that when I met him. It wasn't until I left."

"It doesn't make any difference when. It happened. And you're charmed."

"Well, what does he feel about me? Really?"

Helga takes another deep breath.

"Give me your hand. ——— Good friend. ———How does HE perceive? And I don't go for asking what he's thinking in his head. He's glad he met you. Who is this woman? 'Oh, she's a friend.' Do you know her very well? 'No, not very well.' Do you like her? 'Yes.' Do you love her? This is what I heard – 'Explain love.' And I'm asking, have you ever loved? Have you ever really loved? And he answers, 'Had sex? Explain.' And I said, 'no, love and sex are not the same.' 'Explain love.' He doesn't really know. I did not go for what he's playing in his head. I want to know what is in his heart and in his soul. I cannot invade soul privacy. But I can invade — what this has to do with you. And, Cathy, you are charming. He's telling me, 'She's charming'. But that's as far as it goes. Charming.

"Again the spirit world is saying, 'Just be careful.' Remember the mother you came from. Who says you can't play the game too? Eyes open. Be charming and see where he goes. He's telling you in little ways, 'Please don't have big expectations.' And they're telling me now, Cathy, you are not stupid. You are a very intelligent person. Eyes open. You can write the charming letters and check and see — It's not like you are investigating him. Go within yourself. 'I don't want to be any victim of anything'. And it looks like he's trying to be kind enough to tell you, 'I don't want you to be my victim. I do go and meet this woman. I have gone all over Europe. What did you think?' Remember, he lives in India and he is a guide. And who does he meet? Foreigners, continuously."

"Has he ever been married?"

A long silence, then, "You know, I wanted to say that he was. And then it was — the pictures are funny and vague. Under normal circumstances if he came from a certain thing, he would have followed a certain path. His father would have chosen a bride for him. I felt there was a bargaining of some kind and I don't know what happened. It's just like — I don't get any more picture. I don't know. And whatever it is, I cannot go into that space. Its' like I saw two fathers and they are talking. And I don't know if this boy took off, went someplace, did something. Did he study someplace for a while, did he ever say, because it looks like it?"

"Yes."

"And it was in these studies, all of a sudden, that I can't get the father to pull the son back. I don't know. I can't see. It's like there is a closure on this here."

"He has a degree in English Literature. He taught. He also knows many languages. He speaks Spanish and French."

"I can't see, because I'm not being shown. It's like there's a secret place. And I've always said, 'If I cannot under all Karmic laws, go into this place, just put the shield there.' And that's what I got. You know I don't want to invade something I would have to pay karmic debts for. And I've got the shield here. It's a place I can't go. It's like the boy went somewhere for an education, and when he came back the father had no more control over him. It's like he broke with Indian tradition and in between there, I don't know what there is. It didn't feel like it was bad. It felt like it was a secret place. So did he meet someone? Did he marry when he was gone? I don't know. I don't know. OK. Another question?"

"I don't think I have any more."

"I'm going to ask, 'Are you going to see him again?' The answer is 'yes'. I asked, 'Are you going to be excited about it?' I heard the word, 'yes'. Except–You are just like you were before, but your ears are bigger and your eyes are now open. I also see, —— Which religion over there are you more drawn to?"

"Hindu. He's Brahmin."

"See, he's from that rich class, but how rich, I don't know. That's where the merchants and the teachers come from. But what I sense down here — I also see you at an ashram."

"Where is that?"

"What I saw was the one you were visiting in Kerala. It was up in the mountains. I see you there. Whether you're visiting or staying there, I don't know. The water is safe there and clear. And there is a lake–a LAKE! And wildlife. Sometimes elephants and tigers come. Very sparse, but very peaceful."

"What was the name of it?"

"The Shivernanda–I'm not sure. But all of a sudden I see you there. I've seen you in Bangalore. I see you in Fiji. I see you all around that area of Jaipur, Amber, but I don't see you sitting there. That means 'staying'. Was there another question?

"Mom is going to be all right. Husband? I'm not sure. Until the day he dies, he's unraveling puzzles. But that's his choice. There's not even a pot of glue trying to put you back together. There's nothing. But he's puzzled because he never saw it. I'm asking, 'Did you ever know him?' When you first met him -- if someone had told you, 'Get your eyes open'. You had your eyes so thick with glue. You had an image up here about what he was and that's what happened even in here with THIS guy, but this isn't as strong because you're so much wiser.

"Rejoice because you're really doing what you want. And you don't want another mistake. So keep your eyes open. But can we play? Of course you can — as long as the spider web doesn't pull you in. That's all that matters."

"I'm so vulnerable."

"Are you really?"

"Yes."

"When the spider web says it loves you, you go right into it?"

"Yes, but he doesn't say he loves me."

"OK, then eyes open, eyes open. If the spider web says 'jump in', would you jump in?"

"I probably would."

"But if the spider web puts out sweets, would you jump in?"

"Yes, I'm afraid so."

"As long as you admit and know. Once we are aware, you will be fairly safe. Something has happened between the conscious mind, the subconscious mind, and the super conscious. The subconscious mind is the feeling mind, the automatic mind. Practice, enjoy. Keep your eyes open. Am I telling you, don't — ? Heavens no. Because there's a part of you that absolutely needs this. And how is it happening now? By letters. Go ahead "You're safe. But you do need it. And when you get it right, you'll know that's how it feels. I'm going to come back now."

It was the end of the session, and Catherine was exhausted and her heart was sad. Could all this be true? She didn't feel it, but Helga knew so much about her life and marriage. Everything else was on the mark. Catherine definitely had to take this information and keep it in the back of her mind. It all made sense, but she didn't want to believe it was all a game and that he was trying to get something from her. She had such trust in him. That was evident by the way she felt when they were intimate. How could she be so wrong? Was she?

CHAPTER EIGHTEEN
RUSSELL'S WEDDING

It was May and the first Thursday of the month was the last meeting of the season for The Cecilian Society. This was the musical organization that Catherine had been invited to join twenty-nine years ago. Membership was by invitation only and she had been a proud member all of those years, performing as a singer once a year, serving as president of the society for two consecutive years, working on various committees and opening her home once a year for meetings and performances. Two years before she had written a book of rules, according to the constitution, and a history of the organization. It had been printed and distributed to the members.

This particular Thursday the society met at Alice McCabe's new home on Pequaywan Lake Road. It was located amid a forest of evergreens and on the shore of their own private lake. It was a beautiful spring day and it would be Catherine's last meeting as a Cecilian. After the president concluded the business, Catherine asked if she could speak. Permission was granted and she stood up.

"I would just like you to know that my house is for sale, my piano is for sale, I am getting a divorce and I'm moving to India." She sat down as the stunned members gaped at her in surprise and shock. The president moved quickly to the program chairman, who announced the performers and the meeting continued.

Earlier that same day, Catherine had seen her dentist, Dr. Wainio. She told him she was ready to have her front teeth capped. It was going to cost around $3000, but she had been putting it off for several years. Now she felt she needed to do this before going to India where she wasn't sure what kind of dental care would be available. Five upper teeth were to be capped and her lower teeth bleached and whitened. The latter was done first in order to match the caps. It was a long process and it took many appointments to complete the job.

In the meantime, Catherine was continuing her sorting and packing. Bran kept to himself in the basement watching TV. He offered no help. Everett, Bran's brother, came often to the house. He didn't blame Catherine for divorcing his brother. He knew they had not been happy for many years. He was kind to both of them and often went out to dinner with them at a neighborhood restaurant.

Catherine's mother needed attention also. Every day Catherine picked up her hot lunch and brought it to her. There was grocery shopping to do for her once a week also, and of course her hair appointments every Friday morning. Then there were the doctor appointments; eye doctor, internist, foot doctor, ENT specialist, and dentist, because Mother had all her teeth but were in bad shape and needed constant care. There were also her hearing aids that needed frequent servicing.

Every day was filled with appointments. Her calendar was so jammed, she could barely read it. But she took each day as it came and worked through it. If there was a problem, it seemed to miraculously disappear within one or two days. Catherine felt the Hand of God through this entire period. It was obvious to her that this is what He wanted for her so she took everything in her stride.

Portown called her to come. There was a fax from him. Rather than take it home before reading it, she decided to read it there.

I left this evening for Delhi starting a tour of North India. This is all of a sudden. I phoned you this afternoon (morning there). I disturbed, phone rang twice and picked up. I kept mum because you were not there. I will be in Delhi this night. Tomorrow I will leave for Gwalior by train.It will be in the afternoon, so if you like to say anything, you please use this fax number. I talked about fruits to communicate only, not to say otherwise. It was just symbolic. I enjoyed the nature green grass, flowers with colors and sweet odour and your odour. Aadi

Dear Aadi

Thanks for fax. Sorry about phone and my not answering. So wish I would get one of your calls!

Anyway–hope your tour is good. Back again to Gwalior! You must tell me about the area up there because I haven't been there. When do you return?

Please call or fax me along the way. I miss you so!

Everything is in order for wedding on 10th. My sister comes in on 8th for one week. After that I can concentrate on selling house, etc. I'm taking your advice and thinking a lot, especially concerning your numerous warnings.

I've slowed down. Don't worry anymore.

You take good care. C

Before the date of the wedding there was an appointment with Jack Schilling regarding possible tax problems with the divorce. Roland and Anne celebrated their second anniversary. Cindy, Catherine's sister arrived in Minneapolis and visited with her ex sister-in-law. Catherine had another appointment with Dr. Wainio, and another with Lynn Beechler regarding the house sale. There was her Wednesday morning hour at the Adoration Chapel and the all-important hair appointments for her mother and herself before taking off for the Twin Cities and the wedding. Thursday evenings she went to McCabe Center next door to meet with her Centering support group. She enjoyed the quiet time with these prayer-filled people.

Bran and Catherine drove separately to St. Paul. Catherine's mother drove with her and they checked into the Sheraton-Midway Hotel, where the rehearsal dinner was to be held. Bran opted to stay with Randall and Russell. Cindy joined them at the Sheraton later that afternoon, sharing a room with Mother, and Catherine taking a room by herself.

Catherine saw to last minute preparations for the dinner and then proceeded to the church with her mother and Cindy for the rehearsal. It was a joyous time, as weddings usually are, and Catherine was happy. Russell was marrying a lovely girl, a degree nurse who came from a lovely close family. Julie was obviously very much in love with Russell and he with her. The pending divorce did not seem to overshadow the festivities. Everyone was aware, but no one talked about it. Bran seemed aloof at all the festivities, but that was his usual demeanor.

The rehearsal dinner went off beautifully. Catherine had ordered prime rib dinners and wine at every table. The group was mostly relatives and wedding party, but Catherine always included her best friend, Mary Ann and her husband in any family gathering. Russell's godparents were also invited. It had been years since Catherine had seen them. Jacque had been a nursing classmate and at the time of Russell's birth, she and

Tony, her husband, were living in Duluth. It was fun to renew old acquaintances.

Catherine seated herself next to Brandon and the priest, who was to officiate at the wedding, on her other side. Father told her he had never been at such an elegant rehearsal dinner. This pleased her, but was saddened when accidentally she tipped a bottle of wine and splashed Brandon. He chose to think it was intentional. Everyone seemed to enjoy themselves and Catherine rated the evening as a success.

Afterwards in her room, besides her mother and Cindy, Jacque and Tony and Mary Ann and Harold joined them. It wasn't until later that Catherine learned that Cindy and Mary Ann had talked about her, the divorce and pending move to India. Cindy had expected Mary Ann to help her in a confrontation, but for some reason, Mary Ann left before it began.

Julie had made a hair appointment for Catherine early the next morning. She wanted a comb-out to look well for the photo session and for the wedding. The beauty operator appeared not to know what was wanted or needed. Catherine tried to tell her, but the hair style became worse and worse, until Catherine became frantic with worry. She finally told her to finish quickly. She paid an enormous amount for nothing and the ruination of her hair and left in a state of panic. Luckily Cindy had packed a curling iron that she could use to try and repair the damage.

"What's wrong with it?" Cindy asked when she saw what the operator had done.

"You can't see that she ruined the beautiful job Conny did?"

"I think it looks OK."

"Well, I don't. I'm very angry and I'm worried about how I'm going to look on the photos and at the wedding."

Catherine went back to her room and fussed until she thought it was not right, but presentable. There was no time to fuss anymore. They had to be at the church by 11:30 for photos. There would be no returning to the hotel until after the wedding.

The photo session seemed to take hours. When the photographer wanted the groom's parents in a separate photo, it was uncomfortable as Brandon stated, "No, we are getting a divorce. She's dumping me."

After the photos, Julie's mother and family brought lunch to the church and they all ate their fill in the church basement. It would be a long time before the wedding dinner.

The wedding was beautiful. Julie never stopped smiling. And Russell looked like the ever happy groom. It was not only a wedding ceremony, but a Mass as well. Roland and Anne had had the same in Duluth. Catherine recalled Robert and Kerry's wedding in Fargo in 1989. They too were married in May, on the 27th. Roland and Anne on May 6th and now Russell and Julie on May 10th. She was so proud of her sons. They had made wonderful choices and Catherine dearly loved all her daughters-in-law. Anne and Kerry were good wives to her sons and wonderful mothers to her grandchildren. She believed that Julie would be the same to her Russell. Outside on the church steps a reception line was formed to greet guests. When Mary Ann came out she was weeping, and came up to Catherine to kiss her.

"Catherine, you don't know how lucky you are."

"Of course I do. Why are you crying? "

"How can you leave this family? How can you go off to India?"

Catherine just shook her head. Mary Ann did not understand. Probably no one did. For the first time in years, Catherine felt happiness and no one was going to take that from her. She loved her family. They were precious to her, but they had their own lives. She couldn't live with them or for them anymore. Her life awaited her out there, somewhere in India. She didn't know where, but she knew she would find a place.

At the banquet hall Catherine was able to talk more at length with her friends and relatives than at the church. Kay Reardon had come from Duluth and brought her daughter, Eileen, who was a doctor at St. Paul Ramsay Hospital. Jack and Bonnie Schilling came also from Duluth and brought Sr.

Mary Charles. It felt so good to see them there, sharing this lovely day with her. And there were the relatives too, some of whom she saw very little of, but were dear to her. They were family. Bran's sister was cool to Catherine, but she didn't expect anything else. Evelyn and Catherine were never close. Everett was there, of course, with his daughter and granddaughter. They didn't sit with Evelyn because they hadn't spoken to each other for many years. Byron, Bran's step brother, and Shirley, his wife were friendly. Catherine didn't know it then, but it was the last time she would see Byron, who was suffering from Parkinson's disease and he was not doing well.

There was music and dancing after the lovely buffet dinner. Catherine didn't dance, but held her granddaughter, Kimberly and spun around with her in her arms. She watched with joy as she saw granddaughter, Allison pay dollar after dollar to dance with her uncle Russell.

The only sad part for Catherine was when she realized Randall was no longer at the party. He had taken Bran back to the house because Bran had had enough, and then Randall did not return. He had been enjoying himself and he rarely had that opportunity. But Bran was thinking only of himself and how bored he was. Not for one minute did he consider that Randall might want to stay.

The following day, Catherine, her mother and Cindy checked out of the hotel and drove to Julie and Russell's house for the opening of the gifts.

Again Julie's mom had provided a lovely lunch for the family. Bran had left earlier for Duluth, so Catherine didn't see him. After the gift opening and lunch, Catherine left for Duluth with Cindy and Mother. It was a beautiful day and Catherine always enjoyed driving. They talked mostly about the wedding and reception and the fun it was seeing and talking to family and friends.

Catherine held all these joyous thoughts close to her, but she felt the warmth also of Aadi. She wondered where he was on his tour and if he was thinking of her as she was of him. She held him in her heart and poured out her love to him. For a while a month or so ago, she was frantic for the months to pass so she could be with him again. Now she was calmer and was taking each day as it came. But she missed him and wanted to feel his arms around her, his lips on hers. So many months left to wait for that!

Cindy had an appointment, actually two, the next day. The first was with Helga. She was so impressed with what Catherine had told her about her first reading that she wanted to have one also. Then, as a special gift, Catherine arranged to have Teri give Cindy a massage.

When Helga asked Cindy if she had had an abortion, Cindy told her truthfully, "No".

"But," Helga went on, "I see a son here that you lost."

"I lost a son to SIDS.

"Oh, I see. Your father is no longer living, is he?"

"No."

"Because I see your father laughing with this boy. But he isn't a boy any longer. He is grown up. He wants to know when his birthday is."

Cindy started to cry. "I can never remember his birthday."

"That's all right. That is your way of dealing with the pain of the loss. It's all right."

Although Catherine was not in the room when Helga was doing the reading of Cindy, she heard the tape later and was amazed at this information. Of course she knew that Cindy had lost little Paul Andrew when he was hardly three months old, but the fact that Helga saw it and that she saw Paul as a grown man, was indeed a surprise.

The following day was Catherine's usual 'hair' day, and she had another appointment with Lynn Beechler. The house had to be ready to be shown at any time Lynn or her office called. She and Brandon were to be out of the house until the agents and prospective buyers were gone. This was a great inconvenience because of the total mess she was in trying to pack. But the house was beautiful and people should be able to see this in spite of the lack of order. Her carpeting was white through the living room and dining room. Her draperies were a soft cream and light green. It was tastefully decorated and all the furniture was still in place. Her bedrooms had new carpeting and new paint on the walls. The kitchen had had a new paint job on the cabinets, inside and out and a new counter-top stove had been put in, along with new counter tops. Her double ovens were also only a couple years old. She felt sure there was a family somewhere that would be absolutely delighted with this house.

That evening Cindy did not come to the basement bedroom she was sharing with Catherine until quite late. Then she started in on Catherine.

"Bran doesn't want a divorce. Why are you doing this?"

"It doesn't matter anymore what he wants. I want it. I need it."

"Because of Aadi? You don't even know him."

"I know it looks like that, but I'm doing this for me. It has nothing to do with Aadi."

"Bull shit! Why don't you just go to India? You don't have to get a divorce. Why are you burning all your bridges?"

"What bridges? I do have to get a divorce. I cannot go to India and just live there with a husband back here."

"Why not? You're in the driver's seat. You can do anything you want. He'll let you go. But why get a divorce? You've waited this long, you can wait a little longer."

"No, I can't. And if you're talking about the money, I don't care about that. I'll have enough. I don't have to sit around and wait for the whole thing. I have to do this now."

"You're making a mistake."

"No, I'm not. I'm doing what I should have done years ago. And why are you so against me? I supported you when you got your divorce."

"I'm not against you. I just think, you've waited this long, you can wait until Bran goes. He doesn't want this divorce, Catherine."

"Oh, yes he does. He can't wait until it's all over."

"You're wrong. Mary Ann thinks you are making a big mistake too. And she 'chickened' out the night of the rehearsal. We were both going to try to talk sense to you."

"Really! Well, isn't that interesting. My sister and my best friend. Good-night, Cindy." With that, she turned on her side and closed her eyes. She was deeply upset, not only that Cindy and Mary Ann had joined forces against her, but the thought that Bran had changed his mind regarding the divorce was extremely unnerving. What if he decided not to go through with it, and oppose her? She said a silent prayer and left it in God's hands. She was doing that every day now, as problems appeared, sometimes out of nowhere.

In the morning, Catherine went upstairs. Bran was already up. She asked if she could talk to him. They sat in the living room, facing each other.

"Cindy tells me that you don't want a divorce."

"What?" he asked incredulously. "Yes, I want it and the sooner the better." He was angry and bitterness showed in his tone of voice.

"Fine. Then everything is in place and going according to schedule."

"You're going to have trouble with the IRA. You will have to start taking it out."

"I don't think so. I'm not 70 years old."

"But I am and it's my IRA. You will have to follow the rules."

"Kerry will be taking care of my money and she says that I won't have to touch that money until I'm 70."

"Well, she's wrong. I read it in the rules. I'll call her and talk to her about it."

"Fine. You do that, but she deals with this kind of thing all the time. It's her job. I would think that she would know."

Catherine made coffee for herself and Cindy and took a cup down to her.

"Well, Cindy, you were wrong. I just talked to Bran. He wants this divorce as soon as possible."

Cindy laughed. "It just proves that you are still a poor communicator. You never did know how to talk to him, or to anyone else, for that matter."

That conversation did not leave Catherine with happy feelings toward her sister. She dreaded the long drive down to Minneapolis that day to take Cindy to the airport for her flight home. Very little was said during the drive, and Catherine felt relief to be rid of her negative presence. It was sad, but they had never had much in common. They seemed to come from different worlds, and it was difficult to understand how they had come from the same family. Never were two sisters so totally dissimilar. They were six years apart in age, but it wasn't that. Cindy had lived most of her adult life on the west coast and Catherine in the Midwest. There was a vast difference in mind-set between those two areas. But even as young adults, Cindy thought she knew better than Catherine about most everything. She got herself pregnant at the age of 18 and had to get married. Catherine thought this a great mistake, but supported her by making all the arrangements for her big wedding. She even went dress shopping, trying on many beautiful wedding gowns and finding the very one that Cindy wore. That was the only time Catherine ever donned a wedding gown.

Nevertheless, Catherine had never felt envy. Cindy had had a hard life. She had married a man who was selfish, a womanizer and eventually an alcoholic. She never had enough money and their parents had to pour money into that family to keep it alive. Catherine knew that the money would never be returned, but she didn't resent that. Cindy was her baby sister and she needed help. And although Catherine had problems in her marriage, she never had to worry about money or food on the table. Nor did her husband ever stray to another woman.

But all that was in the past, and yet she and Cindy did not understand one another and Catherine felt sad about that. She suspected that once their mother was gone, they probably would have nothing more to do with each other.

Catherine composed another letter to Aadi and sent it off in the mail.

Dear Aadi

The wedding is over. Everything went very well. The groom's dinner, that I was responsible for, was excellent–also very elegant. I was pleased with the food and service. The wedding itself was very beautiful. We had an absolutely gorgeous day also. It was warm and sunny. The day after was cold and it has been COLD ever since. In fact, yesterday in Duluth it was 30 below average.*

So, this morning when I made love to you, I was so chilly in bed. I imagined we were deep in a forest with soft pine needles for a bed, their strong fragrance tickling our nostrils. The air was crisp and fresh and you covered my body with yours to keep me warm. We held each other tightly and kissed long and deeply. It was all very good and very beautiful.

I am sending some packets of seeds. I don't know if they grow in India. You might like to try them in your garden if you have room–or maybe at the site.

Have you seen this month's issue of NATIONAL GEOGRAPHIC? Big articles on India–her 50 years after independence. If you can't get it, let me know, and I will send you a copy.

Another astronomical phone bill came in. I guess we will have to write more and talk less. You were right–but I miss hearing your voice.

I finished raking the yard and trimming the shrubs. Now I'm waiting for some warm weather to plant a few annuals. I'll take photos afterward so you can see how it all looks.

Take care. I miss you. C

Portown called her the next day and she hurried down to retrieve her fax.

16th May 97

I am back and collected your fax and read you letter. I am very happy to know progress of marrige– Thanks for the informations. I will be soon posting you a letter describing the rituals of a Brahmin marrige in Rajasthan. I will also post some old photographs as you desired. I hope everything is well with you. It will be my pleasure to assist you for the renting or buying the house. Please do not think about that.

I will be soon knowing my programme. Please do not think about time. If I have time, I will give more than a week. A big kiss.Aadi

That made her feel good. It was everything she wanted to know. Each time she heard from him, either by fax or by voice, she felt stronger and more able to do the job that was ahead of her. It was a big one, but there was this bright light at the end of it all. She would be going to Aadi in September and who knows what would happen then? A whole new life would begin for her. And how she looked forward to beginning again.

CHAPTER NINETEEN

PACKING AND DEAR FRIENDS

It was now the middle of May. The wedding was over and things were back to normal. Normal? What was that? Packing, running all over, appointments never ending. There was an Oblate meeting on May 18 which Catherine attended. It would be the last for the year, and Catherine had no idea when she would attend another. She hoped that next spring she would become a Benedictine Oblate when she returned for a new visa.

She tried to send Aadi a fax the following day, but it wouldn't go through. On the morning of the 20th she heard his voice on the phone. She was so happy to be there when he called her. They only spoke for a few minutes and he encouraged her not to phone him that week. It was too expensive. He always asked about her blood sugar and wanted to know if she was in good health. She told him that she would fax him later that day.

Dear Aadi,

Thank you for your very welcome fax. It was so good hearing from you. Thank you also for your kind assurances. You don't know how appreciative I am. I promise I won't take advantage of you. I mailed a letter to you on the 15th along with a few packets of seeds. Hope you like them. My house went on the market Friday. There are two possible buyers I know of, so hopefully it won't take too long.

I've been forgetting to tell you that should you want to call me on Friday mornings I am usually alone from 6:30AM to about 8:15 AM–5:00PM–6:45PM your time. I will call you one day this week, but will have to limit our time. My phone bills are rather large!

This is the hottest month in Delhi. Is it hot in Udaipur? We are still cold- freezing at night, so I can't plant annuals in my flower pots until probably June 1st. I imagine your garden is lovely. Take care and don't overdo if it is hot. C

Your machine wouldn't accept fax on 19th.

It was wonderful to hear your voice this morning. I will heed your advice and not call this week as I had planned. But please write and fax and I will also. After we said good-bye, I put my arms around you and entwine my legs with yours. I kissed you deeply and ached to have you touch me.

Every morning I make love to you. Do you still think of me this way? I am not sure sometimes. I went down to 'our' little house last night and gave Lisa some of my pretty things. It made her cry. I love her as a daughter–she is so very special.

Have you checked out the olive cuttings, lately? I wonder how they are coming along. Have you had to transplant them yet? I look up at the photo of you planting them and send you kisses. I still kiss that photo every morning when I wake and at night when I go to bed. I'm wearing pink today for you.

Nothing out of the ordinary happened that week, except for more appointments. She saw Jacalyn for electrolysis and Melissa to remove splotches on her face. Catherine thought it probably wouldn't be permanent, but she wanted to try. Then there was a meeting with Sr. Martha at the monastery to discuss becoming an oblate. Sister gave her the Rule of Benedict to read and study. If she was still inspired to become one, there would be an oblation ceremony the following March. Catherine hoped to be back for that.

Catherine had to be out of the house on Friday afternoon for there was to be a showing, so she drove to Lisa's and picked up the phone. She dialed India and got Aadi. He wasn't surprised and they talked and made love. At one point she asked him if he made love to her as she does to him every day. He said, "Why did you ask that?" She felt strange about that reply and didn't know how to answer him. It was very hot in Udaipur and she told him she would send some of their cool weather. He told her not to do that because the hot weather was necessary for the monsoon, which they sorely needed.

The house was being shown again the day after Memorial Day observance, so Catherine could do little work there. Instead, she wrote and sent a fax to Aadi and had another session with Meridith.

I mailed a letter to you Saturday, 24 May. It is a long one. I explained our Memorial Day holiday which we celebrated this past weekend. No celebrating or remembrance activities for me, however. I packed and packed and threw out all kinds of things. Today there are 4 showings of the house.

I will go to Lisa's to read, meditate and listen to music. When you asked me what my menu was for the rehearsal dinner, I was so embarrassed. It is silly to think that I could offend you when the event had nothing to do with you. But I felt disrespectful of you just the same. And I thought of that when I chose the menu, but I had very little choice.

Chicken was being served at the wedding, so that was not an option for me. Not everyone eats fish and I would never serve pork. That left only the beef. In India I will make very sure that nothing is ever served at my table that would offend my Hindu families and friends. And whether or not it is warranted, I do humbly apologize to you.

I hope you aren't jogging or playing Cricket in that awful heat. I know you are acclimatized to it, but I can't believe it is good for you to be too active when it is so hot. Please take great care. I loved talking to you. You calmed me down and lowered my stress level. Thank you for that. C

She left her usual lip print on the page and wondered how it faxed through. She never asked him and he never mentioned it.

Catherine always felt good when she met with Meridith. They prayed together and Catherine was able to unload by talking about all the things that were besetting her. The main thing was that she felt God was guiding her and she told this to Meridith, how whenever a problem arose, it quickly dissipated. She had deep faith that God was working with her to accomplish this move to India. And as she had told Aadi, her stress level was high because she was doing all of this herself, with no help from Bran.

Aadi had asked if Bran was helping her to pack and sort. She had told him 'no' that she was doing everything and felt that it was OK because it had been her decision to make these changes in their lives. She believed it was her responsibility. Although there were times when she could have screamed. Bran could have done SOMETHING! At least he could have packed the items that he wanted to take with him. Instead, she had to ask him what he wanted and he kept telling her, 'nothing'. Of course this was not true, because even if he was going to live with their son, there were items from the house that could be used. She finally convinced him to take the sofa and two matching chairs from the living room. And too, she packed a box for him including kitchen ware. Randall would be moving out of Russell's home, so he and Bran needed to set up an apartment and it would take furniture and basic cookware. Catherine saw no sense in selling what was in her kitchen and having Bran and Randall buy all new.

That week, Catherine took her mother to see Dr. Austin for her eyes and she had an appointment with her attorney, Jack Setterlund. When she returned from that appointment, Bran wanted to know what had been discussed. She told him, but he wasn't satisfied. He was suspicious that she or the attorney would try and pull something that would affect him negatively. He called Robert, who tried to allay his unreasonable fears. At one point, Robert told her that her bill was going to be astronomical if "Dad keeps calling and writing to Setterlund. He will charge for his time." She advised Robert to tell his dad that, not her, because Bran was very paranoid already about anything she had to say.

It was June now and the Albuquerques had come from Bombay for their son's wedding. Catherine saw them many times. She couldn't have them for dinner, but they came to her house and she took them to visit her mother. Teresa invited Catherine for dinner at Mahesh's and she gladly went, enjoyed a delicious Indian meal and met more friends of Mahesh. She did discuss with Mathew Albuequerque her idea of buying property in India. He also told her that foreigners were not allowed to do that. Somehow, other problems seemed more formidable than that one, so she decided to leave it on the back burner. If God wanted it for her, somehow it would come to pass.

On the 8th of June, Catherine picked up the phone and it was Aadi. She was so happy to hear his voice. They never talked long because Catherine was always aware that he couldn't afford it. But just to hear him and have him ask about her made her feel so calm. It renewed her spirit and she felt energized to continue the enormous amount of work still ahead of her.

Catherine's hair was becoming a big problem to her. She was losing a lot of it on top. Her mother was completely bald on the crown and Catherine was sure that she was following the same pattern. She had started wearing a hair piece to help cover the thinness. But this week a permanent was scheduled. Marsha, the woman across the street from her, invited her and a few neighbors to lunch as a farewell to her. She enjoyed that very much. Also, Mary Ramsay and Catherine had become close friends and they often went out to dinner in the evening if Mary wasn't too tired. She could confide in Mary and talking helped to dispel the stress, which was building up each day.

She had contacted the ND Blue Cross/Blue Shield and found that it was not as good as the Minnesota plan. Catherine was using Robert's address in Fargo for her U.S. address since he had her Power of Attorney. Although this dismayed her, she decided to call the MN BCBS people and was delighted to learn that she didn't have to change her insurance. She would be able to continue to see her doctors in Duluth and MN Blue Cross/ Blue Shield would take care of it. That was a load off her mind.

The facial sessions with Melissa were continuing and the splotches were disappearing. Also her face was beginning to feel very fresh and young. She had many moles on her back, which she had had removed before, but kept recurring, so she made an appointment to see her dermatologist once again. From Conny she learned of a woman who did eyebrow tattoos. Catherine got excited about that because she hadn't had eyebrows for years and always carried several eyebrow pencils. So she made an appointment to have that done also. After the eyebrows, she had Rose tattoo her eyelids. That hurt very badly, but it went well and she was happy with the results. She had Mary Ramsay shaking with laughter when Catherine told her, "Just wait until you're 60. Your teeth need whitening, you get 'old age' spots, you lose your hair on your head and it starts to grow on your chin. You start to creak all over and it hurts your knees to walk upstairs. Just wait."

Catherine was doing this for herself because she felt like she was becoming a new woman, with a new self-image and finally with self-respect. But she also thought of Aadi, who was so much younger than she, and although he told her that didn't matter to him, she wanted to look her best for him. He constantly asked her to send him photos of herself. He even told her he wanted one of her in her bed. When she told him she had no one to take the photo, he told her to read the camera manual and time-set it. She did that, but the photos were awful and she never sent them.

She called him from Lisa's a couple days after he had called her and then sent him a fax.

> *It was so good hearing your voice! I was sitting at the computer, just finishing a letter to the Indian Consul in Chicago. I'm applying for a one year visa rather than the usual 6 months. Don't know if I'll get it, but I have to try. My friends, the Albuquerques, from Bombay are in Duluth for their son's wedding on the 28th. They brought their daughter and granddaughter along. I've had fun driving them around Duluth. They told me of a place in Kerala where they think I would like to live. Do you know MUNNAR? It's an old* hill

station (7000 ft) east of Cochin. They lived there some years ago and say it is very beautiful.. I must check it out.

Summer has arrived, trees are leafed out, but it is not hot yet. I'll take a photo of house with tree in bloom and send it to you. I fold you in my arms and kiss you many times each day. Please write. I love to read your words, hold the letter in my hands and to my face. C

A few days later, Catherine followed this fax with a letter. She needed to communicate with him, even though the phone calls had to be fewer and shorter in length. It eased her tension to sit and write. During the day she constantly carried on imaginary conversations with him. That lessened her stress also.

Dear Aadi,

It is Sunday afternoon and I am still packing. My desk and table here were such a mess, that I decided to clean them off so I could tell where I'd been. Anyway, I found these photos and decided to send them to you. The photos of me–in bedroom, in office and those taken of me dressed up in wedding outfit etc.were not good. I just could not send them.. I hope you enjoy these of my city and surroundings.

The Indian Consul called me Friday after receiving my visa application and accompanying letter. They (He) was very nice but told me they no longer gave one year visas. So he is sending everything back and I will send it to them again in August. I did not want the visa issued too early.

I remember our conversations with great joy. And I continue to carry on imaginary ones with you. I feel you close to me.

C

There was another call from Aadi on the 17th, after which she sent him another fax.

Dear Aadi–Never think you are disturbing me. Your calls are always welcome. Hearing your voice gives me such joy–you cannot begin to imagine. I was a bit sleepy this morning because – for a change–I made love to you last night before sleeping. And earlier this morning–some time before you called, I awakened and felt you with me, so you were already in my arms when the phone rang. When I exercised later, the sweat was pouring down my body and I imagined it was mingled with your sweat and your semen and it was all very erotic. I kiss your head, your eyes, your nose, your mouth and feel your soft touch. I taste you, smell you, and I am at peace. Take care -Sit in the shade and write to me. All I want is to hear your voice and see your words in my hand.

C

More appointments that week. And now she needed a storage unit to put the things she wanted eventually to be shipped to India. There was very little actually. Only one chair and ottoman from the kitchen area and a small table that Roland had made in workshop at Woodland Jr. High. Of course she intended taking the stain glass lamp she had spent hours and hours making. It had only hung over her kitchen table for a couple of months when she had to take it down so as not to be shown with the house. This she had taken to the Mail Room, a mailing shop on London Road, to have it packed professionally. She took the set of old Noritake china that she had received from Helen Gleason when she died, and some pots and pans.

Most of her things were framed photos of her children and grandchildren. Catherine could not have her wedding portrait renewed. It was terribly faded, but she took it to her friends at First Photo and asked them if they could computer enhance it. She told them to take their time with it and they did not charge her an exorbitant amount. The only thing she was disappointed in was the dark shadows under her eyes. But it was her fault because she hadn't told them that that was the only place that had not faded out. Catherine had 5 x 7s made for each of her sons and had them framed.

Aadi called again on the 21st, the first day of summer. She asked him if he had received the letter with the enclosed blossoms from the crab tree. He said he had. They were still fragrant and he told her that he had kissed them. She wanted to cry because that touched her heart. Again it was a short call, but it was enough to give her joy and hope. Catherine also told him that her divorce was now final. He said that it didn't matter to him. But she told him she didn't wish to keep anything from him, and she wanted him to know that.

There was a meeting of the Merton group, at which she told everyone what she was doing. One woman looked at her in amazement and said, "I thought your husband had cancer?"

"Yes, he does."

She just looked at Catherine and shook her head. Catherine didn't know the woman or the others in the group well enough to explain her motives.

"I am going to live in India." That was all she said. She really didn't care if she had their approval or not. Catherine had peace in her heart and soul that she never expected she'd ever have.

The divorce had gone through without any problem. She read it in the paper before the attorney was able to notify her. He had told her this would probably happen and to watch for it.

The calmness and rightness of her decision had come to her when she first decided to get the divorce. Now it was a fact and she felt a great release and freedom. The bank could start dividing the IRA and that would take a few weeks. Bran worried about it. At one visit to the bank, Bran and Catherine had to separate their checking accounts.

"After all this is over," he told her, "I'm going to shoot myself."

Catherine just sighed and told him, "You'll do what you have to do."

"You don't even care."

How could she answer him? He was feeling sorry for himself and he was trying to make her feel guilty. She refused to let him do that to her. In fact, it wasn't possible anymore, for anything he said, to affect her. Catherine was totally free, legally and emotionally.

She called Aadi and spoke to him from Lisa's back steps. He asked her if she had received his letter and photos. She said, "No, not yet." It was getting closer to the time when he would go to Germany. She tried to come to terms with it in her heart, but it hurt. She never mentioned this to him, however. He had told her the first week of September would be the best time for him, so she had set the first of September as the day she would leave Duluth.

This was beginning to pose a problem at home, because the house had not sold and Bran was getting worried that she would leave him with the house and all the details. She kept assuring him that the house would sell and everything would be worked out. But he was pessimistic and paced the floors at night.

A couple days later, she sent a fax to Aadi, because his upcoming trip to Europe was very much on her mind. She wanted to reassure him and herself, so she sent the following.

Dear Aadi,

You are leaving very soon now for your holiday. Although I understand and am learning to accept, it is still difficult and painful for me. You will understand that I cannot hold you in my arms nor make love to you until you return.

I want everything for you that brings you joy, because that is part of loving, and I do so love you.

Take very good care of yourself. Have a safe and happy journey.

Vaya con Dios,.

C

She was going to miss his calls and his faxes. He had told her recently that she was sexy. He also told her that when he heard her voice he immediately had an erection. Catherine was surprised that he thought she was sexy. But he assured her that she was. But the arousal in him made her smile with great joy. She wondered how their first encounter would be in India. She looked forward to it with great anticipation. But there was a sadness in her now, knowing he would be with another woman. She was going to have to keep busy to keep her mind off that.

Actually earlier that same week, before she sent the fax, she had started a letter to him. Catherine knew it would not be received by him until he returned from Germany, but she wrote anyway of her thoughts and feelings.

She was wrong about his leaving then, but she didn't realize it until later. The Albuquerque wedding was lovely. There were many Indian people attending and Catherine felt good in her lovely sari. In fact, Teresa, who was in a deep green silk, told her that her sari was more beautiful than her own. It was crowded in the little house and it did rain, but eventually cleared so that people could be outside. Judge Bujold did a good job with the ceremony and his wife, Margaret, whom Catherine knew for many years, was there also.

On the second of July a fax came from Aadi. She was surprised. He was still in Udaipur.

Dear Catherine.

I hope you have received my letter. I did receive yours with the photo graphs but without you. It was not good enough. How are you? I hope all is well. I did read your letter last night and thought of you and enjoyed very very much what your doctors said about your health.

I found that foreigners could buy the property (land) for constructio in India and they can sale also.

I will soon fax you or phone you about September programme, so that you can reserve the programme. You could choose Delhi or Bomba as per your own convenience.

A big big kiss.

Aadi

Her time was getting shorter and there was still much to be done. She drove to Fargo the following week. She established a ND residence with Robert by taking a drivers' test and passing it. She talked with Kerry regarding her IRA and her other finances.

Catherine had confidence that she would have enough money to live comfortably, and certainly this would be true in India. There were papers to sign and Kerry and she had to discuss certain investments. She was given a CHEXTRA card, which was a VISA, but could be used to draw money immediately from her checking account. Kerry told her not to worry about drawing money, that she would watch her account and put in more as needed. Catherine gave Robert a letter stating her wishes in the event of her death in India. She stipulated that should he be unable to recover her body, that she be cremated there and her ashes buried next to her father's grave in Calvary Cemetery in St. Paul. She told him if her ashes were not available, for him not to worry about it. They would be somewhere in India and that would be all right with her. She signed her Will and gave it to him for safe keeping.

Catherine returned to Duluth on the 10th of July and immediately checked her P.O. Box. Nothing had come! She wondered where his letter was. And the following day, she sent him a fax.

> *Dear Aadi As of today, no letter has arrived. I can't imagine where it is. No one but Lisa knows I have the box. I have the key and it has no number on it. So no one here could have taken it. I returned from Fargo yesterday. Missed my exercises, but started again today.*
>
> *How are you? Are you back to work yet? I'd like to talk to you again. My phone bills are manageable now. I don't want to pressure you, but I need that date of arrival. I'd prefer Delhi, if that is OK with you. I always enter there so am familiar. If Bombay is easier for you – that is OK too.* House *still on market. So is piano. Oh well, I'm not going to worry about it. I miss you and think of you all the time.*
>
> *C*

Aadi called her that same day. He was very upset that she hadn't received his letter yet.

"Catherine, it was VERY open. No one should read it but you."

"But it must be lost in India, Aadi. No one, absolutely no one could get it here."

"I will write you another one."

"Oh, yes. Please do that. I've been waiting and waiting to get one from you. When you faxed me that you had read my letter one night and enjoyed, I knew what you meant."

"What did I mean?"

"You were referring to that erotic letter I wrote you and then you had to take care of yourself. Isn't that right?"

"Yes," he said very softly.

"I will call you tomorrow from Lisa's."

"All right."

When she called him from Lisa's, he asked her what she was wearing. "White shorts and a blue sleeveless blouse."

"Shorts. I can get my hand up in them."

She laughed. "Yes, you certainly can. Do you want to do that?"

"Yes. Can you feel me touching you?"

"Oh, yes. It feels good."

"Can you take them off? I want to make love to you."

"All right."

Afterward he talked about her trip to India.

"Catherine, it would be better if you come on the 6th or the 7th."

"Oh, not the first week of September, then."

"No, I'll have paper work to do. It would be better if you come later."

"OK. I'll see my travel agent and make the reservations, then I'll fax you the time."

Catherine wondered what she would do with that first week, since she planned to be out of the house and gone from Duluth on the 1st. She called the Procaccinis from home and invited herself. They told her to come. They would really like to have her, so she decided to leave on schedule, only with a Boston stop over.

She drove to Portown on Monday and laid her plans in front of Wendy. Calling several consolidators to get Catherine the best deal, Wendy finally got her flight booked from Duluth to Boston and then Boston to Delhi through Heathrow via United Airlines. Catherine then sent a short fax to Aadi regarding the flight to India.

HAVE BOOKED UNITED #2
LONDON – DELHI

ARR: 6 SEPT 11 PM

I can change this to following day–7 Sept if that is better for you. I have 10 days to decide. Please let me know what you think.

C.

CHAPTER TWENTY
ANXIETIES

Catherine had another reading from Helga on the 15th of July. She began by telling her that deep down Catherine was apprehensive. Helga said that she always felt this way when there were changes in her life. It was not fear.

"And if you think your divorce does not fit into this, you're wrong. Because you thought of a divorce 15 years ago. You thought of a divorce 20 years ago. You never told anyone, but the spirit world is telling me, there was a thought and then it was like, 'I can make it.' And your first thoughts of going to India happened five, seven years ago. They are telling me – you think you do things suddenly, but you do not. There is a thought and then a break. And every time you went to India there was the thought, 'You know, I'd sure like to come back here again for a little longer.' And the apprehension is because you don't have the little support group there that you have here. But the excitement is there. I still see you connected to some ashram over there, because spirituality starts flowing in through here. Yes, it looks like there is all the excitement of the opposite sex, but that doesn't stay. It doesn't stay."

"The excitement doesn't stay, or the opposite sex doesn't stay?"

"As soon as you said that, I got one hand of each. But have fun while you're having it. No one's saying you can't have fun. I'm just not seeing it with a lot of depth. Just be careful. Don't be used. I see a lot of shallow. They showed it to me before and they show it to me still, in that same light. I see–I'm sorry, but what I see is a snake charmer. He's ohhh so charming. His voice and body movements. And as long as you're aware of it, then you can play your game anyway you want. You are the free soul. Part of what I do here is Never to tell anyone how to live. And I sense there is another question on your mind. Your house hasn't sold yet, has it?"

Catherine laughed. "That's it."

"Because they brought up this BIG sign, For Sale, and I knew the house hadn't sold. It's OK. You want it right now, but it isn't time yet. Someone was interested, but didn't have the money. But someone who has the money is not there yet. All your income doesn't depend on this house, does it?"

"No."

"Because what I'm seeing is that there should be a pot here."

"There is."

"Then it's OK, because when it comes, it will be legally taken care of. You can give your Power of Attorney to someone and it will be OK."

"It's already taken care of."

"You can't push these things, but someone is coming. But there are few people these days that can afford this much. But they're telling me, it will sell. It is not a ridiculous range. Don't let anyone push you to lower the price. Bran is going to stay in the house, isn't he?"

"Yes."

"Because I see, he'll be the care-taker. You're free to go now. I just asked why you aren't going yet. They told me two things. One, that you aren't quite settled with the mother situation. It means that, 'You know that if I take off, this might be my good-bye'. And a part of you hasn't quite settled that, but within a month there will be a lot more settled in your mind. When does she go to your sister's?"

"I think around September 1. My sister's not talking about it."

"That's OK too. She'll talk later. You know it's more than you just didn't listen to her. I'm asking, 'What's behind all this?' It's not just the money that she thinks you're leaving behind. It's not that she wants you to stay with your husband. It's–what I'm getting here is–She didn't even like you anyway."

"Really?"

"Because I didn't see any —— But she thinks you're being a fool. There is a part of her that thinks that when you're all done, you'll be crawling on your belly. That's what I'm being shown and you won't have a nickel to your name and you won't know who you're going to crawl to. Somehow this woman sees you like a child. Just go and do your thing. But keep your eyes open, that's all I'm saying. What I see is that she sees you as a 16 year old with the brain as an open cavity. But it's OK, because what I see, this is not you. Yes, you loved the feelings of finally being alive, but you're not stupid. They are not telling me that you should throw this guy aside, just eyes open and purse shut.

"And the other thing, the first was your mother, and the second reason you're not going yet is that two of your kids are having a hard time letting you go. I don't know which two. But I see that inside of you those are the two things holding you back, because you could have left. Do you know what two these are?"

"No. But I went to Fargo last week and Robert was supposed to drive back with me to take the boxes meant for him, but he wouldn't come with me because I was driving. His father told him that I fall asleep driving, so he wanted to get behind the wheel. I told him that I don't fall asleep and I refused to give up the wheel, so he got mad and went back in the house and I left."

"Ah, it wasn't that. He's mad, deep down, at you for leaving. I see a little boy with short pants calling, 'Mommy'. He's hanging on to his daddy's finger so hard, because he feels he is losing you. It doesn't matter that he has a wife. He thinks he's losing his mommy. This is a portion that he has to settle with himself. So, turn on the charm. You've got a month and a half to say your good-byes. Turn on the charm. It's like their dad gave them each a big empty bowl and told them, 'I don't know what crazy thing has happened. I don't know if it's her mind.' He cannot accept any responsibility for any portion of this. So he gave each boy the same bowl, and they're going to look in it and if they see loneliness they will think Dad was right. So, just turn on the charm. These are little boys now whose Mommy is going away. Everybody is worried. It's like he's given everyone the same bowl. Not your mother. He didn't like her anyway. Not really. He didn't give her this 'pity' bowl. That's what it is, a pity bowl. They are looking into the bowl. Dad has this story and Mom has this, and they're trying to make up their minds.

"And I see him commenting down here that you're a nut. The religion, India, something has taken your mind. And maybe there is someone–because he has overheard something and he wonders if there is someone."

"Really?"

"It doesn't matter, because I'm seeing a little bit down here. It's over and done with. It's divorce. But he's commenting you're a nut, and you've taken everything from the boys. He's saying their bowls are as empty as his. Do you see what I mean?"

"Yes, yes."

"I'm just saying, be who you have to be. Be charming, be happy. I'm also seeing ——-Are you still living in the house with him?"

"Yes."

"That's unusual. How did I know this? I saw this house and a chalk line. This is my side. That is your side."

Both Catherine and Helga laughed. "And the other one looks out the window when you leave. He doesn't leave. He watches when you leave. This is the funniest thing. It's like he's never been as aware of what you've done as he is now. I just see the line."

"He's splitting everything. When the water bill came, he told me I take more showers than he does." Catherine laughed heartily as she told this.

"The chalk line gets bigger."

"And I told him that he watches TV all the time and I never do."

"So give him the electric bill." There was more laughter.

"Have you already decided what you're going to take with you to India?"

"Yes."

"Has that been packed?"

"Pretty much so."

"Because it appears I'm going into a storage area."

"You mean I finally got one? I've been waiting."

"I just see a storage area. It doesn't look like it's in anyone's apartment or…"

"Oh, no. I'm trying to find a storage locker. They're all full."

"Well, I see a storage area. Why don't you take your stuff to North Dakota? That's where your US residence will be. So why not move it all there? Because India will not be your permanent address anyway. I asked, and they showed me India cut in half. Half of it folds out, like a card. It's not a hundred percent. I don't see it. It's going to be part time. It has to do with seasons and something else that is not being shown. I don't know what it is. And I feel there is a part of you that needs some of that family tie. Grandchildren or whatever it is.

"Oh, did I say this to you before? I'm also suddenly seeing Australia or New Zealand? I don't know what this has to do with anything."

"Well, you've mentioned Fiji twice. At two different readings."

"You know what I'm seeing? My God. I wonder if you're going to meet someone from Australia or New Zealand while you are in India, or while you are in Fiji. I'm just going to leave it, because it is nothing clear. I just saw a strong —— not now, maybe a year from now, whatever. You're going to have a hard time figuring out that you're free. You're free.

"It feels like you're going to meet someone, either in Fiji or the two of you go there. I'm really getting excited about it. I haven't seen this before, but all of sudden, I'm seeing it. And now leave it at that. My spirit forces have never lied to me. I may have misunderstood, but here I get Australia and Fiji. And someone is laughing beside me. Australia and New Zealand are very important. And I asked if this was a male or female and I got a male, excited. I asked, 'Will she be ready?' And I got, 'Of course.' As time goes you'll be able to see where you're at. I mean with all feelings. Now someone just brought in a daisy chain and I see you sitting pulling petals, 'he loves me, he loves me not', so I have a feeling that this is going to be love."

"No kidding. Hmmm."

"And I ask if it is the man who is so charming. And I get, 'No, we're talking about someone else'."

"Wow!"

"I feel so peaceful with that last portion. If I misunderstood it, I gave it to you in the segments I was given. I saw the maps and I felt the peacefulness. Whereas with that man from India I don't feel that peacefulness. Exciting, yes. Charming, yes. But not peacefulness. I can't get depth. OK, ask question."

"How was my friend's trip to Germany? Is that possible or is that closed?"

"All I'm getting is he had a nice trip. I asked if there are any heartfelt questions in here. And I got the same answer as I got before. He isn't that deep a person to have real heartfelt–He had a good time. He enjoyed Germany. Now listen to me. He enjoyed Germany. 'I've been there before so it wasn't exciting.' He enjoys going. That's his reward for being friends. I have a feeling that she paid for his way. Did I feel love? I–I've never felt real love with this man. I feel sexuality. I feel excitement. I feel the charmer. Do I feel love? No. I don't think he knows that. He knows his game. Did he have a good time? Yes, but it wasn't exciting because he's been there before. He loves to leave India and go somewhere else. He does."

"He called me often before he left and immediately after he came back. He left before I expected him to leave and was back before I expected him."

"OK, did anybody read the fax before he left?"

"I don't know. I was in the travel agency. What do you mean?"

"I don't know. I just saw a fax. I don't know what that was all about."

"There is a letter he wrote over a month ago. I'm very concerned because it has not arrived."

"I think it's lost between here and India. I'm serious. It does get lost. And the hidden message that he sent is that he's waiting for you. Because this is the exciting portion again. Because I didn't say there wasn't excitement."

There followed a long silence, then Helga began again.

"In answer to your question. He had a good time, but I didn't get any depth. He loves to leave India. I asked is he ever going to see this woman in Germany after you get there. You know what I got? 'If she gives me the money and I get the ticket, of course I will.' I get the feeling that she was on a tour in India when they met. He was a guide and she was getting the romantic history of India, and that is where the tie is, somewhere in there. But it feels like she has to pay the costs. OK. Another question."

"I just wondered if I'll ever get that letter?"

"I don't know. Tell him to send another letter."

"He said he would."

"It's so strange. I said, 'Show me the path of the letter.' And I can't find the letter. I saw a letter, but not THE letter. I can't find where it starts and I can't find it in between. I don't know where it is. Didn't he ever write it or mail it or what? OK, another question."

A doorbell rang and Helga realized it was her next person coming for a reading.

"If you thought the spirit world was telling you not to go, they are not. They are just saying keep your eyes open. Be aware. If you think they are telling you that you did wrong by the divorce, they said that it was a long time in coming. And you will not go down any tubes like your little sister thinks. I do sense you're going to enjoy. And when the day comes that you do not enjoy, you can always move back. They're showing me there will be trips back and forth."

Catherine felt somewhat depressed by what Helga had told her regarding Aadi. She couldn't look ahead that far to an 'Australian' excitement. Her heart was still with Aadi. That, and the enormous amount of work still ahead of her. That same day she had an appointment with Rose for the tattooing of her brows and lids. The next day she had to see Mike Altman, the accountant who had prepared her quarterly tax statement for the IRS. Then she had lunch with her old singing buddy, Marge Pettigrew.

She took her mom to see Dr. Wainio because some of the wires holding her teeth together had come apart. This happened too frequently. Later she had lunch with her friend, Mary Hanson. And that evening there was the Thursday Centering support group meeting. She was really going to miss those.

Her old choir director and his wife were in town. They had retired the year before after many productive years at St. Michael's Church. Catherine had enjoyed so many years working under Don Rubertus. Now they lived in Arizona, but came to visit Duluth and friends in the summer. Don and Lorraine took Catherine and Kay Reardon to lunch. It was a happy reunion.

Another Merton meeting on the third Sunday of July, followed by dinner with Mary Ramsay and Laura. The next day the house was being shown again and Catherine had to attend a wake service for a beloved friend from her church. The funeral was the following morning and she attended that also.

Every day without fail, Catherine went to check her post office box. There was nothing. Where was his letter? And why hadn't he written another? And there were no faxes either. She assumed he was on tour. She tried to keep her mind off him for a while because her work load was horrendous and so was her stress level. It would have helped her to hear from him, just a short note or fax. Something!

Her full day at the dentist came when Dr. Wainio got her five front teeth ready for permanent caps. After hours of drilling, temporary caps were glued on and she was able to go home. It had been exhausting. She felt her body was asking, "What are you doing to me? Teeth, Eyes, Face, Hair, what next?" And there was a next. Her internist told her that she had to have a flex-sigmoidoscopy. So the night before she gave herself enemas to clear her bowel and went in the following day for the procedure. It was not pleasant, but she would only have to have one every five years. Then she had her annual mammogram. Those were always painful for her. Another session with Rose for her eye lids and then an appointment with Jacalyn for electrolysis.

It was now past the first of August and the house hadn't sold. She was getting anxious and Bran was at her every day.

"What if it doesn't sell? The house is not sellable. No one wants it."

"It will sell. And the house is sellable. Everything is sellable. There is someone out there that will want it."

"But you're leaving September 1st. What am I going to do if it doesn't sell by then? You're just going to leave me here? Why do you have to leave September 1st? Why can't you wait until it is all over?"

"It will be all over. And I have to leave on the first. I have my tickets. Everything is planned."

"So you're just going to dump all this on me, are you? You're a selfish bitch."

"Look, I've been doing all the work here. You haven't done anything. You won't even tell me what you want to keep."

"I don't want anything. I just want to get out of here."

"Well, that isn't possible just yet. Stop worrying. It all will be taken care of. You'll see."

Catherine bought a statue of St. Joseph and planted it outside in the garden by the house. This had worked for other people, so she tried it. The story went that if you planted a statue of the saint next to the house, face downward, with head to the north, and prayed for his intercession, you would sell your house. It was superstition, pure and simple, but she could use all the help she could get.

Through Mike Kylmala, Conny's husband, Catherine at last found a storage locker. Mike brought his truck and loaded all her boxes, took them to the storage area, and packed them for her. It was a good size and everything fit in very well. That was one problem solved.

Why hadn't she heard from Aadi? This was bothering her. Even if he was on tour, she had to fax him. This waiting was driving her mad with worry.

Dear Aadi,

I know you have been out working. Please call or fax me when you get in. It has been over 3 weeks. Perhaps you have called and didn't find me here. I do need to hear from you. My departure here is getting closer. No letter has come, so that one must have lost its way.

If this gets to you today–please think good thoughts for me and when you go to temple–please pray for me. C

Catherine had a recall from the hospital for another mammogram. They had seen something in her left breast that hadn't been there a year ago. She had no time to worry about it. But it did come to her mind that if it was something, she would have to have surgery. Not only was the timing wrong, she was due to leave soon, but if she had a breast removal that was the end of her relationship with Aadi. She worried more about that than the possibility that it was cancer.

The second series of xrays showed nothing. She was told to come back in six months for another mammogram. Since she had to return anyway for a new visa, this would be no problem. She thanked God for His watchful care of her, and she went home to face a house still full of boxes.

For some reason, the boys were not coming to get what she had packed for them. She was anxious to get the boxes out so that she could get the house cleaned and in some semblance of order. Next on her agenda was finding someone to do the estate sale. Conny gave her the names of two ladies that she knew did this work. Catherine called one of them. Her name was Darlene. She came alone to the house and told Catherine that her co-worker was on vacation and wouldn't be back until the end of August. Darlene said she could start without her. She told Catherine to purchase stick-on tabs, and said she'd be back the following week.

There were many items that Catherine didn't want in the estate sale; tables for her stained glass work, and an antique dresser that had been handed down from her grandmother. These she gave to Lisa. Mike hauled them down to her house for Catherine. All the remaining stained glass she gave to Ada Teske, a friend from the beauty shop who shared her love for stained glass and had become a close friend over the past couple of years. Catherine also gave her the window she had made during her beginning classes. It was a good job and had been hanging in the front entry over the door. There were other items she gave Lisa, knowing that she would value them, and knowing too that her boys wouldn't want them.

Somehow her sons were procrastinating. At some point they were worrying about the division of spoils. They didn't want to feel greedy and grab things. Over and over both she and Bran told them to please take what they wanted. Also they told her that they had no room for all her stuff. This hurt her, because she was giving them antiques that came down from her grandparents plus many, many expensive beautiful things in china, porcelain, crystal and silver. How could they not want them? If the men didn't appreciate them, certainly the women would.

She called and called and called them and they wouldn't come. They kept telling her they would as soon as the house sold.

Another headache was Bran's room in the basement. It was full of tools of every description. He wouldn't even choose sets for each of the boys. He did choose one set for her, which she packed and put in storage. This room alone was worrying her. After it was cleaned out, it needed to be scrubbed and painted. Bran kept telling her that he was waiting for the boys to choose what they wanted. And they weren't coming. He called them. She called them, and still they refused to come. This was beginning to take its toll on her.

And still no word from Aadi. Finally, she couldn't stand it anymore, so she drove to Lisa's on the 11th of August and dialed his home. A young lady answered the phone.

"May I please speak to Aadi?" Catherine asked politely.

"He is not in station."

"Could you tell me when he will be back?"

"Fifteen, twenty days."

"I see. Please tell me. When did he leave Udaipur?'

"!8 July."

"Thank you very much."

She was distressed that he hadn't contacted her in some way. Had he changed his mind? What was going on? The following day she sent him another fax.

Dear Aadi,

I called your home yesterday (11 Aug) and was told you left 18 July and won't be home for 15–20 days more. That is just before I am due to leave. I am concerned, not having heard from you. Have you changed your mind about meeting me? I realize you are very busy and probably took on 2 tours back to back. I hope it is only that. However, if you have decided you don't want to see me, I need to make other arrangements because I don't wish to arrive in Delhi in the middle of the night with no reservations and no one to meet me. Please fax or call me when you get home–use either number and if necessary–leave message on my machine–for whatever you decide. I leave Duluth 1 Sept for Boston. I will be with friends in Walpole, Massachusetts (Paul and Marie Procaccini). You may call me also at their number: 508- 885-3829. I depart Boston 5 Sept via United #2 for India, arriving 11:00PM Delhi 6 Sept. If you are wondering why I am questioning–just know that the last several weeks have been extremely stressful and becoming more so. One short fax or call would have helped me.

C

The Gilbert and Sullivan Singers gave her a going away party one Sunday afternoon in August. It was just after the Merton group met, and she was able to say her good-byes to them as well. It was a beautiful party and a lovely day, so they were all out on the large deck at Dick Stewart's daughter's house. They even had a cake decorated with the Taj Mahal.

Despite many ads in newspapers in Duluth, St. Paul and Minneapolis, the piano did not sell. Robert wanted it, but both she and Bran felt it was too large a gift; that they didn't have the equivalent to give to the other three sons. She told Robert he could have the piano free if he would give each of his brothers $3000. That would give him a $15,000 piano for $9,000. He refused. This was another problem to solve. Finally Roland told her that his friend, Brian, would like to have it. He couldn't afford to buy it, but he would store it in his house until there was a buyer. Catherine wrote up an agreement stipulating that Brian and his family could use the piano, but they were to open their home to any possible buyer. Roland told her that he would advertise regularly in the Minneapolis paper. After the agreement was reached, Catherine called several transfer companies and found one to do the job.

It was past the middle of the month, and the time for her leaving was coming fast. The gals at the beauty shop gave her a luncheon at James' restaurant. She knew this place well, because she and Bran were there almost every night, often with Everett also. Her kitchen had been dismantled and there could be no more cooking there. On that particular day, Catherine saw her beloved piano taken apart and loaded onto a van.

She enjoyed the lunch with many women from the beauty shop. Then she had another appointment with Rosa, plus a final reading from Helga.

"Cathy, I see a man. Your father is in the spirit world, isn't he?"

"Yes."

"Because he says to me, 'My daughter. There is a fear within her. Please assure her that when the time gets long and it gets lonely', it's like he'll be in there. Because there is a portion of you at some inner gut level, some fear of what if you get stuck and you're all alone. And he says he'll be there with you. Now I'm getting such a funny feeling. Haven't you heard from India for a while?"

"No."

"Because all of a sudden I got this void. That's a part of why you're afraid. It's almost like, 'What happens now?' And what I heard is that you are going to go and stand on your own two feet regardless. Whatever it is that is causing this void. I was going in there, and there's nothing. I didn't feel any communication, and I can't tell because he's been on the telephone before. He's sent faxes, I don't know, but I see some fast mail. And now I just saw a void."

"My first word, question, was 'communication."

"Your father knows and he'll be beside you when you are doing some of the footsteps alone. The fear that I get is that it is way down here at gut level. 'What if he isn't there?' But the spirit world is saying they already told you everything is not as exact as–you already knew that. And it's OK. You'll do fine. If he comes across, fine. If he doesn't come across, it's going to be OK too. Because that's not the only people you know in India. When you have a bad day, just remember that tomorrow will be a new day. They are not bad. I see you really enjoying something.

"I asked, 'What is this that I see you so thoroughly enjoying?' And I'm not sure exactly. It's so funny, because that man has faded. He's there, but not a sharp image. You see him, but it's not sharp. And I asked, 'Now who are you having such a good time with?' And it feels like you get involved with something. I felt a learning. I felt an excitement. I don't know exactly what it is, but there are several people that keep going in and out. It's not going to be exactly like you think, but it's not all bad. I do see you pissed. That's the best word I can use to describe it. I asked, 'Are you so mad at the country?' And I got 'No.' Really at yourself, because somehow you didn't listen.

"And I also feel that when you leave you're going to wonder if you'll ever see either your mother or your ex again. Even though you are divorced, he is the father of your children and there is a bond there. In my mind's eye I see this box of tissue. And grieve it out. Do the grieving when you leave.

"Except how come your kids are acting so funny? It's almost like, they were OK with you going, but your kids aren't OK at all now. In fact you've been getting grief. I just see grief from this one, this one, this one. You've got three plates of grief. One of them is giving you a lot of garbage."

"There are four."

"Hm, how come the fourth one doesn't show? There's one that is small, like one of those custard cups. Not much showing on top, but it goes deep. You only see what is on the top. He's going to grieve more. Do you know which one is which?"

"No. I'm not sure. No. They're grieving?"

"Grief. 'Why are you doing this? Why are you leaving?' But this other one over here, the custard cup–yes, he's united with the other three, but inside it's deeper. I asked if he's been verbal and it says 'no'. They don't know if they're going to see you again either. This is how they're acting. And I said, 'She's 65. She'll be back in between.' To them you are falling off the end of the world. Because your kids have not been to India. But you got kid problems now too. Instead of you celebrating that you are finally getting to do what you want, it's rough. Are the kids going to be at the airport? No, all your kids won't be at the airport, are they?"

"No one will be."

"No one?"

"I'm leaving from Duluth."

"I'm seeing a young man. I'm seeing Minneapolis airport. I don't know if he was thinking about it or that he actually was there. I can't get which one is which here. And I asked if he was going to try and talk you out of it, but I didn't get that.

"I'm also sensing that–I don't really know what I'm seeing. It appears that what I want to say, there's something else that is going on in your head. You haven't quite figured out what is what. I see you putting it in your head and then putting it down, and again picking it up. Is that because you don't have a place? You don't have an apartment or a house yet, do you?"

"No. That's not so much what it is. I guess my arrival."

"We touched on that. I'm not sure if he's going to be there."

"It's just that if he doesn't meet me, I have to see my way to getting to a hotel and it's difficult. The arrival is extremely difficult. With the luggage, changing money into rupees, a sea of faces and having to find a kiosk where you hire a car to take you where you have to go."

"In which place are you landing at?"

"Delhi."

"They're telling me, exchange some dollars before you go. I'm sensing that if there is no one there to meet you that is when the forces will come and be with you. You might have to send someone to get you a cab, because I don't want you to leave your luggage."

"No, I would never do that."

"What have you got, four bags?"

"Three."

"Because I saw four. But it might be the purse. Because I didn't see the size. Oh, suddenly I saw one monstrous–Holy Christopher! When I said I didn't see the size, they said, 'Do you want to see the size?' and they showed me."

Catherine laughed heartily. "It's big all right."

"Take a lot of reading material. More than you think you're going to want."

"I sent books already this week. I mailed three boxes for $332."

"I wonder. You know, I saw you so mad. I wonder if some of that gets lost? And you are just furious. What if only two of the three arrived?"

"I would be mad."

"Really, what I saw were fireworks. You were really mad, but remember that is some of the things that happen. Don't have a heart attack. I'm also seeing a learning process. I don't know if it's a literary thing, but I see you writing. You haven't done that for a long time."

"I want to learn Hindi. There's a learning process there."

"Exactly. But you're also going to be writing, journaling. But I also see you mingling with people. And I want to say that's where you felt so good. I'm not discouraging you. I just want to say, that man's face is not clear here anymore. He's over here. I want to say he faded. If he comes, you just grab on to him. You know what I mean. Or else you watch and see how it goes. Give him the freedom to come and go so that you see what he really is. But learn the Hindi and in that process, who knows what you will come across. It's going to be a good experience, but you're going to be ticked off sometimes too. Now why don't we go to your questions?"

"You've answered my questions."

"That's good. OK, ask more. Anything. And I'll just go deeper."

"I'm just thinking of the sale of the house. If it's going to go through. The sale of what's left. The clean-up."

"You're not going to do the clean-up. It looks like you've hired someone. But there's little things that keep appearing, another box, another box. I don't know what they are. It's like I see little things. It does appear that the house is going to sell. I asked if they would be good for the house, and the answer was, 'yes'. They would love the house. But you're grieving the house! There's a portion of you that's grieving about leaving your house. And it's not tears, but it is, this was the house that you'd always dreamt you'd have, but also know that when the day comes that you have to close it down, you will. But there is a grieving. Especially when you don't know what you are going to, one room or four rooms. When you don't know, that makes it even more so.

"Your things. I see you giving away some things that were really important to you. I just see you putting them from one hand into another and you turn your back. So also, the house will go too. I just saw you being OK with that. And I don't know what orchids mean. I just see orchids. To me they are exotic. I don't know what they mean to you. I always think of Hawaii. All I know is when I was talking about the house, it was in a place and someone was giving you orchids. Remember, I told you two or three times, I don't see you staying in India. Maybe you'll learn Hindi, maybe you'll go here, or maybe you'll go there. All of sudden someone is bringing you the most gorgeous lavender orchids. They're just gorgeous! And they're just placing them before you. I wanted to know if they meant something. And I never saw orchids in India. And this felt,–I can smell sea breeze. Very clean smell. And I know what India smells like. It doesn't smell like that. And I still say you're going to meet someone. I don't think he's an Indian. He may be in India or close. OK, another question."

Catherine was silent, so Helga went on.

"Now I'm going to ask you. Have you heard anything from him since he came back from Germany?"

"Yes, immediately."

"OK."

"He called me twice a week before he left."

"And then how long was he gone?"

"I would say about a week."

"And he called when he got home."

"I got a fax and a call."

"When is the last time you heard?"

"Five weeks ago."

"Did he speak of anything when he called, or was it jibber-jabber? Because this is what they're showing me. But there wasn't anything concrete that you could hold on to. Try to think back."

"When he calls, we only talk for a minute. He called on the 11th of July and then I called him on the next day. I was trying to get a date. He was taking a week's time off so that we could travel and I wanted to know when so I could reserve my ticket. He had always talked about the first week of September, but then on that Saturday when I spoke to him, he said it would be better if I came the end of that week because he had office work or something he had to do that first week. That I should come the 6th or the 7th. So I made the reservation. Oh, and I had asked him if it would be better for him if I came in Delhi or Bombay. And he said it didn't make any difference to him, so I told him I'd come in Delhi, because I was more familiar there. And then he asked if there was something I needed to do in Delhi before we left. I said 'no', and if he meant speaking to Sunil, I said, 'no'. And he said, "Well, good. Then we can just escape."

"Did he say what mode of transportation?"

"I talked about that. And he said he'd get a car and a driver. He wanted to know where I wanted to go. I told him Jaisalmer, Jodhpur, and anyplace else he wanted to show me. The following Monday I reserved my ticket and I sent him a fax telling him I was coming in on the night of the 6th, and that I had ten days to decide, and if that wasn't OK, to let me know. And I never heard another word. I called his home on the 11th of August and someone told me he went out on the 18th and he wasn't due back for another 15 to 20 days. I sent another fax saying, 'If you've changed your mind, let me know."

"The fax is at his job?"

"No. At his home."

"His home? Who would pick up the fax if he wasn't there?"

"He told me the faxes are extremely private, and that he picks them up."

"Because I wondered if he had called home. Was he with a tour group then?"

"I would assume that he was, and when it was so long, I assumed that he back to backed tours. Again, it could be something else."

"It could be. It's funny because even when you talk, he's not clear. I don't understand. It's like he's faded. That's the only thing that I can say. I asked if you're going to see him and I got, 'yes'. You're seeing him, but I don't know what exactly it means. I wish I knew. I saw the pictures of him, but I can never hold on to him. He's elusive. He goes here."

Then Catherine told Helga about the fax she had sent him and what were the contents.

"Very definitely I'm going to get a reservation at some hotel, so that I won't be stranded. And if I can change money in Boston, I will do that."

"Regardless, if you come in the middle of the night and there is someone to meet you, you just have to rest. And change the money in New York."

"I'm not going through New York, so I have to try in Boston."

"As soon as you said that, I got the word, 'wise'. We always have to have plan one and plan two. Would this young fellow that you know in Delhi, could he pick you up?"

"Yes, but I wouldn't call him at the last minute. He does not have a car. He'd have to order one. He lives an hour from the airport."

"Oh, I didn't know."

"And I didn't want that complication if Aadi came to meet me."

"Exactly. It's understandable if you just make reservations for a hotel. And somehow take a cab or a bus to it."

"Oh, there are no buses. Ahiiii! This is like no other terminal. It's just like my son, Robert, told me not to take five thousand dollars in travelers checks. He said it was too much and to just use my Chextra Card. I told him there were few, if any, ATM machines in India, and certainly not in the small places where I'd be traveling, and I had to have cash. The small hotels do not take credit cards. He said, 'Take a thousand and then wire Kerry for more'. Well, where am I going to wire from?"

"That is absolutely the truth. I asked if the five was sufficient, and it felt like at first it was going to cost you more money because you were moving from here to here. And then it kind of settles down. That feels wise.

"Any other questions? The thought has come, if your mother passes away, will you come home? And the answer is 'no'."

"Really?"

"I don't think so. I just saw that everything would be taken care of. I don't know if you would be flying back. If you can, you will. But I don't see it. It was like everything was taken care of."

"My mother asked that and I told her that I would rather that she ask if I was coming out to Oregon to see her when I came back in March."

"This thing with your sister is going to ease off. It was like the pile was this high and now it is getting smaller. I saw it as a manure pile."

"It sure has been."

"But it's not as steep as it was. It'll ease off."

"I had this feeling after talking to her this week, that after Mother dies, I'll have no more contact with her."

"That might be, but right now I'm seeing it's not as bad as it was before. It was really yucky! Just think of it as 'I don't have to play on the top of this pile.' Is your mother excited about going?"

"I don't know. I know she worries, but then she worries about everything anyway."

"Because I felt excitement. Fear, yes, but excitement. I know you don't get as excited so much as you get older, but I see excitement here. And I asked, 'What is she excited about?' And somebody says, 'Well, remember, you don't have to go out in the cold snow now.' She forgets that she is that old. She's not going to be dancing in the street. Has she said anything to you about how she feels about this?"

"My going?"

"And divorce and all that? Because I saw the mouth going."

"What she said first when I told her about the divorce was, 'Is he going to give you half?' That was the first thing she was worried about, if I was going to have enough money. When I told her the divorce was final, she said, oh that's the first time that it's happened in her family. I said, 'What are you saying?' And she said, 'Well, I guess there were some cousins in St. Louis.' I said, 'Mother, your nephew, two nieces, your other daughter, your grandson, and now another grandson. What do you mean I'm first?"

"In her, this little family, you were the first. She never thought you would. She's the mama right here. And wherever it was, she couldn't see past. You've bitched to her before and it's like, 'If things were like this before, what are you doing it now for? Things are better now.' This also means she's thinking about it or talking about it. She's puzzling over things."

"I explained a lot to her, but she listens to my sister and she said, 'Your sister thinks you're making a big mistake.' That was way back and now she says, 'I just want you to be happy'."

"And really, that's it. And again, do I see happiness in India? Yes. Do I see you being ticked off? Yes. Are you going to be sorry you went? Only on certain days. But come on, it's not bad. And on the whole, I want to say, it's exciting. Why do I get this gut feeling? You know it would be different if you had been 35 and could have done this. But at our age, it's like, 'Why do I go off and do these dumb things? I come home exhausted.' Remember you may be dead tired in between there. So then, take a good book and read for a while.

"I asked if there was anything you were going to miss. I saw you missing some western cooking. Well, when this happens, for gosh sake, make it yourself. And once you got a taste of it, you went right back to the other. It was a strange picture. I never had better fruit and I never had better vegetables than I had in India. You can make a blah dinner, which is ours in comparison to theirs. You can do that. That's what I saw. Any other thing at all? Has anything crossed your mind?"

Again Catherine could think of nothing.

"I still see–I don't know what you're doing, but I see you in Bangalore. I don't know what you were doing, but you were so excited about Bangalore. What it feels like, you're meeting somebody."

"Could it be a relative?"

"Could be. I don't know. You're meeting somebody."

"I have a cousin who is doing business with Indians in Bangalore."

"Ooh, I just got goose bumpies. You're going to meet someone there. I said, 'Let me just move all over the country,' and all of a sudden I was in Bangalore. You were so tickled. It was great. I'll travel with you sometimes in mind and spirit. You are doing some of the things that some of the rest of us only dream about. I couldn't go and live down there, but some part of India is a part of my soul too. I absolutely loved it when so many hated it. It feels good. Basically I don't see anything horrible. Go with God. Enjoy and do the things you really want to do. But that man is not over here like he was a month ago when you were here. I can't bring him up as sharp. Do you see him? Oh, yes. I don't know what it means. You'll probably figure that one out later."

CHAPTER TWENTY ONE
FAREWELLS

Catherine went to Portown Travel to see Wendy. She was determined to make a hotel reservation for her first night in Delhi. She simply couldn't wait any longer to hear from Aadi. It seemed like he had dropped off the end of the earth. If only she hadn't been so occupied with moving, selling, doctoring and everything else that was going on in Duluth, she might have been able to figure it out. But her mind was very full of all the immediate problems and finding ways to solve them.

Wendy sent a fax to an Ashok hotel but didn't get a return. Catherine asked her to make the reservation by phone, which she did. The Albuquerques had asked her to come for another dinner at their house, and when she told them she worried about changing dollars, they had the answer. Mathew exchanged $50 worth of rupees for her. This was a god-send. She could fly into Delhi without fear of having to change money and she had a hotel reservation. Now, Aadi or no Aadi, she would be OK.

She tried to dismiss Aadi from her thoughts. It worked most of the time because she was so busy, but when she finally went to bed at night and when she woke in the middle of the night as she had been used to doing, her thoughts were always of Aadi. There was a great sadness within her and there seemed to be no joy or anticipation any more. She was leaving and that was how it was supposed to be, but there was no excitement.

Bids had come in for the house and one of them was so low that Catherine began to cry. Then another one came in.

This was from a young couple with three adopted children and a golden retriever. Catherine saw that as a signpost from God. They were the ones He wanted for their house. Brandon and Catherine agreed on their bid although it was lower than what they had hoped for. Lynn Beechler contacted them the next day and told them that the buyers were able to get the financing and it was done. The house was sold. Of course, it wouldn't be absolutely definite until the closing, but that would be in October after Catherine had left. Because she would be going to a foreign country she had to sign preliminary papers, but Robert would be at the closing in her stead with her Power of Attorney.

Immediately they called the boys and told them to come because the house had sold and they had to take their things. Russell and Randall rented a van, which was difficult to find because so many were being used for students going back to school. They had to pack Roland's things as well. Brandon started to take the bedroom set apart and was having difficulty with it.

"Why don't you wait now for the boys to do that?" she asked him, as she watched him sweating over it in exertion.

Suddenly he stood up with a terrible look of hatred on his face. He raised the hammer over his head and said, "I could kill you. I could kill you."

"Go ahead," she said resignedly. "Go ahead and hit me."

He lowered the hammer and went back to the bed. Another time as they were out in the garage trying to assemble the items to be put in the garbage, he told her that he wanted to shoot her and then kill himself. The pressure was getting to both of them. There was such a huge pile to go to the garbage, but he wouldn't allow her to place but a few items at a time for it to be picked up. She argued this point every week, but finally got it all hauled away.

When she had gone to Fargo, Kerry had told her that the family would have a get-together for her so that the children could see her again and they could all say a final good-bye.

Catherine looked forward to that and she drove to St. Paul on the last weekend before she was to leave. It was strange because it seemed to her that the boys, or their wives, were not happy about this. First she was told that she was to go to Russell's house. When she contacted him from Carmel and Al's house, Russell told her that she was welcome to go to his house, but Julie would be working and he would be home late. What was this? They were going to use his house, but neither of them would be there?

She contacted Roland and he told her to come to his house. She drove there and wondered what was going on and she felt that she should not have come. Roland seemed reluctant to talk about it. It seemed that Julie felt that Anne should do it and Anne, who was pregnant again and had Katie to look after, thought it would be easier for Julie. Catherine just wanted to drive back to Duluth and forget the whole thing. This was supposed to be a happy last time together and instead it had become another stress-filled situation.

Anne came home from the market and a little later Robert and Kerry showed up with Allison and Jacob and also with lots of food. The two daughters-in-law put on a beautiful luncheon and it was suddenly a very lovely reunion. Randall was there and then a little later, a car drove up and Julie arrived. There seemed to be a bit of a strain between her and Anne, but it was covered up. Russell had to work, so he never did come. But Catherine saw her grandchildren again and was able to kiss and hug all of them before she left. Anne and Kerry had done their best to give her a lovely send-off and she was very grateful to them. She was also grateful to Julie for coming. Catherine dearly loved all her daughters-in-law and wanted to see them happy. With two of them living near each other, she hoped they would become close friends as well as sisters-in-law.

Cindy arrived in Duluth and began the job of packing up Mother. She contacted a van company and arranged for her furniture and belongings to be picked up. Many of her clothes were donated to St. Michael's 'Used a Bit' shop. Some of the ladies on Mother's floor gave her a farewell tea. Catherine was invited to that as well. Afterwards, Cindy arranged for the ladies to come to Mother's apartment and take what they wanted of what was left and would not be taken to Oregon.

In the meantime, Robert had expressed the desire of having Catherine's dining room table and chairs. She was delighted to give this to him. The chair seats had been covered in petite point, which had taken Catherine twelve years to complete. She hoped Robert and Kerry would cherish them. Five days before she was due to leave Duluth, Robert informed her that because the dining room set had no matching hutch, they had decided not to take the set. Now it had to be sold in the estate sale. But the chair seats? Catherine had no intention of letting those go. Cindy went with her to a fabric store where she bought a floral print to cover the seats. The seats were removed and taken to Mother's apartment, where Cindy reupholstered all of them. Catherine helped, but Cindy had done this before so it was her expertise that was needed. They worked steadily until three o'clock in the morning. The following day Bran helped Catherine put the seats back on the chairs. When Robert came to pick up his things and saw the chairs, he said he liked the set better now that the seats had been redone. Catherine just shook her head and didn't offer them to him again. They went into the sale along with Mother's dining room set. Cindy had also recovered those chair seats, but they were only four and an easier job. Both sets looked very nice and Catherine felt they would sell for good prices.

The van came to take Catherine's mother's things to Oregon. Barbara was hired to clean the apartment before it was given up to the manager. Then Catherine saw her mother and Cindy off at the airport. It was not a tearful good-bye, but Catherine wondered if she would ever see her mother alive again. She promised her that she would visit her when she came home in March, and that as soon as she had an address she would write and phone.

There were many last minute things to do. Catherine had gotten estimates for the cleaning of all the carpets and the walls of Bran's office, which was permeated with smoke. They chose the middle priced estimate, but the work would not be done until after the estate sale. Darlene, the woman whom Catherine had hired to do the sale, was not working out. Catherine had a section of the basement filled with items to be sold, but instead of pricing as she tagged each item, the woman only put on the stick-ums. Also, as Catherine was busy, she would interrupt her by asking what she wanted for a particular item. Finally, Catherine gave her a check and told her that it was not going to work. Darlene was aghast.

"But, Mrs. Forrest, we have done this many times and people are always pleased with our work."

"I'm sorry, Darlene, but I don't see this as a professional job. I'm leaving in three days and I have to be sure this is going to be taken care of. I don't understand why you aren't pricing as you go along."

"When my partner comes, we will do that."

"I'm sorry, but that seems like a waste of time to me, handling everything twice. And you don't seem to know what you can get for some items because you ask me what I want. This is your job. You should know without asking what I want. I'm sorry, I'm going to have to let you go. I hope this check covers your time."

"Yes, it is fine."

Catherine went to the phone book and started calling estate people. Of course, at this last moment, they were fully booked until October. Catherine couldn't let it go that long. She was leaving on Monday and on Saturday, she got a call from a woman who did estate sales. Her name was Nancy Benninghoff. It turned out that they had a mutual friend by the name of Jim Stearns. When Jim heard that Nancy was going to Catherine's to look at the items, he told her to take good care of Catherine, that she was a nice lady.

It was obvious to Catherine that this was another intervention from God. Nancy herself could not do the job, but she contacted someone who thought they might be able to do so. Catherine liked Nancy very much, who agreed with her that the woman she had hired before was not doing a professional job. Looking over the items, Nancy gave her an idea of what she could expect to get and it wasn't much.

The problem of the basement was still looming. The boys took very little from Bran's room. He decided to let Mike Kylmala take what he wanted and also told the nuns next door at McCabe to come and take what they would like. Sister Teri came and was delighted with many tools and Mike felt like he was in heaven with all the things that he took.

Mike told Catherine later that he felt guilty taking as much as he did and promised her that he would help Bran with the cleaning and painting of that room and do anything else to help him after she was gone.

There were last minute dinner invitations. Bev and Bonnie gave a lovely dinner party for Bran and Catherine at Bev and John's house. Mary Ramsay and Catherine had their last dinner out together. They had become very close and they hated having to say their farewells, but Catherine promised to write often and let her know how things were going for her, especially where Aadi was concerned. That is, if she ever saw him again. Wendy and Suzanne at Portown Travel took her out to dinner also. She loved those gals. They had been so supportive of her. Sisters Mary Charles, Teri and Mary Stephen took her to breakfast and gave her lovely gifts.

Catherine expressed to the Benedictines at the breakfast that she thought she was doing what God wanted, because she had felt His Hand behind everything that she had been doing, but she wondered now if she really had heard Him at Kovalam Beach. Or was this move just a selfish one and her desire only? They reassured her and told her that it was natural to question when one made big changes in their lives. They reminded her that she was a prayerful person and to trust in God and in His guidance. She really needed to hear that. Mary Charles had been afraid for her safety when Catherine had told her of Bran threatening her with a hammer. She had wanted her to sleep at the Barn, but Catherine didn't think that Bran would actually harm her. Now he no longer seemed angry, only resigned.

Catherine wrote out everything to be done after she was gone, and in the order in which they were to be accomplished. She had the names and phone numbers of people to contact, such as the carpet and room cleaners, Barbara Harthan, the lady who cleaned regularly for them, and Mike Kylmala, who was to clean and paint the basement floors, particularly Bran's tool room. She labeled furniture and items that were not to be sold. Some were going to go with Bran to the Twin Cities. Other items, such as the basement refrigerator, the large upright freezer, the washer and dryer and one bedroom set were being sold to the new owners. Catherine tried to make it as easy as she could for Bran. All he had to do was to go down the list. When the first was finished, he was to contact the second and so forth. Mike also told Bran and Catherine that he would gladly help him to move to the cities and Bran was to call him for his help when that was needed.

But Bran still felt Catherine was abandoning her responsibility by leaving him until the house closing. She was at the very end of her endurance. Even if she hadn't been committed to leaving with airline tickets, she could not have done any more. Lisa took her to dinner on the North Shore. It was wrenching for both of them. Lisa cried and held tightly to Catherine's hand, and Catherine was choked, with tears running down her cheeks. Lisa was the daughter she never had. They were now closer than they had ever been since they had met in 1986, over ten years ago. Being able to confide in Lisa regarding Aadi, and using her phone and her house had cemented their relationship. She would leave carrying Lisa's love in her heart wherever she went.

It was the 31st of August, the day before she was to leave. The couple that Nancy Benninghoff had contacted came that afternoon to see what there was to sell for the estate sale. They didn't seem very impressed, thinking there wasn't much there. They told her it would be more of a garage sale than an estate sale, but they agreed to do it. They would handle all of it; setting up, pricing, advertising and selling. Anything that didn't sell, they would remove and add to another sale. Bran was to leave the house and have nothing to do with it. That was the last problem Catherine had and it was solved. Truly she felt God had handled everything for her. She could now leave knowing she had done all she could for her sons and for Bran. Her house would be cleaned and freshened for the new owners.

One last thing Catherine did before she left was to light a candle and walk through her house, which had been her home for thirty years, a home where she had raised her sons, a home that she had loved from the moment it was conceived and became a reality to now when she knew it was time to let it go. She thanked her house for the many good years it had given her and her family. And she asked its blessing on the new people who were to inhabit it soon.

As Catherine lay down in her bed for the last time, she heard a message over the radio that Princess Diana had died in a car accident in Paris. She ran to the TV and heard the sad news again in more detail.

Finally she went back to her bed and arose at 4:30 AM. Her three heavy bags were packed. All she needed to do was shower, dress and leave.

It was 5:00 AM and Sister Mary Charles drove up the driveway to take her to the airport. Catherine's car stood there, an Oldsmobile with 90,000 miles on it. Everett told her he would sell it for her because Bran had no wish to do that. It would sell before Catherine even left the States. Now, Bran stood watching as the bags were loaded into Sister's car. Catherine went over to Bran and put her arms around him. He stood like a statue.

"Good-bye, Bran."

"Take care of yourself."

With that, Catherine got into the car. It was still dark outside and she did not look back, either at Bran or the house. She was on her way at last.

At the airport Catherine got her bags out and proceeded to the NW counter while Mary Charles went to park her car. When Catherine got her bags on the luggage shelf, she wondered about over-weight because they were so heavy, she could barely lift them. When the woman ticket agent lifted them, she became very angry.

"These have to be weighed," she said.

Catherine nodded. "Yes, I know."

Coming back to her after she had weighed them, she was angrier then before.

"This is way over-weight. You'll have to remove some things."

"Look, I'm going to live in India. I need everything. Just tell me the overweight charge."

"India!" she cried incredulously. "You will have to pay three times this amount on your international flight."

"Yes, OK. But what do I owe here?"

"One hundred dollars."

"Fine. Here it is in traveler's checks."

The agent took the money and became more civil. Catherine got her boarding passes to Minneapolis and to Boston and took only her purse and carry-on with her. Mary Charles was waiting for her and when they proceeded to the upper floor, Conny and Mike were there to see her off as well.

Conny was sobbing uncontrollably and Catherine tried to comfort her. They were very good friends and they had helped Catherine innumerable ways over the past months. And Mike was still going to help Bran. This also was a comfort to Catherine, because she knew Bran was feeling lost and abandoned. Mike and Conny would be good friends to him also.

"I wish you were going to be in Boston longer than four days, Catherine," Mary Charles said. "You look absolutely awful. You are completely exhausted and I'm worried about you."

"I'll be fine, Charles. Please don't worry."

"Well, I do. And you will be in my prayers every day."

"I know that, and I will need them."

"Let us hear from you as soon as you are settled over there."

"I will. I promise."

They called her flight and she hugged and kissed each one of them, then entered the security section and went to board her plane. It was only a half hour flight or less to Minneapolis, where she needed to change planes. Her best friend, Mary Ann was there to meet her. They went to a small restaurant and had a light breakfast.

Mary Ann asked her if she really had said good-bye to Aadi. Catherine confessed that they had been in contact for many months until early in July. She told Mary Ann that she had tried to back away from the relationship, but couldn't, that she was in love with him. But she also told her that she hadn't heard from him, and didn't expect to see him again. When Mary Ann heard what Catherine had written to him the last time, she predicted that he would be in India waiting for her. Catherine was not at all sure. In fact, she was numb and couldn't think or anticipate. She felt like a zombie. Mary Ann walked with her to her gate and watched as Catherine presented her boarding pass, and walked on without a wave or a backward glance.

Her flight was only two hours and somewhere along the way, she remembered that she had not shown her World Perks card to a NW ticket agent. Her flights would not be given credit toward future flights. Upon landing at Logan Field in Boston, Catherine did not see the Procaccinis so she went immediately to the baggage area. She didn't see them there either, and there was always a wait before the baggage came in, but she purchased a cart and found her flight number indicating where the baggage would be coming in. Just behind that area she saw an office for over-weight luggage and wondered if hers would be there. She found another office with NW agents and was able to show her World Perks card and boarding passes and get credit for her flights.

"Catherine," she heard her name called. It was Marie.

"Hi, Marie."

"I've been looking all over for you."

"I had to see the ticket agent here."

"Well, the luggage is coming in. What does yours look like?"

"Oh, Marie, I have three heavy bags. I had to pay over-weight charges."

"They are coming in now. Your friend called this morning. He said he'd meet you."

"What?" Catherine asked, dumbfounded.

"Your friend in India. He called and talked to Paul. He said he'd meet you."

"Oh!"

"Catherine, are you all right? You look awful."

"Yeah, I'm OK. I've had a very rough time, Marie."

Then she spied her luggage and Marie helped her get it off the moving trolley and onto the cart she had purchased. No carts were free in the United States. You had to pay a rental fee wherever you went. After loading her bags, they walked out to the street and waited for Paul to drive up. He had a bad back and Marie and Catherine didn't want him to lift, so they struggled with the heavy luggage and finally got it in the car. Marie told Catherine to sit in front with Paul, which she did.

"What did my friend say?" she asked them.

"Tell her, Paul. You spoke to him. Tell her exactly what he said."

"He sounded very nice, Catherine. First he asked to speak to you. I told him you weren't here yet, but would be coming this morning. Then he said to tell you that he would meet you in Delhi. He told me his name, but I don't remember."

"His name is Aadi Abhimani. I'm very surprised. I never expected to hear from him again. OK. Thanks, Paul."

"Catherine, tell us what has been going on."

"Oh, Marie, it's been a long six months. I can't believe I'm finally here and on my way to India. You have no idea what I've been through." She started talking and talked non-stop until they got to Walpole. There, Marie fixed lunch and Catherine continued to talk and talk and talk. These were her dear friends who loved Bran as well as her, so she felt she could unburden herself. She began by telling them of her trip to India in January and the experience she had had at Kovalam Beach and then on through all the months that followed including the divorce, of course. After lunch, she was still talking and suddenly she fell asleep. When she woke, sitting in her chair, Paul was sitting there watching her.

"What happened?" she asked.

"You fell asleep while you were talking."

"Oh, God!"

Marie came out on the porch where they were sitting and put her arms around Catherine.

"We are so glad you came to us. You are exhausted, Catherine. We are going to take care of you these few days you are with us. What would you like to do?"

"I want to see your kids and I would like very much to go to a Benedictine Abbey at Hingham. Would that be possible?"

"Sure, I know where that is. We will drive up there. Do you want to go anywhere else?"

"No, I just want to be with the two of you and I desperately need rest."

"We can see that."

Every morning Marie took long five mile walks. Catherine opted to go with her. It felt good in the early fresh air and the two were able to talk, but Catherine did most of it. She told Marie about Aadi, how they had met and how she had fallen in love, knowing all the time that there was no future in it for her.

She poured out her soul to Marie and Marie listened and understood. Although both Paul and Marie cared for Catherine and Bran, had traveled extensively with them, they knew that there had been problems in their marriage and that Catherine hadn't been happy for many years. Often, as Catherine talked to Marie, she cried and it felt good to release her restrained emotions. She felt the love and concern flowing to her from her friend and she was happy she had decided to come here before going to India.

Marie arranged a dinner so that Catherine could see all her kids and grandkids without having to travel to visit them. She was especially happy to see Lisa, Marie and Paul's only daughter. And there were Jay and Julie with their two little daughters and Rick and Joyce. EJ was a young man already. He was Lisa's son before she married Bob. Catherine knew EJ since he was a toddler of three. She felt good with this family whom she only saw occasionally, but there was a place in her heart for them just as she knew they also cared about her.

Two days after she arrived Marie drove Catherine to Hingham. It was a beautiful drive to the coast, just south of Boston. There they found the monastery where Sister Mary Charles had visited a few times and painted an icon for their chapel. They made their way into chapel and were able to attend Mass with the monks. It was a beautiful experience and Catherine was delighted to see the icon hanging there. They perused the bookstore and gift shop and Catherine sent Mary Charles a post card telling her that she had been there.

The following day Marie made an appointment for Catherine to have her hair washed and set. The outcome lacked Conny's skill, but she needed to do that before going to India. Also, Marie helped her repack some of the luggage. Catherine left a pair of high heel shoes that she knew she would never wear again. Still the bags were full to capacity and she dreaded landing in Delhi with such a load.

Then it was time to depart. Again Marie and Catherine got the luggage into the car without Paul's help and they took off for

Boston's Logan Airport. She hugged and kissed them both and thanked them for taking such wonderful care of her. They said good-bye outside the terminal because it would have been too much of a hassle to find a parking place and then get the luggage to the terminal. There was a sky cap handy and it worked out very well.

The Procaccinis drove away and Catherine followed the sky cap to the United Airlines ticketing counter. Here again, the agent had to weigh her bags. However, this agent was kinder to her and asked if she wouldn't like to purchase another bag, thereby distributing the weight among four, which would lessen her over-weight charges. Catherine said 'no' to this suggestion and paid out $300 in fines. She received her boarding passes for Boston and Newark because that is where she would depart for Heathrow in London. She had a long wait until flight time, both in Boston and again in Newark, but she no longer cared. Her luggage was safely aboard and she wouldn't see it again until she landed in Delhi. And Aadi would be there to meet her.

CHAPTER TWENTY TWO
DELHI

"Taxi, Ma'am?"

"No, thank you."

"Car, Ma'am? What hotel?"

"No, thank you."

"Taxi, Ma'am?" "Taxi?" "Taxi?" "Taxi?"

She shook her head over and over, and finally they stopped asking her. But so sure were they that she would need transport, that they began to close in on her, each wanting to be the one she chose. With the heat and the closeness of their bodies, she began to feel claustrophobic. She was losing her advantage of standing out in a crowd, which she needed in order to be found by her friend, whom she knew was there looking for her. Her vision was also being blocked, making it difficult to watch for him.

"Please," she begged, "Move off. I'm waiting for someone. Someone is meeting me."

They moved a slight distance away, but continued to watch her and wait for her to change her mind. They knew she had been standing there a long time, and they were sure that she had been forgotten. She knew better. He had sent word that he would meet her, and she knew that he would be there. She faced in one direction only, the direction from which he must come. She knew this also, for she stood on one side of the periphery, and there were few people behind her.

And then, there, there he was at last, walking toward her, the familiar figure she remembered from eight months ago, a figure she only saw for two days and one evening, but every minute detail of him had been constantly recalled and treasured.

He was not a large man, nor tall, just somewhat over her own height of 5'3", with fine features and bone structure. His skin was light brown and his hair, white and black. He was balding, but there was hair above his ears which encircled his head. He wore a full, well-trimmed beard and mustache. His nose was slightly wide at the nostrils, and his eyes were dark pools with flecks of gold.

They greeted each other by the formal act of a handshake. His eyes searched hers then, and were full of concern.

"How long have you been standing here?" he asked.

"My plane was a half hour early," she replied.

He closed his eyes as if in pain. "We've been here since eleven. It's now past midnight."

"I know," she said. "You've been looking in and I was already out."

"I'm sorry."

"It's all right. You're here now.

"We left at six this morning. We should have left earlier."

"No, no. it's all right. Really it is. But are you sure you want to be here?"

"Yes," he assured her. "Wait here. I just come." He moved off and was immediately swallowed up by the crowd. It never thinned out as planes continued to arrive, discharging more and more passengers.

He was back as a white Ambassador car pulled up and the driver stepped out.

"This is Chain Singh," he said, but did not introduce her.

She nodded and smiled at the driver. As they moved to take her luggage, she warned them of the weight. They struggled with it and she was embarrassed. Who but Americans travel with so much? But she had packed for a stay of six months and was sure that she would need all of it. They wrestled with the bags and finally got the large piece into the trunk. The carry-on fitted in the front seat. She got in the back, making room for him.

"Do you want to stay in Delhi?" he asked. "Or would you like to go on? Chain says he feels up to driving if that is what you want."

"No," she said. "We are all tired. Let's stay here tonight."

"All right." He leaned forward to Chain and spoke to him in Hindi. Chain acknowledged with a nod and the car moved off into traffic.

"Does he understand English?" she asked, indicating Chain.

"A little."

"Aadi, I want to ask you again. Are you sure you want to be here? Do you really want to do this?"

"Yes," he answered. "Now it is all right? We stay at Indian hotel? It's not far."

"That's fine. Whatever you choose is fine." She didn't tell him she had made a reservation elsewhere, before, when she thought she would never see him again, and thought she would be arriving alone with no one to meet her.

The drive through the streets of Delhi was familiar, yet unfamiliar. As many times as she had been here, she was still lost. It was the same everywhere in this country. Her sense of direction, usually so sharp, got hopelessly lost in India. The lights of the city were dim and pollution hung in the air like yellow fog in front of the driving lights and formed thick halos around the street lamps.

There was no conversation in the car. The situation felt strange, awkward to her. She was unsure of him and unsure of herself. She felt tired, yet not sleepy, nor was she excited and exuberant as she should be. Eight months ago, seven, six, five, four, three months back—all of that time she yearned for this moment, anticipated it, saw it in her mind as a bright shining time of fulfillment. Where was that feeling now? She wasn't even asking herself that question. She would not for a long time to come.

Now, as on the plane, she simply reacted automatically to what was happening around her. She fully trusted this man, and without any conscious thought whatsoever, placed herself entirely in his care. A month ago she had written to him, assuring him that she had no intention of becoming a burden to him, that he was in no way responsible for her or her decisions. Yet, here she was in Delhi only two hours and with him just under a half hour, and already she was depending on him completely.

The hotel was dimly lit, but the bellboy came out to bring in the luggage. Again she was embarrassed. She needed all the pieces because she didn't remember what had been packed in each, and she thought she needed to open all three.

"Don't lift it," she told the boy. "There are wheels. WHEELS. Pull it." But her instructions were in vain. The boy did what he always did.

Aadi had gone ahead to Reception, a dark area paneled in wood with more dim lighting. He beckoned her to come, and she signed the register giving her passport number. She handed Aadi all the rupees she had on her, about fifty dollars' worth.

They took the elevator, she, Aadi, and Chain, to the 13th floor, and followed the bellboy to two rooms across the hall from each other. She saw her bags in the room on the left, so she entered it, vaguely wondering if he was going to share the other room with Chain. Then he came.

"Is it all right?"

"Yes, fine. It's just fine."

He looked at her. "Do you want me to stay with you?"

"Yes," she said. "I'd like that." A third time she asked him, "Aadi, do you really want to be with me?"

He answered, "I wouldn't be here if I didn't want to be here." He closed the door behind him and walked toward her. She faced him and as he opened his arms to her, she walked slowly into them, feeling their familiarity holding her, not passionately as she remembered, however. As they kissed, it felt tender and sweet to her, but again there was no passion, no urgency in either of them. Vaguely this registered to her, but she dismissed it as exhaustion in both of them.

"I'm afraid," she confessed to him. "It's been so long, and I want, more than anything, to please you. And I'm so afraid of being compared to other women and falling short."

He just looked at her. Then, "We don't have to do anything. We can just talk."

"No," she told him. She needed and wanted the intimacy. Later, months later, she would realize they should have talked and waited.

"I need to clean up." She told him.

"Yes," he said. "I just come." He opened the door, and left the room to give her privacy.

She began to unlock and open her suitcases. She took out a few things which she laid on the bed, then found her toiletries, a bath towel and a nightgown. Without locking the door to the corridor, she went into the bathroom. She was afraid he would come back before she had showered and find the door locked.

He did not return however until she was out of the bathroom. She waited in her long cotton pink nightgown. It was a color which she knew he liked and she had chosen it for their first time together.

"Come" she called, at the sound of his knock.

He entered, closed and locked the door behind him. As he turned to her, she rose from the bed on which she had been sitting.

"I have some things for you," she said, indicating the items on the bed. There were CD's and cassette tapes of music she enjoyed and thought he would also like. And she gave him a wool sweater.

"This was a sweater I bought a long time ago, not for you, but because I thought it was beautiful and I liked it." It was a lovely shade of lavender which she knew he wore well.

"Thank you," he said as he set the gifts aside. Then she handed him a package wrapped in brown mailing paper with his name and address on it.

"This is for you. I didn't expect to see you again, but it was purchased for you. There is a note inside explaining. I packed it intending to mail it in India."

It was heavily wrapped and sealed with tape. He used all his strength and tore it open. It was a book on gardening.

"Thank you," he said again as he looked through it quickly and then set it aside with the gifts.

"May I use your shower?" he asked.

"Yes, of course.

"Oh, there are no towels.

"Please, use mine.

He closed the bathroom door and she listened to the water running as she lay on her bed awaiting him. When he returned, he wore a yellow and black horizontal striped T-shirt and a pair of dark blue and red striped briefs. He walked over to her bed and stood looking down at her. As she watched, he removed his shirt first, then his briefs. His body glistened in the soft light and appeared darker than his face. There was a sprinkling of black hair on his chest. His pubic hair was black and his penis and testicles were a deep chocolate brown. This was the first time she had ever found a male body to be attractive and exquisite.

He turned to her and she slid down on the bed to take his erection into her mouth. He smelled fresh and tasted clean and sweet. She loved the feel of him and began to stroke him with her tongue while moving up and down his phallus with her lips. He bent over and braced himself on the other side of her in order to watch her. After a while he lay beside her.

"You are so beautiful," she whispered to him. As he reached to touch her breasts, she slipped her gown off over her head. He made a motion with his hand and arm to let her know that he found her beautiful also, but she knew he was only being kind. Her body was no longer young; she was obese and her belly was disfigured with two long surgical scars. Tears welled up in her eyes.

"I wish I were beautiful for you," she said.

He began to touch her pudendum and she opened wide to accommodate him. She felt no shyness, no awkwardness, only complete trust.

Afterward she lay next to him, on her side, facing him as his left arm encircled her. Her emotions were all on the surface then and tears streamed down her face.As she began to doze off, he removed his arm from around her, left her bed and crossed over to the other one. With a sweep of his arm he cleared it and spread himself full length upon it and fell into an exhausted sleep. She had forgotten completely that she snored, and that she had packed tapes for her nose to prevent this annoying habit from disturbing him.

In the morning they made love again. And later, after his shower, he sat in a chair in the lotus position with only the towel wrapped around his loins. He wore the white cotton thread of a Brahmin, the highest, or priestly caste of a Hindu. He began a prayer chant from a tiny book he carried with him. She kept perfectly silent, and as she listened, her heart opened and felt the sacredness of the moment.

Afterwards they dressed and she watched him repack his things, fitting her gifts into his bag. Then she espied a flat box about 6x3 inches with a pink ribbon adorning it. 'Oh,' she thought, 'He has a present for me.' But it went into his bag and her heart skipped a beat. She never saw the package again.

They met Chain downstairs for breakfast, but Aadi disappeared while she and Chain ate. It was difficult to converse because Chain knew very little English and when he did speak, the English was so heavily accented, she couldn't understand him. Then Aadi returned.

"Aren't you going to eat breakfast?" she asked him.

"No, I don't eat in the morning. Just tea."

He talked in Hindi to Chain. Although she didn't understand the language, she heard the word, 'Lufthansa.'

"I've arranged for the bags to be brought down," he told her. "I have an errand to run, so please you wait in the lobby."

"All right," she said, but her heart was starting to ache. She knew instinctively that he was dropping off the pink ribboned box at the Lufthansa office. It was for his German girlfriend. Did she work for the airline? She wondered.

She was not a people watcher, never wanting to stare at anyone for she always felt self-conscious when people did that to her. So she sat in the lobby feeling very alone, and watched the clock as one hour turned into two. Her heart was crumbling and she held back the tears so as not to make a scene, but she was very, very hurt.

"How can he do this? After our first night together? Oh, God, he doesn't want to be with me. Oh, God!"

Still she sat, and waited, the pain inside her becoming all consuming. It wasn't that she felt he had abandoned her. He would never do that.

CHAPTER TWENTY THREE
RAJASTHAN TOUR

They were on their way now to Jaipur. Nothing was said about why they had been gone so long or where they had been. Catherine held her tears and disappointment in check. This was no time to show her displeasure at what was happening. She would bide her time and see what transpired. Arriving in Jaipur, Aadi directed Chain to the Arya Niwas Hotel. It was a pleasant place, with a garden and verandah in front and a clean, vegetarian restaurant. It was privately owned and the owners lived on the premises. Catherine and Aadi had a room with its own verandah and an attached bathroom. It was nothing elaborate or elegant, but it was clean.

The first night in Jaipur Catherine dug into her large suitcase and pulled out a fat candle which she had brought to enhance their love-making. It was called 'Passion' and was scented with ylang-ylang, vanilla and rose petals. She wanted to make the room beautiful, but nothing seemed to work. It was hot and Aadi didn't care for A/C during the night. They used the fans sparingly. She also took out her small cassette player and asked Aadi if he would listen to tapes she had brought.

They were a pair of healing tapes called, 'Freeing the Female Orgasm'. Catherine had repressed her feelings for so long and although she could give herself freely to Aadi, she was having trouble reaching an orgasm. These tapes were beautiful and took the partner of a woman through all the steps of healing to the release of her inhibitions. Aadi said he would listen, but after only five minutes or so, he told her that he could do that. The player was shut off and he proceeded to touch her as he thought he had been instructed to. Catherine enjoyed his gentleness and perseverance, but the exercise had not followed through to the healing that Catherine needed so desperately.

The next day she put away the player and the tapes. She would never take them out again, because she knew he was not interested. Her heart was crying out for understanding and love, and it was being deprived again.

Aadi took her sightseeing to the City Palace and museum. She had been there before, but enjoyed it all the more this time because she was with Aadi. He took her to the Nahargarh Fort overlooking the city of Jaipur, a site she had never been to before. Also they visited the cenotaphs of the Jaipur maharajas at Amber.

One evening they stopped at a supermarket and Aadi advised her to buy a small electric water jug. With this they were able to make their morning tea without going to the restaurant. It was a fine idea. And every morning, he asked about her blood sugar. Because it was quite low, he purchased mangoes and fixed them for her each day. She had never seen this done before and decided it was the perfect way to enjoy the delicious fruit. He gently rolled the mango between his palms until it was very soft, then removed the stem and made a small opening at the top. She put this to her mouth and sucked the ripe juice and pulp until only the stone and peel was left.

She cashed traveler's checks only in small amounts as Aadi advised her. Then she handed the cash over to him, from which he paid all their bills. It was very inexpensive because Aadi was known wherever they went and it was still low season, so they were given deep discounts at all the hotels. Food was cheap and she paid not only for herself and Aadi, but for Chain also. Chain joined them every morning for breakfast, of which only he and Catherine partook. Aadi was content with his early morning tea until lunch time.

One day in Jaipur they were driving down a particular street when Aadi told Chain to stop. He got out of the car and said he had an errand to do and would be right back. A policeman told Chain that he had to move the car, so they drove down a block and a half before finding a parking space. Catherine worried that Aadi would not find them, so told Chain to go back to the spot where Aadi had left them to direct him to the car. It was very hot and Catherine sat in the back seat with the windows open. Soon there were beggars at the windows putting their hands in and asking for rupees. Catherine locked the doors and closed the windows, but the beggars continued to look at her with their pitiful faces.

She was not about to give them anything, knowing this was an act and she was immune to their entreaties. However, it was getting later and later and neither Aadi nor Chain came back. Catherine was feeling isolated and abandoned once again. Where was he? What was he doing? Was he looking for places or things to do so that he didn't have to be with her? She turned it all inward. She was used to being rejected. She had had a lifetime of rejection. But it hurt. It hurt very badly because she hadn't expected this from Aadi. She loved him and he was anything but loving toward her. Gentle, kind, yes, but not caring and loving.

Over an hour passed and still she sat in the hot car, sweating and trying not to look at the beggars outside her windows. An hour and a half and still no Aadi. The tears were rolling down her cheeks when he finally showed up with a package in his hand. It was large and he asked her if she would put it in her hand bag. It was too large, so he put it in his bag in the front seat.

"What's the matter?" he asked her, evidently noticing her emotional state. "What were you thinking?"

"Nothing. It's all right. You're here now."

Aadi took her to a nice restaurant in the city. It was air-conditioned and they sat in a booth. Aadi ordered for the two of them. When the food came, she noticed him pick up his fork and knife and hold them the European way. He was very deft at this and her stomach turned over with distaste. It was ridiculous, but she knew he had learned this habit in Germany with his girlfriend. As she watched him use the fork in his left hand, pushing the food on with the knife in his right hand, she lost her appetite and ate very little of the delicious lunch.

Their last night in Jaipur, there was another incident between them. He had made love to her, but he seemed uninterested in having her make love to him. She was confused and became adamant about pleasing him. He finally said, "All right then, go ahead." But his voice wasn't gentle. He seemed angry. After she had brought him to an orgasm, he went to his bed and went to sleep immediately.

Catherine didn't sleep for a long time. Why had she been so insistent? Why hadn't she just let it go? She had forced her will on him and he had become angry. This whole tour was not what she had expected. She was so hurt and upset that she went out onto the verandah and cried. But the mosquitoes were fierce out there and she had to return to the room.

The next morning she decided to talk to him about what had happened the night before. He lay on his bed and she sat on the edge of hers.

"I want to talk to you," she began. "Last night I felt like a prostitute. I am well attuned to rejection, Aadi. And that's what I felt last night. What is wrong?"

"Now you have hurt my feelings."

"How have I done that? I wouldn't hurt you for anything."

"Because I couldn't have another erection again so soon."

"Aadi, it wasn't that. You didn't want me."

But he refused to get into a discussion or explanation. He turned the conversation around until she felt she had been in the wrong. And she had been by insisting when he had wanted nothing more. She left it at that but felt more frustrated and uncertain of herself.

Aadi told her they were on their way to the painted havelis of Shekhavati. She followed the map as they drove along. She was numb with fatigue and emotional grief. She couldn't think anymore, only react. It was certain that she was not enjoying herself. Catherine tried to tell him that she was ill, but she either was unable to convey her thoughts adequately or he just opted to ignore what she was trying to explain to him. He hardly spoke to her, but talked freely and often with Chain in Hindi. She felt even more left out and isolated.

On the way they stopped at the Samode Palace, now a hotel. Aadi took her through the rooms and then they sat on a lovely verandah waiting for lunch to be served.

"I've never spoken to anyone about this before, but I'm telling you because you are a nurse."

Catherine looked at him, wondering what he was going to disclose.

"What's wrong?"

"I have a problem with my foot. It does this…." He showed her with his hand how his foot sometimes did not pick up completely.

"How long have you had this?" she asked him.

"About five years."

"Five years? Why haven't you done something about it?"

"I thought it would get better. Perhaps I injured it jogging or playing Cricket."

"Do you remember hurting it?"

"No. I never had any pain."

"What does your father say about this?" She knew his father was a professor of Ayurvedic medicine.

"I haven't discussed it with him."

"But hasn't he asked you about it?

"No, because I walk naturally."

Catherine didn't want to tell him that he does not walk naturally. She noticed his leg or foot the day she met him, and wondered what was wrong with it. Suddenly, she got scared and wondered if this could be the onset of Multiple Sclerosis, but she didn't express her concern.

"I don't know what it could be, Aadi. But tonight I will examine your leg and foot."

When the buffet was ready, they entered the dining room and enjoyed a lovely meal. Afterwards as they were walking out of the palace grounds, Aadi brought to her attention a particular leafy bush.

"Look," he said, as he placed his finger on a leaf, which closed immediately with his touch. She wanted to say, but felt shy, "I open up when you touch me." The moment passed and they went to the car where Chain was waiting for them.

Arriving in Nawalgarh, Aadi looked for a place called 'Eco Farm'. He had heard this was a nice place to stay and was run totally on solar energy. When they found it, they drove off the road onto a small lane and came to a lovely enclosure. There were several cottages with thatched roofs and brick walls. In the center was an open sitting area. The owner's name was Ramesh. He was very tall and thin with a black mustache that curled at its tips, and he wore diamond studs in both ears. This was his first meeting with Aadi and they got along very well. It turned out that Ramesh was also a tour guide, and spent months in Europe every year.

They were given one of the cottages, which Catherine liked immediately. The only problem was the Indian toilet, which she found difficult to manage. Squatting was extremely hard for her because of her arthritic knees. But she liked the setting and felt the charm of it.

Ramesh and Aadi were talking Hindi in the sitting area when Catherine went out to join them. Ramesh immediately began to speak in English to include her in the conversation. She felt grateful to him especially since Aadi seemed to prefer speaking in Hindi.

Another couple arrived; two women from Delhi. One was from the French Embassy and both spoke French and

English. They seemed to keep to themselves and Catherine had nothing to say to them. Ramesh called them all to dinner in the dining room. At some point, Aadi began to speak to them in French. Catherine heard the embassy woman speak about another woman called 'Michelle'. Aadi picked up on it and spoke also of her.

"How do you know Michelle?" asked the woman with a surprised and condescending look on her face.

"I stay with her whenever I am in Delhi." Aadi answered.

Catherine's heart gave a lurch, but she smiled because she was glad Aadi had let the woman know he was no flunky. The dinner was served on plates made of leaves. Afterwards everyone retired to their own cottage. Again Catherine noticed that there were twin beds in their room. When she had seen the room earlier they had been placed together. Now they were separated. Aadi must have requested this. It made her sad. She wanted more than anything to have a night sleeping next to him as she had imagined they would when she was still in Duluth.

After he lay on his bed, she went to sit beside him to examine his leg and foot. Both were perfectly straight. Why did the foot turn in when he walked? She held the foot in both hands and asked him to push as hard as he could. He had good strength in the leg. Then she asked him to do the same with the other leg. As far as she could tell, the strength was the same. Then she tested the strength in both arms as well. They seemed to be perfect.

"What are you thinking?" he asked her.

"Nothing. I'm just comparing."

"You have some idea what this is."

"No. I'm no doctor and nurses never diagnose. You need to see someone. Are there good doctors in Udaipur?"

"Yes."

"I'm wondering about that, because I remember your telling me about the man who was your friend who died after heart surgery in Udaipur. It sounded like the doctor had botched the operation. Aadi, you need to see specialists."

"What kind?"

"First, have an internist give you a complete physical. Then you need to see an orthopedic man and a neurologist. And do it soon. Five years is a long time. If it isn't taken care of, you could have permanent nerve damage. Will you see someone soon?"

"Yes, I will."

"Good." She kissed his foot and his leg and he took her in his arms.

The next day they went sightseeing to the important towns in the Shekhavati area. Catherine had had no preconceived idea what the painted havelis were like. Now, she was absolutely captivated. There were frescos all over exterior walls, on doorways, under roof and window over-hangs. And colorful drawings and paintings that had escaped weathering. They were breathtaking in their scope, an absolute delight. Some buildings had portraits, others religious figures and symbols, others, signs of the times, such as trains and carriages. Many were western figures in western clothes. They walked and walked and Catherine took many photos. Once they entered a school, which was also filled with the unique art. They were told by the principal that the boys studying there were being taught to respect this heritage from another era.

It was sad because the owners of these dwellings were rich and had moved away to the big cities of India and left their houses in the hands of a few servants. The paintings were becoming faded and many were wearing away from the facades in decay. No one was interested in the preservation of this art. Catherine was dismayed to see shopkeepers paste signs over them. Others had smashed into painted walls to make doorways.

Aadi asked her if she would like to stay another night there, and she agreed. She enjoyed the Farm very much. And that gave them an extra day to see more of the painted havelis. Ramesh had told Aadi the best towns to visit.

Their last night at the Farm became the first time when Catherine was able to laugh and feel joy. They had gone to sleep, when suddenly she heard Aadi make some sound. He was sitting up and brushing something off him.

"What happened?" she asked.

"Something fell on my leg."

"Oh my God! What was it?

"I don't know."

She lit the bedside lamp and they looked, but did not get out of their beds. It felt creepy. What could it have been? Suddenly, she let out a small cry. "Oh."

"What?"

"I don't know what it was, but it was crawling on the wall next to my bed."

They both looked up at the ceiling and the thatch."Do you suppose there are animals living up in there?" she asked.

"I think so."

"Oh, I don't know how I'm going to sleep now. Aadi, I hear something up there."

"I don't hear anything. Here, change beds with me."

She did, but continued to stare at the ceiling. "Aadi, I see something. It is running back and forth. Do you see it?"

Suddenly he was sitting on the side of the bed. "Oh, it was just a small rat."

"Rat?" she almost screamed.

And Aadi started to giggle. Then she started to laugh and the two of them got a bit hysterical. He got up and went to the window seat where there were many pillows. Throwing them all off, he said, "Come, we'll sleep here." Here there was no thatch, but a curved ceiling covered in some kind of plaster. There were two tiny windows to the outside in this little cove, but they were not open. Catherine crawled in first and Aadi lay beside her. She had finally gotten her wish to lie next to the man she loved.

But there was hardly any room. She couldn't turn or move an arm or a leg. And neither could he or he would have fallen on the floor. She lay awake for some time before exhaustion overtook her. When morning came she felt in terrible need to make love, but she said nothing to him. He awoke and went to one of the beds and fell upon it and slept. Oh, God, how she needed him

A knock came on their door and she woke Aadi to answer it. He opened the door and spoke to a servant

"He is bringing tea." Aadi told her. "I'm going outside." With that he went to sit just outside their door where there was a small table and two chairs. Catherine ached. She wanted him so badly, she could think of nothing else. Her body was throbbing, but she didn't tell him.

If he had just touched her, she knew she would have exploded. She went into the bathroom, used the toilet and showered. After dressing, she went out and found him reading a newspaper. It was then his turn to shower, pray, and dress.

They said their good-byes to Ramesh and thanked him, but never told him about the incident of the little creatures in their cottage. Aadi told her later that it was a nice place, but some kind of netting should be put under the thatch to prevent animals from falling on the guests.

Bikaner was their next stop. It looked like a small city, clean and beautiful. Aadi again directed Chain to Ram Puria, a lovely pink sandstone haveli. There was a large courtyard, the enclosure intricately hand carved. There were two storeys with a balcony encircling the courtyard. Aadi was shown a room on the ground floor and he told her to see if she liked it. Then the servant took her to other rooms above. Aadi asked her if there was another room she preferred to this one.

"No, I really like this," she told him. It was a long suite. The door opened to a small foyer. Off to the left was a sitting room with stuffed, period furniture and many antiques. Further on was the bedroom, with twin beds. The bath was at the opposite end, to the right of the foyer. There was a sink and a bathtub. Catherine wondered where the toilet was and suddenly saw it. She started to laugh and called to Aadi to see it.

"What is it? What is funny?"

"Look! It's a throne!"

And they both laughed. From inside the bathroom there was a narrow stairway, a flight of some dozen steps, at the top of which sat the toilet. There was nothing else there, and there was room for nothing else. It was very strange using it and looking down the stairs.

The two of them enjoyed a lovely dinner that evening at the haveli and listened to Indian musicians in the courtyard. In the dining room there was only one other couple. The four of them seemed to be the only guests at the haveli.

They had gone to her bed and he entered her to bring her to an orgasm. He was gentle, loving and very considerate. When she asked him, he sucked her nipples, giving her great enjoyment. Always, when they were like this together, she felt complete, like a whole person. Afterwards, he knelt above her and masturbated, coming to his own orgasm on her chest. She was intrigued to see the penis open and spurt the white creamy seminal fluid. Too, she was surprised to feel the heat of it on her skin. She leaned forward then and licked the tip of his penis to cleanse it. With his hand Aadi smeared it all over her chest and abdomen and then laughed and told her to shower. It had been an especially intimate evening, and Catherine felt warm and loved.

The next morning, she went up to breakfast alone and when she got back to the room, he told her that he would not be going sightseeing with her because he was having some loose motion problem. He told her he would have Chain take her to the fort and palace museum. Before she left, he asked if she had any medication to take. She found some Pepto-Bismol tablets in her bag and gave them to him. Then she took off with Chain.

It was disappointing not to have Aadi with her and she had to rely on local guides at the fort and the museum. Both sites were absolutely magnificent, particularly the fort. Chain was kind and always watched out for her and she was grateful. He was a very nice man. Catherine only wished they could converse. She found it impossible to decipher his heavily accented English. And he could not understand her.

They left the following day for the long journey across the Thar Desert to Jaisalmer. They drove all day, stopping at various places to have food and use facilities. Aadi was conscious all the time of buying water and soft drinks, making sure that she had enough fluids in that hot, dry climate. Watching the map, counting the miles traveled and the miles yet to go, Catherine found the trip long and the roads not very accommodating to fast travel. Chain was an excellent driver and a most careful one. He never hurried, but kept a steady pace.

Into the dusk of evening they drove and then the night was upon them. There was little traffic and the silence of the night was awesome, the stars in the heavens very bright. Off in the distance, to the west, Catherine noticed clouds and heat lightening.

"Look, do you see that?" Aadi asked her.

"Yes, heat or sheet lightening."

"We are traveling toward the Pakistan border. That could be Indian guns at the army bases."

"I don't think so, Aadi. It looks like lightening to me."

"But it doesn't move. I think it is from the army bases."

"Well, you know this area. I don't. But I've often seen this kind of thing in my country. And it is lightening. The heat from the earth hitting the cooler air in the atmosphere."

"I've never seen this before," he told her.

"Well, maybe you are right. I certainly could be wrong."

They continued to watch the lights until they came to a rail crossing. There was a station master at the road.

"Why don't you ask this man if he knows what the lights are," Catherine suggested. Chain spoke to the man and reported to Aadi.

"It is lightening, just as you said," Aadi told her.

After many hours they saw the lights of Jaisalmer in the distance. The long journey was almost over. Towering over the city were the lights of the fort. Chain drove them to the Gorband Palace Hotel, where they were to spend two nights. Here, after their showers, they felt much at ease and comfortable. There was a TV, which Aadi turned on and they viewed some of the rituals surrounding the funeral of Mother Theresa of Calcutta, who had died a few days before. They watched as Hillary Clinton, wife of the President of the United States, laid a wreath at her coffin.

They spent two nights in Jaisalmer, sightseeing only one day and a half. The fort was a 'working' fort. People lived and worked in it. Aadi, Catherine and Chain walked together, Aadi pointing out places of interest, architectural styles and ornamentation. Late in the day, they went out on the desert to the cenotaphs of the Brahmins to watch the sunset from that point. There they happened to meet the couple who had been staying at the haveli in Bikaner the night before.

The man started speaking to Catherine as he recognized her also. They talked for a short while, and then he confessed a total lack of understanding for the Hindu beliefs.

"You must speak with my friend. He will gladly answer your questions," she told him.

As Aadi approached them, Catherine told him that the gentleman would like to know more about Hindu beliefs. Aadi, the consummate guide and intelligent, well-educated Brahmin, began to explain his beliefs to the amazement of the Italians.

"I have never heard this before." He told Aadi. "Never has this been explained to me like this. I am very grateful. You are Indian. Do you live here?"

"I live in India and Europe." Aadi answered.

Catherine's heart gave a leap. "What's he talking about?" she thought. "Is he just putting on airs? Is this just part of his spiel as a tour guide? What does he mean, that he lives in Europe? He can't be serious."

They watched the sunset, then made their way carefully down the hill, Aadi holding Catherine's hand to assist her descent. They drove to a restaurant in the city and Catherine was delighted to see they were on a rooftop. It promised to be a romantic evening. The moon and stars were shining brightly, with not a cloud in the sky and they had a full view of the fort on the hillside. She was just about to tell Aadi how happy she was to be there, when Chain joined them. Catherine was so disappointed, she could have wept.

"Why did Chain have to join them for every evening meal?" she wondered. "Especially this lovely night when the setting was so right for two loving people?" Obviously, Aadi didn't feel the same and Catherine was crushed. It was just a place to have a meal. There was a table not far from theirs with people in conversation. Aadi became an eavesdropper and told her they were Spanish.

Back at the Gorband Palace, Aadi sat on her bed with his arm about her as they both watched the TV screen. At some point, Catherine's head nodded, and perhaps she began to snore.

"Oh, you are falling asleep." Aadi said. He got up and moved to a chair next to the TV and Catherine lay down, falling immediately into sleep. There was no loving that night or the following morning.

After breakfast they drove around Jaisalmer, viewing architectural facades, then took to the road for the distant city of Jodhpur. Crossing the desert once again, this time traveling southeast, Catherine looked at the desolation and told Aadi that although she liked Rajasthan, she didn't think she could ever live there. He didn't comment.

Arriving in Jodhpur, they drove to the home of Aadi's friend, Chandra Shekhar Singh, who had a small tour company and opened his haveli to guests. Chandra Shekhar came out to the car and explained that his home was filled and to please come the following day. This was where Aadi always stayed when he came to Jodhpur. They were directed to a small hotel not far from Chandra Shekhar's haveli and there they stayed for one night.

Aadi took Catherine to another house belonging to his 'uncle,' he told her. They had walked there from the hotel and Chain was not with them. At the house, his 'uncle' was not in, but he spoke to the woman of the house. After a time, they walked back to the hotel, finding a small out-door restaurant nearby. As they sat and waited to be served, Aadi told Catherine that there was to be an eclipse the next night and it was a time for Brahmins to stay awake and pray and after it was over, to take a shower. Catherine told him she would gladly stay awake and pray with him. She looked forward to the new experience. The food finally came, but it was more of a snack than an actual meal, and it wasn't very good, but they were both starving, so they ate everything and then went back to the hotel.

Catherine lay in her bed while Aadi took his shower. Then he came to her.

"May I sleep with you?" he asked.

"Of course," she replied, as she moved to make room for him. They made love but, as usual, he did not sleep with her.

In the morning they showered and prayed and as they were getting their luggage ready for departure, Aadi noticed spots on the sheets of her bed.

"Oh," he said. "I must wash the sheet.

Catherine was aghast. Wash the sheet? Suddenly, she was incensed. "I'll wash it," she told him.

"No, it's all right. I will do it. It will only take a minute."

"I will wash it. It came out of me," she said somewhat angrily

"It came from both of us," he told her.

Nevertheless, Catherine went to the bathroom, wet a towel and proceeded to wash out the stains. A short time later, Aadi inspected the area.

"See? It is dry already."

Catherine's heart was beating fast and she had all she could do to hold back the tears. Why was it so important to wipe out all signs of their loving? He wasn't known at this hotel. She could understand if it were at the home of his friend, but a hotel? It was probably unreasonable, but she felt that he was ashamed of having been with her and needed to hide the fact and destroy the evidence. Once again her emotions were on the surface and she was crushed.

They went sightseeing after breakfast and visited a beautiful garden as well as the fort. Here, at the fort, Aadi walked ahead of her, talking and pointing out items of interest to Chain. She had a hard time keeping up with them and a few times, Chain waited for her when Aadi had turned a corner and was out of sight.

After sightseeing, Chain drove them to Chandras Shekhar's haveli, where they were made very welcome. Chandra Shekhar was smiling and hospitable to Catherine, telling her that this was Aadi's home whenever he was in Jodhpur. Aadi showed her their room, which had twin beds set close together.

"This is your bed," he said, pointing out the one on the right. "I'm going out for a while. You rest and I will come back for you."

"OK," she agreed. After closing the door, she lay on her bed and wondered where he was going. She didn't sleep, but thought over the morning at the hotel where she had washed her sheet and also wondered why he hadn't walked with her at the fort. She was feeling left out again and isolated. There was a knock at her door and she could see through the translucent window in her door that it was a servant. Catherine opted not to answer and lay there waiting for Aadi to come to her. He never did.

It got later and later and Catherine wondered why he hadn't come. Another knock came at the door. This time she answered it.

"They are waiting for you," the servant said.

She freshened up and went out. In the courtyard she found Mrs. Singh talking with some people. Catherine wondered if this is where she was supposed to be. Mrs. Singh invited her to join them and introduced the people, who happened to be old friends of the family. Catherine felt ill at ease and wondered why she was there, and where was Aadi. Then she saw him. He had come looking for her. Evidently he had been talking with Chandra Shekhar somewhere else in the haveli.

"Would you like to take a walk?" he asked her.

"Yes," she told him, then excused herself from Mrs. Singh and her friends.

"I was looking for you," he told her, "but you were asleep."

No, I wasn't asleep. I was waiting for you to come."

Chain drove them to the market area and Aadi and Catherine got out of the car and walked along the busy streets among hundreds of evening shoppers. It was an interesting market to Catherine, especially the area beneath the roof. It appeared to be one giant warehouse, but had the atmosphere of being outside. They walked along many vegetable sellers, grains and fruits, metal ware and finally Aadi stopped at a spice shop. Here, the shopkeeper was effusive. His enthusiasm for his spices was most engaging. They sat at his invitation, while he showed them his scrapbook of the many letters from people around the world who had purchased his spices. There was also a photograph book with photos of his numerous customers. When he wanted to take their photo, both Aadi and Catherine declined. From there they walked back to the car.

Arriving back at the haveli, dinner was set and everyone took places at the table. Aadi did not sit near Catherine, but sat at the opposite end next to Chandra Shekhar. She spoke very little, as the others seemed to know each other and she felt like a stranger among them. When they were nearly finished with their meal, Aadi got up and spoke to Catherine across the Singhs and the other guests.

"I'm going to my uncle's house for the night. I'll see you tomorrow." With that, he proceeded to their room, and returned with a bundle of clothes and left. Catherine sat with a huge lump in her throat, unable to finish her dinner. She was embarrassed and deeply hurt.

"Why didn't he tell me this," she thought, "when we were alone? Why did he have to embarrass me in front of all these people? We had so much time – walking and even in the car. I wouldn't have minded if he had said something in front of Chain, but here! I am mortified. It is as if he was telling me, in front of all these people that he didn't want to be with me."

As quickly as she could, Catherine excused herself and retired to her room. There, she wept and lay on her bed for the remainder of the night. She couldn't sleep. She thought over and over about the position he had placed her in. Why had he brought her here if he wasn't going to stay with her? She could have stayed at the hotel and been more at ease. Here she felt that he had abandoned her and had done so before an audience. She could understand if he didn't want his friend to know that they were sleeping together, but then why bring her here in the first place? Catherine wanted to pack her things and go back to the hotel. She hated this haveli. She hated these people. She wanted to run, but she couldn't. She had no car and no money. Aadi had all of it. She was stuck, so she cried and waited for the morning.

At first light, Catherine took her shower and packed her things. Leaving her room, she found Mrs. Singh who wanted to give her breakfast. Catherine declined and Mrs. Singh asked her to wait for Aadi on the front verandah as she was expecting more guests and needed Catherine to vacate the room. Catherine took her bags out to the verandah, but left Aadi's in the room. A servant brought it out and finally Mrs. Singh asked her to sign the register with her passport number.

Catherine had had laundry done the day before, but had no money to pay Mrs. Singh for it. After an hour, Chain drove up and Aadi came up to the house.

"Good morning. How are you?' he asked, all smiles. Catherine did not smile in return. She was upset and couldn't wait to leave.

"Please pay for my lodging. And I also have a laundry bill."

"Don't worry about that. These are my friends."

"They are not my friends. Please pay them."

"Relax, it is all right."

"Pay her, Aadi. I insist that you pay her. I was a guest here, not a friend."

Mrs. Singh came out to greet Aadi and they spoke in Hindi. He did not give her any money however, and Catherine was angry. Chain put their luggage into the car and they drove away. Most of that day, Catherine kept very quiet. She was hurt beyond belief and was afraid of sobbing if she opened her mouth. Why, why Why had he done that to her? She kept asking herself and had no answer.

They were on their way now to Mt. Abu, the highest point in the Aravalli Hills. Aadi hadn't told her this. Chain had. Again she wondered. Why hadn't Aadi told her where they were headed? Why did Chain, the driver, have to give her that information?

By the afternoon Catherine had gotten over her fit of peevishness and began talking normally to Aadi. She was still hurt, but she chose to look ahead, knowing that their tour was almost at an end.

The road to Mt. Abu was winding and steep. The landscape was beautiful and she enjoyed it. Arriving at their destination, Chain parked the car and Aadi walked Catherine around the small lake, called Nakki, which meant 'fingernails'. The lake had been dug with people's hands and fingernails. They were actually alone for this short time and Catherine felt good to spend this quiet, private time with him.

"Don't you feel sorry for the fish?" he said to her. "It must hurt to have a hook in their mouth."

Catherine thought what a wonderful, sensitive man this was to worry about one of God's least creatures. At one point there was a secluded spot. Aadi took her hand and drew her to him and kissed her. It was a very special moment to her and she forgave him in her heart for the hurt of the night before.

It started to rain, a light drizzle, so they proceeded to the car and then drove around the small town looking for a suitable place to stay for the night. There were many small guest hotels and Catherine thought it would be nice to stay in one of them. They stopped at one and Aadi told her to follow the boy and look at the room. It was large, but had a musty smell. He showed her another and still she wasn't satisfied. Aadi then directed Chain to a modern hotel, where they found very nice accommodations. Again, Aadi had her check out the room. When she got back, she found him waiting in the lobby.

"It is a lovely room," she told him. "But it has the beds pushed together." By this time she was sensitive to his obvious wishes to sleep separate from her.

"That's all right, isn't it?" he asked.

"Yes, I like that."

They then proceeded to check into the hotel, after which they went to their room and showered. Catherine was surprise to find the beds had been pulled apart. She said nothing to Aadi, but another piece of her heart was torn out of her

In the dining room they found Chain. Obviously Aadi had told him to join them. They sat at a table for six. Aadi sat on the opposite side from her and at the far end. Chain sat across from her. It felt strange and again a band tightened around her chest. Afterwards, Aadi and Catherine made their way upstairs to their room. He made love to her, but she was hurting badly

She awakened early the following morning, and went to the window to look out. Aadi was still asleep and she enjoyed watching the way his hands were folded beneath his cheek as he slept on his side. After a half hour, she bent over him and kissed his forehead. He awoke with a smile on his face. She went to make their morning tea and he showered and prayed. After she was dressed, they sat facing each other.

"This is our last day, isn't it?" she asked him.

"Yes," he said.

Suddenly the tears started rolling down her cheeks, and she began to sob. She couldn't control them.

"I'm sorry," she said to him. "Please excuse me." And she fled into the bathroom. He kept calling for her to come back. She couldn't do that. She needed to pull herself together.

"You shouldn't hide your feelings," he told her when she came back.

"I'm all right now," she told him. "Let's go."

After breakfast there was sightseeing of the Jain temples. Catherine was no longer in a mood for seeing them. All she could think of was that her tour was finished. She ached all over. Her emotions were raw, and she was totally at a loss as to what was going to become of her. She was completely exhausted emotionally and certainly she had not recovered from the months prior to her coming to India. She needed rest for her body and spirit, but she saw no way of finding it.

The rain had stopped and the hills were a beautiful green as they drove out of the area and onto the plains. She continued to follow the map and then Aadi told her they were going to Kumbhalgarh. That was the fort where he had promised to take her when she came to Udaipur. He hadn't forgotten.

They arrived in the afternoon; the fort within walls and on a high promontory. It was a magnificent sight.

"Aadi, I'm out of film. Is there somewhere I can buy some?"

"No, not here."

Chain parked the car and Aadi took Catherine alone to the wall where they climbed many steps to get to the top and then walked along it for a great distance. It was an easy climb and they took it slowly, enjoying the view of the hills surrounding the fort area. And there was the fort itself on the highest elevation. They could see school children climbing there, but no one was walking the wall as they were, and it was comforting to Catherine to be alone with Aadi this final time.

It was very warm and when they made their way down again, they found a small shop selling cold drinks. There they saw film also on sale and Aadi told her to get her camera in the car.

"What are you going to do?" she asked.

"Get your camera. I'll buy the film."

Returning with her camera, she watched as he put in the new roll.

"Wait here," he told her and started running back the way they had come.

"Don't run. It's too hot."

He didn't listen. He kept going. She followed at a leisurely pace and then realized that he was going all the way to the top of the wall where they had been. She could see him running in the distance and she felt a sense of warmth because he wanted her to have a remembrance of this place. And her heart was sad, knowing they were soon to say good-bye.

Catherine met him half way on his return. His shirt was wet with perspiration as he handed the camera over to her.

"Thank you, Aadi. But you shouldn't have run in this heat and it wasn't necessary to go all the way to the top."

"The sun is going and it was difficult to get a good photo shot. Come, we must go now."

As they drove away, they looked back at the fort and the wall. Aadi had Chain stop and he grabbed the camera to take more photos from the distance. Then they were on their way again, this time south on the road to Udaipur.

The sun made its journey over the Aravalli Hills and soon it was dark. At one point, Catherine touched Aadi's chest to see if his shirt was still wet. He seemed to be disturbed by the touch, and she realized she was being too intimate in front of Chain.

During the entire trip Aadi had not once held her hand as he had when she first visited Udaipur. Now, she felt the need to do this and took his hand in hers on the seat between them. There was a newspaper in the car, which he took with his left hand and covered their entwined hands. Catherine thought that it was a bit silly because there was no way that Chain could see their hands. It was dark and he was busy driving against all the lights of the on-coming traffic. But she said nothing and just held on as if her life depended on this hold.

Vaguely Catherine wondered what hotel he was going to take her to, but her mind was not functioning. She was just going along and letting him do the thinking. Her heart was aching and that was all she felt. The rest of her was numb.

Driving into the city, she recognized a few areas and suddenly it was very evident to her where they were. He had taken her to this place on his scooter the one night she was in Udaipur. She remembered they had gotten off the scooter and walked, and now Chain was driving up this same small, winding, narrow street. He stopped and Aadi opened the door.

"Come," he said, "Relax, it will be all right."

Catherine followed him out of the car and they proceeded down the narrow street to an open door. It was dim, but she remembered that it was the house of his friend, Jannu. Aadi's friend was standing there in the reception area, and Aadi went up to him.

"She's to have a room and she's to eat with the family," he told his friend.

"Perfect," his friend said. "Come." The two men walked across the courtyard and Jannu showed Aadi one room and then another. Catherine didn't move. Aadi called to her then.

"Come, see which room you like."

She looked at one, which was quite large and then when she saw the smaller one, she decided to take that one.

"I'm alone and I'll only be here about three days, so this will be fine," she told them.

Chain brought in her luggage, which took up much of the room space.

"I'll see you tomorrow," Aadi told her.

"All right," she said, and closed the door to the outside. Sitting on one of the twin beds, she sighed. It was over. She was in India and now on her own. It was black outside her windows. One was open with a screen and she listened to water gently lapping on the side of the house. A peace filled her and she knew suddenly that she would be all right.

CHAPTER TWENTY FOUR
KANKARWA HAVELI

Totally exhausted physically, mentally and emotionally, Catherine had found a place of refuge. She didn't know the night she arrived how long she would be staying, but it felt good and she knew she would be able to rest there. The small room suited her and although she couldn't see the lake for the darkness outside her window, she heard the gentle waves lapping at the foundation of the building. It soothed her and she was soon asleep.

The next morning the owner, the man called 'Jannu', came to her door and told her to go up to the roof and have her breakfast. She found the stairwell and remembered her climb to the roof when Aadi had brought her there in January. She sat at a table and a servant brought her a menu. She ordered something very simple; a banana, a dish of curd and a cup of Indian tea.

After breakfast she unpacked a few items for her bath and settled in. Aadi arrived later and told her that the room rent was Rs.400 per night, a discount of 50%. Catherine gave it no thought at all, trusting that Aadi would do whatever was right for her. He didn't stay long, but once in her room, the door was left open. Aadi looked at her and said, "I must be very disciplined now." She understood then that no one was to know of their intimate relationship, and that she was not to expect anything further from him in that way.

At noon Jannu came to her door and told her to come, that lunch was being served on the roof. The kitchen was there and a dining room, although at breakfast she had eaten outside. She followed Jannu to the roof and met the rest of the family who lived at the haveli; Jannu's brother, Subhash, his wife, Suchana and their three children, Divyarishi, 9, Tapasya 8 and Diksha 5. They all smiled at Catherine and tried to make her feel welcome, but she noticed that she was the only guest eating with the family. Jannu filled her plate and she watched as they ate, with their right hand only and served with their left. No one used a spoon, only fingers, so she did likewise. Only small portions were doled out, so there was no waste of food. More could be taken, but again it was served in small portions. These people were totally vegetarian, so ate vegetables, dal and chapattis as their main fare. Catherine found the food delicious and filling.

The first evening at the haveli she was once again summoned by Jannu to climb to the roof for dinner. It was after dark, the stairs and rooftop dimly lit. The scene was as she had remembered it from January when Aadi had brought her there and she was so enthralled by the beauty. There again was the Lake Palace, where she had spent two nights, it seemed now, so long ago. The Jag Mandir Palace in the farther distance lit in diffused light, and just near the haveli on the hillside, the City Palace. The lake shimmered with the glow of lights surrounding it, and Catherine took in a sharp breath as she experienced once again the magnificent view.

Jannu led her to a table outside where a candle was lit and food was served to the two of them. She dined only with him as the family gathered in the kitchen and ate there.

"Jannu, would it be all right if I stayed on a few more days?" she asked.

"Perfect," he answered. "How is your room? Would you like to see another?"

"Oh, no. I like my room very much. Listening to the water is very soothing to me. I lived near water all my life. The state I come from has ten thousand lakes."

"Ten thousand! Where in America is that?"

"Minnesota. It is in the middle of the United States on the Canadian border."

And so began Catherine's life in India, most particularly in Udaipur. Three days became five and then ten, and Catherine realized she was not ready yet to move on. God had directed Aadi to bring her here and she knew instinctively that she needed to be here to recover from the turmoil of the past nine months.

Aadi came every day and she looked forward to seeing him. He never spent more than ten minutes in her room, and then asked her to join him in Reception where they would talk with Jannu. Occasionally he would kiss her briefly when he arrived but she ached for him all the time. He brought her pens and a notebook, and when she expressed a need for a frame for her icon of the Blessed Virgin, he measured it and had a frame made for her.

There were three niches, 'takhs', they were called, all deep shelves in her room. One opened to the lake with both a window and a screen. Another had a screen above it opening to the courtyard, but she kept the wooden door on it closed for privacy. Here she kept her medications, her purse and a few other supplies. The other takh was on the opposite wall with a rod above it to hang clothes. It was here that she decided to place her icon, her crucifix, a Shiva idol, Tibetan prayer bells and gong. She prayed and meditated before it every day.

The icon, a favorite of Catherine's, was a print of 'Our Lady of Compassion'. The artist was Sr. Mary Charles and Catherine often had watched as she painted it in the barn studio. It was the largest icon Mary Charles had ever done and had to be lowered to the ground through a large window on the second floor of the barn, and transported by van to Minneapolis. The original now hung in the chapel of St. Olaf"s Church. Catherine had seen it there also and loved it very much. She purchased the print from her friend, who found a tube so that it could be rolled and protected for the journey to India. Now it looked out at Catherine from the simple frame that Aadi had made for it.

It was the centerpiece around which everything else was added. Her bible and a few prayer books were laid there along with a 5 x 7 framed print of St. Benedict that Mary Charles had given her as a 'going-away' gift.

"Catherine," Aadi said one day, "your shrine needs a lovely cloth. Do you have something to put there?"

"Why, yes I do as a matter of fact. And you are right. It does need something underneath." She remembered there was a piece of Chinese silk in a shade of deep pink that she had packed for an entirely different purpose, but it would suit well here. When it was all rearranged, the effect was lovely.

She was delighted with the simple decor of the room and learned very early that it was Jannu's tasteful ideas that went into all the areas of the haveli. Her bathroom was at one end of the room, just beyond a beautiful arch extending the width of the room. There was a door for privacy, but it was open above to the 15 foot ceiling. To compensate for that and also to add a touch of Rajasthan, Jannu had fashioned a canopy over the bathroom area in a simple cream color fabric to match the walls and accented with a border of a typical Rajasthani design in red. The bathroom itself was tiled in white; floors and walls, with a comfortable white porcelain western toilet, a built-in white sink and a shower area with good plumbing and 24 hour hot water. Surely these bathrooms here at Kankarwa Haveli were the best in India except for the five-star hotels, where you paid western prices and expected western comfort and amenities.

Outside her window there was a wall and steps leading into the lake. People from the neighborhood gathered there, washing clothes, bathing and shampooing their hair. Men came early in the morning and the women and children later. All day there was a constant flow of chatter and laughter, mostly of children playing on the steps and in the water and the incessant pounding of women beating their clothes. Catherine wondered about all the pollution and how these people survived it. There were open sewers running along the streets and all eventually emptied into the lake. She watched as men and women brushed their teeth and no doubt urinated and defecated there as well.

Eventually, Catherine was shown all the rooms for clients at the haveli. Each was unique, decorated in simple, yet elegant style of traditional Rajasthan. Two rooms were decorated with old frescos on the walls and floors. One of these rooms was under the magnificent dome of the haveli. Here as you lay in bed you could look up into the lovely circular space created by this example of Rajasthani Hindu architecture. No telephones and no TVs were in any room to disturb the tranquility of the haveli. There were two levels above the ground floor with a total of thirteen rooms for guests. The family rooms were primarily on the second level with a 'puja', or worship room and a private storage room on the third.

The building was entered from a large double doorway of the original heavy black wood and impressive closures. Just inside the entrance on the right was a desk for Reception and on the left, cane chairs, or 'mudhas', for sitting and relaxing. Soft cream-colored walls were accented by the jewel tones of blooming bougainvillea and other greenery in the courtyard and on all levels of the haveli. The floors were of the original stone; blackish stone of Kota at the entrance and in the courtyard, gray stone of Chittor in most rooms and on the roof, and another stone, Nimbhara, from Madras in other rooms. Heavy pillars were made from Sajjangarh stone, very strong and utilitarian. Many of the floors in the rooms were covered with colorful darri rugs.

Catherine learned much about the history of Udaipur, this family and the haveli from Jannu as she spent many hours talking with him in the reception area. A 'haveli', she was told, is a mansion with a courtyard and found only in the state of Rajasthan. This particular haveli had been in the same family for 180 years and had been built for the family use when the Maharana of Mewar needed the services of the men in Udaipur.

Rajasthan was once a land of numerous kingdoms, ruled by maharajas and maharanas. The latter is found only in the once princely state of Mewar, because the maharanas were warriors as well as kings, and were the last hold-outs to the Mughal Empire. They fought for their freedom and never capitulated, or formed alliances by marrying their women into mughal families. The capital of Mewar was Chittor, and time after time as the city was sacked and destroyed, the women sacrificed themselves to flames rather than give themselves to the enemy. When the royal princes gather now, the Maharana of Mewar sits higher than all the others, bestowing the ultimate respect due to him.

The royal house of Mewar dates back to 728 AD. It is very proud of its history, especially for being Hindu and for never losing its honor to the Mughal Empire. In 1567, when Chittor was captured and plundered for the third time, Rana Udai Singh fled to the Aravalli Hills. As the story goes, there he came upon a sage who advised him to build his new city on that very spot. Udai Singh wisely followed the advice and the beautiful city of Udaipur now stands majestically on the shores of Lake Pichola. It is a city of white; walls, houses, shops, temples, palaces, all nestled in a valley surrounded by the Aravalli hills, the oldest mountains in the world and which divide Rajasthan northeast to southwest. Shimmering water from five lakes and a profusion of luxurious gardens render this the most charming, romantic city of all India.

Kankarwa Haveli acquired its name from the family village located 60 km from Udaipur. This family of Rajputs is descended from 16th century Maharana Udai Singh of Udaipur. They are known by the surname of Singh, but the family name is Ranawat, meaning 'son of Rana'. Rajputs were all descendents of the rulers and were given land titles in the villages, a village fort from which to defend, and a house in the city. They were in charge over the entire village or villages and reported directly to the ruler. This privilege of 'thakur' was given to the oldest son and passed down to his son.

For some years this haveli was rented out to a school for boys, but was reclaimed in 1995 to renovate it into a guest house and a city home for the family. Janardan, better known as 'Jannu', was the prime mover, although every decision was a communal one including the entire family. Mama and Papa lived primarily in the fort, or castle, in the village of Kankarwa, but often visited the city. The oldest son, Subhash moved from the village immediately with his wife, Suchana and their three children to occupy a room at the haveli while the renovation was being done.

Viburaj, the second son, oversees the family farm some distance northeast of the Village of Kankarwa. He is married to Prem and they have a small daughter, Uma. Jannu is the third son and not married. A fourth son, Nirhendra , or 'Nirhu', works the family farm lands with Papa in Kankarwa Village.

Jannu attended college and at one time it was his desire to become a doctor. However these plans never materialized and he subsequently worked in a travel agency. It was through this experience that he learned the needs and desires of western clients and used this knowledge in the remodeling of the haveli.

There are many havelis in the old city, and travelers are drawn to these converted homes where the cost is less than hotels and where they can experience a life of simplicity and graciousness. Often guests, planning to stay for 2 or 3 days, remain weeks and even months, as it proved to be just that in Catherine's case. There are many repeat clients and many referrals.

When the family heard that Catherine wanted to learn Hindi, they were delighted and the children were anxious to teach her. She wondered about that, but Aadi was enthusiastic about the idea and brought some books for her to study from. She already had a few that she had bought in the States, but it was good to have more. The children were delightful and very friendly. They came to her room often and started calling her, 'Auntie'.

Every day Catherine worked on the Hindi alphabet, writing it and trying to pronounce each one correctly. She found it a beautiful, phonetic language, but it was difficult to twist her tongue in an unfamiliar way. There were two 't's, two 'th's, two 'd's, and two 'dh's. Another 'd' sounded like an 'r' and again the tongue had to be placed just right for that pronunciation. Catherine didn't do very well at the beginning and one day Tapasya kept shaking her head and finally yelled in her ear.

"Tapasya", Catherine cautioned her, "I can hear. I just can't pronounce it right."

It wasn't long before the children decided to give her homework and enjoyed correcting her work. They loved giving check marks, which to them meant it was right. Then five pointed stars became the fun of the day as they filled her pages with them. As they became more familiar with 'Auntie', they decided to play school with her and soon Hindi became just another subject. Catherine was given simple math problems and lessons in English.

"Hey, this is MY language," she told them. But all to no avail. One day she was required to memorize an English poem. She really enjoyed it and she was becoming very attached to the children, especially Divyu who was the most demonstrative. Tapasya was somewhat reserved and Diksha seemed quite remote much of the time. Catherine felt that with her she was on trial, but knew that eventually she would warm up to her.

Suchana also tried to help with the Hindi, but Catherine knew she needed a language teacher because she didn't seem to be making any progress in the present situation. Catherine felt the kindness of this family and realized very soon what honest people they were. They were very spiritual and prayed as a family every morning before the children went off to school. Subhash went about the haveli after puja, sprinkling water to bless the house. Again in the evening they would gather in the puja room and pray before the evening meal. Catherine wondered why she was never invited to join them, as Aadi had told her that he had mentioned to Jannu that she was very spiritual also.

Every day she would listen for the sound of Aadi's voice in Reception and her heart would fill with joy upon seeing him. He came often to play Cricket in the courtyard with Divyu, who was an avid fan of the game. And Catherine soon realized that Aadi was an important person to this family. They always referred to him as 'Aadi bhai sa', an honorary title meaning 'elder brother'.

Soon after her arrival at Kankarwa, Aadi came to tell her that he was going to Mumbai on family business and that he would be gone for two days. Catherine felt devastated, and although she knew she was over-reacting, she couldn't help herself. On the third day after Aadi left, Catherine started looking and waiting for him to come to the haveli. When he didn't come, once again she felt devastated. Her heart was longing to see him and she ached all the time. Then on the fourth day she happened to meet Chain and stopped to talk with him. She never mentioned Aadi to him as she was careful never to bring up his name to Jannu or anyone else. It was important to her that no one suspect there was or had been anything between them. She knew without Aadi warning her that he felt this strongly, and she was determined to protect his reputation in this city, which was his home and place of business.

"Hello, Chain. How are you?"

"Fine. You?"

"Good, Chain."

"Aadi come in morning."

"Aadi? What do you mean?"

"Aadi in Bombay. Come back tomorrow."

"Oh, yes, I see. Thank you for telling me, Chain."

So she knew then he had not yet returned and her heart went back to normal. Catherine felt this chance meeting with Chain was a blessing that God was watching out for her, that He knew her heart and how she was suffering. She immediately gave thanks to Him in a silent prayer.

She was having many sleepless nights, waking and sobbing. Catherine knew that it would be difficult to have an intimate relationship with Aadi, but felt that if he really wanted to be with her, he would find somewhere they could be.

"What is happening to me?" she asked herself. "Is this what I want? I love this man, and it is hopeless. There seems to be more anxiety and pain than joy and happiness. I keep praying for a miracle–a closeness with this man–that he will open his heart to me.

"God has been so good to me, answering all my petitions in the positive. Will this just take some time? Do I need more patience? This Aadi Abhimani is such a good man, a kind man. He took such great care of me in spite of his remoteness. I want to get to the bottom of this relationship. What happened to change it?"

Jannu had encouraged her to walk about the city. At first she told him she was afraid she'd get lost, but he just laughed at her and told her to go and move about. Finally she started off one morning after breakfast. It was a fascinating experience, walking in the narrow streets with no sidewalks, dodging people, cows, donkeys, dogs, goats, an occasional elephant, many scooters, cars, buses, and motor-driven rikshas. There were children in various uniforms headed for school and younger children squatting over the open gutters along the sides of the streets doing their daily. She also had to be careful where she stepped because there were numerous cow paddies, which were left to dry and eventually picked up to be used for fuel. The lower caste ladies, or the 'sweeper class', were out cleaning the streets with their brooms, picking up the litter. Catherine noticed how colorfully they were dressed, heads covered with a long veil, which was tucked into their waists then draped over shoulders and head. They were heavily ornamented also with silver bracelets and bangles on their ankles and wrists, nose rings and earrings.

Store fronts lined the streets, Hindu shrines and temples were in great abundance. Smiling faces of shopkeepers and warm greetings from children met her at every turn. Catherine's eyes were assaulted with the bright fabrics in hues of pink, red, yellow, orange, purple and blue seen only in Rajasthan. There too she saw bangles in glass, gold and heavy silver; earrings, nose rings, toe rings, finger rings. In almost every other shop miniature paintings were exhibited and sold. Hand-loomed fabrics of every description were to be found; embroidery, appliqué and mirror work, shawls and carpets in great profusion. There were a few fixed-price shops, government controlled, but for the most part, bargaining was the customary practice.

Markets in the early morning had an abundance of appetizing vegetables and fruits, some common to Catherine, others uncommon. Each farmer used his own scales and weights, selling from a cart or sitting on the ground. She saw carrots a deep red in color, and various shapes and sizes of eggplant, known here as 'brinjal', snow white cauliflower (gobi), juicy red tomatoes, freshly picked spinach (palak), bright green sweet peppers and many varieties of hot peppers (chilies), potatoes (aloo), onions (pyaj), thick, heavy ginger, some so fresh they were still pink and reminded her of shrimp, peas in their pods (matar), cabbage, and beans. Mouth watering papaya, watermelon, mangoes, pineapple, grapes, oranges and sweet limes were to be found also.

Catherine never lost her way, and walked in different directions each day in order to learn more about this part of the city which was once walled in and had several gates. The closest gate to the haveli was Hathipol, or Elephant Gate. It was an easy walk there, first passing another landmark, the Clock Tower. Close to Kankarwa was the famous and important Hindu temple, 'Jagdish Mandir'. The idol here was known as 'Jaganath', an aspect of Vishnu, in black stone and ornately dressed several times a day by the priests. Women and men chanted morning and evening and as people arrived, they clanged the bell which resounded throughout the temple area.

A longer walk was to Surajpol, where there was another profusion of markets. Here was a fine sweet shop, shoe stores, and shops selling pots and pans. Located between Hathipol and Surajpol was Delhi Gate. Many streets led off from Delhi Gate, the best known was the Bapu Bazaar; dress shops, photo shops, shoe stores, card shops, and so many others too numerous to remember.

Walking in another direction from the haveli, Catherine found herself in the Muslim section. She wasn't too sure where she was going, but traveled in a huge circle, passing the steel market, where a sect of Muslims known as Borhas worked and lived. These men wore distinctive white lacey pill boxes and the ladies were attired in long skirts, blouses and short capes with attached bonnets, their heads always covered.

Soon Catherine found a route that she continued to follow every day. It passed the Jagdish Temple and went deeply into the old city behind the City Palace in the opposite direction from Hatipol, and beyond shops to a residential area. Eventually she came out on Lake Palace Road, where she walked along hotels and found Sajjan Niwas Garh or the Gulab Bagh (Rose Garden), as it was known. It was an immense garden with many trees, plants, walkways, buildings and on the far side, a zoo. This was a true haven for Catherine. She loved walking there enjoying the magnificent old trees, flowering plants and shaded paths. Sometimes she would run into wild dogs that were not friendly and she tried to avoid those areas where they were found. One path she traveled became a spiritual arbor for her. The trees overhead formed a canopy and diffused light penetrated here, making her think of it as a gateway to heaven. One day she brought her camera and captured the sight. Always she prayed when she walked, but in this special place she felt God's love and spirit touching her soul.

From the Gulab Bagh she walked toward the City Palace and found the boat landing for the Lake Palace Hotel. It seemed so long ago now that she had been there as a guest and had met Aadi for the first time. Memories crowded her mind as she recalled meeting him in that spot for a night 'on the town', giving him an embrace in thanksgiving for a beautiful evening, and jumping behind him on his scooter the next morning in full view of a group of Americans taking a bus. Catherine followed the road upward to a part of the City Palace known as Fateh Prakash, where there was a restaurant and a room filled with crystal. Climbing along the winding road, she passed the Zenana, once the palace of the queens and now the residence of the Maharana Arvind Singh. Further along were the royal crimson gates leading to the Shiv Niwas Palace Hotel, which opens its elegant arms in a crescent-shaped facade; a magnificent swimming pool surrounded by trees, flowers and a graceful fountain, as the main focus. Pool side tables and chairs accommodate guests and visitors alike for ala-carte or buffet dining.

The last landmark on her route was the City Palace Museum, fronted by an immense square where at one time a hundred elephants stood for inspection. High above the entrance she saw the sun emblem indicating the House of Mewar. Walking down and out of the main gates, she was once again in a market area, but making a sharp left turn she followed a residential lane that led directly to Kankarwa Haveli. Catherine walked this route at a good pace and it took her an hour and a quarter from start to finish. She thought it was perhaps a total of five miles.

Soon a routine was established. Catherine would arise at 5 AM, meditate, then dress and go to breakfast at 7. By 7:30 she was in the streets of the old city. This is where she met Chain when he told her Aadi was due home from Mumbai the following day.

Catherine felt it was a blessing from God, meeting Chain and receiving that message. She waited and waited for Aadi to come to the haveli, but he didn't arrive until nightfall when Jannu and she were on the roof after dinner. Her heart started to sing with joy upon seeing him. He sat next to her and she noticed a wad of cotton in his right ear.

"Why do you have cotton in your ear?" she asked him.

"I have an ear ache and my father put in oil."

"Oh, I'm sorry. When did it start?"

"This morning on the train. I think I put the cue tip in too far when I was cleaning my ear."

Aadi and Jannu conversed in Hindi most of the time, but Catherine did not feel left out. It was, after all, their language and they felt most comfortable in it. Just Aadi's presence, hearing him and seeing him and being with him was a blessing to her.

The next morning the strangest thing happened to her. As she washed her face she noticed her left ear hurt to the touch. She pulled on the lobe and it hurt even more. Aadi's right ear was infected and now her left ear hurt? This was crazy, but just coincidence? She went on her walk as usual.

Also in her routine, was coming home, as she now thought of the haveli, taking a shower and washing her hair. She was using Menoxidil for her balding, and needed to apply it every day. What she didn't realize was that by washing, setting, and drying it every day, her hair was losing all its natural oils and after some months started to break. Eventually she stopped the Menoxidil also because it was not growing new hair.

After her personal clean-up, she washed clothes, hung them up on a rod in front of her window, then wrote letters and in her journal. One day she hung some clothes on the rod over her shrine. Jannu happened to stop in and just stared at the sight.

"Catherine," he finally said, "Would you hang laundry in your church?"

Oops! "Why, no, Jannu. Of course not."

"Then why hang up wash over your shrine?"

"You are absolutely right. I wasn't thinking. I just didn't have enough room on the other rod, but I'll take them off immediately."

"Do you have another cloth? One to hang over the shrine?"

"Why, yes I do. I never thought of it."

"It would look nice."

So digging into her large suitcase she found another cloth, a cotton piece in pink that she had purchased when she had visited Manipur, a state in northeastern India, a few years back. But this cloth was stiff, so she decided it would look better under her shrine and the silk piece draped above, which is what she did and once again the effect was beautiful, more so than before. She called Jannu in to see it and he heartily approved.

Aadi did not come to the haveli the day after he returned and Catherine wondered how his ear was. When she found the reception area free that evening, she tried to phone him, but the call wouldn't go through. She was unaware at the time that she needed to dial 0 before the number. Then the next day Aadi came by holding his ear and asked her to look at it.

He bent down and she tried pulling the lobe aside, but without an otoscope it was impossible to see into the ear. Jannu laughed and said the ear was just fine.

"I had so much pain last night I could not sleep. I could not lie down."

"Aadi, you need an antibiotic," she told him. "Are you taking one?"

"No, I've never taken antibiotics."

"Aadi, an ear infection can be very dangerous. I have some Doxycycline. Will you take it?"

"All right."

Catherine went to her room and found the full, unopened bottle that she had brought with her from the States, in the event she would need to have a good antibiotic. But it was very necessary now for Aadi to have it.

"How do I take it? With tea, water?" he asked.

"It doesn't matter. And start taking it now. You are to take two every day until they are all used up. This is a ten day supply."

"But do I take it at meals or after?"

"It doesn't matter, Aadi. Just take them. And you must take all of them, even though you will feel well within 24 hours. It is important that you continue to take all until the bottle is finished."

"All right I will do that."

Later she was discussing Aadi's ear infection with Jannu.

"When he was in so much pain, why didn't he go to a doctor?" she asked.

"Oh, Catherine, you don't know Aadi's father. He believes in Ayurvedic medicine only. He would be very angry if Aadi went to a medical doctor. And oh, he is strong, very strong minded."

"But Jannu, his ear was swollen in front and in back. I was very afraid of mastoiditis, which can spread to the brain. It was important for him to have antibiotics and I know this will help him, especially since he's never taken any before. Just so he takes all of it so that it completely kills the infection. Otherwise it could recur."

The following day Catherine noticed her left ear no longer hurt and when Aadi came to see her he told her his pain had left him. It was then she told him about her ear ache and how it too had disappeared that very morning. They both laughed about it, but Catherine knew that it was more than coincidence. It was another connection with this man. She was sure of it.

The days passed and although they were full and Catherine was getting her much needed rest as well, she was not happy. She missed Aadi all of the time and ached when she couldn't see him every day. Always she wondered where he lived and didn't understand why he never showed her or invited her to his home. However, she never brought up the subject, waiting for him to suggest it. On her walk she would look at one house after another wondering if he lived in it or nearby. She was sure that she was in the right area, but there being so few street names, and knowing his address had no street attached, there was no way she could find it on her own. Certainly she would never ask anyone, especially not Jannu.

One afternoon she sat talking with Jannu in Reception. He mentioned that Aadi wanted some clients who were to stay at Kankarwa, to have their rooms when they arrived early and have the rooms late on the day of departure. Jannu was somewhat upset because allowing that meant he would lose money having to hold those rooms from the night before and not being able to sell them the following day until evening. He said Aadi pleaded, so he agreed. Suddenly, Catherine became aware that perhaps Aadi had taken advantage of his friend asking special favors for her, and she became teary-eyed.

"Jannu, is that what Aadi did with me?"

"What do you mean? Auntie, say again." By this time he too was calling her 'Auntie' because it was easier for him to say than 'Catherine', and also out of respect for an older person.

"Jannu, Aadi brought me here and told you. He didn't ask you. He told you to give me a room and that I was to eat with the family. No one eats with the family. Just me! Besides, because of Aadi you gave me a 50% discount. I'm sure you didn't expect me to stay this long."

"Auntie, I trust Aadi. He is 'bhai sa'. I knew he wouldn't ask me to have someone who isn't good for the haveli. There is no problem. You can stay as long as you want."

"But Jannu, let me pay more for my room, and charge me for my food."

"No, Auntie. Just leave it."

"Jannu, I don't want to be a burden on the family."

"Auntie, you are no burden."

At this point Catherine excused herself because she was going to cry and didn't want to do so in front of Jannu. Obviously she was not herself yet and became emotionally upset very easily.

As she climbed to the roof that evening for dinner, Suchana stopped her outside of her door.

"Auntie," she said, putting her arms around her, "You NO burden. You just like my mama. You NO burden."

Catherine cried then and held this sweet little lady in her arms. Suchana, without her platform shoes barely reached Catherine's throat, she was so tiny. Obviously Jannu had talked to her about their conversation. It was a very close family, and they shared everything.

CHAPTER TWENTY FIVE

BIRTHDAYS AND VISITOR

"Good Morning, Auntie"

"Good morning, Hansraj. I'll have my usual; curd, banana and chai."

"Auntie, no banana."

"Do you have an orange?"

"No, Auntie."

"An apple?"

"No, Auntie."

"Hansraj, do you have any fruit?"

"No, Auntie."

"All right. Just the curd and chai then."

The next morning on the roof Hansraj came to her smiling, bringing her two bananas.

"One banana, Hansraj."

"But, Auntie, you didn't have one yesterday."

Catherine found that very sweet and very typical of Indian culture, but on another plane, it was hysterically funny. When she told Jannu about it, he laughed so hard, she thought he'd fall out of his mudha.

"He knows what you eat every morning. But he doesn't tell me in the evening when I go to market if we are out of bananas. He doesn't think."

Catherine was sitting in Reception with Jannu one afternoon when a man walked in and Jannu introduced him as 'Sanjay'.

"You are Catherine, Aadi's friend?"

"Yes," she answered warily.

"Your faxes came into my shop."

"What?"

"Oh, oh, Auntie," laughed Jannu. "Nothing secret now."

She could have died right then. Certainly she wished she could disappear somewhere. Into this man's shop? Aadi had told her the faxes she sent were very, very private. Private? Aiiiiii! All the lip marks on the faxes and some very, very personal communication. What was wrong with Aadi not to have warned her? She couldn't wait to see him.

He came that evening and as they sat on the roof, Catherine brought up the subject.

"Aadi, I met Sanjay today."

"Yes?"

"Aadi, you told me my faxes were very private."

"Yes."

"But they came into his shop and he could read them!"

"No, he doesn't understand much English."

"Aadi, you know they were VERY personal and the kisses on them!"

"Relax," he laughed, "It is all right."

"All right? Do you know how embarrassed I was when Jannu told me who he was and Sanjay said he got my faxes in his shop?"

"Believe me, it is all right. Relax."

What could she say? He took it lightly, so she had no choice but to do likewise. Aadi took her to the bank the next day and Catherine was upset to the point of weeping. He introduced her to a man at the Bank of Baroda by the name of Mr. Jalla. He was very nice, but there were so many people crowded into a tiny space, all waiting for his attention. Catherine sat across from his desk and there were four people plus Aadi seated immediately to one side of the desk.

"How much money do you want?" he asked her.

She couldn't believe it. All these people watching and waiting their turn. Nothing was private.

"Two thousand dollars," she answered, handing him her passport and visa card.

"TWO thousand?"

"You don't need that much," Aadi told her.

Catherine was embarrassed and angry. Why were they questioning her? She didn't think it was anyone's business how much she withdrew from her American bank.

"Believe me, Catherine," said Aadi. "You don't need that much."

"How much can I get then?"

"Just take one thousand," Aadi advised.

She agreed to that and the paper work was completed. Then she had to go to a specific teller to get her cash. Aadi went with her and helped her to count all the bills. By the time she got out of the bank, she was shaking.

Aadi took her then on his scooter to his garden on the east side of the city. It seemed a long way to her. They stopped at a walled-in garden the size of two house plots. Aadi opened the padlocked gate and they entered what seemed to Catherine an almost dense forest. There were so many trees and they followed a path which led to a deep, good-sized pool, which was not for swimming, beside a cleared area. Behind this was a shed. A man was working around, but he left soon after Aadi and Catherine arrived. She spied roses and many flowering plants.

Bougainvillea grew along one entire wall. When she asked what color they were because at that time there were no blooms, he told her there were all colors. Toward the back of the garden an entire area was planted with vegetables. Aadi pointed out the various fruit trees and showed her the bee hives in them. He said they didn't bother anyone and he just left them. There were more plants that were not in pots and needed a spot in the earth, but he told her there was no more room.

Catherine noticed there was an empty lot behind the garden back wall and suggested that he expand and buy the property there.

"Oh, no. It is very expensive."

"I'll buy it for you," she told him.

"No, I couldn't do that," he said.

She then opened her purse and asked how much she owed for the car and Chain's services during their tour. He told her and being so unfamiliar with rupees, she told him to take what was needed. Aadi counted it out and showed it to her.

"Please take money for your services also," she told him.

"No," he answered.

"Aadi, I told you that I would pay you because I didn't want you to be losing money by escorting me on this tour."

"No. I will not take money from you." He was adamant, so Catherine didn't argue with him.

Back at the haveli Aadi became very animated and started shouting at Jannu.

"She's mad at me!" he told him.

"What are you talking about?" she asked. "I'm not mad at you."

"At the bank you wanted to cash two thousand dollars."

"Yes I did, but I was, and still am, upset that my business was being held in front of all those people. I'm used to doing my banking in private. I don't appreciate everyone knowing my business, and I was embarrassed about arguing in front of them also."

"But this is India and two thousand was too much."

"OK, but I need to have cash to pay bills."

"You're in India now and your bills are not that high. Believe me."

Of course Aadi was correct, but she didn't realize it yet and she could still feel all the eyes of those strangers on her as she was conducting her affairs.

Aadi came into her room with her and sat on her bed next to her. He stroked her arm and told her that Jannu had told him how emotional she gets at times. So Jannu had noticed her crying on the roof too? Often at night after dinner, she would stand looking out over the water at the Jag Mandir Palace remembering when Aadi had taken her so forcefully into his arms and kissed her. She could still feel his strength and the gentleness of his kiss. How she wished she could return to that moment in time.

"Catherine, why don't you talk to Jannu?"

"Aadi, I can't just pour out my guts to him."

"You can talk to him."

"No, I can't, Aadi. I cannot."

"All right."

"Aadi, can I take you to dinner for your birthday? Would that be a problem?"

"No problem if I'm in town, but food is not good in restaurant."

"How do you usually celebrate your birthday?"

"The family prays before the goddess and we have friends come for dinner."

"Oh, I see. Aadi, how do you feel about my staying here for a while?"

"It is fine. You must do what is right for you."

"Aadi, you wouldn't take money from me for the tour. I would like instead to take you on a tour of my country. Would you like that?

"Who doesn't want to go to America?" he laughed.

"When would be a good time for you?"

"May or June would be best, but it is very difficult to get visas to the United States."

"I'll go to the embassy with you in Delhi."

"All right."

"I want to call the States. Where can I do that?"

"Come, we'll ask Jannu."

Jannu advised Aadi where to take her and they set off walking. She was surprised they went down to the Lake Palace Road, which was quite a way from the haveli. Catherine thought they would just stop in one of the numerous shops close by. But when they arrived, she realized it was Sanjay's shop, 'Shiva Telecom'. Sanjay dialed for her and she spoke to Robert, assuring him that she was fine and giving him her address and the phone number at Kankarwa.

Aadi was in conversation with Sanjay and then phoned a friend of his. Catherine could not understand the Hindi, but noticed Aadi becoming more and more agitated. He raised his voice and stomped his foot. At one point, he turned around to her and asked her if, in the United States, people drove vehicles through parks. She shook her head, and he continued to argue with the person on the phone.

After hanging up the phone, Aadi continued the conversation with someone who had just entered the shop. Again he became upset, as this person obviously did not agree with him either. Then he explained to her that no cars and trucks were allowed in the Gulab Bagh and now they wanted to change the law, thinking that more people would use the garden if they could drive in. Of course she agreed with Aadi that having vehicles in the garden would destroy the ambiance and serenity that now prevailed.

They left the shop and Aadi was tense and seething. She wanted to take him in her arms and comfort him. She wanted to make love with him to ease his tension, but she wasn't even allowed to touch his arm or hand. He barely spoke on the way back to the haveli.

"I'm all right," he assured her at one point, as she looked at him with concern. But as soon as they entered the haveli, Aadi burst out telling Jannu of the situation. Jannu made light of it and told him to relax, but Catherine knew that gardens were almost sacred to Aadi and the thought of defiling one with unlimited vehicular traffic was making him very upset

Catherine was becoming more and more desolate. There was no intimacy between her and Aadi. Not even in his garden, in the privacy of all those trees, did he even move to embrace or kiss her. She felt confused and abandoned.

While talking with Jannu one day, he mentioned a friend of his whose name was 'Dagmar'. She was German and a high profile travel agent in Germany. Jannu told her that Dagmar's husband was of some Italian aristocracy and they had four daughters, including one pair of twins. He said that Dagmar's husband was an architect and they had lived in India for some years. Then the family lost a great deal of money and Jannu suggested that Dagmar go into the travel business since she already had many connections in India. She took his suggestion and was now making a lot of money. Dagmar was in India now, he told Catherine, and would soon be in Udaipur. At some point he also told her that Dagmar was in love with someone else and he had advised her to live a parallel life and that way maintain and prolong the relationship. Catherine's heart and mind did one gigantic leap. Was this Aadi's German girlfriend?

Aadi was scheduled to go out on tour. He told her he would come to her to say good-bye the next day, but after waiting until nightfall, Catherine felt depressed and saddened that he hadn't come. She started off to Sanjay's shop to call the States and met Aadi on his bicycle. She was very surprised to see him.

"I was just coming to see you," he said.

"I thought you had already left."

"No, I leave tonight."

"I was walking down to Sanjay's, but let's go back to the haveli."

"No, I have many things to do before I leave, so I will say good-bye now."

Catherine was desolate. There, standing in the road, she could not touch him and she wanted so much to feel his arms about her. She rested her hand on the handle of his bike and he looked down at it. Suddenly she realized this might not look good to other people in the market, so removed her hand.

A few days later, Dagmar arrived. Catherine stayed in her room and tried to see her without being seen. She was slim and blond, not particularly attractive, with a rather 'washed-out' look, but Jannu had told her that she was 55 and looked younger than that. Jannu spent the afternoon talking to her, but Catherine didn't go out to meet her. When Catherine was called to the roof for dinner, she realized that Dagmar and her client were joining her and Jannu. It was very difficult for Catherine to eat, but she didn't have to converse with them because they were talking about where the client was going to visit, and what he was going to do. Suddenly, Dagmar and Jannu looked up with smiles on their faces. Catherine had her back to the door, so she didn't see Aadi enter. She nearly choked on her food. He sat next to her in the closest empty chair and asked her to say something in Hindi. She felt embarrassed and said nothing. Divyarishi came in and immediately jumped on Aadi's lap. Ridiculously Catherine wished she could do that and felt envious of Divyu. Then he also got interested in the subject that Dagmar, her client and Jannu were discussing and joined in the conversation. Suchana came in, sat next to Catherine on her other side and shortly motioned for her to leave with her. Catherine went to her room totally devastated.

"Was Aadi going to visit Dagmar in her room?" she wondered. But a knock came on her door instead. Aadi came in and said it was late, but he wanted to know how she was. He kissed her good-night and said he'd see her the next day. He had brought his clients to Udaipur.

Catherine was having a particularly difficult time. She found herself crying much of every day, weeping silently on the roof after dark and waking in the night to cry again. Obviously she was extremely depressed. In spite of her daily routine, her constant thoughts of Aadi and the deterioration of their relationship were affecting her most adversely.

"If he showed me any of the passion and loving he did in January and over the phone," she told herself, "I would feel better, but I have nothing now except his concern for my physical needs. My emotional needs are bereft."

Perhaps she should go to Delhi, but after sending Sunil a fax, she hadn't heard from him. Catherine also thought of Belgaum and decided a visit with Asha and Ramu might do her some good, although she was afraid of becoming a burden on them.

On the morning of the 14th Aadi brought his three American clients to Kankarwa. Aadi came to Catherine's room and told her that he was having a luncheon the following day and he wanted her to come with Jannu, and told her that his clients would be there also. He didn't know at that time where it was going to be. She was pleased that she was being included in his birthday festivities. Jannu told Catherine later that Aadi had wanted his luncheon at the haveli, but Jannu had not agreed to that. Jannu said Suchana was too busy with the children and 20 or more guests would be too much for her. Suchana was an asthmatic and not well.

After they were settled in at the haveli, Aadi took his clients sight-seeing, and then dinner was served to them in the dining room, but without Aadi. When Catherine went up for dinner, she decided to join them, as they were the first Americans she had seen since she had arrived. She had talked to other clients at the haveli and although she met many British and Australians, it was like 'being home' talking to her own countrymen. They were lovely people; two women friends and a young man who had joined them in India. It was a high class tour, staying at prestigious hotels and traveling in their own private van.

The older woman, Ann, asked Catherine what she did there in Udaipur. When Catherine told her that she walked every day, Ann expressed her wish to join her in the morning. Catherine was delighted to have her company. They met for breakfast and started off on Catherine's favored route. It was a very interesting experience

"Are you enjoying your tour?" Catherine asked Ann.

"Oh, it is wonderful. We have seen so much and Aadi is an excellent guide."

"What have you done here in Udaipur?"

"We went to the City Palace, also had a boat ride on the lake. We saw a beautiful garden and went to Eklingji and Nagda yesterday. And we had tea at Aadi's uncle's house and also visited Aadi's home. It is so beautiful with many plants and trees and he has a library filled with books on gardening."

Catherine was astounded. He had brought these strangers to his house and never her?

"So you met his parents?"

"Oh, yes. His mother made us tea. She looks much older than his father who is close to 70, Aadi said. She doesn't speak English, but his father does. I wonder how old Aadi is."

"What would be your guess?"

"Probably in his 50s. He is balding and his hair is gray."

"He will be 43 tomorrow."

"Really!"

"If you look at his skin; his hands and face, you can see that he is still young."

"Then the luncheon will be in celebration of his birthday."

"Yes, Ann, but please don't mention his birthday. It would embarrass him."

"I won't. In fact, I won't say anything to the others until after we leave. You know, I wondered why he wasn't married, because Indian men marry early. I thought perhaps he might be homosexual."

"Oh, no! I assure you, he is not," Catherine laughed.

"Well, then he told us he goes to Europe to live two or three months every year and that he travels for three weeks also with a girlfriend. It was good to hear that he has some fun. I asked him if he'd rather be given dollars for his tip at the end of the tour because he could use it in Europe. He said he'd like that."

Catherine wondered how to dress for the birthday luncheon, and decided to ask Jannu's advice.

"Jannu, should I dress in a sari?"

"Oh, no Auntie. That is too formal. It is for lunch."

She decided to wear a skirt that Suchana liked very much and decided to adorn herself with Indian jewelry; ankle bracelets, bangles, necklace and earrings.

"You look smart, Auntie," Suchana told her.

Jannu hired a car and they drove to Aadi's garden where he had decided to hold the party. There she met his parents, his sister, and his 'uncle', 'auntie', and 'cousins', whom she had had dinner with in January. They remembered her and it pleased her. His mother did look very old to her, but she found his father good-looking, bald just as Aadi was, and charming also. Catherine opted to sit next to him when they ate.

Chairs had been arranged and a blanket on the ground. A buffet had been set up and the food was delicious. Catherine enjoyed talking to the Americans and with Aadi's 'cousins'. His 'aunt' invited her to come to visit. Catherine told her that she would enjoy that.

Aadi was dressed in pajama and a lovely gray silk 'kurta' (long shirt, with long sleeves and high neck, open part way down the front). His mother was in a beautiful silk multicolored sari in subdued colors. But his sister wore a lovely blue cotton sari and 'auntie' wore a deep pink. It was obvious these women always wore saris, so for them it was not a formal occasion.

When it was time for the Americans to leave, Aadi arranged for Catherine to ride back with them in the van. They stopped to pick up a few pieces of art work they had ordered the day before and then they proceeded to the haveli. Aadi came later in the afternoon, still dressed in his kurta and pajama, to take them to the airport. The van was driving to Jaipur, but the clients were flying. Aadi came to Catherine's room to say good-bye.

She opened her suitcase and handed him a gift-wrapped package.

"Happy Birthday, Aadi," she said.

He tore open the package, and found a beautiful garden book which Catherine had purchased in the United States. Aadi skimmed through it hastily.

"Thank you very much. It is a beautiful book. I must go." He took her in his arms and kissed her then. "Good-bye. I will see you in a few days."

"Good-bye, Aadi," she said and watched as he walked across the courtyard to Reception, where he disappeared from her view. Her heart plummeted. Again she felt desolate. Every time he left she felt a piece of her went with him.

Three days later it was Diksha's birthday. Catherine was on the roof for breakfast when Divyarishi came up and told her to look down into the courtyard. As Catherine did so, Diksha was looking up. "Auntie, Auntie, see my dress," she called. Catherine immediately ran down the three flights to see her properly. Diksha was wearing a frilly white dress instead of the usual school uniform. She looked just darling.

"Oh, Diksha, you look so beautiful," Catherine told her. "Happy birthday, Sweetheart. Have a fun day at school."

"Thank you, Auntie."

Later in the afternoon, Catherine helped to blow up balloons and hang them in the dining room. Ten children came for the party of cake and snacks. Even friends of Tapasya and Divyarishi came also. It was good for Catherine to see all the smiling, happy faces and she joined in the merriment.

That evening Catherine called Delhi to talk to Sunil and ask him if he had received the fax she sent him. He told her he had sent her a letter by courier, but it had never arrived.

"Mom," he said, "Aadi Abhimani called me today from Jaipur."

"Oh? Why?" She asked cautiously.

"He said he had seen my mom and that you were fine."

Catherine could hardly believe it. What a lovely, thoughtful thing for Aadi to do. Also, he must have been thinking about her. It made her feel warm inside.

Chain came to the haveli and picked up a package from Jannu. Catherine was sitting in Reception at the time, so she overheard the conversation. Although it was in Hindi, she understood that Jannu was describing Dagmar to Chain, so the package obviously was to go to her. Where was she? Was Aadi with her?

The next afternoon Catherine went to Reception to give Jannu money for Sanjay for her phone calls, and there sat Dagmar having chai and chatting with Jannu.

"Chai, Auntie?" asked Jannu.

"No thanks," she declined, and went back to her room.

When she went up for lunch, Dagmar joined them, and Catherine found she could not dislike this woman. She seemed very pleasant, charming actually. And she certainly was friendlier than Catherine felt toward her.

Dagmar told Jannu she was leaving a pile of frames at the haveli. She had ordered them but they were not to her liking, so they were being picked up by another woman that evening. Dagmar only spent a few hours at the haveli that day, Jannu having given her a room to use.

In the evening the 'other woman' came and picked up the frames, but first Jannu invited her to have chai on the roof. Catherine saw her, but was not introduced to her. After the woman left, Jannu told her that this was 'Concha', a Spanish travel agent, was a very, **very** good friend of Aadi Abhimani. Concha had gotten Aadi into the business. Catherine nearly choked. Did he bring all his women to Kankarwa? Suddenly it seemed very humerous to her.

It was good that some humor entered her life, because most of the time she was in great pain. She worried constantly now of Aadi being with Dagmar, and she had no basis for this assumption. Yet she cried all the time. She was in such distress that she could hardly pray. Catherine loved the haveli, loved the family, and loved Udaipur, but because of Aadi she was in constant turmoil. It wasn't his fault, she told herself. It was hers alone. And she didn't know what to do.

Jannu had a surprise visit from his cousin, Banni, from Jaipur. He was a young doctor of medicine and had finished his studies only recently. Catherine suddenly thought this was an excellent chance for her to glean information about doctors and hospitals in India. If she could talk to him privately, she could find out what would possibly help Aadi with his leg and foot.

"I'd like to ask Banni a few questions," Catherine told Jannu.

"Go ahead, Auntie."

"But in private? Would that be OK?"

"Go into your room." Catherine led the way to her room and once there, she needed to know if their conversation would be kept in confidence. Banni assured her that he would.

"Banni, would you write down for me the top orthopedic surgeons?"

"In India?"

"Yes, in India."

"All right."

She gave him paper and a pen and he proceeded to write as he also spoke to her. Catherine was sure that she had given him the impression that the problem was with herself, although she gave no description of any malady, nor symptoms of a disease. She wanted to be perfectly sure that her questions could not be linked in any way to Aadi.

"Now, please give me the names of the top neurologists and neuro-surgeons in India." He continued to write and elaborated as to where these doctors practiced. Catherine also wanted to know the approximate ages of the surgeons, and when she inquired about anesthesiologists, he said that each doctor used the ones in the particular hospitals where they worked. Finally she asked about the top hospitals in the country. Except for a very few private facilities, the best was in Delhi, The All India

Institute of Medical Sciences. The private hospitals charged Rs.9, 000 per day and were located in Mumbai, Madras and Delhi.

"Thank you so very much, Banni, for all this great information. Best of luck to you for your future studies and in your examinations."

This felt like a blessing from God, otherwise how would she have been able to learn about doctors and hospitals? Certainly not from a layman, for each had their own experiences to refer to and hearsay, none of which was a reliable source. She copied the information in a readable form and planned to give it to Aadi at the earliest possible opportunity.

Other visitors to the haveli during this time were more members of Jannu's family. His parents arrived and his second older brother, Vibu with his wife, Prem and their baby daughter, Uma. Catherine was told that Vibu and Prem had been waiting eight years for a baby and due to the prayers to Sati Mata, their household goddess, Prem conceived and Uma was born. The baby was named after Sati Mata and the family came to Kankarwa Haveli to perform special prayers in thanksgiving to the goddess for this blessing.

Although Catherine was beginning to feel like 'one of the family', there was still a reserve both on her part as well as on the family's. She ate regularly now with them for lunch and for dinner. No longer did Jannu and she eat by themselves on the roof. All ate as a family and Catherine felt very good about that. However, she wondered why she was never included in the family puja room.

She was very impressed with their spirituality. Except for the children, each fasted one day a week and prayed before meals. Sometimes, Catherine noticed, each took a tiny particle of each food they were about to eat and placed it aside. This was to be offered in the puja room. Suchana made a special chapatti every morning and took it on a plate down to Reception. There she waited for a cow to wander by and offered the chapatti to the animal. As the cow took the food from her, she placed her hands together and bowed before the sacred animal.

Despite her unhappiness over Aadi, Catherine felt that she was indeed in the right place, that God had led her here for a purpose. She was learning new things every day and if her heart were not so heavy, she would be truly enjoying herself.

CHAPTER TWENTY SIX

A REVELATION AND A FESTIVAL

Out of deep depression and despair, Catherine woke in the night and decided to read all of the correspondence she had ever received from Aadi. She skimmed through her own also, as she had kept copies of most everything she had ever written to him. Suddenly she gasped. There it was in front of her and she had totally missed it until now. Stupid! Stupid! All of it came together and she understood at last.

She remembered her last reading with Helga, who told her that she couldn't 'see' Aadi. "Where is he?" she had asked. Catherine told her that he was on tour in India. And Helga had shaken her head. "I don't see him. It's as if he has disappeared." But of course he was not in India. He was in Europe!

Aadi had told Catherine that he was going to Europe the first week of July, but he didn't go until the second week, and Catherine had thought he had gone and come back. Then she recalled his telling the Italian tourists in Jaisalmer that he lived in India **and** Europe, and she dismissed it at the time, wondering why he had said that. Then Ann, Aadi's American client, recently told her that Aadi spends two to three months in Europe every year.

So he had been in Germany when she was trying to contact him. She never thought his 'summer holiday' was for that long a time. He must have returned just prior to her arrival in Delhi. Now it became clear to her regarding his remoteness or indifference, the gift he obviously sent back to Germany via Lufthansa and his change in attitude toward her from his correspondence and phone calls.

"Oh, God," Catherine thought, "He didn't want me. He just came from **her**. He was all used up. And I thought it was something I'd done or not done. Seeing my ugly body must have been a 'turn off' too after being with her. Oh, God, why did it take me this long to see it?"

What she still didn't realize was that she had been and continued to be in a state of recovery. The emotional, physical, mental drain of the past many months had taken its toll. She had been unable to decipher simple logic. Now she was blaming herself and the effect was devastating.

Catherine went through a private hell realizing the truth. She wept, prayed, thought about the sequence of events over and over again, and wept repeatedly. She went totally berserk; everything became exaggerated in her mind. She carried on one-sided conversations with Aadi and finally recovered from that state of turmoil with a better perspective and a calmness which surprised her. Catherine was grateful that Aadi had not returned yet, otherwise she knew she would have ruined their relationship with anger and churlishness.

But she was deeply, deeply hurt. Her heart was broken, but she also realized that she had been at fault not understanding the length of time he actually spent in Europe. Aadi had not deceived her. He had told her what he felt she needed to know and no more. It was she who had made the wrong assumptions and had come to false conclusions.

Catherine was in her room one late afternoon when Jannu pounded on her door.

"What are you doing in there?" he yelled. "Come out."

She opened the door. "What's wrong?"

"Your lights are not on. What were you doing?"

"Lying down."

"This is not a time for sleeping. Come out. Sit out here."

Catherine followed Jannu out to Reception and thought what a kind, thoughtful man this was. Of course she could not confide in him, but he was very astute and must have noticed her depression, and was watching out for her.

"Auntie," he said, "You must put the past behind you. You are here now. Be happy."

"You don't understand, Jannu. And I can't talk about it."

A few nights later she was on the roof when Aadi arrived. She was so happy to see him, but held herself in check. Catherine always restrained her emotions regarding Aadi when others were present. She couldn't allow anyone to suspect her feelings for this man. Every week her sister called to report on their mother's condition and how she was faring in Oregon. Cindy never wanted to hear about what she was doing, and seemed interested only in her relationship with Aadi. Catherine refused to discuss him because there were people in Reception listening to her every word. So Catherine became adept at hiding her feelings and side-stepping awkward questions.

Jannu had asked Aadi to buy her a new flash attachment to her camera as it was not working and Catherine thought it was no longer usable. In her room Aadi presented her with the attachment, which he had bought in Delhi, and although it was not the same brand, it did work on her Canon. Aadi wanted to show her, which he did, but when he wanted to snap her photo, she declined and snapped his instead.

"How much do I owe you, Aadi?"

"Later," he said, and took her into his arms and kissed her tenderly. She felt wonderful then and responded in kind. It was the first time in so very long that she felt an intimacy with him. And it wasn't long before she noticed his arousal, but that was not acted upon.

"I talked to Sunil in Delhi," he told her.

"That was so nice of you to call him."

"But I saw him at the office in Delhi. I assured him you were fine."

"Thank you, Aadi. I wonder, is there a possibility that we could talk privately somewhere? Other than here at the haveli? Because you don't stay in my room very long, and I have some things I need to discuss with you."

"Yes. I will call you tomorrow morning and set a time and place."

Catherine waited all the next day and she never heard from him. The following day she was on her walk and had just exited the Gulab Bagh when she saw him coming toward her on his scooter. He had two young boys riding behind him. He stopped to talk with her.

"I was just coming to get you. I couldn't come yesterday. Did Jannu tell you I called?"

"No, I didn't get the message."

"Please wait here. I will be right back."

She stood at the cross-roads, a busy intersection on Lake Palace Road until he returned. Catherine felt very conspicuous, as men stared at her and she was aware that they had seen Aadi talking to her and would observe them taking off on his scooter. He arrived shortly and they proceeded in a direction with which she was unfamiliar. She wondered where they were going because it seemed so far.

"Are you taking me all the way to Jaipur?" she joked, not realizing that they were not going in that direction.

"It is not far now," he replied.

Actually she was enjoying the ride. She had to hold on to him and that felt good. Indian women never held on to men on scooters. They balanced holding onto the seat, but Catherine was not that confident and she loved holding him and feeling him next to her. Then she knew where they were. He was heading for his garden. Catherine had prayed for this meeting and had asked the Holy Spirit to guide her so that she wouldn't say anything that might damage their relationship. When they were settled in the small clearing beside the pool, Catherine began.

"Aadi, I have three subjects to cover, that's why I needed this time. First of all I want to talk about our tour of Rajasthan. It was a good tour, Aadi and I am so grateful for the time you took out of your busy schedule. Also I am grateful for the great care you took of me. You were always concerned about my blood sugar and saw that I ate regularly and that I had plenty of fluids.

"But something was missing, Aadi. I couldn't understand why you were so distant at times. It wasn't until just a few nights ago that I realized you had just come from Europe before meeting me in Delhi. I had no idea you spent that much time there."

"I told you a long time ago."

"Yes, you wrote that you spent your summer holiday with her, but I thought that meant a week or two, certainly not months. Aadi, if I'd realized that you had just come from her, I would not have allowed us to become intimate that first night. You were all used up. You didn't want me. But I remember asking you three different times if you wanted to be with me, and you assured me you did. But something was wrong and I knew it.

"Aadi, I wanted so much to sleep in the same bed with you, but every night I was dismayed to see single beds. Sometimes I felt abandoned. Especially in Jodhpur. Aadi, why didn't you tell me privately that you were not going to spend the night with me? I was so humiliated in front of all those people when you got up from the table and announced you were going to your uncle's and you'd see me the next day. We had all that time in the market and also in the car when you could have told me."

"I'm sorry."

"It's all right, but it was just one more thing."

"So it was all my fault."

"No, I'm not saying that. I'm not accusing you. I'm explaining how I felt and I just needed to talk about this. Aadi I didn't understand what had gone wrong between us. I thought it was something I'd said or didn't say. I thought maybe it was the sight of my body that turned you off. But you knew in January how

I looked. Now I realize finally that you had just come from her and you didn't want me. Aadi, is Dagmar your German friend?"

"Dagmar! Dagmar is Jannu's friend. I hardly know her. Besides she is married."

"Oh, thank God. You see, not being able to talk to you, my imagination ran away from me."

Catherine and Aadi had been sitting side by side on the ground. At this point, he got up and moved to a chair in front of her. Immediately she felt him distancing himself from her.

"Aadi, don't you want me to touch you?" she asked.

"You can touch me. I just moved because the sun was in my eyes."

Now Catherine had the sun in her eyes looking up at him, but she made no comment on that.

"Aadi, please don't think I'm angry with you. Disappointed in our tour, yes, but it wasn't your entire fault. I do wish you had told me that you had just come from Germany, but I was ill, Aadi. You have no idea what I went through all those months. And the last two when I thought you didn't want to see me again, when I needed you the most, you were gone and I didn't know where.

"I was so exhausted, Aadi; physically, emotionally, mentally. I wasn't functioning normally. Our communication broke down and I never said anything. If I'd been my usual self, I'd have spoken up immediately about the twin beds. At Jodhpur I should have asked to be taken to that hotel we'd stayed in the night before. At the Eco Farm, Aadi that morning after we'd spent the night lying in that tiny window seat, I wanted you so badly I thought I was going to go out of my mind. I needed you so badly and you went to sit outside. It was an indication that even at that early stage of our tour, I couldn't talk to you. It was my fault. I should have told you. Instead, I suffered, because I knew if only you could have touched me, I'd have gone completely wild. I'm sorry for all the times I didn't speak up. I'm sorry for the time I insisted on having my own way and then felt like a prostitute."

"When was that?"

"In Jaipur. Don't you remember, we talked about it the next morning? Aadi, I just needed to get this all out. It is a part of my healing. I've been ill. I didn't know how ill until I started recovering at Kankarwa. It was so kind of you to bring me there. They are so good to me."

"They are good to everyone. They are good people."

"Yes of course. But I'm closer to them than the other clients. I am the only one who eats with the family. And I know that is because of you. I'm so grateful that you brought me there, Aadi."

"You know, I feel responsible for the break-up of your family."

"Aadi, in the first place, my family is not broken up. I got a divorce. And you were not responsible for that. My marriage was over a long time ago. Aadi, how do you visualize our relationship? What am I to you?"

"You are my intimate friend. But it is not based on the sexual. It never was."

"OK, I guess I can live with that. Do you suppose we could travel together again, here in India? Because there is so much more I want to see."

"Yes, when I can find the time. I feel you are in India looking for something spiritual, answering God's call. Perhaps you should go to an ashram like Rishikesh."

"Aadi, I'm not looking. I am already spiritual. As I believe you are also. I only know God called me here, but I don't believe it was to join an ashram. I do know of a couple of Catholic ashrams that I may visit sometime in the future however, but I'm not ready for that now."

"Why haven't you gone to see Sunil?"

"I'm not ready for that either. Besides, I'm worried about how to explain my coming here. I don't want him to know of our relationship."

"I don't want that either, Catherine, but you have to see him."

"I will when I can."

"Is that all?"

"No, it is not all. I also want to tell you that I got information for you regarding specialists that you can contact about your leg. Jannu's cousin, they call him 'Banni', is a young doctor and visited the haveli. I took him into my room and questioned him at length. I asked him first for complete confidentiality and then I let him conclude that I was the patient. I have a list of doctors and hospitals for you.

"And Aadi, I'd like to go with you to see these doctors. I know what to ask and you don't. And if you should need surgery, I definitely would wish to be there to make sure everything is sterile and to be with you every step of the way. This is my area of expertise, Aadi. How do you feel about that? Are you open to my going with you?"

"Yes."

"You have to take care of this right away. You can't put it off any longer."

"All right. I will make an appointment as soon as I have time. Chale?" This meant, 'we go now?'

"Not yet, Aadi. I told you I had three things I wanted to talk to you about. This last thing–are you open to going with me to America?"

"Yes, but I want to do it leisurely, not using an itinerary."

"Fine. I'd like that too. I'm so anxious for you to see my country, Aadi.

"Are you all right, Aadi?" she asked him. "Are we all right?"

"Perfect," he answered.

They left the garden then and rode the scooter to the place where he had picked her up.

"Is it all right I leave you here?" he asked. "I have to go to office."

"Yes, fine. I need to finish my walk." With that she got off the scooter and they said 'good-bye'.

****

All Hindu feasts follow the Hindu calendar and most are movable. In October the feast of Dussera is observed for ten days. It celebrates the triumph of good over evil which is played out in the great Hindu epic, THE RAMAYANA. Just following Dussera is the great festival of Diwali, probably the most joyous except for Holi. Lamps, candles, fireworks, and decorations similar to those of the Christian festival of Christmas are seen everywhere. The candles and lamps symbolize the lighting of the way for Rama returning from his adventures. Diwali is also dedicated to the goddess Laksmi, the Goddess of Wealth. Hindus celebrate also by buying gold, kitchen utensils, saris and especially sweets. The merchants are very busy during this happy time.

Catherine decided to gift the children on this occasion. She asked Jannu what she could buy them.

"Auntie, that is not necessary. Just your blessing, please.

"Jannu, I want to buy the children something."

"Then buy some sweets."

"That isn't enough. Come on, Jannu, help me out here."

"Auntie, I have to talk to Bhabhi sa about this." 'Bhabhi sa' is the Hindu word for brother's wife, and is what Jannu always called Suchana out of respect.

After some time Jannu told her that it would be all right for her to buy them some clothes. He took her to the Bapu Bazaar, a huge market place near Delhi Gate and named after Gandhi, who was called 'Bapu' by those who loved him and were close to him.

Catherine was so surprised to find Osh Gosh B'gosh. But that is where Jannu took her and she found some lovely things for each of the children. That evening Jannu and Divyarishi were going to walk to the market near the clock tower, so Catherine tagged along. They went into one particular shop and looked at fabric to buy Suchana a new suit. Catherine chose a beautiful iridescent silk in pink tones and bought it for Suchana. Divyu and Jannu chose a cotton material for her.

Rajput ladies wear a suit called a 'poshak'. The orthodox, or very traditional Rajput ladies do not wear saris. A poshak consists of a gored skirt (lahga), a very short blouse with tight elbow-length sleeves which laces in back (kachali), a kind of vest (kurti) with no sleeves, no opening, but slips over the head and falls to cover the hips and has side slits. Over all this, Rajput ladies wear an 'odhna', which is a long filmy veil tucked into the waist under the kurti and covers the front of skirt to the floor. It is then wound around to the back on the left side under the arm and covers the head, falling over right shoulder to the front where the end is tucked into the left side of the kurti. It is a very beautiful attire and many wear poshaks even if they are not Rajput. The odhna is used to cover the faces of the ladies at marriages, in the villages, even in the home, and it is done in respect for their husbands.

Firecrackers were going off all over the area with loud bangs, and even some occasional rockets could be seen in the sky. At times the noise was deafening, but Jannu said it was very quiet this year compared to past Diwalis. As she sat in Reception, Catherine noted a guest couple leaving the haveli for dinner. They returned almost immediately, the man visibly shaken and holding his head.

"What happened?" she asked, walking up to him.

"I was hit by a firecracker. They just throw them anywhere. It is very dangerous out there! It could have been my eye."

"Here, let me see," she said, and looked at the small wound on his forehead. "Come into my room and I will take care of it. I'm a nurse."

The man was so very grateful for the treatment of a little antibiotic cream and a Band-Aid. He and his wife went out again and had no more accidents.

That evening, Catherine dressed in a sari for dinner, and the children were excited to see her in one. "Of course I'll wear another tomorrow, for Diwali," she told them. She was just returning to her room, when Tapasya came to her and told her that Aadi bhai sa was waiting downstairs for her. Catherine's heart skipped with anticipation. She was so happy to see him. He followed her into her room and she showed him all her purchases for the children and Suchana. She also showed him the sari she planned to wear the night of Diwali.

"It is very good, and you look very nice in sari tonight."

"Really? You like me in a sari?"

"Yes."

"Will you be here tomorrow night?"

"Of course. It is Diwali. I am so tired," he told her, "And I have a sore toe."

"Let me see," she said. "It looks like an insect bite," she observed examining it.

"Yes, I was working in the garden without shoes."

"Aadi, soak your foot in hot water."

"My father told me the same thing."

Catherine smiled. "Well, do it. It will feel better."

"I will."

She was sitting on the end of the bed facing him in a chair. He pulled her to him and she knelt on the floor in front of him.

"No, sit on my lap," he insisted.

"But I am too heavy."

"Please. Come."

She did as she was bidden and he held her fast and kissed her tenderly. Her heart swelled with love for him. Everything felt so natural between them and that night, as she went to sleep, she held him in her arms as she had done in Duluth.

The day of Diwali was a busy one. The servants were getting things ready, cooking special food and the air was heavy with anticipation.

"Jannu, I want to buy something for Aadi. Will you help me?"

"All right, Auntie, let's go."

Again they went to the Bapu Bazaar, where Jannu led her to a cloth merchant for men's suiting. Here he asked for material to make a kurta. Most of the material they brought out was unacceptable to Jannu's taste. He said over and over, "Not for Aadi bhai sa". Finally they displayed a raw silk and Jannu was pleased. There were two shades of tan, and Catherine chose the lighter. Then they proceeded across the street to buy material for the pajama.

"Jannu, don't you think a cream color would go best with the tan?"

"No, Auntie. White! It must be white. Besides, after two washings in India, white is cream." He laughed and she just shook her head and laughed with him.

"OK, Jannu. Whatever you say."

On the way home they stopped and bought boxes of sweets. Catherine bought one for Aadi and one for the family.

By the time the evening puja began Catherine was dressed in her green silk sari with pink elephants and a gold lame blouse. The children were also dressed up in colorful costumes and Suchana wore a deep blue poshak trimmed in gold.

"Jannu," Catherine had asked earlier, "Could I join you for puja tonight?"

"Auntie, I'm sorry, but only family members can go into the puja room, and only certain family members, not all."

"Oh."

"You see, Auntie, Sati Mata told us we must be very careful. This house was not lived in for a long time and we had it blessed before we moved in and do it every six months. We don't know if anything bad might have happened here, so we take precaution. Sati Mata told us which family members can go into the room and no one else is allowed. I'm sorry, Auntie."

"That's OK, Jannu. I understand. Thanks for explaining."

As Catherine waited on the roof for the family to finish a very long puja, the servants placed candles all over the roof edges. Every foot or so there was a candle. Then they were lit and the effect was absolutely dazzling. Clients dining on neighboring roof tops told the family later that Kankarwa was the most beautiful house on the lake. When puja finished, the family came up and sweets were distributed to all, clients included.

Then the children started running and the servants and Jannu got out the fireworks. They lit Roman candles, sparklers, swirls and rockets. The children were so excited and Catherine was worried that someone would be injured. She went close to a Roman candle that Divyu was lighting and he warned her.

"No, Auntie, too dangerous! Stay back!"

So the adult backed up and watched the child light the candle. She felt very warm for Divyu as he moved to protect her. It was so incredibly sweet it brought tears to her eyes.

Somewhere between all the excitement and commotion, the family found time to eat. Then as the Lake Palace started their display of fireworks, Aadi arrived. He was dressed all in black in a fashionable Jodhpur jacket. Catherine thought he looked very handsome. Jannu made some remark however that led her to believe he didn't approve of Aadi's attire. Later she was to learn that Jannu did not like black.

"Would you like to go for a walk?" Aadi asked Catherine.

"Oh, yes," she replied.

"Let us go then." They descended the stairs and Catherine asked him to come to her room for a moment.

"I have a Diwali gift for you," she told him.

"I have one for you too," he said, and presented her with a small box of sweets.

When he saw the material she had for him, he was dismayed.

"But it is only the exchange of sweets," he told her.

"Well, today is like Christmas and I felt that I wanted to give gifts to everyone. Do you like the material?"

"Oh yes, but you should not have spent the money."

"It is all right. I wanted to do this. And here is a box of sweets for your family," she said as she handed it to him.

"Thank you very much," he said and kissed her. "Shall we go now?

All right."

When they got to Reception, Aadi pulled his scooter into position and motioned for her to get on. She was surprised because she had thought they were going to walk about the neighborhood. Instead, Aadi drove to the Bapu Bazaar.

Hundreds of people were there, walking elbow to elbow one way on one side of the street and walking the opposite way on the other side. Every shop was well lit hoping for last minute shoppers. Over the street were hung glittering streamers and twinkling colored lights. Music blared from loud speaker systems, making it impossible to converse. Aadi led Catherine into the crowd and they proceeded to walk the length of the bazaar. They walked along, enjoying the festive atmosphere, and at one point, Aadi met a friend he hadn't seen in fifteen years. It was that kind of evening. As they walked together for a while, Catherine fell in step with the man's wife, who smiled at her, and Catherine wondered what the woman was thinking of her relationship with Aadi.

After coming to the end of the bazaar, they took a parallel street back to where they had left Aadi's scooter. He took her back to the haveli and she thanked him, but would have given anything if she could have hugged and kissed him for the special evening adventure he had just given her.

Three days later he was gone. He had come to pick up his gifts that he had left on Diwali. A group was coming into India and he was to meet them in Delhi. He looked very animated and she was happy for him that he enjoyed his work so much. Aadi said he didn't know where they were going or how long he'd be gone. He kissed her briefly and left hurriedly. Little did she know she would not see him again for two and a half months.

CHAPTER TWENTY SEVEN
A NEW LIFE OPENS UP

Suddenly Catherine's life became very busy. Her skills as a nurse were called upon. The family needed her help. A few clients became good friends. She felt at last that this was indeed the place God had chosen for her, and where she was to begin her new life's journey.

Divyarishi became a very beloved friend to Catherine. He enjoyed coming in her room and every evening he wanted to be there when she checked her blood sugar. He watched very carefully as she pricked her finger and placed the drop of blood on the monitor. Divyu observed also the medication she took following the test. Some evenings he would call to her to remind her.

"Auntie, blood sugar? Wait, I come."

Soon he wanted to set up the test for her and she allowed him to do this, but warned him never to touch the blood sample or the lancets that pricked her finger. She insisted on cleaning that up herself, instructing him that it could be dangerous to touch someone else's blood. Then he would take her pill out of the bottle and watch as she swallowed it. This became a nightly routine and she became very attached to this charming little boy.

Divyu loved Cricket and always got someone to play with him in the courtyard. Often the ball would hit Catherine's door or windows and sometimes she wondered how the glass didn't break because the hit was so strong. One afternoon she stood watching as he swung the bat but did not see his sister, Tapasya behind him. The bat hit her in the mouth. Her mother and father both came running, as did Catherine and Jannu. Suchana and Subhash didn't know what to do but hover over her.

"Jannu, get some ice cubes," Catherine ordered. He immediately called a servant to get them from the kitchen. Tapasya was crying, Catherine checked and found her teeth were intact, although the upper lip was swelling very fast. The ice cubes came and Suchana and Subhash tried to hold one to her mouth, but the ice was melting in their hands.

"We need a towel," she told Jannu, which he produced from the linen supply. Catherine placed a cube in the towel and gave it to Tapasya to hold for herself. This she did and she quieted down.

Chai was being served in Reception and the children always drank hot milk instead of tea. There was no way Tapasya could drink from a glass, so Catherine asked Jannu if there were any straws.

"No, Auntie, no straws."

"Then tell someone to bring a teapot down here and she can drink from the spout."

Jannu laughed. "Oh, Auntie, she won't do that!"

"Please ask for one and we'll see."

"All right. But she won't do that." He called upstairs and they came with the small pot. Catherine poured the milk into it and handed it to Tapasya.

"Put the spout into the side of your mouth, Sweetheart, and pour slowly."

Tapasya did as Catherine instructed and enjoyed her milk. Catherine and Jannu exchanged looks and she could barely hold back her grin.

The following day she noticed Tapasya toying with a piece of skin on the underside of her lip that obviously had been cut by her teeth.

"Darling, come into my room and I'll fix that," she told the little girl. Catherine had a very sharp embroidery scissors, which she took out and washed first with soap, then used an alcohol sponge on it. It wasn't sterile, but it was the best she could manage. Tapasya was shaking and obviously afraid.

"Tapasya, I am going to cut that little piece of skin off, and you must hold very still. But I promise you. I promise you, it will not hurt."

The little girl was still scared, but she didn't move as Catherine cut the skin from her lip. Tapasya then smiled and thanked her, and from that day on they were closer friends than before. She too came often to Catherine's room and would draw pictures for her. Of course Hindi lessons were going on as well as the other 'school work' Catherine was required to do with the children.

She often tried hugging and kissing the children. Divyu always complied, and Tapasya also, but this was alien to their culture. Only family members did this, not strangers or outsiders. Diksha squirmed away every time Catherine tried to embrace her. She was a very independent little girl and also very smart. Catherine did not feel badly about this; she just bided her time for Diksha to get to know her better and feel more at ease.

Just after Diwali all the servants left to go back to their villages. The haveli was full of clients and there was no one to clean rooms and no one to cook except Suchana. The situation was desperate. Jannu and Subhash started cleaning rooms and Catherine decided that she could help in the kitchen for breakfast.

Generally, only breakfast was served to guests, and never lunch unless Jannu had a special request for a group. Dinner was served occasionally to a guest or guests and again sometimes for a group. However, the food was vegetarian and it was the same as the family ate. There was a menu for breakfast, but not for dinner. A concession was made for clients who wanted eggs for breakfast, but these were prepared on a separate stove with separate utensils. It reminded Catherine of a kosher kitchen.

At first she just started handing out menus and taking breakfast orders. Then she noticed Suchana never went near an egg, so Jannu was doing all the egg dishes. Catherine decided that she could do that. After all, how many times had she made breakfast for her family in the States? She certainly knew how to make eggs. Clients asked for omelets; plain, cheese, cheese and tomato, masala (with onion, tomato and chili powder), for fried eggs, boiled eggs, and scrambled eggs.

"Auntie," Jannu said sharply. "How many eggs are you using?"

"Two. Why? Isn't that what the menu calls for?"

"Only two? But how did you get that big omelet?"

"Watch me," she told him, laughing to herself. Earlier she had seen omelets made by the servants that looked like small envelopes. The only problem she had was getting used to not touching anything else while she was cooking the eggs. At first, Suchana constantly had to remind her.

"Auntie, wash hands," after she left the stove to do toast or get something from the refrigerator.

Finally she got herself organized so that she didn't have to stop and wash all the time. There was also, what Catherine considered, a bad habit of toasting all the bread before fixing the hot food.

"Jannu, the toast should be served hot at the same time as the eggs or the porridge. The juice can be made first and then stirred just before serving."

"Really, Auntie? You sure?"

"Yes, I'm sure."

So the three of them, Suchana, Jannu and Catherine, made a team, and breakfast went smoothly and quickly. She had never worked as a waitress, but she certainly had had experience cooking and serving in her own home for many years. She found she was enjoying this work immensely. It gave her a sense of purpose and most of all, Catherine felt she was finally able to repay the family for their many kindnesses to her.

One of the great pluses of this job, if it could be called that, was meeting and talking with the clients. Many wondered if she owned the haveli and if not, how it was that an American was working there? She would laugh and tell them that she lived there and was helping out. Catherine met people from all over the globe and it became very fascinating for her.

Jannu eventually got more boys to work in the kitchen and to clean rooms. But most were from the village and had to be taught. However they did not speak much English and she didn't know Hindi, so at times Catherine would use sign language along with the English and showed them how to do things.

"Auntie," said Jannu one day, "I think it's time you take morning walk again."

"But Jannu, how are the boys going to manage?"

"They will. They are becoming addicted to you."

"You mean too dependent."

"Yeah." Jannu told the boys after breakfast that the next day they would be on their own, but Jannu would take all the orders.

"Oh, Auntie," one boy said, "How we work without you? We scared."

"You will do fine. Jannu and Suchana will be here. Really, you will be just fine," she assured them.

Catherine resumed her morning walk, but found she missed working, so she decided breakfast was more important and went back to the roof by 7:30 every morning. Most clients came later for breakfast, but there was always an occasional early riser. Which was the case of a young Frenchman by the name of Francois. He was tall, dark, and good-looking and was working in Mumbai. Francois had decided to take a few days holiday in Udaipur, and he and Catherine enjoyed a lively conversation every morning. He told her to be sure and call him when she came to Mumbai and they would have dinner. She promised she would. Some weeks later as she took an order from a young woman, she was surprised by her question.

"Are you Catherine?"

"Why, yes I am."

"I'm from Mumbai. And Francois sends you his greetings. He told us about this haveli and that we had to stay here."

"That is wonderful. I hope you will enjoy Udaipur. Please give Francois my best when you see him."

One day a young Swedish girl from Delhi who was staying at the haveli came to sit in Reception. She was very fair skinned with long blond hair. Catherine took one look at her and became concerned. She went to her room and came back with a thermometer.

"I think you are ill, dear. Your face is very red. Please, may I take your temperature?"

"All right. Yes, I'm not feeling well."

Her temperature was over 102 degrees, and Catherine became worried.

"Is someone here with you?"

"No, I'm alone."

"Which is your room?"

"She's in 216, Auntie," Jannu told her.

"What is your name?" Catherine asked her.

"Sarah."

"All right, Sarah. You need to be in bed. Please go now and I will check on you later. Do you have any aspirin? Take two of them and try to rest."

That evening, Catherine knocked on Sarah's door. When she didn't get an answer, she tried the door and found it unlocked. Sarah was lying on her bed with all her clothes on and burning up with fever.

"Sarah, I'm going to take your temperature again." It was now 104 degrees.

"You need a doctor and I'm going to have one called for you. In the meantime, I want you to get out of your clothes, take a shower to cool off and then lie here with only a sheet covering you. I will be back soon."

Catherine left and found Subhash in Reception.

"Subhash, please call a doctor for Sarah in room 216. She is very ill. I will stay with her until the doctor comes."

"All right, Auntie, right away."

Catherine returned to Sarah with a basin and a small towel. Sarah had showered and washed her hair and was lying in bed. Her face was inflamed with fever.

"Now, Sarah, I'm going to sponge you down. The doctor is coming, but until he gets here, I will take care of you. I'm a nurse, Sarah, although I haven't practiced in a long time, but I know we have to get that temperature down. Now just relax and I will sponge you."

Catherine did this until the doctor arrived. He checked her temperature, took her blood pressure and got a short medical history from her. He diagnosed the disease as infectious diarrhea and ordered medications for her.

While Subhash sent out for the drugs, Catherine prepared tea and toast for Sarah. She needed fluids and food. Sarah sat up to eat and drink and Catherine was able to get her to drink mineral water as well.

Room 216 was a twin bedded room, which gave Catherine an idea.

"Sarah, I don't want you to be alone tonight, so I'm going to sleep in this bed just in case you might need me. Is that OK with you?"

"Oh, yes, please stay with me, Catherine. I'd really appreciate it."

"Fine. I'll get into my robe and come back. By then your medication will be here. The antibiotics will start working right away and you are going to feel so much better tomorrow."

Catherine learned that Sarah was working in the Swedish Embassy in Delhi as a nursemaid for the children of a secretary. She told everyone that she was visiting an aunt because it seemed to be an easier story for her to tell. Before Sarah left Udaipur she asked Catherine to please call when she got to

Delhi, and Catherine promised she would, because soon she had to visit Sunil and would enjoy seeing this young girl again.

In room 204 there was an older man named David who moved in, it seemed, for the duration. He brought in a refrigerator and decorated the room to his taste. By profession he was an interior designer from London. Jannu knew of him from old because David had been coming to Udaipur for some years, although this was the first time he had decided to stay at the haveli. Jannu told her that he had a relationship with a young Indian boy and that he was ruining this boy's life by spoiling him with many western clothes and trinkets. Jannu thought it possible that David was homosexual.

The boy, Hamed, came often to the haveli and to Catherine it looked like he was an errand boy for David. From what she observed she agreed with Jannu that David was homosexual and in love with Hamed. David left every morning for Lake Palace Road where he had bought a jewelry shop for Hamed, and decorated it to catch the eye of foreign tourists

One evening when David returned he sat in Reception and started a conversation with Catherine.

"A shopkeeper whom I don't know, came into my shop today. He asked where I was staying and when I told him 'Kankarwa Haveli', he got very excited."

"Really? Why, David?"

"He said, 'Oh, that's where that American lady is staying.' I said, 'Yes, there is an American lady living there.' He said, 'Do you know that she left her children and her husband to come to India'?"

At this point, Catherine started to laugh. What a small town this was!

"Well, David, how did you respond?"

"I told him your children were all grown up, that you had grandchildren and I thought your husband was dead."

David said this with such dignity and obvious disdain for the man that Catherine laughed heartily. "Good for you, David. And my thanks."

She told Jannu and Suchana about this at dinner and both of them were alarmed.

"Auntie, you must be careful what you tell people. You must not let them know your private life."

"All right, but I know exactly where that came from. Do you remember that Irish lady and her daughter that were here?"

"Oh yes, Auntie," said Jannu. "They were very friendly with the shopkeepers."

"Yes, and they even had dinner at that house across the lake. They were very impressed with the fabrics he had."

"Auntie, what did you tell them?" Suchana asked.

"Well, I was in a funny mood and when they asked, I told them how I came to be in India. I told them I sold my house, got a divorce and moved here."

"Oh, Auntie," cautioned Jannu, "You must be very careful. Don't tell anyone personal things."

"Yes I agree. You are absolutely right. I'll be more careful from now on."

One day she noted some droppings on her bed and had also seen them behind the bathroom door. She wondered what they were.

A few weeks earlier Carol had sent her a package of candy; Tootsie Rolls and some chocolates. She had them in sealed plastic bags on her window takh with her purse and medication. The children and even the adults came for hand-outs when they heard what she had received in the mail. Catherine was incensed however, because much of what she had ordered had been stolen by Customs. After that she told her sister to make a list of everything in the box and make sure it was on the packing label.

Catherine always got up at 5 AM to say her prayers. As she sat meditating in the dark one morning, she heard a rustling sound coming from the window takh. She became concerned and flipped on the light, and the rustling continued. A drape covered the area of the takh, and when she pulled it aside, a rat jumped out of her purse, jumped to the floor and ran out under her door. Catherine nearly lost it. Could there be anything worse than a rat? She didn't yell, but she felt sick inside knowing where that rat had been and also knew it had been in the candy. Then she realized that the droppings she had noticed earlier had been rat poop and that it had been on her bed made her shiver with disgust.

"Jannu, I've got a problem," she told him at breakfast.

"What, Auntie?"

"There was a rat in my room this morning."

"Oh no, Auntie. We've never had rats in the rooms."

"Well, they are in my room, because I saw it jump out of my purse. I've also found droppings around my room."

"Auntie, aren't you living right? Why would they be bothering you?"

"Come on, Jannu. This isn't funny. I hate rats! And they are coming in under my door."

"OK, Auntie, I will fix the door.

That evening the entire family came into Catherine's room. They told her it was possible it had built a nest in her luggage. She certainly didn't need to hear that, but the family men searched her luggage and the contents of the bags in the takh. Holes had been made through the plastic bags, so the rat had gotten to the candy.

"Take it out," she told them. "I don't want it."

"But, Auntie, the rat only took one piece at a time. The rest is OK."

Catherine became almost hysterical. "Out. Please, get all of it out. I don't want it. I feel dirty, my belongings contaminated. Ugh!"

"Auntie, we change your room," Suchana said.

"Yes, Auntie, we move you now," Jannu agreed.

"Oh no," replied Catherine. "That will not do because the rat will come here and scare a client. It must be taken care of with me in this room. It would be terrible for clients to know there are rats here."

"But, Auntie," said Subhash, "Every Indian house has a rat."

"Really! Well I don't want one in my room and we should get a trap so there aren't any more here."

"I will do that, Auntie," Jannu said, "But you know they come in from the lake and the street."

Jannu fashioned pieces of wood to fit under the door sill where the stone had worn down. He sent a servant out to buy a trap and placed bread in it to entice the vermin. It worked beautifully. They caught one rat after another in the back store room. Catherine was in Reception when Subhash called to her.

"Auntie, Auntie." She got up and went to see what he was yelling about. Catherine was surprised to see him jumping up and down with glee.

"Teen, teen, Auntie."

"No! Three in the trap?"

"Yes, Auntie. Come, see." Sure enough the trap or bread had caught three at one time. The servants took the trap out to the lake, drowned the rats and brought the trap back to put more bread in it. This went on for a few days until there were fewer and fewer rats in the haveli. However, Catherine was still being plagued with a nightly visitor. Although the candy was gone, a rat continued to get through the wood barricade and enter her room.

"Jannu, I can't take it anymore. I can't sleep at night worrying that the rat will come on my bed."

"You want to move?"

"No I don't want to move. I want you to take care of the problem. Fix the door!"

The next day Jannu put a slab of concrete in front of the door. Certainly the rat could not move that. For extra protection, Catherine stuffed a towel under the door from the room side. She was finally able to sleep with complete confidence that she would no longer have a nightly visitor. However when she opened her door the following morning, there again were rat droppings on the slab, but she was satisfied that it had not gained entry.

Divyarishi told his mama, "How **dare** that rat come in Auntie's room! I'll **kill** him!" Catherine nearly wept for love for that little boy.

Another guest at the haveli was a young Argentinean woman, Deborah Peters, who had lived in England and then had decided to move to India. She now made her home in Darjeeling and was studying Buddhist teachings. Friends of hers from France arrived and also stayed at Kankarwa Haveli, but Deborah stayed on after they left. Catherine and Deborah became friends and every afternoon they would have tea in Catherine's room.

It seemed pests continued to plague 202, which was Catherine's room. Suddenly there was an infestation of ants. Catherine kept no food in her room now since the rat incident, but the ants made a trail from her open window above the lake, across her wall and floor to the doorway. When Deborah saw this, she immediately asked Jannu for a spray, which he readily supplied.

"Auntie," Jannu teased her again, "You don't live right. You are doing something wrong!"

Deborah sprayed the entire route of the ants and with another application the following day, the problem was solved. Catherine enjoyed Deborah very much although she found her to be somewhat of a cynic. She was living on a very tight budget and had to move from Kankarwa to a much cheaper hotel. Before leaving Udaipur, Deborah gave Catherine a gift of hand-made sandalwood incense, knowing that Catherine used incense every morning at meditation. They promised to stay in touch and Catherine felt very sad when Deborah finally had to leave for home.

A mother and daughter came to stay for a few days before traveling on to Australia. They were from England and Catherine heard from them about a lovely haveli near Jodhpur called 'Narlai'. It sounded so beautiful that Catherine wanted Aadi to take her there for a few days, and dreamt about this happening. Sometime after these women left, Catherine received a lovely note from the mother, thanking her for the lovely breakfasts she had served them every day. She told Catherine that the eggs were cooked exactly like she fixed them at home, and extended an invitation for her to visit should she ever travel to England.

Catherine also received a note of gratitude from Sarah Svensson's mother in Sweden. Sarah had written her mother of her illness and Catherine's nursing care. Again there was an invitation to visit if she were ever in Sweden.

Jannu was very pleased with Catherine's contribution to the haveli. Not so much for the breakfast help, which was certainly appreciated, as for her interaction with the guests. He told her that the clients felt more at home than in a hotel and were most comfortable being able to talk to another foreigner with whom they could relate.

Catherine felt the haveli was her home now and the family took her in as one of them. When people asked her where she lived, she told them and stated that these wonderful, good people were her family.

One morning Catherine did not appear for breakfast and Jannu came to her room.

"Auntie, are you all right? You didn't come this morning."

"Oh, Jannu, I'm sick. I feel awful and I have diarrhea."

"Should I call a doctor?"

"No, no. I'll be all right, but I can't leave my room."

"Would you like something to eat?"

"Yes, but just tea and toast, no butter."

"Perfect. I'll send it to you. And, Auntie, whatever you need, whatever you need, you just ask."

"I know, Jannu. Thank you."

"Remember, whatever you want, it is yours."

"Yes, darling."

Suchana came to see her as did the children. All were concerned, but Catherine had medication to take for this possibility and she was soon well again.

Catherine was missing Aadi very much. She wept when she prayed and often after dinner on the roof. There she would sit alone and look out over the beautiful lake to the Jag Mandir Palace where Aadi had kissed her for the first time. The tears rolled down her face and her whole body ached for him. He had called Jannu a couple of times that she knew of because Jannu had mentioned it casually. Jannu went to Aadi's house many times to oversee the building extension, since Aadi was out of Udaipur. Catherine never questioned Jannu, nor brought up Aadi's name, but she learned that he did not approve of some of the items Aadi had decided to put in the house. One was a bidet, which Jannu said Aadi's German girlfriend had insisted had to be installed.

"Who's going to clean that?" Jannu said to Catherine.

"Auntie, they are Brahmin. Servants aren't allowed in the house for fear they will touch something. And who will use that bidet? His parents? No, Auntie."

"How big is the addition?"

"Just two rooms. And he chose granite for the bathroom. I don't like it. White tile is much better."

Catherine ached with loneliness for Aadi and still looked around when she walked for where his house might be. Of course the area was so congested, it was impossible to discern where one house ended and another began.

Her walking was becoming more and more difficult also. Her left leg was getting numb and stabbing pain would hit it before she had gone very far. Soon she had to stop her exercise altogether. She felt sad because she missed the walk, especially in the Gulab Bagh and her special spot where she felt so close to God.

Her prayer time became a torment until she finally stopped praying and offered her pain to God as her prayer. There she sat and wept and wondered, "Where is my God?"

CHAPTER TWENTY EIGHT
A VISIT TO DELHI

The holidays were fast approaching. It would be Catherine's first Christmas in India. First on her agenda was to write her holiday letter. She sent it to Robert to have it lazer printed on Christmas stationery. He didn't receive the letter and she had to rewrite it. Eventually he mailed all the printed stationery with the envelopes for her to sign, write notes on and address After all the letters were completed, she sent them back to Robert to mail from the States.

Flights out of Udaipur to Delhi were full to capacity from Diwali onwards. When they finally thinned out, Catherine was still unable to visit Sunil because she was needed at the haveli. Aadi had been gone for five weeks and Catherine was beside herself with loneliness for him. She thought of him constantly, aching for the sight of him, remembering his touch, his wonderful, clean smell, the sound of his voice, and the sweet taste of his mouth when he kissed her. She kept his picture hidden, but looked at it many times during the day and kissed it.

Jannu had mentioned that Aadi had called a couple of times. Once he had told him to tell Catherine that he had seen and talked to Sunil. Another was to tell him that he had a group tenting in Nepal and it was freezing with constant rain, and he was miserable. When Catherine heard that, she imagined how it would be if they were together keeping each other warm.

Catherine was also waiting for a shipment of medications that she needed and knew she couldn't go to Delhi without them. Jannu then told her of his idea to place a short history of the haveli in each room with a list of services. They talked about what should and should not be included, then joyfully, she wrote the text, of which Jannu approved. He decided that it should be printed on handmade paper. When she told him each should be signed, he thought a signature stamp would facilitate this.

"No, no, no, Jannu," she admonished him. "It must be hand written, each one."

"Oh, Auntie, that's a lot of signatures."

"Come on, Jannu. Not so many. One in each room and maybe 10 signatures a day, but probably not that many as people stay longer than a day."

"What do you think of the paper rolled up with a ribbon?"

She winced. "Jannu, don't get cute. Just place the letter on the bed where it is readily seen."

"In an envelope?"

"Don't waste your money on envelopes. They aren't needed. Just place it on the bed in full view where they will read it right away. Envelopes will be placed in their luggage or put somewhere for a later read, and the envelope discarded."

Jannu took her carefully printed text to be typed. When it came back, there were so many typographical errors, that she was dismayed and frustrated. This was India, she needed to constantly remind herself. Sometimes she wanted to scream. She certainly needed to learn patience. But Americans were not known for that virtue. They wanted everything yesterday. Jannu's idea of a letter in the rooms did not materialize.

Catherine's medications arrived and Jannu made plane reservations for her. She called Sunil and left for Delhi on December 9th. Before departing, Suchana came to her.

"Auntie, how long you be gone?"

"Not long, Suchana. I want to be home for Christmas."

"Oh, Auntie, you must be home for Christmas. This is your home. This is your family. You not a foreigner. You my auntie. I love you." And she took Catherine in her arms and hugged her.

"Oh, Suchana, I love you too. And I love this family. I will come home soon, I promise." Catherine was very touched. Never before had she heard an Indian say the words, 'I love you.' She felt very blessed.

Just as she was about to leave the haveli, Suchana handed her a small packet of batti to be eaten on the plane. Batti was a Rajasthani bread made with flour, salt, and a little ghee. It was kneaded as for chapati, but made into balls and baked in a special batti oven. Catherine loved it and it was a good travel food, certainly better than the cardboard boxes of sandwiches they handed out on the plane. Suchana also gave Catherine a tin of very special sweets to be given to her 'brother', Sunil. She considered Sunil her brother because she thought herself a daughter to Catherine.

Sunil met her at the domestic terminal and she was surprised that he had a car, a Maruti, and that he was driving.

"It's a beautiful car, Sunil."

"It's not new, used."

"That's OK. It looks like it's in good condition. How is the family?"

"All fine. Aadi called."

"Yes, so I understand."

"He came to the office too. He told me you were fine."

"Yes, I am, Sunil. I love Udaipur and the family I'm staying with is very good to me. I couldn't get here earlier because I was needed there. I help with breakfast and also talk to the guests to make them feel more at home."

"How did you decide to go to Udaipur? I thought you would come to Delhi."

"Aadi took me on a tour of Rajasthan and we ended up in Udaipur. He took me to Kankarwa. They are friends of his. And I found that it was just the place for me to recover from the divorce and all that has happened to me over the past several months."

"What is wrong with his leg?"

"What?" Catherine asked incredulously.

"Aadi's leg. He walks funny."

"Did you say anything to him?"

"Yes. I asked him about it."

Catherine was completely aghast. "And what did he say?"

"He didn't answer me."

"Nor am I going to talk about it." She couldn't believe Sunil had the audacity to ask such a personal question of a man he barely knew.

"Sunil, I need to have those boxes I sent you before I left the States."

"Catherine, I couldn't get them from Customs. You will have to go there and get them."

"Why? I mailed them to you."

"They think that I want them for selling."

"Oh for heaven's sake! OK, you'll have to take me there so I can pick them up."

"I'll do that."

"Sunil, I also want to buy some new walking shoes. Mine are all worn out on the insides. Could you take me to a market where they sell Reebok or other well-known walking shoes?"

"Yes, I will do that

When they arrived at the house, Mita was waiting for them and Catherine was greeted warmly.

"Sunil," she said, "This is for you, a present from Suchana to her brother." Catherine handed him the box of sweets, which he opened immediately.

"My favorite," he said as he proceeded to stuff his mouth. Mita, Piku and Catherine looked on as he continued to eat without offering any to them.

"Well," Catherine said, appalled at his behavior, "Aren't you going to share any of it with us?"

"Oh, yes. Here. Have some."

In many ways Catherine's visit to Delhi was a disaster. She had been there so many times and knew what to expect, yet it distressed her when confronted with reality this time. She was used to sharing a bed with Mita and Piku, but now she missed her little room and her privacy at the haveli. Also, Delhi was cold and it seemed to seep into her very bones during the day. But at night there were big heavy quilts to sleep under. After the luxurious bathroom she was accustomed to she took her turn in the tiny space with no hot running water. There was a bucket of water with an electric coil in it to heat it. She had to be careful to turn off the power and then take it out of the water by the wooden handles. There was also a bucket with cold water and by using a small pitcher she mixed the two and poured it over herself for her shower.

Mita and Sunil both went to work and Piku, of course took off for school. Catherine was left alone to her own devices for the entire day. There was no one to talk to because Sunil's mother did not speak English and she did not come upstairs, nor did Catherine go down. The cold was so intense that she bundled up with all her clothes on and stayed in bed all day. She had a book to read and her prayers, and then out of boredom, she fell asleep.

Sunil's family ate mostly fish and rice, but also chicken and mutton. Mita knew that Catherine was now vegetarian, but she didn't seem to know what vegetables to cook besides those loaded with carbohydrates. The food she served was very poor, but Catherine realized the woman was very pressed for time. One day she served raw cabbage, which Catherine had a very difficult time eating. Mita called it 'salad', but it was plain with nothing on it, simply grated and raw. It was obvious to Catherine that this woman needed help. Besides, she could tell that Mita was extremely unhappy. The family situation had gone from bad to worse.

Tapa continued to rule the house and refused to allow Deepa to visit. Mama followed whatever Tapa dictated. Sujeet,

Sunil's brother refused to pay rent to Sunil for the house that he bought for them. He was jealous that Papa had left the house to Sunil and blamed Mita for insisting on rent money.

One day Laxmi, Sujeet's wife came to the house weeping, asking Sunil to talk to Sujeet. They were having marital problems. Sunil refused to listen to her and told her to go home. Laxmi did not go home, but went elsewhere. Sujeet came looking for her, accusing Mita of hiding her. Sunil was not at home and Mita got the blame. Sujeet was drunk and yelling. He then went downstairs to talk to Mama and Tapa and Mita followed. Catherine stayed upstairs with Piku and tried to take his mind off the trouble by working with him on his English lesson. But Piku and Catherine could hear the row going on below them. Sujit was both yelling and sobbing. Sunil finally returned and talked to his brother.

It was that time of the season for school conferences. Both Mita and Sunil took a leave of absence from work in order to go to St. Columba's with Piku. Catherine was delighted to go also. The school is an immense complex in Delhi. The parents met in an auditorium and listened as one of the Christian Brother's lectured them on how to be good parents. Catherine was appalled and felt this was insulting. After the lecture, they were to form small groups and discuss questions that had been handed out. Then one representative from each group was to relate to the others the findings of their group. Mita and Sunil opted out of this exercise, much to Catherine's relief, and the three of them went outside and proceeded to the classroom where they were to meet with Piku's teacher.

They had to wait for some time, but found Piku with boys from his class playing in the school yard. Here at school, Piku was known by his given name, Udaiyan, not the baby name that he was called at home. When his teacher appeared it was a woman, who was called 'Ma'am'. She sat behind her desk and parents and their children formed a queue. Catherine was once again appalled because the teacher related the bad points of the child as well as the good to the parents, in full view and hearing of all the others in the room. Catherine remained at the back of the room when Mita and Sunil's turn came.

Afterwards they went home where Mita and Sunil descended on Udaiyan with great anger. They yelled at him, admonishing him for not paying attention to Ma'am and for not getting the grades that he was capable of. They pulled his hair and twisted his ears, screaming at him, and calling him, 'Stupid'.

"Stop that!" Catherine ordered them. "What is wrong with you? Wasn't it enough that he was embarrassed in front of all those other students and parents?"

"Mom, he's not doing his work and he's being very naughty in class. He doesn't pay attention."

"Listen to me, both of you. Piku is a smart boy. I know because I've been working with him on his English. He learns very quickly. And his grades are mostly A's with a few B's. If he's disruptive in the classroom it is because he is upset with his family life here. And both of you are to blame for that."

"What do you mean, Catherine?" asked Sunil.

"I'll tell you what I mean. This situation with Mama, Tapa downstairs is intolerable. It is frustrating to both of you and you are taking out this frustration on your son. Sujeet comes here drunk, screaming and crying and your son hears all of this. Sure, it was going on downstairs, but we could hear it. If you think this is upsetting to you, believe me it is more upsetting to a child who does not understand and feels his family is being torn apart. He feels insecure and he's acting it out in school.

"Get your act together here. Your son's life is at stake. Sunil, your wife is unhappy. She doesn't have to say anything. I can read it in her face. And now your son is inattentive at school. This is not his fault. It is yours. Do something with that sister of yours downstairs and talk to your brother. This must not go on. If nothing else, live apart from the rest of your family. Sell this house and split it four ways. This is your main concern. Right here. Your wife and your son.

"And stop abusing the boy. Believe me he will listen better if you sit him down and talk nicely to him rather than hurt him physically. That is no way to treat the son you love. Get your lives in order and treat him with respect. You owe that to him."

"Mom, I can't sell this house. It was Papa's and Mama wouldn't go anywhere else. This is her home."

"Then leave them here and you move."

"I don't have the money and Mita doesn't give me her money."

"What?"

"She spends her money and doesn't give it to me."

"Mom," Mita said, "I spend my money on food and things for Piku."

"What?" Sunil asked, and continued to speak and then rant at Mita in Bengali.

"Why are you yelling at her, Sunil? And what are you saying?"

"I don't want you to know. That's why I'm talking in Bengali."

"Fine, but let me tell you. Your wife works out of the house and she also works here in this house, cooking, cleaning, washing and taking care of both of you, besides having to put up with the disrespect she gets from your mother and sister. I don't know what you think she's spending her money on, but it certainly isn't herself. I haven't seen any new clothes on her in a long time."

"Mom," said Mita, "Ever since we lost all that money in the business, Sunil is very different."

"OK. I can understand that. Sunil, you took a beating from that crooked agent in Texas, but you can't allow that to ruin the rest of your life. Take a lesson from that and go on. You have a job which you like and you have your health. You have a good wife and a beautiful son. Be grateful."

"Yes, Mom. Yes, you are right."

Sunil took another day's leave in order to take Catherine to Customs. He had the forms that were needed to identify the boxes. The building was huge, made of cement with no paint, no carpet, and no heat and of course, high ceilings. They went from office to office waiting their turn, then getting a signature and going to the next one. Catherine was frozen to the bone, the chill working its way from her feet upwards. Finally they were directed to a large open room with a long desk where several government workers sat looking at the papers people presented to them. There were many men, who of course never stand in queue, but push ahead of everyone else, their hands outstretched. Catherine was well accustomed to this from standing in post offices. Luckily Sunil was able to push ahead also. Catherine, being a foreigner, was stared at, but no one was about to give room for her. The last paper was signed at last and they moved down the desk to where other workers were handling boxes.

Again they waited for her boxes to be brought to this room and a man began opening them.

"What is this?" he asked.

"My personal belongings," Catherine told him.

"You are going to sell these things?"

"Certainly not. I'm living in Udaipur and I need them for my personal use."

The man rifled through all three boxes, then tied them up once again.

"Come back after lunch," he told them.

Catherine couldn't believe it. Why couldn't they have them now? But by this time it was almost four hours they had been in the building, and she was exhausted.

"All right, Sunil. Let's go to lunch."

"But there is no place around here, Mom."

"We have a car and driver, so what is the problem? I'm tired and cold and hungry. Let's go."

They found a nice restaurant and had their lunch. Evidently all the government workers were also going for lunch, because she saw so many of them at the same restaurant. By now they were so familiar to her, she felt like inviting them to join them.

Back at Customs, Sunil presented a paper and the boxes were brought down to them. However they were not allowed to take them.

"What is the problem now?" she asked Sunil.

"I don't have my ID with me," he told her.

"Why do you need an ID?"

"Because the boxes are addressed to me."

"Oh my God, Sunil. What now?"

"He says he wants a copy of your passport and visa."

"Where do we go for that? Is there one in the building?"

"No, Mom, we have to find one outside."

"This is insane, Sunil, and I'm ready to scream!"

Several blocks away they found a copy machine, came back and were given the boxes. Catherine decided that everyone was covering their ass. No one had computers and the piles of paper were monstrous. Who would ever look at any of it again? It was worse than her bank in Udaipur. Sunil took Catherine home, then went to the office, where he finished off his day.

The shopping expeditions were no less frustrating.They went in the Maruti after Sunil came home from work, changed clothes and grabbed something to eat. Taking Piku with them, he sat in the front seat next to his father. There were no seat belts and Catherine was worried about whip lash for all of them, but was more concerned about Piku in the front seat.

"Sunil, why don't you take some driving lessons?" she asked him.

"Oh, I had fifteen, Mom," he told her.

"Well, Sunil, you need fifteen more. Your driving is atrocious. And why do you continually blow your horn?"

"You are supposed to do that so people in front know you are coming."

"I know the horn is used a lot, Sunil, but you don't have to sit on it when there is no one ahead of you."

Five blocks from home, they ran out of gas. Catherine and Mita helped to push the car to the side of the road and Sunil went with a riksha to get the petrol, which is what they called it in India, as the British did. This was a comedy of errors and Catherine didn't know if she wanted to laugh or cry. Sunil returned with the petrol and they continued their journey.

Then she watched as he pulled out to cross in front of oncoming traffic.

"Sunil, what are you doing? You can't make all those cars stop for you."

"Oh, yes, Mom. They have to stop for me because I put on my signal."

"It is dangerous driving with you, Sunil. They have the right of way, even if you signal, you must wait for them. And for heaven's sake, get seat belts. Piku is in a very vulnerable seat. He can go right through the windshield if you have to stop suddenly."

I am careful not to stop like that."

"Well, Sunil, what if someone hits you from behind? You don't have any control over that. Please get seat belts. It is so important. You know they are mandatory in my country because they save lives."

Finally they arrived at a market, but they had only a half hour to shop as it was near closing time. Catherine went to three shops; Reebok, Nike, and Adidas. None had a woman's shoe to fit her. The largest size they carried was 6-1/2 and Catherine wore an 8.

"Mom, buy a man's shoe."

"Certainly not, Sunil. Men's shoes are specially designed for a man's foot. Besides they are huge and clunky and too heavy to walk in. Let's look for a salwar kameez."

Again they could find nothing but 'free size' which fit larger Indian women, but not Catherine. Foreigners' bone structure was broader and heavier. It was hopeless.

"Why can't we go to Connaught Place, where they sell to foreigners?"

"That's too expensive, Mom. They sell the same thing in Indian markets, but less money."

"Sunil, I don't believe it. Sure, many small foreigners can fit into these Indian sizes, but the majority cannot. You can't tell me there aren't places in Connaught Place that cater to tourists."

The argument was worthless because it was closing time, but they had stopped at one shop earlier and Mita had bought Catherine a sweater which she badly needed, so the excursion wasn't completely unfruitful. Then Catherine insisted they find a nice restaurant and have a good dinner.

Another day Sunil took leave so that he could take Catherine to the Immigration office. They were early so as to be the first ones in queue. However when the doors opened, Sunil was not allowed in and Catherine proceeded on her own. She filled out a form and requested immigration status. After two hours of waiting, she was asked for her passport, which she gave up in the hope that soon she would be seen by an official. Another hour passed and her passport was returned without any explanation. She approached one officer and asked to be seen by someone.

"What is it that you want?" he inquired. "Your visa cannot be renewed."

"I'm not asking for my visa to be renewed. I want to speak to someone about living in India on a permanent basis."

"You will have to speak to that man over there," he pointed in one general direction.

"Which man?"

"Wait half an hour. He will be back."

Catherine waited again and no new person arrived. She went into the hall and asked the same officer again. He looked at her as if he had hoped she had left. Then he pointed to a door in the hall and told her to enter there. The door was slightly open, so she walked in. It was an office where a man sat behind a desk and was conversing with a man and woman sitting in front of him. She sat on a sofa so as not to interrupt.

After some time the people were still talking to the official and five more people entered the office, walked to the desk and interrupted. The officer said something brief, motioned for them to give way. The couple sitting at the desk left and Catherine was asked what it was she wanted.

"Give me your passport," he said. Catherine handed it to him.

"I cannot renew your visa."

"I know that. That is not why I am here."

"Then, what do you want?"

"I want to live in India. I want immigrant status."

"Why?"

"Because I've been coming to India for many years and I want to live here."

"Ma'am, you have to have a purpose."

"I have a purpose. I love it here. I am healthier here. I love the people and I'm already living in Udaipur."

"Ma'am, you have four choices. You can join an ashram. You can open a business. You can marry an Indian, or you can go to an accredited school."

"What happens when I finish my studies?"

"You can keep failing."

It was hopeless. Another four hours wasted. Catherine was totally frustrated. All she wanted to do was go back to Udaipur. She needed to call Sarah Svensson at the Swedish Embassy, which she did. Sarah came to Sunil's house with her sister, who was visiting her from Sweden. Mita served them chai and sweets and Sunil enjoyed meeting the girls. Sarah informed Catherine that soon they were going on a short tour and planned to be in Udaipur on Christmas night. Catherine was delighted, but sorry it would only be for one night. She promised to reserve a room for them at the haveli.

At last the week was up and Catherine, numbed by the cold and frustrated with the family situation and bureaucratic nonsense, boarded the plane for home. She also made quiet note that Sunil did not send anything to Suchana in return for her gift of sweets to him.

Her plane was late arriving in Udaipur, but Chain was there to meet her. She was so happy to see him. Arriving at the haveli, the servants stood in a row, all smiles and grins. She was surprised to see Hanraj, who had been gone since Diwali.

"Hello, Auntie."

"Welcome back, Hansraj. Where is Jannu?"

"Just a minute, Auntie," said Mahipal. "I call him." He went to the phone and called upstairs for him. As Jannu entered the courtyard, Catherine rushed to him and hugged him. This was not an Indian custom and the poor man just stood still with arms at his sides.

"Auntie," he said, grinning. "Welcome home."

"Oh, Jannu, thank you. You have no idea how happy I am to be home."

"Did you have a good time?"

"Not at all. It was awful, but I'll fill you in tomorrow."

"The kids waited up for you, but they finally fell asleep."

"Oh, I have a few little things for them. I can't wait to see them."

"Auntie, khana?" He asked. "Food is ready."

"No, thanks, Jannu. I ate on the plane, but I'd really like some chai."

"Hansraj, make chai for Auntie"

When the tea arrived, Catherine was surprised that Jannu wasn't joining her. "You don't want chai?"

He laughed. "It's late and my mama always said if you drink late at night you will do soo-soo in your bed."

Catherine laughed with him and felt warm and happy to be back with her family. When she entered her room, she saw that it had been cleaned and her beds had been made up with fresh sheets. She closed her doors and sighed with relief, knowing peace and comfort once more, and feeling the love of this good family surrounding her. Truly, she was home. Added to that was the knowledge that God had blessed her by bringing her to Udaipur rather than to Delhi. He knew she would have had a breakdown had she gone there first.

CHAPTER TWENTY NINE

CHRISTMAS AT THE HAVELI

"Auntie, Auntie, Auntie," the children cried as they ran to Catherine's room the next morning. She opened the door to them and gave them all hugs. They were so sweet and genuinely pleased to have her home. She took out the presents she had bought for them; Barbie dolls dressed in saris for the girls, and cars, trucks and a helicopter for Divyarishi. Then off they went to school.

She also got a great welcome from Suchana, who greeted her with smiles and a wonderful hug.

"Auntie, I so happy you home. My husband is gone, but I am happy because you here. You are just like my family; not American, not foreigner–my Auntie!"

Despite her happiness to be home, Catherine was thinking constantly about Aadi and aching for the sight of him. Jannu mentioned that he wasn't expected back until late December or even January. That he wouldn't be there for Christmas was a blow to her. She missed him so much that she woke in the night and wept and wept. How could she go on like this? She was being torn apart, but the family made it possible for her to meet each day with hope in her heart.

Back she went to the breakfast crowd, handing out menus, taking orders and preparing whatever was needed. It felt good to be helping out again, and continually meeting new people from all over the world. She told Jannu about Sarah and reserved the only room that was left and paid for it.

"Auntie," Jannu told her, "If a better room becomes available, she can have that."

"Jannu, I need to talk to you about my rent."

"Why?"

"Because you could be getting more now with so many clients. Please can I pay you more?"

"Auntie, I don't ever want to talk about this again. If you are here twenty years from now, your rent will never be more."

He was so emphatic, that Catherine said no more.

She began to think of how she was going to decorate her room for the holidays. One day she asked Chain to take her to a nursery where she purchased a small tree and four poinsettias. When she asked the nursery man what kind of a tree it was, he just said, 'Christmas tree.' But what kind? Because she didn't remember seeing that particular evergreen before. She didn't get an answer from him except, 'Christmas tree.' The poinsettias were disappointing. Evidently all the good ones had been taken. These were quite small; two white and two red, but they looked very nice in her little room.

Thinking about gifts for the family at the haveli, she decided to visit the CIE shop across from the City Palace. It was Kashmiri and she knew it would be expensive, but went there anyway and purchased cashmere sweaters for Jannu, Subhash and Aadi. She found a lovely Kashmiri shawl for Suchana and then bought papier mache ornaments for her tree. In the Bapu Bazaar she found toys for the children, Christmas wrapping and cards. She looked and looked for Christmas lights, but found none.

Divyarishi's birthday was the 27th of December, and Subhash's on the 31st. The children had Christmas holiday break for a week beginning on the 21st, so Divyu begged to go to the village. Subhash took him, with the promise they would be back on the 26th so that Catherine could have the entire family join her Christmas celebration.

Christmas Eve Catherine dressed in a sari for dinner and Jannu gave her a cassette of Indian music. He advised her to buy a better player than the one she brought from the States, so she decided to do just that, giving herself a Christmas present.

On the morning of Christmas, Catherine had prayed, made up her room and had Aadi's photo on her bed, thinking of him with love on this special day. She went up for her breakfast and when she came down, saw Jannu and Tapasya in the courtyard.

"Merry Christmas, Auntie," "Merry Christmas, Auntie."

Catherine smiled happily and wished them the same. When she entered her room, the first thing she saw was a huge envelope on her bed, next to Aadi's photo. She never locked her door, but she never expected Jannu would enter without her presence.

"Oh, my God!" she said aloud, and immediately put the photo away. Her door was open and she could see Tapasya outside at some distance.

"Tapasya," she called to her.

"Yes, Auntie?"

"Did you put this envelope here?"

"No, Auntie. Jannu Kaka."

Catherine's worst fears had become reality. Jannu had seen the photo. He could not have missed it. What did he think? He was so astute. Would he say anything to her? If so, how would she answer? She looked out and saw both Tapasya and Jannu still in the courtyard.

"Please come in. I found something here on my bed."

They entered her room and sat down. Catherine opened the envelope and found the largest Christmas card she had ever seen. It was signed, "The Kankarwa Family." She read every word and then saw a package inside the envelope. It was a heavy silver necklace and a pair of earrings with three red stones in each. She was completely stunned. The gift was not inexpensive.

"Oh, this is just beautiful," she said. "Thank you so very much."

"Auntie," Jannu said, "Divyu told me to get something really nice for Auntie. I hope you like it."

"I do, I do. I will enjoy wearing them very much. You are so good to me."

Later in the morning, a hired car took her to church where she enjoyed Christmas Mass in Hindi and English. The church was decorated in Indian style, with much glitter and lights. A huge crèche was set up to the left of the altar, and although the figures did not conform in size, it was done with love and care, and the congregation flocked to it to touch and worship there. After Mass, she had the driver take her to the Bapu Bazaar where she bought a new radio/cassette/disc player. She found only one cassette tape for Christmas, and bought that also.

When she returned, Suchana found her and wished her a Happy Christmas. Catherine then thanked her for the necklace and earrings.

"Auntie, would you like a cake?"

"A cake?"

"For Christmas."

"Oh! No, Suchana. No cake. I just want to be with the family and eat as we usually do."

"Auntie, I make Kata?" Suchana knew that Catherine loved it.

"Oh, yes, Suchana. Please. I'd really like that."

"All right, Auntie. I make."

Kata was also known as Karhai, a thick yellow soup made with 'charge' or buttermilk. When yogurt is blended with warm water, it separates and the curd is taken off to be rendered into ghee. The thin liquid that remains is buttermilk (charge, as they called it at the haveli), and into this is mixed besan (chick-pea flour) and spices. Sometimes small pakoras, like dumplings, are made and dropped into the kata. Either way, Catherine was very fond of it. When batti was also made, the batti was crumbled on the plate and kata was poured over it. That plus a vegetable of some kind, a dal and a hot green chutney, made an excellent meal. This is what Suchana prepared for Catherine's first Christmas dinner in India. She wore another sari that evening.

Late on Christmas night Sarah and her sister arrived. Their plane had been delayed, so they had little time to be together, but spent time in Catherine's room until they all felt the need for sleep. Catherine set her alarm because the girls had to leave very early and she wanted to see them off.

"Catherine," Sarah said at the haveli doorway, "When I tried to pay for the room, they said it was already paid. Did Jannu do that?"

"I did, Sarah. It was my present to you. Merry Christmas."

"Oh, Catherine. Thank you. That was so nice! I love you."

"I love you too, Sarah. Have fun on the rest of your holiday, and be sure to keep in touch."

"I will. I will write you from Delhi."

Catherine got a card from Sarah from somewhere in the south. She had gotten ill again, but had recovered.

The next day Subhash and Divyarishi returned and Mama and Papa also arrived with Papa's sister-in-law from Jaipur. Vibu's wife Prem and little Uma also came. Catherine dressed in yet another sari and opened her door to receive the family. When she asked Jannu how everyone was going to fit in her little room, he told her, "No problem, Auntie." He had two durry rugs laid on the floor and pushed the beds together. It was a cozy gathering, with the ladies sitting on the floor, the men on the bed and in the one chair. Catherine had a plate of sweets which she passed around and then proceeded to give out the presents. She had written a personal note on a card to Mama and Papa and wondered if Papa would be able to read it. Catherine put on the Christmas cassette and was dismayed to hear that it was mostly jazz, but the children loved it, especially Tapasya who wanted to dance to the music. Catherine got up and twirled her around and then did the same with Divyu and Diksha. It was in a tiny space, but it was fun and everyone enjoyed the evening.

Divyu's birthday came the following day and of course Catherine had to dress in sari for that occasion. When Papa saw her, he smiled and came to her.

"Auntie, you just like Indian lady. You no foreigner. You not of our family, but in our hearts, you are family." Catherine was so touched, she wanted to cry.

"Thank you, Papa. That means so very much to me."

Divyu was beside himself with joy because he got a bicycle. He had been riding one that was too big for him and now he had his very own for his size. "Auntie, Auntie, look," he cried to her, as he wheeled around and around the courtyard.

Big plans were set for the evening birthday party. All the haveli guests were invited as well as friends of the three children, of the parents and of Jannu. Divyu had made a list of the people he wanted there and after the immediate family, he asked that Aadi be present. Of course this was impossible because Aadi was out of station, but Catherine's heart clenched when she heard how much he was desired to be part of the celebration. A catered buffet was set up with a separate table for liquor and soft drinks. Only a few of Divyu's little friends came because it was a holiday and many were busy with their own families and festivities. Of course the Lake Palace, the Jag Mandir Palace and the City Palace were still lit up, but there was a fireworks display only on Christmas night.

Because of the holiday season, Catherine continued to wear a sari every day when she worked, taking orders for breakfast from the clients. One morning she noticed a foreigner as being obviously an American.

"Where are you from?" Catherine asked her.

The woman looked down her nose and answered her very haughtily, "New York".

And then to Catherine's surprise, the silly and proud woman asked, "Where did you learn your English?'

Obviously she thought Catherine was Indian due to her working as waitress and wearing a sari. Catherine decided to answer her in equal terms.

She looked down her nose, answering in the same manner. "Minnesota." And walked off to the kitchen to give her order.

In the kitchen, Catherine related the incident to Jannu, who laughed uproariously. For days following she was accosted by his friends.

"Auntie, where did you learn your English?" And they would laugh.

Then came New Year's Eve, which was Subhash's birthday. The family was together once again for his celebration, which consisted of dinner and good wishes. Catherine did not tell anyone that her birthday was just a few days away on the 3rd, but she received many cards from the States which she placed on the window takh in her room.

One evening she was talking to two young men from the States who were staying at the haveli. They talked about having spent time in Thailand when they were growing up and how they remembered the Christmas tree they decorated. When they were describing it, Catherine suddenly realized her tree was the same type, so she took them to her room where they immediately recognized it as a Norfolk Pine like they had as children.

Catherine was feeling very low on her birthday, not because no one was aware of it, but because she missed Aadi and he didn't remember her on her day. She was in the kitchen in the evening when a call came for her, which she answered and heard Teresa Albuquerque on the phone. Teresa was inviting her to come to Bombay soon before they went to Goa.

She knew she had to leave India to return to the States for a new visa before the middle of February, so she decided to plan a trip to Bombay to visit the Albuquerques and then on to Belgaum to see Asha and Ramu.

Before that occurred, a woman came to the haveli from Cairns, Australia. She was British, but had left England twenty years earlier because of a hopeless love affair with a Sikh. Neither family would understand their relationship, so Robina moved to Australia. Even to this day, this couple spoke to each other every day, although he was married and still lived in England. Robbie had planned to stay at the haveli for three days and felt so at home, she remained for three weeks and became a good friend of Catherine. They shopped together and spent time having chai and exchanging histories.

On the 9th of January, Catherine ran into Chain in Reception.

"Hi, Chain. How are you?"

"Fine. Aadi come here?"

"Aadi? No, Chain, I haven't seen him."

"He home last night."

"Oh, thank you for telling me, Chain."

Catherine wondered how long it would be before Aadi made an appearance at the haveli. Surely he would come to see and talk to Jannu. That evening there was a knock on her door and when she saw him, she began to cry. It had been ten weeks since she had seen him.

"Oh, Aadi. Come in. I'm so happy to see you."

"How are you?" Catherine noticed immediately that he said those same words differently than he had before. The sweet, loving emphasis was no longer on the 'how', and she suddenly felt bereft, that something was irretrievably lost. He made no move to touch her, but she needed his arms around her.

"Aadi, please hold me," she said.

He took her in his arms then and kissed her, not passionately, but fully on the mouth. Then he sat in her chair and they talked for a short while, and Catherine gave him his Christmas presents; two shirts, a cashmere sweater and a neck scarf.

"I will take only one gift," he told her.

"What?" she asked incredulously. "But they are all for you."

"Whose birthday?" he asked, seeing the cards by the window.

"Mine, Aadi."

"But you never told me when your birthday was," he accused.

"Oh, Aadi, I've told you at least three times when you have asked me." She wasn't about to let him get away with that! He jumped out of his chair and ran to the door, and opening it, yelled out at Jannu in the courtyard.

"I forgot her birthday! I forgot her birthday!" he said as he went out to join Jannu.

Catherine sat where she was and felt disappointed when he ran out, making his visit such a short one after being gone for so long. Her heart was aching. Jannu and Divyu came in her room along with Aadi. He began to sing 'Happy Birthday' to her and Jannu and Divyu joined in.

"Auntie, you didn't tell us it was your birthday," Jannu said.

"Oh, Jannu, it was of no consequence. There were already other birthdays and Christmas, so it didn't matter. After all, I wasn't here for your birthday either, on the 11th of December, because I was in Delhi."

"But you should have told us. We would have had a cake."

"A cake I don't need," she told him laughing.

"But the kids would have enjoyed."

Aadi left then without any of her gifts, telling her he was not going straight home and he would pick them up the next day. Of course he did not show up the following day and it would be many days before he took his gifts. She was heart-broken and very sad. What had happened? Why was he so distant? What had changed him? The situation seemed hopeless to her, as though the last year had been a fantasy. Was that it? Had it all been a dream? Or had there been a deeper meaning that somehow now was broken?

Again the depression set in. She wept and prayed, read over all their correspondence of the past year, and wept more. Deep down she knew she was feeling self-pity and hated herself for it, but it came with all the hurt and sense of loss. Rejected again! Undesired and unwanted by the third man she ever loved. The loss of unfulfilled dreams seared her soul.

It was Sunday, the day after Aadi had come to see her. Chain picked her up for church and waited until Mass was over. He then drove her home, but suddenly she wondered where he was going, because he didn't follow the usual route to the haveli. As they drove down one street, he told her.

"Aadi house."

"Aadi's house? Where, Chain?"

"There, Auntie." He stopped the car across the street and pointed to it.

"You go in?"

"Oh, no, Chain. I've not been invited. Please, let us go. But thank you for showing me."

She could not see the actual house because of a high wall surrounding it. But there was a large green wooden gate and she noticed a tree behind the wall with branches reaching to the sky. They drove on and Catherine made note of where in the old city it was located. She had walked so close to where he lived, but never down that particular street. It was near the Gulab Bagh and just off Lake Palace Road. The area was known as 'Chhoti Brahmpuri', or 'small Brahmin place.'

Catherine was very touched that Chain had shown her Aadi's house. Certainly she never talked to him about Aadi, and yet he must have known that Aadi was special to her. His kindness to her in showing her where he lived touched her deeply. "Chain knows my heart," she said to herself, and held her tears in check.

"Jannu," Catherine said, as they sat together in Reception, "Would you start looking for a house for me?"

"You want to shift?"

"It's time, Jannu. I need to get my things out of storage in Duluth and have them sent here. I would like a place of my own. Perhaps two bedrooms, a kitchen, bathroom and living room and maybe another bedroom that I can use for a workroom and do stain glass."

"Auntie, I think you should go into a flat or a double house so you are not alone."

"Oh, no, Jannu. I have envisioned a separate house, one floor with garden all around it."

"But, Auntie, that isn't safe. You must be around people. I will ask Aadi if he knows of a place."

Yes, it was time for her to move. She felt stronger now and able to cope. Always Jannu and the Ranawat family would be there to support her emotionally or physically. But she now wanted privacy and a home of her own.

Catherine started to make plans for a trip to Mumbai and Belgaum. Jannu learned there was a small plane that flew to Belgaum instead of her taking a train or bus. Even Ramu was unaware of that when she contacted him. He had advised her to come by train from Mumbai. Jannu called the travel agency he used and made all the arrangements for her. She would leave at the end of the month and spend a few days with the Albuquerques, then go on to Belgaum and visit Asha and Ramu for a week and a half. More reservations had to be made also for her journey back to the States, for she needed to be out of India before her visa had expired.

Aadi hadn't come around and Catherine was beside herself with loneliness for him. She was walking again and praying in her special place in the Gulab Bagh, where she was always alone and could weep in private. On the way home, as she walked up Lake Palace Road to the City Palace, she looked out over the Lake at the Hotel where she and Aadi had met and felt tears coming again. It would soon be a year after that momentous occasion. She was now in India, living a new life and she had to come to terms with the reality of the present. Only then could she hope for any happiness in the future.

He came at noon. He was suffering from a sore throat. Catherine was in her best spirits, conveying only light-heartedness. Aadi responded in kind.

"I'm leaving soon for Mumbai and Belgaum. Do you think it is possible that we could spend a day together before I leave? Go somewhere and maybe have a picnic?"

"Yes, we can do that."

"I think it would be fun. Aadi, we haven't had time to talk for so long. I've been worried about you. Have you seen a doctor about your leg?"

"Yes, but I couldn't see P.K. Sethi because there was a three week waiting period for an appointment. I did see Dr. Katju."

"The older man. What did he say?"

"He said there was nothing wrong. I just need to do exercise."

"Really! What kind of exercise?"

Aadi pulled up his trouser leg and showed her by tensing his muscles.

"That's it?"

"Yes. You see, I am fine. An x-ray showed nothing wrong. I will bring it for you to see."

"Aadi, I'm so proud of you for going to see the doctor, but you are not fine. This is why I asked to go with you. You didn't know the questions to ask, and I'm dismayed that this doctor didn't do more examinations. Please, Aadi, see someone else. I think this doctor is past his prime."

"What do you mean?"

"I mean he is too old. Go see a neurologist or neurosurgeon, one on the list I gave you. And I so wish you would take me with you."

"I will go. I promise."

"Aadi, do you want to come to the U.S.?"

"Yes, but I may have difficulty getting a visa."

"I'll go with you to the Embassy. You mentioned earlier that May was the best time to go. I wonder if you could possibly go sooner, because it would save me money by waiting there for you."

"No, come back here, then we'll go."

"All right. I'll do that. I told Jannu recently that I want to find a house of my own. Aadi, how do you feel about that? Are you comfortable with my living in Udaipur?"

"Yes, you must do what is right for you"

She told him what she had in mind regarding a house, and he promised to talk to Jannu about finding one for her. Their conversation continued on in a light vein and then she was in his arms and kissing him.

"You will get my sore throat," he told her.

"It doesn't matter. This is more important. I've missed you so."

After he left she was exuberant, her heart singing. "Thank you, God," she prayed, "I love him so very, very much.

This day was Suchana's birthday and Catherine was happy to join with the family that evening in a quiet celebration over dinner. She truly loved this little lady who was so very kind to her. Catherine knew that Suchana didn't understand how she could get a divorce after so many years and leave her children and grandchildren. This was completely alien to Indian culture. She had tried explaining it to her one time, but in the end, Suchana just accepted without understanding, and the rest of the family evidently did likewise

CHAPTER THIRTY

VISITS WITH OLD FRIENDS

Catherine awoke the next morning with chills, fever and diarrhea. She lay in bed and didn't get dressed for meals. Jannu saw to it that food was brought to her room. It was all bland as she ordered and she was able to tolerate it. Jannu wanted to call a doctor for her, but Catherine had medication for this in her bags, so refused his kind offer. She felt good in another 48 hours, and was surprised when Aadi came to see her.

"Why didn't you call me?" he admonished her.

"Call you? For what reason?"

"Jannu told me you were ill."

"So, it was only for a couple days."

"But you should have called me. You got it from me."

"Aadi, you had a sore throat. This was a stomach upset. They were not related."

"I wish you had called me."

"That is very sweet of you, but all I did was lie in bed and use the bathroom. Aadi, are we going to have that day together?"

"Yes, when you get back."

"But there will be so little time between my return from Belgaum and leaving for the States. And then too, you may be gone on tour."

"No, I will be here."

While they were talking, Jannu came in and sat on her bed and showed Aadi brochures of washing machines, asking his opinion of what to buy.

Aadi told him he needed to buy the expensive Japanese model that heated the water.

"You don't need a machine for that," Catherine said. "You already have hot water here. Besides, you don't need hot water to wash."

"For white clothes you need hot water," Aadi said.

"Not if you have the proper soap," she countered.

"Come on, Aadi," Jannu said. "Let's go and look at these machines."

They left and Catherine just shook her head. Two men deciding what washing machine was best for a woman to use. What did they know? And why didn't Jannu ask for her advice? What did Aadi know? When did he ever use a washing machine? But then, perhaps he used one in Germany.

It was 4:30 AM and Catherine was awakened by a pounding on her door.

"Auntie, Auntie!"

"Yes, all right. Just a minute."

She slipped on a robe and opened the door. Hansraj stood there and a man behind him had an arm full of flowers. It was dark outside and she couldn't seem to get her bearings.

"Hansraj, what is going on? No, no, flowers are not for me. I don't get flowers. For someone else."

But Hansraj kept insisting, then handed her a card. It was addressed to her and she saw that it was from Lisa.

"Oh, I guess they are for me." She took the bouquet from the man and closed the door. Opening the card, it read: 'Happy Thanksgiving, Merry Christmas, Happy New Year and Happy Birthday. Love life terrible. Love, Lisa'. Catherine looked at the bouquet and was amazed at the size of it and the quality of the flowers. But why were they being delivered at such an hour? It seemed crazy. She went back to bed.

"Auntie, Auntie," this from the children a few hours later. She opened the door and the children burst in to see the flowers.

"How did you know I got them? It was so early."

"Jannu kaka."

When she saw Jannu later she had to ask how he knew of the delivery so early in the morning.

"Auntie, Hansraj didn't know who Catherine Forrest was. He only knows you as 'Auntie'. So he called and woke us up."

"Oh no! I'm sorry. But why did they bring them at such an hour?"

"Auntie, do you think Udaipur has flowers like that? The man brought them from Ahmedabad on the bus."

"You're kidding! On the bus? But it must have taken all night for him to get here and I never even gave him a tip!"

"Auntie, you need a nice vase for the flowers. I will find one for you."

Jannu gave her a lovely Rajasthani vase and the flowers looked beautiful in it. However her enjoyment was short-lived. She was soon to leave for Mumbai. Divyu came and asked if he could take care of her flowers while she was gone and she gave them to him. Surely they would be no more by the time she returned, so let the children have fun with them.

Catherine started packing for her trip south. Jannu got her tickets for her, and she contacted the Albuquerques and Ramu to appraise them of the dates of her visits with them. Ramu told her that he and Asha would be in Puttur for their grandson's 'Uppanyanma', the Brahmin thread ceremony. But she was to come anyway and Preema and Vimal would take care of her.

The day she was to leave, Suchana took her aside in the kitchen.

"Auntie, before you go, you go with Jannu Bhana and get me Whirlpool."

"Oh, Suchana, you do need a washing machine. Of course I'll go with Jannu."

"Yes, please, Auntie. You tell Jannu Bhana."

Catherine was all packed and there were several hours yet before she needed to leave for the airport. She went out to sit in the sunshine of the courtyard with Jannu.

"Jannu, before I leave, let's go to the market and buy a washing machine."

"What?" he asked, scowling?

"A washing machine. Suchana needs one. She is not well and she has so much washing. It would help her. Let's go."

"Not now. Later."

"But Jannu, I want to do this before I leave."

"All right, Auntie. Not now."

Catherine could see that he was upset and didn't want to do this, but she was determined, so she sat there until he finally said, "Let's go." They took a riksha to the market and shop where he had been once before. The manager was not in, but Jannu and Catherine went from machine to machine looking at them. She was appalled at how cheaply they were made.

"Jannu, this is a Whirlpool, and I've used them for 40 years, but I've never seen any that were so poorly made. The covers are so light and flimsy; I don't know how they will last."

"Auntie, Indians won't pay for quality. These are made for the Indian market. Come, let's go."

They left the store and Catherine thought they were going to another shop, but instead they went back to the haveli.

"Jannu, what happened? Why couldn't we buy a machine?"

"Auntie, just a minute." He went to the phone and called someone and talked for some time.

"Those machines," he told her later, "were too expensive. They were more than they were the last time I saw them with Aadi. I just spoke to the manager and he said to wait ten days and prices were coming down. Then I'll buy one."

"Ten days. OK. I'll tell Suchana."

Catherine went upstairs to find Suchana and she could tell by the look in her eyes that she was disappointed.

"Only ten days, Suchana. When I get back from Belgaum, you will have your machine."

"All right, Auntie."

Catherine left on the evening plane for Mumbai and after retrieving her luggage, she looked about for Mat, whom she thought was going to meet her.

"Catherine?" a voice from behind her. She turned and recognized Louis, Mat and Teresa's son-in-law, and husband of Sunanda.

"Lulu!"

"You remember me?"

"Of course. How are you Lulu? And Nanda and Sarita?"

"All fine. Come, I have a car."

They drove to the Albuquerque's where Catherine was heartily welcomed. She was given a lovely big room at the front of the house, mosquito netting covering the large bed.

The next day Teresa took Catherine shopping for a salwar/kameez. Sunanda had told her mother where to go because Teresa always wore sari and didn't know what shops would have salwar suits to fit Catherine. The largest sizes seemed to be 'free size' and once again Catherine was dismayed at being unable to get into them. Finally they arrived at one lovely shop and Catherine found salwar/kameez to fit her. They were all similar with Chikan embroidery, beautifully made, and Catherine bought three of them; one in white, one pale yellow and another in a rust color. All had long sleeves, but of very light weight cotton material and Catherine was happy.

One day Teresa made Goan fish for dinner and Catherine thought she had died and gone to heaven. It was so delicious. She made a pig of herself, but couldn't stop eating the wonderful fish curry, which was bright red in color and very hot. Mat enjoyed watching her eat.

"Catherine, how can you eat that without chapati? It is too hot for me."

"Oh, it is just wonderful, Mat."

She finished the entire meal, having eaten most of the fish curry herself. Outside of Udaipur she would eat eggs and fish, but not meat. And this particular recipe of curry was the best she had ever tasted. She had watched Teresa make it with dried hot peppers in a grinder, but didn't take note of the other ingredients.

After three days, it was time to leave these lovely people, who were soon going to their home in Goa. Catherine boarded a Spanair tiny plane for Belgaum. The plane held six passengers including the pilot. One seat was next to the pilot and the other four faced each other, two by two, knees touching. It was a new propeller plane however and Catherine felt safe in it. But it took several hours to reach their destination.

Since Asha and Ramu were not in Belgaum, Catherine hired a riksha at the small airport to take her into town. Through an interpreter she was able to tell the driver where she needed to go. The driver had a difficult time knowing where to go and all Catherine could say was, 'Ayodhyanagar' and 'Dr. Ambedkar Road. After several stops whereby the driver asked directions, Catherine recognized the statue of Dr. Ambedkar and knew where she was, thus directing the driver to Ramu's house.

Preema and Vimal were so happy to see her and had worried as to how she would find her way. As soon as she entered the house, Catherine felt at home again. These people were family. Although Preema knew little English, she and Catherine were able to communicate very well and Catherine enjoyed being alone for a few days with these loving, attentive servants. Preema cooked many different dishes for her and taught Catherine some of her recipes. It was an enjoyable time.

Asha and Ramu returned and once again it was a joyful reunion. It was a leisurely visit, early morning rising with tea, then a bit later a lovely breakfast. Ramu walked about the house every morning dusting the furniture, then walking for a while in the garden. He was living a sedentary life now that he had had another heart attack. Catherine could not convince him that by-pass surgery would be the answer for him. He was afraid.

"Dinu was very worried when I had the attack in Ankola. He had a heart specialist come and examine me. That doctor wanted me to have surgery immediately. But I called my doctor in Calcutta. He told me I didn't have to have it, that I could just cut down my activity and get plenty of rest."

"Ramu! Your doctor in Calcutta! You haven't seen him in years! What does he know of your condition now?"

"He is a good doctor."

"Maybe so, but he is not here to examine you, so how can he give you the proper advice? Ramu, by-pass surgery is almost routine now. I know there are excellent hospitals in Bangalore. Your son lives there. Why don't you check out a physician there?"

"No, I'm not going to have surgery. I can just rest and take things easy here."

So the women of the household watched him closely, cooked foods without saturated fats and waited on his every whim. He took naps after each meal, but he did not give up his drinking. Every night he sat with his bottle of whiskey and sipped out of a small glass with water.

Catherine's visit was over all too soon. When Ramu called the airport to find out when the Spanair plane would be arriving in Belgaum for a return flight to Mumbai, he learned that they had to leave the house immediately in order to take the flight. Spanair had not called the Shenoy number, which Catherine had given them in the event of a change of flight time. Asha and Ramu hurried to get the car out and Catherine said brief good-byes to Preema and Vimal.

It was a long distance to the airport and Ramu was very anxious that Catherine would miss her flight. He became very nervous and agitated, which was bad for his heart condition and Catherine tried to calm him down, telling him not to worry.

They arrived at the airport only to learn that the plane had not yet arrived and no one was there to check her in. Ramu relaxed and then Asha and Catherine did also, because they were very concerned that Ramu would have another heart attack. They waited over an hour and finally the plane arrived as did the ground personnel to check luggage and passengers. Catherine hugged Asha and Ramu, thanking them for their warm hospitality and inviting them to visit her in Udaipur.

Again the plane was full; pilot and five passengers. Mineral water and box lunches were supplied to each, just as on the trip down to Belgaum. Once again Catherine enjoyed the flight and landed in Mumbai, where she had to take a bus to another building for her return flight to Udaipur.

Home at last to the city where she now lived, she retrieved her luggage and looked in vain for her driver and car. Had Jannu forgotten to send her one? Other taxis stood waiting to take passengers to Udaipur, but no one came for her. Finally, a taxi driver came up and asked if he could drive her into the city.

"No, I'm waiting for my driver."

"Where are you going?"

"Kankarwa Haveli."

"Oh, I know that place. They don't send cars out for anyone."

"Yes they do. They know I'm coming."

"Madam, I know that man. He is not sending anyone."

It was getting later, so Catherine went inside to call the haveli.

"Oh, Auntie," the servant answered. "Car coming right now."

She went back to stand outside and the other driver tried once again to get her fare.

"Car not coming. Take my taxi. I know that man. He not good."

"I know that man also! I've been living there for six months!"

"Oh, yes, yes, very good man!"

Jannu laughed when she repeated this exchange to him, and he often told others how drivers liked to influence tourists to go to hotels where they are given commissions. Kankarwa never paid commissions to anyone.

"Jannu," Catherine called to him. "Did you get the washing machine?"

"Oh, Auntie, come! You must see."

Catherine followed expectedly and was dumbfounded when he led her to the Common Room.

"Look, Auntie. A new TV!"

"A new TV! Jannu, what about the washing machine?"

"Oh yes, we will get that after some time."

"I don't believe this! Jannu, why a new and bigger TV? You only have one channel and Suchana needs a washing machine!"

"Yes, yes, Auntie, but look how nice this is."

Catherine shook her head. It was hopeless! Now there were only two days left before she had to leave for the States. Where was Aadi? She had been looking forward to his taking her on a picnic. But he didn't come. Was he on tour? He had told her he would be in Udaipur. She didn't dare ask Jannu. Finally, when no one was about, she made a call to his home only to learn he was not at home. Catherine was determined not to call him again. But she couldn't keep this promise with herself. She wept bitterly during the day and night, and felt totally miserable. On the afternoon of her last day, only Suchana was in Reception and Catherine once again dialed Aadi's home.

"Where are you?" he asked. "In Delhi?"

She was flabbergasted. Delhi? "No, I'm still at Kankarwa."

"When do you leave?'

"At six."

"I will come."

Aadi finally arrived at 5:15. Her room had been vacated to make it available for clients. Servants had taken her luggage and other personal things which she planned to leave at the haveli, and put them in the family storeroom. All that was left was her cassette player and speakers, which two servants were boxing up when Aadi finally arrived. He handed her two packets of plastic he'd had in his pocket.

"Here, this is your Christmas present and your birthday present."

The servants were still in the room and Catherine didn't want to open and look at her gifts until they had left. When they finally did, she closed the door and opened the packets.

"Oh, Aadi, this is beautiful," she cried. In her hand were a pair of silver earrings and a silver necklace with blue glass. They didn't match exactly, but they went together very well. The style was definitely Rajasthani and Catherine loved them.

Her room was devoid of all her belongings and she felt somewhat displaced. But Aadi made himself comfortable in a window seat and they talked for a short while. He brought up the political situation in Iraq and the United States role in the Gulf War. The Indian press was not favorable to the U.S. position and obviously Aadi agreed. Catherine tried to offer the view of her country, but Aadi was adamant, saying that this war was also bad for India.

After several embraces, Aadi and Catherine opened her door and proceeded to the reception area for it was almost time to leave for the airport.

"Will you come with me to the airport, Aadi?" she asked.

"No, I am expecting someone at my home."

Chain arrived and the whole family, kids, Suchana, Jannu and the servant boys walked with her to the car. The children demanded kisses over and over. Suchana hugged her and then she was off, tears streaming down her face. At the airport, Chain took her luggage out of the car. She paid him for the trip as well as the trip back to the city.

"Chain," she said, "please take care of Aadi." She then said her 'good-bye' to him and went into the terminal.

CHAPTER THIRTY ONE
TWO HOMECOMINGS

Sunil found Catherine at the domestic terminal in Delhi, and took her to his home for several days before she took off for the United States. Happily, she found the family situation much better than her last visit. Due to the war in the Gulf, the airlines had to reroute their flights, and Catherine arrived in London ten hours after departing Delhi. Her flight was seven hours into New York, where she had to change terminals and experience a four hour delay. The grueling trip continued with another four hour delay in Detroit for bad weather. Arriving in Minneapolis, Catherine learned that her flight to Fargo had departed, so she called Roland, who picked her up and took her home for the night. Early the next morning she boarded another plane for the short flight to Fargo. Her bags were delayed, but finally made their way safely to Robert's the following afternoon.

In Fargo, Robert advised her against renting a car for the duration of her visit in the States. Instead he shopped for a car for her and decided a Mercury Sable would be just right for her. Catherine went with him to the dealership and bought one, choosing a metallic green. It was great to have wheels again and be independent. After three days with Robert, Kerry and the children, Catherine drove to St. Paul to spend one week with Carmel and Al Wawra. During this time she shopped for gifts for the children at the haveli. She also spent time with her other three sons. After that, she drove to Duluth and stayed with Lisa. Robert had made appointments for her with her dentist and several doctors.

Catherine was most concerned about the recurring pain in her left leg. She thought it was due to a pinched nerve in her spine, but the orthopedist she saw in Duluth told her, "No, you have bursitis," and gave her a cortisone injection into her hip, and prescribed an anti-inflammatory drug. He told her that would solve the problem. She was very skeptical of his diagnosis and treatment, but had no one else to turn to for a solution. Other examinations were good, with no concern except for her diabetes.

On Sunday, March 8th, Catherine became a Benedictine Oblate, which is a layman with a prayer life, following the Rule of St. Benedict, and connected to a monastery, in this case, St. Scholastica of Duluth. She was thrilled to be part of this community, after living next door to Benedictines for thirty years. Catherine dressed in a lovely black and gold sari and spoke the words of oblation with the five others who joined that same day. It was the highlight of her entire trip. It began with morning prayers at the monastery, meeting Sr. Mary Charles and attending a beautiful liturgy. Afterwards they joined the sisters for brunch in the dining room, and ended the day with an oblate meeting and oblation ceremony in the chapel.

The second week in Duluth was spent at Mary Ramsay's home. It was good to have time together and 'catch up'. During this time, Catherine saw many friends, especially Conny and Mike Kylmala. Conny gave her a much needed permanent and dye job and the three of them enjoyed dinner together one evening. Catherine called a trucking company and arranged to have her belongings removed from storage and shipped to India. The company told her it would take 4 – 6 weeks to arrive in Bombay.

It was the festival of Holi in India and Catherine vividly remembered how Aadi had 'painted' her over the phone the year before. It had been so much fun that she hoped to have the same experience this year. She called him, but learned he was not at home. It was bitterly disappointing.

A few days later Catherine flew from Duluth to Portland, Oregon to visit her mother. Mike Kylmala took care of her car so she didn't have to leave it in the Duluth airport. Cindy met her at the airport and informed her she would be leaving for California in a couple of days and would not be home before Catherine left. Catherine was stunned and deeply disappointed. She had blocked off an entire week to spend with both her sister and her mother.

"Cindy," she said, "I'll never again come for this long a visit."

"I knew you would react this way! You're going to take this out on Mother!"

"No, I will always come to visit Mother. This has nothing to do with her."

Cindy left and cousin Joe Angeletti flew in from California to spend a day and a half with her. It was a very special time. And one day Cindy's daughter, Monica and her daughter, Katy, came from Seattle for a short visit. It helped to pass the time. Catherine found her mother happy and in good spirits, and pleased to see her, of course. However, there was little conversation because Mother wanted to watch her TV. She was still smoking as much as ever. And Cindy surprised her by coming home in time to take her to the airport.

Catherine arrived in Duluth and found her car in the parking lot. Mike had had it washed and it was ready for her. She drove to Lisa's and stayed with her again. She was lonely for her family in India, so phoned them and talked to Jannu, Suchana and the kids. In an email from Divyarishi she learned that Jannu had bought a dishwasher for the kitchen. Catherine was really upset. She emailed back.

'DISHWASHER? DISHWASHER? DISHWASHER?' in increasingly larger print. She hoped Jannu would get the message that she was angry that he hadn't bought a washing machine for Suchana.

She phoned Aadi and spoke to him. It was so good hearing his voice. He had been out of station and had just returned. She was hoping he would decide to visit the United States with her this year. He always said he would, but never committed himself.

Her last Sunday in Duluth, Catherine went to the monastery for Mass, and had brunch there with Srs. Mary Charles, Teri and Mary Stephen. Later she had a good visit at the Barn, and an early dinner with Sr. Mary Charles and said 'good-bye'. The following day was Russell's 30th birthday, so she called him to wish him happiness. It was his 'golden' birthday.

At 5:30 AM March 31st, Catherine's newest grandchild was born. Anne had a Cesarean Section due to the baby coming breach. Both mother and baby were fine; another granddaughter for Catherine and second daughter for Roland and Anne. They named her Bailey Kathleen. Kathleen was in honor of her other grandmother and Catherine was not hurt by this, only pleased because she loved Kathy DeBoth. On Randall's birthday, April 2nd, Catherine drove to Fargo to see her grandchildren there for a last time. Then she left for the Twin Cities, where she spent most of one day holding her new grandbaby. What a joy, with baby in one arm and the other around Kimberly, the 2 year old.

Catherine had sent her passport via Fed Ex to the consulate General of India, asking for a business visa. She had heard nothing from them and she was getting anxious as the time for her departure was drawing very near. Finally, in desperation, she phoned the consulate and learned the passport was still there. She informed them of her impending departure for India and they sent it back by Fed Ex on the very morning she left for the airport. They did not give her a business visa, but another six month tourist visa. This meant she would have to return to the United States after only six months to get a new visa. They would not renew one in India.

Her whirlwind visit home was over and on April 9th she arrived in Delhi where Sunil met her and took her to his house for a few hours. Then back on a plane for Udaipur, where she was met again and transported to her beloved family at Kankarwa Haveli.

Jannu had sent a car to the airport for her and she was treated royally on her return. Catherine enjoyed watching the children's eyes light up at the many gifts she had brought for them.

"Jannu, I must now find a house. My belongings have been shipped and should be in Bombay within six weeks."

"All right, Auntie. I'll place an ad in the paper and we'll find you a house."

"I'd like to live in a separate house, Jannu, with a garden around it."

"Auntie, that is not safe. You must be in a house with other people."

"Oh, Jannu, I want to be alone."

"Auntie," Jannu said with exasperation, "You will be alone, but it is best for others to be close. Just wait and see."

There were several calls to the haveli from various home owners. Many of them Jannu dismissed outright.

"This is in a new area, Auntie, but there are many break-ins there and houses are too far apart. You would not be safe."

And again; "Auntie, this is too far from the haveli."

"Auntie, this is in Muslim area. Not good for you."

Finally, Jannu saw a possibility and they went there to see if Catherine would like it. The landlord saw immediately that she was a foreigner and raised the rental price. Jannu had been talking to him in Hindi so Catherine didn't know what was going on. It was only obvious that Jannu became very angry.

Forget it!" he yelled at the landlord. "Come on, Auntie, he just raised the rent because you are an American. Let's go."

Jannu found another house, a side-by-side, owned by two brothers. One brother was living in Jaipur and wanted his house taken care of during his absence. It was set back somewhat from the other house although they shared one wall. It had a lovely garden all around it and although the kitchen was small, Catherine liked the house. Jannu made arrangements for her to meet the owner when he came into Udaipur. However, something else occurred that changed everything.

"Auntie," Jannu said, coming to her room, "the family is leaving for Jaipur. Divyarishi is to have a hernia repair. You will be in charge with Mahipal. OK?"

Catherine suddenly felt bereft. It was not that she was being put in charge, but that the family was leaving. "Jannu, for how long?"

"A week, maybe two. Do you mind being in charge?"

"No, of course not, but I'm going to miss all of you. And what about my house?"

"Auntie, Aadi is back. I saw him last night. If the owner comes before I get back, Aadi will take you there and help you."

Catherine had heard when she came back that Aadi was 'out-of-station' with his German girlfriend. She wondered how often the woman came to India. Catherine wondered also if the woman was coming here because Aadi planned to visit the U.S. this year with Catherine, and not go to Europe as he usually did. Strangely, Catherine felt no jealousy, only a sense of rightness because she wanted nothing but joy for this man she loved. There was sadness however, for Catherine realized that she would never be loved by this man and that caused her heartache. But she did have faith that Aadi would help her with the house.

For a long time Catherine toyed with the thought of writing a book; something more than the everyday writing in her journal. She opened a notebook and began. She didn't know if she could do this, as she was especially afraid of writing dialogue. Nevertheless, she took pen in hand and found the words flowing easily. She completed the prologue and then it came; words, dialogue, all from her heart. It was as if she was bursting to tell her story and it was insistent on being told. Catherine always knew she could write, but this was a surprise which gave her joy, courage, and self confidence.

The family left the following day and Catherine felt sad, for she missed them immediately. The haveli was not the same without them, especially the children. She had no doubt however that she and Mahipal could manage the haveli. After all, it was summer and there were few clients due to the heat.

Catherine called Aadi and asked him to go with her to see the house in Bhopalpura, the area in Udaipur where it was situated. He didn't come to her until the following day and she was anxious, not only for the house, but because she hadn't seen him since she had gone to the U.S. They left for the house on his scooter. It felt so good to place her arms around him, even though it was for her safety only. It had been ten weeks since she had seen him last and her body ached for the sight of him, the sound of his voice and the feel of him. But he was strangely quiet and when Catherine tried to start a conversation, he barely answered her.

"Aadi, I hope you like the house. I certainly do." She had to direct him at one point, for she saw it in the distance and he had started in another direction. When they arrived, they walked through the house and Aadi spoke in Hindi to the owner. Then they walked across the property, in front of the brother's house and into the next street.

"Where are we going?" Catherine asked.

"To the sister's house," Aadi answered.

She was surprised that the sister lived just behind the houses of the two brothers. The lady answered the door and ushered them into a parlor. They all sat down and the lady started asking questions of Catherine.

"Why do you want to live here?"

"I like the house very much," Catherine answered.

"But why here in Udaipur?"

"My friends are here."

"You don't know the language, how can you manage?"

"I'll manage just fine."

"How will you get your food? The markets are all over. Vegetables are not in the same place as meat."

"Excuse me, but I am vegetarian, and I'll find the right markets."

"Why don't you live in Travandrum?"

"I don't have any desire to live in the south. I plan to live in Udaipur."

"What would you do if the lights went out?"

Catherine was getting exasperated with these questions. She answered, "I'd wait until they came back on."

The woman said something in Hindi and got up and went into the kitchen. Catherine had been waiting for Aadi to open his mouth to back her up, but when he finally spoke, she was astounded.

"She's very rich," Aadi told the brother, referring to Catherine.

"What?" Catherine asked.

"You are," he said.

"Excuse me, but I am not rich. I suppose you think that I am as an American living here, but I assure you, by American standards, I am not."

The brother left and followed the sister into the kitchen. Aadi was quiet and Catherine felt uneasy.

"What is going on, Aadi? Don't they want me to rent the house?"

"We'll see."

Tea was brought in and they drank it and left. The brother stayed with his sister, obviously to talk over whether or not to rent to Catherine. Aadi and Catherine walked back to the rental property where they were to wait for an answer. She was upset, not only about the house, but for the strange attitude of Aadi.

"Aadi, I only got a six month visa again, so I'll have to go back to the U.S. Are you coming with me? We could go in a month or so."

"Oh, no. I can't. There are many weddings I have to attend here."

"Weddings! But Aadi, you said you would go with me! When can we go?"

"We'll go before the end of the year," he assured her.

But Catherine was not convinced. Also, he was very restless and kept walking away from her. She couldn't figure out what he was thinking. Then the brother came back and spoke to Aadi. Evidently there was a man who wanted to see the house and they planned to show it to him before deciding who to rent it to. Catherine was disappointed, but still optomistic. She was sure she would hear from him that evening or the next day at the latest. But it was a false hope. She was not contacted again.

The next day Catherine tried calling Aadi, but was told by his father that Aadi was not home. She left a message, but Aadi didn't return her call. She was devastated because she felt he had betrayed her, that he did nothing to help her get that house. Also she was sure he was avoiding her. Alone in her room, she wept and prayed.

Another call to Aadi was answered by his father. He asked if she was calling from London and when she told him 'no', he informed her that Aadi was not available. This hurt Catherine terribly, but she continued to phone him at other times of the day and evening. Finally, Aadi answered and told her he would be coming to her the following morning.

Catherine waited expectedly, but Aadi didn't show up until the afternoon. Conversation was minimal. He obviously felt pressured. He didn't want to go to the U.S. with her, but didn't actually say so. He was upset when he realized that she had bought a car for that purpose. She let him know that she knew his German friend had been to India and that it was fine with her.

About this time a young French couple arrived on their honeymoon and became very attached to Catherine. Their names were Franck and Delphine. They were very sweet, and wanted her to spend time with them. Catherine explained she was in charge at the haveli and couldn't take time to travel with them.

"Please, Catherine, come with us to Ranakpur," Delphine pleaded.

No, Delphine, I cannot go, but when you come back I'll have a lovely dinner prepared for you on the roof. Just the two of you by candle-light. Very romantic."

"Catherine," she said, "You must have dinner with us."

"Delphine, this is your honeymoon. This is for you to enjoy. You don't need a third person."

"Oh, but we do! We want you. Please, you must join us."

Catherine arranged for the dinner for the couple, but she rejected the idea of joining them. She decided to join them the following evening and that pleased them. Also, Catherine thought Aadi might enjoy meeting this couple and conversing with them in French, so she placed a call to him.

Mr. Abhimani answered the phone. "Where are you calling from" he asked.

"From Kankarwa," she answered.

"Aadi is not available," he told her.

Catherine was crushed. It was obvious that his father was once again screening his calls, and she felt insulted.

Jannu's second oldest brother, Vibu, arrived to take charge at the haveli because Mahipal had to leave. Vibu, however, did not speak very much English, but he had a great sense of humor and he and Catherine got along very well. Vibu had a wife and child at his farm some distance from Udaipur. His wife, Prem, called him frequently during his stay at the haveli and Catherine got the impression she wanted him to come home.

It was getting extremely hot and Catherine was feeling the heat, this being her first real summer in India. Jannu called occasionally, and finally she got to talk to him.

"Auntie, how are you?" he asked.

"Fine, Jannu, but it's so hot."

"Oh, Auntie, move into 204. It's cooler there. Do that right away."

"OK."

"Otherwise, everything OK?"

"Yes, Jannu. But I miss you and the family."

"We are coming soon, Auntie."

That very day the boys helped her to move her belongings across the courtyard to room 204. It was not only much larger, but it was so much cooler, facing only the lake at its far end and having thick, insulating walls. There was an antique desk in the room which she immediately took over for writing and many takhs (niches) in which to place many items. At the far end was a large takh, which she decided to use for her puja area because it faced west, which was auspicious. Jannu had told her east or west was correct, not south or north.

Vibu decided to go back to his farm for a few days and since there were so few clients, Catherine felt confident she could manage without him. However, she did call Aadi and asked him to please stop by to give her a hand, since she would be alone. He told her he would, but he never showed up.

Catherine got along very well with the servant boys. She knew enough to manage well on her own and was good at it. Bapu was one of the boys who worked in the kitchen and also did cleaning of the rooms as well. Catherine enjoyed him and started teaching him English. It was difficult. He was 21 years old and quite slow. Although he knew the alphabet, he couldn't understand how to 'sound-out' letters to read words. So she tried memorization with him and that too was extremely slow. She did get him to answer 'yes' instead of the Hindi 'ha'. However, it was difficult to erase the subservient manners he had acquired in the village.

"Sorry, Auntie," he would say, and pull both his ears.

Catherine had noticed this when he talked to Vibu and had been appalled. He had gone down on both knees and pulled both ears when talking to him. Vibu had looked down upon him as if he were a king looking upon his subject and Catherine was totally dismayed by this sight. Of course she said nothing because this was not her culture and she had no right to interfere.

Another observation she made was that the servants never sat in chairs, but on the floor or squatted. When they were alone, Catherine asked Bapu to sit across from her when she was teaching him English and he did so.

One day a call came from a man who worked for Fed Ex. He had helped Catherine ship packages to the U.S. for Christmas and he knew she was looking for a house.

He told her of one that was available right on Lake Pichola, so she contacted Aadi so that he could go with her to see the house. That was the last she heard of the place. Aadi found out that the owner did not want foreigners renting there so didn't bother taking her. Catherine was very upset. Jannu never told owners ahead that she was a foreigner. It seemed to Catherine that Aadi was sabotaging all her efforts to get a house.

Aadi came to the haveli on the 10th of May dressed in white pajama and dark blue kurta. He looked so handsome, Catherine's heart swelled with love for him. She showed him her new room and explained that Jannu had told her to move to this room because it was cooler. Her other room got morning sun as well as afternoon sun and had become unbearably hot. He seemed to like it. Aadi gave her a hug, but did not kiss her. She tried to talk with him about the houses, also about their relationship, but he constantly evaded the issues and finally told her she was 'negative'.

"Aadi, I just want to know where you are coming from. How do you feel about me? I am in a great deal of pain because I don't understand you."

With that, he got to his feet and left the room. Catherine was shocked, dismayed, and terribly hurt. He had run away.

The following day the family returned. She was so happy to see them, she wept. Jannu took her to see another house, but it was too expensive and she didn't like it either.

Then Jannu found another house and took her to see it. At last it was something both of them liked and felt good about. It was on a busy street, but set back and was on the first floor, actually the floor above the ground floor where the landlord and his wife lived. The landlord was a retired veterinarian. The house was large, spacious and clean.

CHAPTER THIRTY TWO

A HOUSE ON SAHELI MARG

So a new chapter had begun in Catherine's life. She had a house, a place to call her own. She had only to wait for her belongings to come from the States. And yes, she needed furniture, which Jannu was already ordering for her in the market. In the meantime she was happy at the haveli with the family except for her deep depression knowing that Aadi would probably no longer be in her life.

Dr. Nanavati, her landlord, came to the haveli to finalize the rental agreement with Jannu. Catherine was to pay Rs 8,500 ($218) per month for the apartment. It was done in dark green marble floors with a large kitchen, a living room, a wide entry hall running the full length of the house, a guest bedroom off the hallway and a full bedroom at the end. A lovely sunroom was also at the end of the hallway and a terrace which opened to the bedroom as well as to the sunroom. There were three bathrooms, only one of which had a western toilet however. There was another room off the hall which opened directly to the front door and also into the front room. Catherine opted not to rent this room. There were shelves in each room, but no cupboards and no closets for clothes. This would be a problem because of the dust. The kitchen had a pantry, but again there were open shelves and no cupboards or drawers. This seemed to be the norm of every Indian home Catherine had looked at. As a matter of fact, the haveli kitchen was not at all convenient either.

On May 19th Aadi showed up at the haveli. He came to Catherine's room and sat down. He said nothing, but pulled her into his lap and started kissing her passionately. She was stunned. Then he got up, went to the door, locked it and came back.

"Take off your clothes," he said, as he began to undress. She did as he told her and they went to her bed and made love. He then dressed and left without saying a word to her. It was very strange. After so long! No emotion, no caressing, no kisses, nothing, and suddenly? Passion? What was going on with him? What was he doing with her head?

Catherine talked to Cindy that week and learned that Brandon was ill. She faxed Robert and learned that Bran had cancer of the prostate and was to have surgery on May 26th. He was wearing a Foley catheter with a urine bag attached to his leg. Catherine felt sure he was feeling very scared, so decided to phone him. The connection was very poor and they could not hear each other. She felt so sad for him and prayed for him.

On May 24th the family began a 24 hr. reading of the Ramayana, the Hindu holy book. This was done as a blessing on the family and the haveli. A kind of altar was set up in an area off the courtyard and Brahmin priests came to do the readings. Members of the family also took turns reading aloud, and while the reading was going on, family members sat around following with books. Catherine did not feel it proper for her to intrude. However, on the last day, she was in her room and a knock came on her door.

"Auntie," the children were calling her.

She answered the door and there they were. Three bright faces smiling at her.

"Come, Auntie. Jannu Kaka wants you to join us."

"Oh, really? Ok, but I have to dress properly first. I'll just be a moment."

Catherine quickly put on better clothes and combed her hair and went out to the area where they were praying. She shed her shoes and walked into the enclosed spot where the family was seated on the floor and sat down next to them. They smiled in greeting. This was the closing ceremony and Catherine found it beautiful and she felt so honored to be a part of this sacred moment. Afterwards, everyone was talking and laughing. Sweets were handed out and shared by all. It was very festive.

Another happy experience for her was taking the children to the circus. They had heard the circus was in town and had asked to go, but wanted Catherine to take them, no one else. Jannu asked her if she minded taking them and of course she was delighted to be asked. Subhash drove them to the area and the four of them totally enjoyed the evening. The children were an absolute delight and Catherine loved every minute with them.

June arrived and Catherine learned that Brandon did not have surgery after all. The surgeons felt he was too weak and would not survive, nor would he survive chemotherapy or radiation. Since phoning was unsuccessful, Catherine wrote to Bran, telling him she had heard of his latest problems and if he needed her, she would return to help him. Robert was terribly worried about losing his father and conveyed this to Catherine in a fax. He also faxed, asking her to give Randall $10,000 to build a house.

Catherine was shocked. $10,000? My God! She had already given him that amount from the sale of her diamond. Robert stated that she 'OWED' Randall for taking care of Bran in his illness, since she had abdicated her responsibility by divorcing Bran and leaving the U.S. Shock again! He was placing a guilt trip on her which she did not deserve. She faxed Robert that she was hurt by his words, but agreed to give Randall the money. He faxed back that he would not do so because of her attitude. She decided to let it go for the time being.

In the meantime, she was hearing nothing at all from Aadi and her heart was breaking. He was constantly in her prayers and in her thoughts. She had no one to talk to about him. She wrote in her journal and spoke to God and wept daily. Her work continued at the haveli. She did not consider it work because she enjoyed it so much; meeting people from all over the world and helping the family with breakfast everyday. It was a joy for her. She expected to continue this after she moved to her house. Jannu had expressed this also, telling her,

"Auntie, you must come to the haveli everyday."

It wasn't that he wanted her to work, just that he felt she would be lonely at her house and have nothing to do there. God Bless Jannu. She loved him so much and the rest of the family. They were so good to her, looking out for her, taking care of her. She felt so safe and so loved. God had blessed her; bringing her to this place, this family. Indeed, He was watching over her.

Then came the news from an agent in Bombay that her shipment had arrived. Catherine had to go there and claim her belongings. Jannu contacted the agent and found out where she was to go, then called a hotel. She overheard him making the reservation and felt so protected.

"No, it's not for me. It's for my AUNTIE! Will she be safe there? Are you sure?"

She left Udaipur for Bombay on June 7th and was met at the airport by Lulu, Theresa Albuquerque's son-in-law, who took her to her hotel. It was a small hotel near the Fort area where the warehouses were located. It was clean and she felt safe. She always ordered room service for meals, but often walked outside and down the narrow streets. Catherine phoned and met with her agent regarding the paperwork.

Then on June 10th she spent most of the day at the Port Terminal Customs House. It was an immense warehouse and stifling hot. Her shipment stood in a crate and she had to stand watching while workmen unpacked it, placing everything on the floor. Sweat poured down her face and down her entire body, soaking her clothes.

A Customs official arrived with papers in hand and proceeded to have every box opened for inspection. Catherine had anticipated this and had in her possession a photo of her stained-glass tiffany lamp, which she had had professionally packaged to prevent breakage. She took the photo from her purse and showed this to the official, pointing out the particular carton which she knew contained the lamp.

"Please, sir" she pleaded, "Do not open this box. It contains this stained-glass lamp, which I had professionally packed so it would travel without breaking. I would not worry now if Bombay were its final destination, but it has to travel to Udaipur, and I'm afraid it might break on the way if the box is opened here. Please, sir, I assure you, this is all that is in this box. Please do not open it."

The official looked at the photo for a long time and at the carton and finally decided not to have it opened. Catherine felt a debt of gratitude, especially as she watched while her things were put back into the crate any old way without any care whatsoever. Then she had to wait interminably in that sweat-box to pay custom fees and ended up paying 'baksheesh' as well before she could leave.

It was so good to be back in Udaipur. Suchana, Subhash and the kids took off for Sikar to visit Suchana's parents. Suchana hadn't been home for three years. Sikar was a city NW of Jaipur about half way to Bikaner. Jannu and Catherine and one of the servants ran the haveli, but there were no guests due to the heat and the haveli having no A/Cs. But this was the time for major work to be done, such as painting of all the rooms, cleaning floors, light fixtures etc. Some mattresses were being refilled, mudhas (cane chairs) repaired, painting of kitchen, reception area and all hallways. Outside of the haveli, Jannu made a parking place for their new Maruti car.

After the family returned, Jannu and Catherine decided to buy computers. They shopped in the market and took notes of various types, then came back to the haveli and phoned Roland for his advice. The shop carried COMPAQ, but also an Indian copy, a model called 'PHILLIPS'. The quality was the same and less money. Catherine learned that Indians could copy anything and could FIX anything. Bran had so many tools to do things with, but Indians only used one or two and managed to do exactly the same. They never threw anything away either. It was amazing. Catherine decided she didn't want multi-media, but thought Jannu should have it for the children. He bought a very good printer, but she bought a laser printer. Roland told them a 14 inch monitor was too small, but Jannu thought it was OK for the haveli. Catherine ordered a 17 inch for herself.

"Jannu", she said, "Please let me buy you the 17 inch, whatever the difference is, I'd like to pay it. I think you would be happier with it."

"Oh, Auntie, I don't know. I'd have to ask the family. I can't make that decision on my own."

"Then please do that, Jannu. Ask them, because I want you to have the 17 inch."

"All right, Auntie."

Windows 95 was included with Compaq but was extra with Phillips. Jannu talked the dealer into giving it to them free, also free dust covers and free internet license for Catherine. Jannu opted for no internet. The laser printer was reduced Rs.3,000 saving her $75. Her total cost came to $2,200, which included installation and teaching.

That evening a knock came at Catherine's door and when she went to answer it, she found Jannu, looking a bit shy, almost sheepish.

"Auntie," he said, very shyly.

She knew immediately he had talked to Subhash and Suchana about the monitor. Catherine gave him a big smile.

"They said, 'yes'."

"Yes, Auntie, it's OK," Jannu said, all smiles, just like a little kid.

Catherine was so happy that she could do this for him, for this wonderful young man who had done so much for her. Now she had to purchase a computer table and chair, but Jannu told her he'd help her find one in the market. He really enjoyed shopping, and was a good shopper, having excellent taste.

On July 9th Catherine shifted from Kankarwa Haveli to her new house on Saheli Marg. Her shipment had arrived and Chain Singh had helped her with the boxes, unloading them and sorting them out. He had brought his son-in-law, who was an electrician, to put up light fixtures and photographs for her. Indian structures were made of concrete, so walls had to be drilled to make holes for nails. Then plastic sleeves had to be placed inside for the nails or screws to hold before a picture could be hung. It was quite a process and Catherine had a lot to learn besides being very grateful to Chain and his son-in-law.

Jannu had had her beds and mattresses made and delivered and she had purchased extra sheets, although she had some packed in her shipment from the States. Now she wanted plants to fill her terrace, but Jannu had told her to wait for Aadi to take her to the nursery. Well, she would have to wait now for him to return from Europe. In her guest room, which faced east, she set up a puja shelf, where she prayed morning and evening. Catherine was very lonely for Aadi and cried every day at prayer. Perhaps it would have helped had she had someone to talk to about him, but there was no one.

Chain was a big help to her in her loneliness. He brought his brother-in-law, Bhagwat Singh to visit her with his wife. They invited Catherine to their home for dinner and when she arrived, their whole family was present.

Catherine was learning to manage her home as well as work at the haveli. Chain took her to the market to shop for vegetables and fruit and to other shops for staples. Jannu had arranged for a rickshaw to pick her up every morning at 7:30 to take her to the haveli where she happily worked in the kitchen and on the rooftop taking orders from the guests and helping with breakfast. Then the rickshaw took her home again at 11:30.

Catherine had been eating a rather substantial breakfast at home, but Jannu told her he'd never speak to her again if she didn't have breakfast everyday with them! This seemed crazy to her because rarely could they sit down together, it was always 'on the run', because the clients had to be served first, so the family had to grab a bite when possible.

At her house, she cooked now and washed clothes in a bucket like all Indian ladies. It was hard work. She had purchased two drying racks to hang her clothes and bedding on and placed these on her terrace. Indian cooking took a long time because one had to cut up everything first and then masalas had to be made separately. Catherine didn't mind. She loved Indian cooking, but to cook only for herself seemed like too much work sometimes. She never made chapatis for herself, finding that really too much work for one person, so ate only vegetables. It was a good diet for her.

Her days were full and she didn't get to her computer until 9 PM. Also, she had told Jannu she wanted to study Hindi, so he arranged for her to take lessons from his cousin's wife who lived only a short distance from her house. Her husband was a Brigadier General in the army, and when he was home, he was stationed in Udaipur, so she didn't work. But he was just recently transferred to Kashmir and of course families do not go to border areas as they are not safe. And Kashmir was a big hot spot. 'Lucky', the general wife's name told Jannu she was planning to go back to teaching, but he asked her to consider 'tuitions' instead. Catherine had never heard of this word before, pronounced 'tutions', until she was in Belgaum and heard that Ramu's granddaughter had 'tuitions' everyday to supplement her regular college courses. It just meant private study. At the same time Jannu was telling her his Auntie needed Hindi lessons, so he set it up for Catherine and Lucky to meet at Catherine's house.

Lucky spoke beautiful unaccented English and she and Catherine got along very well. They arranged to meet everyday except Sunday at Lucky's house, which was a mere 15 minute walk from Catherine's in a very posh neighborhood called 'Polo Ground'. Lucky and the General also had a male golden retriever, which Catherine immediately took to, having had two of them in Duluth. The dog, named 'Misty' seemed to know right away he was loved because he wagged his tail and gave her wonderful greetings every time she arrived. He was always up on the roof and she was afraid he would jump right down to greet her.

Lucky started Catherine with a child's Hindi book. Although she had learned the letters earlier, she had never mastered them. Now she worked on the vowels, the pronunciation and the writing. She had homework everyday. At first it was just writing the vowels, one at a time, an entire page full. Then she was given vocabulary also, and from the list of words, she was learning to build sentences. Catherine tried out simple words at the haveli with the family and servants and they were thrilled to hear her.

Catherine found that she was listening more intently to conversations around her, and was picking up words here and there. She felt she had a whole new life ahead of her, a far more satisfying one than the one she had left behind.

Catherine noticed one day that Mahipal was no longer working at the haveli and asked Jannu about it.

"Oh, Auntie," he said, "We had to let him go."

"Why, Jannu?"

"Auntie, when we were in Jaipur and you were here with him, he was stealing from us."

"Oh, NO!" Catherine gasped. She was appalled. "How did this happen and I not know about it?"

"Auntie, he was very smart. He waited until you went to sleep, then he went into the puja room and stole money and jewelry."

"Oh, Jannu," she said, and began to cry.

"Don't cry, Auntie. We learned something from this."

The puja room was always kept locked, but somehow Mahipal had found another key. He had also gotten Hansraj involved as a 'look-out'. Mahipal had been fired on the spot. The family had trusted him. He had worked for them for two years. His sister had recently married and they had gifted her with Rs.10,000. Jannu said they didn't know how much Mahipal had taken but it was about Rs.40,000, which amounted to about $1000 plus gold jewelry. Mahipal's family kept calling the haveli, making threats because they didn't believe their son and brother had done anything wrong. Jannu was becoming more and more angry. Suchana finally told him to call the police. Jannu knew that once the police were involved, that would be the end for that boy. But he finally had no choice. Jannu told Catherine that the police went to Mahipal's house and threatened his father to give up his son and if he didn't, the police would destroy the man's house, so the man gave up Mahipal. Some days later the police came to the haveli to ask for Hansraj's address and that is how Jannu learned that Hansraj was involved with Mahipal. Obviously Mahipal had cracked under police pressure. Jannu believed both boys were too stupid to have mastermined the operation, and there had been someone outside of the haveli who was running it. Later still Jannu learned that another shopkeeper well-known to Jannu had known Mahipal to be a thief and had never told Jannu about him. Catherine knew these people and thought it unconscionable that they had never warned Jannu.

One day after Catherine returned from her Hindi lesson, the family came to visit her. She was so happy. It was Suchana's first visit. Jannu's mama came also, as she happened to be at the haveli. Papa had been there too, but had gone back to the village. Catherine loved Papa. He was always so loving and kind to her.

"Auntie, you must learn Hindi," he had told her.

"Oh, Auntie," Suchana exclaimed, "Everything is so clean!"

"Yes, Suchana, I cleaned especially for you," Catherine laughed. And she had. The kids started running around because they were familiar with the house and loved it there, playing hide and seek. Suchana tried to control them, but Catherine said, "No, Suchana, let them be. They can do whatever they want here. It's OK."

Catherine was becoming more and more annoyed with her landlord. In the first place, he was nosey. He constantly wanted to know where she was going and when she would be back. When someone came to her door, he came out to see who it was. He even came out in his bathrobe. Another thing, several times he brought relatives to see her apartment. This upset her, but she was gracious about it. One day he told her he had hired carpenters to make amaris (cupboards) for her in her bedrooms and in her kitchen. This pleased her, but she soon realized they were not very skilled at their profession. They took forever to do their work. They arrived at 1 PM and worked until 6 PM. This was before she had begun her Hindi lessons. She was tired when she got back from her work at the haveli and didn't want to stand and watch them do their work, so she usually sat and read in her sunroom.

One day she went into her kitchen to get herself water from her refrigerator and noticed black finger marks on the door of the fridge. She couldn't believe it. They had actually been in it! She reported this to Dr. Nanavati. The stupid man believed the workers when they told him they had not done so. Another day she had fallen asleep in the sunroom and when she had awakened, found another man sitting in her bedroom while the two workers were making cupboards. He jumped up when she walked in. Catherine immediately went downstairs and called Dr. Nanavati, but only his wife was there.

"There is another man upstairs," Catherine told her.

Mrs. Nanavati went up with her and after talking to the man, told Catherine he was the boss.

"Well, I want all of them out of here," Catherine told her.

The next day Catherine confronted Dr. Nanavati.

"This is taking much too long," she said. "I can't take this anymore. I want them out of my house. The job they are doing is very poor work anyway. I don't think they know what they are doing."

They only have two hours of work left," he told her.

"OK, but I want you to come up with them and be with them the entire time. I don't have the time or the inclination to stand and watch them. I don't trust them. They also left one of my windows open and didn't tell me and mosquitoes came in."

"Well, you must check your windows," he said.

Catherine was incensed, but she let it ride. "Just be sure you come up with them tomorrow," she said.

The following day the workers came, but Nanavati was not with them.

"Where is Dr. Nanavati?" she asked them when she answered the door.

"He's in the city," they told her.

"Well, then, you are not coming in," she told them, and closed the door.

Dr.Nanavati came the next day with the workers and they finished their work. However, she noticed her walking shoes were missing from in front of her door. They had stolen them. When she reported this to her landlord, he assured her that the carpenters would never do such a thing. She decided her landlord was a total idiot. No one else came up to that level except the landlord and their cleaning lady, who had been very trustworthy and working for the Nanavatis for many years and Catherine liked her. This lady had never taken anything from inside Catherine's home and there were many things she could have slipped into her pockets. No, the shoes were gone when the carpenters left.

Jannu told Catherine to padlock every room in her apartment. At first she thought this rather silly, but after thinking about it and realizing Nanavati's behavior, she decided Jannu was right, so she bought padlocks for every room. She had to return to the U.S. in September to renew her visa, so she wanted Nanavati to understand her position.

"Dr. Nanavati," she said, "I'm leaving for the United States to renew my visa. While I'm gone, I don't want anyone, and I mean ANYONE, in my apartment. I don't care if it's a long lost relative of yours or the Prime Minister himself! Do you understand? This is MY house, not yours! I pay the rent here. It is mine. I don't want anyone in here, not even the cleaning lady. No one! Do you understand?"

"All right, Madam, all right." he said. "How long will you be gone?"

"About a month," she told him. "And when I come back I don't want any more intrusions. I want my privacy. No more people coming to see my apartment. Do you understand?"

"Yes, all right, Madam," he agreed.

Catherine carried on with her everyday life, but her heart was breaking. Aadi was in Europe and she wept at her prayers every morning. She remembered her first days when she had arrived in India and the hopes she had when Aadi had met her in Delhi. Then the disappointment that had set in when she realized he didn't care for her after all.

Another disappointment came. Lucky's husband informed her he wanted her to join him in Kashmir, so suddenly Catherine was without a Hindi teacher. This was a real blow because the lessons were going along so well and Catherine was learning the language and enjoying it so very much. She tried learning it on her own, working with the books which Lucky had given her, but it didn't work out and Catherine lost interest.

She went to the U.S. and got her visa renewed, this time for a year, but she was required to leave India after six months. She saw her family as well as doctors and returned to India in time for the Hindu festival of Diwali. Catherine was on the roof at the haveli when Aadi arrived. She hadn't seen him in four months. He stayed only long enough to present her with a gift, a heavy, old silver candlestick, which he said was a gift for her house. His beard was long and he looked wonderful to her. Now that she knew he was back in India, Catherine ached for him to come to her, but he didn't. He hadn't seen her house yet, and she was weeping everyday for him.

On the 30th of October, Aadi invited Jannu and Catherine to his garden for a party. His American clients were there also and to Catherine, he looked beautiful. He was wearing pajama and kurta. His parents were there as well as his sister and his little nephew and the aunt and uncle whom Catherine had met on her first visit to Udaipur. Someone had cooked a wonderful meal and they all sat around and ate heartily. Catherine rode back to the city on the bus with the clients.

A couple days later, she was at the haveli when Aadi arrived with his clients. Again he looked so wonderful to her. While he played with the children, she left to go home. Jannu had wanted her to stay for dinner, but she couldn't face being with Aadi and not talking to him. She had hoped he would come to her house before leaving Udaipur with his clients, but he didn't.

It was early November and Catherine was working at the haveli and writng at her computer at home. Aadi was back in Udaipur again and came to the haveli to hear an artist, who was staying there, play the Sitar. He was quite famous. When Aadi saw Catherine he told her he'd come to her house the following day, but he did not show.

On November 13th, it was the 12th in the U.S. and Catherine's mother's 95th birthday. She called her mother in Oregon and told her how sorry she was for all the times she had hurt her, for when she was nasty to her and told her that she loved her. This was the first time in years that Catherine had felt those emotions toward her mother. Her own emotional state was so fragile right then; she was having a hard time holding it together.

Aadi finally came to Catherine's house one afternoon. He told her he'd been there the evening before and had called her name from outside. She hadn't heard him. Evidently she had gone to bed. Aadi never touched her. He told her he had been to New York City for two weeks and she was shocked, but said nothing.

"How is your family?" she asked.

"Fine," he told her, "the construction is still going on. Everything is in a mess."

"Nevermind, Aadi, I know I'm not welcome there. I never will be. And it's all right. What have you done about your leg?"

"Nothing yet."

"Aadi, you must do something soon."

"Yes, I promise I will."

The following day at the haveli Jannu was watching her closely.

"Auntie," he said, "Do you want to die?"

"I am so depressed. I am getting worse, and I don't know how to get out of it."

"What happened?"

"Nothing HAPPENED. You always ask that. LIFE happened."

"Did you hear from home? Is something going on there?"

"No, no everything is fine there."

"Then it is something here that is troubling you. What?"

"My life. There is no joy. Only despair. No hope."

"Do you want to live?"

"No. I always felt life was sacred. I never approved of abortion, euthanasia. But I'm scared. I keep thinking of ways I can end my life."

"You must forget and be happy."

"Stop it. I can't just turn off and 'be happy'. That isn't possible."

"Auntie, tell me. Why are you like this?"

"Jannu, I can't talk about it."

"You know, Auntie, if one stays in a dark room, all alone, and talks to no one, he will go mad. Open the door and let the light in. Then it will be all right."

"I've tried that, but it doesn't work."

"Tell me. Come on."

"I can't. I called you the night before last because I just needed to be with someone who cares, but I knew you couldn't come because you were alone here. And I almost called you again last night, but I knew you couldn't come."

"Auntie, it has to be one of three families. This haveli, Chain Singh and his family, or Aadi Abhimani. Which is it? Has someone here hurt you?"

"Oh, God, Jannu. This haveli, this family has been the only hope I have of sanity. If it weren't for you and the family, I'd have died before now."

"All right then, it is either Chain or Aadi. Which is it?"

"Jannu, do you have any idea how much I love you? Not as a woman loves a man, not as a mother loves a son. I think of you as my little brother. (He laughs) The brother I never had, but who cares about me and protects me. Mothers always look out for and protect their children, but in this case, you do that for me. You are the most honorable of men. I respect you, I treasure you. I cherish you. I don't ever want to hurt you."

"You won't hurt me, Auntie. You know how we feel about you. We have never accepted gifts from anyone until you came to us. Always before….."

"Yes, yes, I know. You've told me all that."

"I didn't worry about asking you for a blazer when you went to America. I wanted to ask you how much it cost and how much were the shoes, but I knew it would hurt you if I did, so I let it go. You give from the heart and expect nothing in return."

"I need to give to those I love."

"So, tell me. Who is hurting you? You know, I have a good relationship with Aadi, but there are areas that we don't talk about. He has his life and I don't say anything."

"But he is your bhai sa."

"He is older than me. It is an honorary title. He is not my brother. I don't think of him that way."

"Jannu, I don't want to put you in the middle."

"No, no. I won't be a middle man."

"I don't mean that. I don't want to hurt you by anything I could tell you."

"So, it is Aadi. Listen, Auntie. Last spring when you went to Bombay and Belgaum. He asked me when you were coming back and when you were leaving for the States. I told him. But Auntie, I heard him telling you that I never told him. He lied and I told him that was not right. He made some excuse that he didn't remember, but I shook my head and said that was not the way to act. Last week, we were sitting here and he wanted me to call you and tell you he couldn't make it to your house. I told him, forget it. I am not his secretary. To call you himself. The phone was right here. Chain can tell you. He was here having tea with us. Auntie, this is his way."

Catherine proceeded to tell Jannu how it all started, with his interest in her, not the other way around. She told him about the Ranakpur visit, the visit to the site, the hug on the hill, planting of olive cuttings, the private boat on the Lake, the hug and kisses on the Jag Mandir, the conversation in the Lake Palace coffee shop, the way he was sending kisses across the table at her, the way she felt, the letter she wrote asking him to come to Goa, her feelings when he didn't show, and his phone call from Jaipur, asking her to call him, her questioning why her, etc., the faxes, letters, phone calls.

"Auntie, did you never have a feeling that anything was wrong? You are as old as his mother."

"In the middle of a beautiful letter, he wrote one sentence telling me that he had a German friend of many years and that he goes to her every year on his summer holiday. I was hurt, but I figured, well, holiday once a year. I had no idea the holiday meant months instead of a week or two. I didn't realize that until after I got to India. Not until October actually. I really fell apart when I understood that."

"Auntie, did you ever give him money?"

"No, never."

"Good. He is very smooth. He knows just how to talk."

"We were supposed to go to the US this spring."

Catherine told him the history of how he reacted when she got back and expected to plan a date as to when to go. "When he came to my house Friday, we were talking about American politics, and I asked him if he had gone to my country. He told me he had gone to New York."

"Yes, he went with Toni."

"What?"

"From Myths & Mountains."

"Not the German girl?"

"No, he went with Honey to Spain & France."

"Honey? Do you mean 'his HONEY'?"

"That's her name…Honoria or something."

"You saw her. Is she pretty?"

He waved his hand back & forth, like a so-so.

"Auntie, he has many women. None of them are attractive."

(Thank's Jannu. I needed that. !!!!!)

"Just forget it now. Go on with your life."

"I can't just go on. I poured out all the emotions that had been stored up in me all of my life. You can't put toothpaste back into a tube. It's like that. I love him. And he knew from the beginning that I was falling in love with him. Is this Toni attractive?"

"Auntie, she is OLD!!" He pulled his upper lip back and pulled at his teeth. Catherine sat in shock.

"He is mentally ill, Auntie. He has been going down for three, four years. I don't know what is wrong. His mother cries all the time about him. His father is worried and can't do anything."

At this point Jannu decided he would come to her house the following day and they would continue their conversation then, because the haveli was getting busy with clients and it was getting difficult to talk privately.

The next day Catherine made tea, then started by telling Jannu that she had told Suchana about Aadi the day he came to the haveli, the day after Diwali with a gift of a silver candlestick for her house. She told him she broke down seeing him after

4 months, that she was crying when Jannu came up for lunch and saw her. After lunch Suchana asked her what had happened. And Catherine told her she loved someone and he didn't love her and when she asked who, she told her it was Aadi. She told Suchana how it had all started, but now he has the German girl and he doesn't care about her. Catherine had made her promise not to tell Jannu because she was so afraid it would hurt him.

Then she gave Jannu the letter to read that she had written to Aadi.

Jannu took some time reading the letter, then told Catherine, "Aadi's father HATES that 'Uncle' where Aadi goes all the time. If it was possible to get away with killing Uncle, he would. He hates him that much."

Catherine was so surprised to hear that 'Honey' does not stay at Aadi's, but at Uncle's.

"Mr. Abhimani told Aadi to bring her to their house, not to Uncle's. His parents want him to marry her. His father said, if Aadi loves her, to marry her, and it would be OK with them. They want him married. He is the only son. Honey comes to India every year, and of course Aadi goes to Germany every year. She works for Lufthansa in maintenance or something and Aadi gets a 75% airfare discount."

Catherine wondered how she did that when he didn't fly with her as companion, e.g. from Delhi to Frankfort and back? Does she claim him as her spouse?? Is she his wife???

But Jannu told her more about Toni, that they were seen in Rishikesh, not sure if just smooching, intimate touching or fucking. She didn't want to ask too much about that. Jannu said that Catherine saw Aadi's mother, and Toni looked that old, plus she had very ugly protruding upper teeth. God, this made her want to vomit. He told her the Spanish gal who got Aadi into the business, was Concha. She loved him and wanted to marry him.

"Now he has an English woman, maybe the same one he brought to the haveli recently. She is VERY wealthy," Jannu told her. "And I think he is with her now."

They talked about his foot and leg. She told him about it. Jannu said he always disliked the way Aadi walked, that it was a "lazy" walk. She knew what he meant, but it never bothered her. Funny, but Bran has an odd walk also.

Catherine asked Jannu if he thought less of her because of all this. He told her he had never met anyone like her, that she was so intelligent and that she could write like that! He also told her that he only had an inkling early on that she might be one of Aadi's victims, but then he decided she wasn't. But somehow it never left the back of his mind. He said, now that she knew the truth, and she could keep on with the relationship if that is what she wanted, but there was no future in it. Catherine just shook her head.

"I'll never let him touch me again, as if he ever wanted to!"

She told Jannu that she couldn't stop loving just like that, but it was definitely over, and she told him again how worried she was that she was hurting him.

"Auntie, Aadi is NOT my best friend, and I am not his. The man that is his partner in the site near Ranakpur is his best friend. That man knows everything there is to know about Aadi. Aadi arranged his marriage"

"Oh, and Aadi was worried about my finding a house in Udaipur. Now I know that he sabotaged the house on Bopalpura and the house on the lake."

Jannu also told her that Aadi's best friend had built a house near his garden, and had a first floor apt, which Jannu thought would be good for her. Aadi did not want that, so his friend never got back to Jannu regarding it. Jannu said that Aadi evidently feels threatened by her presence there. Well, too bad. He brought her to Kankarwa. Now she had made her own place there.

Catherine told Jannu how she felt being 'dumped' on him by Aadi, and why she was always asking to pay more rent.

"I was always aware that you left your family at night to eat with me so that I wouldn't be dining alone. It did not go unnoticed and I appreciated it. I also want you to know how well cared for I felt when you knocked on my door one evening and told me to get up, that it was no time to be sleeping (5:00 PM). My light was not on, and you told me to come out of there and come to Reception and talk."

"You, know, Auntie," he said, before leaving, "I think we knew each other in a past life. Because we are so close in this one."

Although Catherine learned so much from Jannu during this conversation which was derogatory about Aadi, it somehow was healing. She no longer felt like destroying herself. She felt rather a great pity for this man whom she still loved. He didn't know what love was. Unless he just loved the German girl and found release with all the other women he came in contact with. Whatever! It just seemed sad to her.

For the first time in a year, Catherine felt better. Jannu noticed it and told her so. She called Meridith Schifsky, her spiritual advisor, and had a long talk with her. This also helped her. When Jannu mentioned the word, 'victim,' it reminded her that Helga had told her that Aadi was warning her so that she wouldn't become one of his 'Victims.'

CHAPTER THIRTY THREE

A WEDDING, A DEATH, AN ACCIDENT

One door closed, another door opened. At the haveli there was a young couple from the Netherlands, not married, but traveling together. The young man's name was Peter Locke. He was a photographer. His lady friend's name was Frances Bakker. Catherine met them at breakfast and enjoyed talking with them. Peter was photographing three hotels for a Dutch women's magazine and asked Catherine if she would write the text for his photos. She was more then surprised at this request.

"Peter," she said, "How can you ask me that? You have no idea if I can write or not," she told him.

Oh, I'm sure you can," Peter replied.

Catherine just looked at him.

"Well, Peter," she said, rather amazed, "I happen to be a writer, but I want you to see something of my work before you decide. Jannu has some of my writing and you can look at that." She asked Jannu for the letter she wrote some time ago for the haveli which he was going to have printed to place in the rooms. He found it and showed it to Peter, who was very pleased.

"Yes, Yes, Catherine. I knew you could write. You will do just fine. I'll tell you what I want."

So Catherine started this writing job and found it exciting. She wrote about Kankarwa Haveli, about the next door property, Jagat Nivas, and about a jewelry shop at the Shiv Nivas Palace Hotel. Peter and Frances took her to dinner at the Trident

Hotel and they discussed the project. They also talked about their coming trip to Gujarat and how Peter wanted Catherine to write about that.

"But Peter, I've never been to Gujarat."

"That's OK. I'll fax you all the information from Holland and you can write it and fax it back to me. "

"Well all right. I don't know how that's going to work, but I'll try," she told him.

Peter was pleased with what she wrote for the hotels and took the materials with him when he left. Catherine heard from him again from Holland in several faxes, but they were very jumbled and difficult to read and follow. Finally she contacted Aadi.

"Aadi, I have to write about Gujarat for this photographer in Holland. He has sent me faxes of where he has traveled in Gujarat, but I can't follow it very well. I'm wondering if you would come here and give me your knowledge so that I can write sensibly about these places."

Catherine was thankful that Aadi came and did exactly as she requested. They sat in her computer room and she took copious notes as he spoke of and lectured on all the places that Peter and Frances had traveled to. Afterwards, she wrote at great length about this wonderful state and wished she could travel there to see it herself. With great excitement, Catherine sent it off to Peter via Fax the following morning. She was surprised to get a phone call from Peter, who was extremely upset.

"Catherine," he said, "You didn't copy my words," he said.

"What? Copy your words? What are you talking about, Peter?"

"I sent you faxes, Catherine. I expected you to copy my faxes."

"I don't understand, Peter. Why would I copy your faxes? I thought you wanted me to write about your travels. In the first place, your faxes were practically unreadable. I've never been to Gujarat. I had my friend who is a travel guide come to my home and lecture me on the places you went so that I could write knowledgably about them."

"No, Catherine, I wanted you to correct my writing."

"Wait a minute, Peter. You wanted me to correct your English?'

"Yes, Catherine."

"Well, excuse, me, Peter. That was not my understanding at all. And it is certainly not what I want to do. I have neither the time nor the inclination to do that. I am not an English teacher. I am a writer. I will not correct your English, Peter."

Catherine heard nothing more from Peter Locke and she received no remuneration for any of her work. She did hear from Frances occasionally however and a few years later learned that Peter had committed suicide in Majorca.

It was the end of her first full year in India. It didn't seem possible. She had had many heart aches, but she had found a family to love, who loved her and protected her and this was most important. And most of all she knew God was watching out for her and above all, loving her.

The family came to Catherine's house for Christmas and gifted her with beautiful gold and enamel earrings. For her birthday they gave her a matching pendant. She had shopped at CIE, the Kashmiri shop in front of the palace, and bought beautiful sweaters for Jannu, Subhash and Papa, and shawls for Suchana and Mama. Jannu had helped her find clothes for the kids in the market. The family had come to her house all dressed up and it was a very festive and happy time.

A new year had begun and Catherine was now 67 years old. Jannu's cousin, Chhoti was to be married this month and everyone was excited and planning for the happy event. Catherine was invited of course and Suchana and Mama took her to a shop to be fitted for a beautiful poshak to wear for the wedding occasion. It was a rani pink with blue and gold embroidered peacocks. Catherine loved it and was thrilled to be wearing it. She went to the wedding house in a rikshaw with Mama, having dressed at the haveli with the help of Suchana. When she got to the bride's house, Mama, who spoke no English, pointed to a room for her to go into and Catherine proceeded to enter it. There she found many Indian ladies she didn't know, but she sat with them for some time. After a while, she got up, left the room, and walked about the house. She went upstairs and found Jannu's uncle, who talked with her for a short time. Then suddenly a door opened and to her surprise Suchana, Prem and Mama came out and greeted her, but passed her by.

"Hello, Auntie," they said, as they passed, smiling. Catherine was shocked and dismayed. What was she expected to do? She was alone. Why didn't they include her?

Again she wandered about the house and this time ran into Kiddu, the bride's brother. He showed her where the ceremony was to take place and where she was to sit.

"Auntie," he said, "You were supposed to be here all this week. Where were you?"

"But Kiddu, no one brought me here. I didn't know."

"Oh, Auntie, You were invited to everything. All the dances. Everything."

Catherine had watched at the haveli as the women had left to go, but Suchana and Mama had not asked her to go with them, so how could she have gone? She felt strangely left out now. More women arrived and found places to sit. Catherine decided to find a place in the area of the ceremony so she could watch. Her family was no where about. When they did come in they did not ask her to sit with them, so she sat alone. Her heart was breaking.

Earlier when the groom arrived, Catherine had gone outside to see him and was thrilled to see this beautiful man upon a caparisoned white horse come prancing up to the house all decked out in white. He was not only gorgeous, but very handsome. He was led into the house to meet his bride, who was dressed in red and gold, and they went immediately into the family puja room.

Eventually the bride and groom arrived, one hand of each bound together. The bride's face was completely covered by her veil. They sat in front of a priest, the bride's parents on one side and only ladies were present in the hall. The ceremony began, and lasted for some time. At one point the bride and groom arose and walked about the small fire, first the bride leading the groom and then the groom leading the bride. This was done several times. Evidently the priest spoke to them, lecturing them in their duties as married couple. They did not exchange any kind of marriage vows.

Afterwards, everyone disbursed and went outside for food. At this point the family finally came up to Catherine and told her to eat.

"Auntie," Subhash said, "We'll be back, but you have food."

Catherine was dismayed. Where were they going? They were leaving the bridal house and leaving her there. She was alone again. So she went to the buffet table and picked up a plate and filled it with food. Catherine was just about to walk away with her plate when she was accosted by some woman.

"You aren't supposed to eat here," she said.

"Excuse me?"

"You are to eat down there," she said, pointing to where the men were eating.

"But the men are eating there," Catherine said.

"Yes, but that's where you are to eat. This is vegetarian."

"I'm vegetarian," Catherine told her.

"Oh! All right, then," the woman said.

By that time, Catherine wanted to throw her plate in the waste bin. She had lost her appetite. She was sick to her stomach. She was alone and felt she had been rudely treated. All she could do was stuff down her food and wait around for the family to return so she could leave. She saw Lucky at the wedding, but no one else. The men were in a separate area and she didn't spy Jannu. Later she learned he didn't even attend.

The family returned and asked her if she had eaten, and then they got into a car to go home. They were going to drop her off at her house, but she reminded them that her clothes were at the haveli, so she had to go there to change and pick up her purse. From there, someone took her to her house. Catherine was very happy to return home. It had been a most disappointing, miserable evening. Much later she learned that the family had brought the bride and groom to the puja room at the haveli while Catherine was having food at the bridal house.

Six days later Catherine was awakened at 11:30 PM by the ringing of her phone.

"Hello?"

"Auntie," It was Jannu. "I'm sending a rickshaw for you. Come right away."

"Oh, Jannu, what has happened?"

"Papa is no more," he said in a choking voice.

"Oh, Jannu! I'll be right there," she said, her heart breaking. Catherine quickly dressed and ran out into the street to await the rickshaw. She didn't think to pack anything. All she could think of was to get to the haveli as quickly as possible. She knew Mama and Papa had been there, so Papa must have died there at the haveli.

When she arrived she found they had placed his body in the alcove next to the courtyard. It was completely covered and Mama was sitting beside it moaning. Catherine stood there for a moment in respect and grief, and then backed away. Jannu found her and told her they were all leaving for Kankarwa.

"Auntie, you are in charge. You can close the haveli if you wish."

"Oh, no, Jannu. I won't close. I'll run it. Don't worry. Everything will be fine. Please don't worry. I'll take care of everything."

"Then, Auntie, here are keys to the storage room. Keep the money in there."

"OK. Oh, Jannu, I'm so sorry. I loved Papa. Now just do what you have to do for him. I'll take care of everything here. Don't worry."

Suchana came downstairs, crying and walked into Catherine's arms.

"What can I do for you, Suchana?" she asked.

"Just take care of my house, Auntie," she said.

"I'll do that, Suchana."

The family left, taking Papa's body with them to the village of Kankarwa. Catherine's heart was so sad, and tears fell as she watched the cars drive away. She decided not to take one of the guest rooms, but to sleep in the Common Room where the TV and computer were located, so that all the rooms would be available to be rented. That room did not have a bathroom, but there was one at the end of the hall which the extended family used when they came to visit. This suited her just fine.

The next morning after breakfast she told Rupender Singh, or 'Bungie' as he was called, in Reception, she had to go back to her house and pack a bag for clothes and her medications. She went by rickshaw and informed her landlord also of the situation, so that he knew she would be gone for some time.

"From now on," she told Bungie, "I'll be keeping a record of all our guests, when they arrive, in which room they stay, for how long, and how much they are charged. I'm going to put that in the computer."

"But, Auntie," he said, "I keep record of that in my book here."

"Yes, I know, Bungie. But I want to keep my own record also. And you will hand over all monies to me."

"Yes, Boss told me."

"Good, then we understand each other."

Catherine had the feeling that Rupender Singh was not happy that she was keeping her own record of guests and charges, but she wanted to make sure he had no chance to cheat the haveli. At this time there was a full house and it was possible to skim, so Catherine was going to keep a very careful watch on this boy.

Everything went smoothly except for one incident. A group of Americans arrived one evening, as expected, led by their travel agent who was Canadian. As they were allotted their rooms they became agitated and upset, running from one room to another. They were all middle-aged, but were acting like children preferring that one's room to the one they were assigned. It was ridiculous. Catherine finally got them settled and was able to confer with their travel agent. He was exasperated.

"This is a very difficult group," he told her.

"I can see that," she said, laughing.

"The company never told them at the beginning that they were to have middle class accommodations. They are expecting 5-star all the way and it's been very difficult."

"Well, this isn't 5-star, but it's a beautiful property, don't you think so?"

"Oh, yes it is. And we'll be here three nights."

"Well, breakfast is on the roof at 8:00. I'm sure you'll enjoy it. Have a good night."

The next morning Catherine served the group on the roof and they seemed to be enjoying the food. But the agent came to her afterwards.

"Ma'am," he said, apologetically, "I have to tell you, they want to leave. They don't like it here."

"Didn't they enjoy their breakfast?"

"They didn't say. Believe me, that was a compliment."

Catherine laughed. "I guess they would be happier at the Trident."

"Yes, but they can't afford that hotel. I'm so sorry, but we have to leave."

"Sir, that is perfectly OK. I don't want anyone here who is not happy. Just take them and leave."

Catherine told Rupender Singh to make out a bill, but he was aghast.

"But you can't let them go! They have a reservation for three nights!"

"They don't like it here, so they should go. Let them go! Give them the bill."

Instead, Rupender picked up the phone and called Kankarwa Village to talk to Jannu. Jannu told him the same thing.

"Let them go."

That night Catherine was surprised by a visit from the travel agent.

"Ma'am", he said, "I took them to the Shakarbadi Hotel and they didn't like that either. So I took them to the Trident, but before I could leave the bus and make arrangements for some kind of deal, they ran out and made their own reservations ahead of me. I told them they didn't have enough money to cover this, but they said they were going to sue me and my company if they couldn't stay there."

"Oh my! I think you will be very happy to be rid of these people. These are indeed ugly Americans. Would you like some tea?"

One day Vibu phoned to ask Catherine if she had a photo of Papa. She didn't, but she remembered that she had taken one of him and it was still in her camera. Catherine didn't say anything because she didn't know how good it was or if it was the type of photo he was looking for. The two weeks passed quickly and the family returned. Subhash and Jannu had their heads and faces shaved of all hair and they looked so much alike to her now except for their body frames. Catherine's eyes teared up when she saw them. They brought Mama back with them, and all went immediately to the puja room. Then food was served. It was the evening meal.

"Auntie," Jannu said, "Please don't go home. Stay tonight."

"All right. I'll stay. I need to fill you in on everything anyway."

The following day Catherine showed Jannu the computer record and gave him the monies from the storage room. Everything was in order. But Jannu wanted her to stay another night as well, so she did.

After a few days Catherine asked Jannu if he was able to talk about Papa and tell her about what had happened in the village. He assured her he could do that comfortably.

"Auntie" he began, "We took Papa to Kankarwa. We bathed him and dressed him in white and I sat up with him all night. The next morning we took him to the cremation site. Auntie, it was awful knowing someday we would be in that place too. After the cremation, we all take baths and change clothes."

"Is everyone at the cremation?"

"No, Auntie, only the men. At the fort, many people come and have tea and food. Everyday hundreds of cups of tea are served. Relatives come from far away, Jaipur, London – Papa's sister lives in London and Mama's relatives from Alwar. We said extra prayers so that Mama could come back here with us. We didn't want her to stay at Kankarwa alone, as is the custom after a husband dies. Now she can no longer wear colorful clothes or jewelry. She cannot go to any parties or any celebrations for a year."

"In my country too, Jannu, there is also a time of mourning for widows, usually a year. I'm glad you brought Mama back here. It will be good for her to be with all of you, especially with the children."

Another month passed and Catherine was standing out by the gate waiting for Bunji to come with the scooter to take her to the haveli. She stood for about 15 min, wondering where in Hell he was. Suddenly, behind her, a large white Jeep stopped and she saw Jannu coming out of the passenger seat, all bloody and pale-faced, and falling into her arms.

"Oh, Auntie," he cried. "I'm hurt." She held him and then they sat on the ground.

"What happened?" she asked.

"I don't know."

She cradled his head and kissed his cheek, murmuring, "Oh, Sweetheart, oh, Baby!"

Jannu said Subhash was coming. She thought he had come for her on a scooter and had an accident, and that Subhash was coming in the car. But Jannu had been driving the Maruti. They waited for Subhash, who came on a scooter with Satish, the juice walla near the haveli. Then Jannu got back into the Jeep, along with Subhash and Catherine got on the scooter with Satish. They followed the Jeep to the government hospital and when she walked into the emergency room, she had the culture shock of her life.

It was grey, dark, filthy, cubicles with no doors or curtains. No sheets on the gurneys, if they were gurneys at all, maybe just black padded tables. Jannu sat at a table as a doctor (?) asked him questions and took some notes on small pieces of paper. The doctor had a stethoscope around his neck, so she assumed he had the proper credentials. He told Jannu to wait in one of the cubicles. Catherine and Subhash helped him to stand and took him on both sides to walk to the table, where he sat and moaned. His nose was bleeding and he complained of his chest hurting very badly.

The doctor never took his BP, nor did he listen to his chest. They had to take Jannu to another room, where he had to lie down, and that was extremely painful for him. There, a woman, (nurse? doctor?) got ready to suture the cut on his nose. She did wash her hands first, but did not put on gloves. She took a sponge and washed his nose a little with water, no antiseptic. Then she took a forceps and a needle holder and a needle that could have stitched a cut on the arm rather than a fine, facial wound. The black thread, (silk?) crinkled up as she pulled it through the cut. She placed the forceps on the black padded table, which certainly was not clean, and picked them up again to continue to sew or make the knot. Catherine's training in asceptic technique was screaming.

Next they had to take him to x-ray, which was a long way and there was no wheelchair, no gurney. Subhash and Catherine walked him down two long halls and two short halls, some of which smelled heavily of urine. There was a pile of feces on the floor, which they had to avoid as they walked three abreast. Finally arriving at x-ray, it was a one room cubicle with an antiquated x-ray machine and one table. Jannu had to stand for the chest x-ray, and Catherine noticed the machine barely gave out a light when activated. She wondered what kind of x-ray it would produce. Only one picture was taken. Then they walked him all the way back to Emergency.

He was complaining of his hand hurting and the doctor then ordered an x-ray of the hand. Back they walked him to the same room. Jannu saw that she was crying and he got upset and shook his head at her, and gave her a piercing look. She had to hold it all in, but she just couldn't bear this treatment in this horrible place. Catherine asked Subhash if they couldn't please take him to a private hospital. Subhash just laughed and said they were worse. She couldn't believe it. Nothing could be worse.

Jannu told her to go to the haveli because Suchana was alone. But just about that time, Suchana arrived with Yogi and Kiddu. She took over and ordered Catherine back to the haveli. Catherine couldn't believe it. She was the only one with medical training and she was asked to leave. Of the two cousins who came with Suchana, one had fainted, the other had vomited, but Catherine was asked to leave. So she kissed Jannu on the cheek and left. The juice walla took her on his scooter back to the haveli.

She went upstairs and did the breakfast thing. Luckily there weren't too many, because she was shaking and crying and very upset. Vibu and Nihru arrived from the village and the boys left immediately for the hospital. They didn't bring Jannu home for about 2 more hours. He was walking, but supported by his brothers. There was a cast on his left hand and a larger bandage on his nose. Evidently, they took an x-ray of his face also and found bone chips of his nose, but work couldn't be done due to the swelling.

They placed him in the Common Room, but to Catherine's surprise, not for rest, but to receive guests. This was a new experience for her. People started coming in a steady stream, relatives and friends, and going up to see him. Vibu was sitting in Reception and Catherine felt she had to say something to him about this.

"Vibu, Jannu needs his rest. He shouldn't be seeing all these people."

"Oh, Auntie," he laughed, "This is our custom. Everyone wants to see him and talk to him."

Catherine went upstairs and looked into the room to see what was going on. Jannu was propped up, with Suchana on one side, Mama on the other. People were sitting in front of them, talking and talking. She couldn't believe her eyes, and went back downstairs to Reception.

"Vibu, this is not good for Jannu. I'm telling you this as a medical person. He desperately needs his rest. Please, can't you stop people from going up there? And get those people out?"

"No, no, Auntie."

Some time later some friends of Jannu's, whom Catherine knew, arrived and asked her about him.

"Auntie, how is Jannu?"

"Oh, please, he is so tired now. Could you please come back tomorrow?"

"Sure, Auntie. We'll do that." And they left.

Again later, Tapasya came down and in a very authoritative voice to Catherine said, "Mama says 'Do Not send anyone else upstairs'."

"Tapasya, I haven't sent anyone upstairs."

"Mama says, 'Do Not send anyone upstairs'."

"Well, Excuse ME, Tapasya! But I have not sent Anyone upstairs!"

Catherine arrived early the next day and helped with breakfast, then took over in the Reception area. She did not go to the Common Room to see Jannu, but was terribly anxious to know how he was doing. In the middle of the day, he asked for her to come. When Catherine appeared in the Common Room, she found him once again surrounded by Suchana and Mama. She sat at the foot of the bed and just looked at him, tears welling up in her eyes and falling down her cheeks. Jannu said nothing, but he watched her and with one finger, touched his cheek, indicating he saw her tears.

There were not many clients at the haveli as it was the end of the season, and Catherine had the idea that it would help Jannu if he could lie in a tub of warm water. She told him this a few days later and mentioned this also to Suchana. There were enough men around so that they could easily help him into one of the two tubs. It would really make him feel good, she informed them. But Catherine learned that Mama vetoed this immediately. Why? Why? It was only much later that she figured it out that Mama did not trust Catherine and was jealous of her, and was not about to take any suggestion of hers to treat her son. To Mama, Catherine was a foreigner, and Mama was a lady from the village with village ideas. Catherine's heart was breaking because she knew that a water bath would be so good for Jannu and she wanted so much to help him, to ease his pain. But it was not her place. She was an outsider.

Catherine made another friend. Her name was Julie Savage, a British lady. They found they had so much in common loving India; they talked and talked and talked. Julie's husband had died and she lived alone now in the Cotswolds. Her house sounded so lovely. While they were enjoying breakfast one morning, Toni Neubauer, Aadi's friend, arrived to stay at the haveli. Catherine had to serve her breakfast and it was painful. She had thought the pain had passed, but she found it had returned as she looked at this bleach-blonde woman who smoked and whom she knew had spent three weeks with Aadi in NYC. Catherine confided in Julie about Aadi and this woman, so at last she was able to talk about her feelings.

Jannu mentioned Toni also, but Catherine told Jannu that Toni wasn't as bad looking as he had made her out to look.

"Well, Auntie, maybe she had something done to her teeth. They used to stick out more."

"Oh, for heaven's sake, Jannu!"

Toni stayed at the haveli, but Aadi's clients were staying at the Lake Palace, so he didn't spend much time at the haveli. Catherine only saw him once or twice with Toni and it hurt her. Toni's company was called, 'Myths and Mountains,' and was a very successful business, located in Lake Tahoe, Navada.

Before Julie left for Ahmedabad, she spent a full day at Catherine's house, and they talked and talked, promising to keep in touch after Julie left for home. Then Julie took Catherine for lunch at the Shiv Nivas Hotel and they watched the Gangaur festival from the rooftop of the haveli.

A couple days later, Aadi came to the haveli with his clients. She was surprised and very touched when one woman told her that Aadi had talked and talked about her. This woman had gone alone with him to Chittor. Catherine had wanted to go there with him for some time because Jannu had told her there were so many stories to be told about the fort, but that was never to be.

Six months had gone by and Catherine had to leave India according to her visa. She decided to visit Nepal, first flying to Delhi, then into Kathmandu and then to a resort in Pokhara. When she arrived in Delhi, Sunil informed her she couldn't leave for Kathmandu as scheduled due to a strike by Royal Nepalese Airlines. So Sunil got her ticketed on Indian Airlines the following day, but she had to waste a day in Delhi.

Sunil and Mita took her shopping for salwar kameez, but by the time they got to the shops, they were closed. It was always the same when Catherine came to Delhi. She was never able to get what she needed there. Either the shops were closed, or the shops did not carry the large sizes for her. Indian frames were much smaller than western frames.

Mistakenly, Catherine brought up the subject of Aadi and Sunil told her that he was a 'bad man'.

"Sunil, what are you talking about?" she asked him.

"Mom, IVT has black-listed him."

"But why?"

"He's pulled some games with IVT and they are disgusted with him. They have already advised Travel House not to use him, so his work load will diminish."

"This is terrible, Sunil. What did he do?"

"He agreed on not taking escort payments with Reet and then telling Toni that he wasn't paid for his services. Toni sent a scathing letter to IVT. Reet told him to come and take his money. So now IVT is black-listing him with all other companies."

Well, something didn't sound quite right to Catherine. She worried about Aadi and if this was all true, he was destroying himself. Sunil seemed very insensitive to her feelings, so she kept quiet. Also, Catherine was upset to learn Sunil had booked her at a 5-star hotel, the Annapurna, in Kathmandu. She had wanted to stay in a guest house in the Thamel area of the city. He arranged for a travel agent to meet her when she arrived and that was the best she could hope for.

Arriving in Kathmandu was a hassle with long lines at the airport going through Customs and then changing money. Finally she was out and found her agent awaiting her. He took her to his office where she explained where she wanted to stay. Again she was obviously not understood, and he placed her in a 3-star hotel, clean, good, but not in the area she had requested.

Catherine spent three glorious days in Pokhara, at Fish-Tail Lodge on Phewa Lake. From the mainland she took a raft to the island where the lodge was located among wondrous trees, flowers, and plants; a profusion of color everywhere. And Catherine had never seen so many butterflies in all her life. The lodges were circular and self-contained, with walkways lighted at night. There was a reception hall and a dining hall, all beautifully kept. The food was excellent. Catherine was very pleased and happy to be there. She did think of Aadi however and wished he could be there to enjoy this with her. She thought to write him a letter, and drafted one to him.

When she awoke the following morning, she looked out at the mountains and to her great disappointment, they were masked in haze. Her guide arrived to take her high up to Sarankot, north of Pokhara to view Fishtail Mountain and Annnapurna South, but again, disappointment due to haze. Her guide was very nice. He also worked as a captain in the restaurant at the lodge. He took her to a cultural museum and to a Kali Temple, also to see White Water River, the water white due to all the minerals. They visited a Tibetan Refugee Center, where a Buddhist priest took Catherine into a prayer room and showed her books and pictures of goddesses and a large one of the Dalai Lama, also photos of former Dalai Lamas. In one building, Catherine turned one huge prayer wheel. Then her guide took her to a very old part of Pokhara and showed her where the Newar caste people live. They were business class people and lived in joint family groups in very distinctive houses.

At lunch in the lodge, Catherine met an American family. He was of Swedish ancestry, his wife Ethiopian, their three children very dark skinned. He had worked in the American Embassy in Dhaka since August 1997, and was being transferred to Cairo. They invited Catherine to visit them there. Such lovely people, but Catherine didn't think she'd ever travel to Egypt.

As she waited for her guide to take her on a boat ride, Catherine noticed there were many Japanese tourists at the lodge. And as always, Japanese were taking scads of photos. Again she was wishing she could share this beautiful spot with Aadi.

Catherine phoned Jannu to tell him she would be returning a day later than expected. She also wanted to know how his trip was to Sati Mata. He had gone there after he had recovered enough from his accident to pray and give thanks for saving his life. Jannu and the family had such great faith in Sati Mata.

On the last evening at the lodge, Catherine had just finished her evening meal and was getting up from the table, when suddenly she felt a terrible stabbing pain in her left flank. She gasped and grabbed at the table and finally made it back to her room. The pain continued and Catherine realized she was having a kidney stone attack. She had no pain killers with her, so she had to bear with the pain, which lasted five hours. Her flight to Delhi was without incident, but as she was getting into the car to go to the airport in front of Sunil's, the pain started again.

When she arrived in Udaipur, she was still in pain and told Dr. Nanavati, who took her to the small hospital across the street on Sahali Marg, just near where they lived. The doctor there sent them elsewhere for exams and by that time, Catherine had no pain, so she decided against any more doctors and went home. Sometime later, Jannu had her seen by another physician for a sonogram, but no kidney stone was found. Evidently she had passed it.

The entire month of April of that year was filled with emotional grief for Catherine. She learned that Aadi was entertaining his German girlfriend in Rishikesh and Haridwar. Hours of praying and weeping; she was writing of the time when she and Aadi were telephoning and remembering these moments brought fresh tears. Catherine wondered if she would ever know joy again.

During this time she heard from Cindy who asked her to come to Oregon to 'baby-sit' their mother so Cindy could have a three week vacation. Catherine wrote her a long letter explaining that although she dearly loved their mother, she no longer was able to care for her in that capacity. Mother had money and Cindy could find someone to take care of her for that period so she could take a vacation, if it was that necessary. Cindy was furious with Catherine and told her so. Their relationship deteriorated from that point on. At some later date Cindy told Catherine she hoped she would get to the point where she would not care if Catherine was dead or alive. Cindy did find respite care for their mother so she was able to take her vacation time when she wanted it. She also took $2000 of Mother's money as monthly rent or care. Catherine didn't know which. She only knew she herself had never taken anything from her parents that she hadn't paid back in full.

Jannu called one night, pretending to be someone else and asked her to come to the haveli the next day. She went for lunch and found Suchana very ill with asthma. Catherine did not talk to Jannu about her feelings regarding Aadi. There was enough worry already at the haveli.

Early in May Catherine was still weeping and praying for joy and peace, but she heard that Aadi was back in Udaipur. She placed a call to him and he said, "I will come to you." She felt better hearing his voice and knowing she would be seeing him. She called Bran and talked to him. He wanted to read her book. Catherine also called Robert and told him she'd be back in the U.S. in August.

When Aadi arrived, he told her he had seen two neurologists and he needed Vitamin B12 because he had pernicious anemia. He also said he had a dent in his cervical spine at C5, which was causing his foot and leg problem. Catherine thought that was ridiculous. That made no sense at all. Cervical spine did not affect the legs! He had not had an MRI. She wished he had taken her with him as she had requested of him long ago because she knew what questions to ask and he didn't. After a while they watched a video Catherine had on sex, but only for a short time because he led her to the bedroom, where they made love. It was wonderful to be with him again, and he was not rushed. Afterwards they bathed together and then she made tea. Catherine at last felt some joy.

She saw him the following day at the haveli where he filled her plate with food. She thanked God for this one more encounter. Her heart was so full of love for this man, and just seeing him and talking to him gave her so much joy. She prayed to make herself more important in his life. However, just the fact that he came five times a week for injections had to suffice. He didn't always make love to her at those times, but he would hold her in his arms and kiss her. Then, some days passed and he didn't show up. She called him several times and finally got him and he told her that he needed injections only twice a week for five weeks. He thanked her for calling, but hung up quickly.

Aadi continued coming for injections when he needed them, and Catherine continued to hope and pray for a love which never came. She no longer despaired, but lived in a kind of indifference, doing what she had to do, and coping with the loneliness

At this time Catherine was reading Thomas Merton's ASIAN JOURNAL. So often Catherine felt rejected by God, although she knew deep in her heart that God never rejected her, never abandoned her. But she had felt rejected all her life by her parents, especially her mother and certainly by the man she married and recently rejected by her sons. Now rejected again by the man she loved.

It was early June and the family was making plans to come to Catherine's house for lunch. Only Subhash, Jannu, and the kids came however. Mama would not come and Suchana was having problems with her asthma and was getting ready to go to Hyderabad to see a particular guru who dispensed a fish, which was supposed to cure ailments such as hers. Catherine's lunch went well and when she saw Suchana the next day, Suchana told her she was praying for her that Aadi would love her. Catherine dearly loved Suchana, and blessed her beautiful heart.

Catherine received a letter from Brandon, which was not pleasing to her. She started to answer it, but erased most of it. Why did she still feel it necessary to explain herself or her actions to him? They were divorced over two years already. And perhaps she should be thinking the same of Aadi – it's Over, it's Over, it's Over. But God help her, he still held her heart and thoughts. Then she wrote to Brandon

It was the middle of June and Catherine was getting anxious to go back to the States to see her family there, but she didn't want to leave India either. She was torn in both directions. She found herself busy every day writing and eating too much, which was a sign of depression, but her pain was less.

One day Catherine made dal batti for Aadi, also chutney. He told her many times it was 'delicious', and her batti was 'fantastic'. Her power went out, but later they watched THE FAR PAVILIONS. He had to leave before the end, but it was a lovely day. It was his last injection. He told her he'd call if he was coming the following week, then he gave her a few kisses and hugs and left abruptly. Catherine wondered if he would show up, and prayed and cried again as loneliness took over her days and nights. He did come however and took lunch with her, showered and took a nap in her bed. There was no intimacy, but it made her happy that he felt comfortable to be with her in her home. Then she wondered again if he would come again the next week. She was hopeless! In the meantime she had shopped for gifts to bring back to the States. It was soon time for her to leave.

Occasionally, like a day in early July, Aadi came to Catherine, watched videos, talked, had lunch and spent the whole day with her, giving her hugs and kisses before he left, and telling her he would bring food for their next lunch in a few days. Catherine's heart nearly burst with love after such a visit. She heard from Mary Ramsay, who cautioned her regarding Aadi, because she didn't want Catherine to be hurt any more. Mary was afraid for her. But after that one day with him, she felt that he liked her and that they were comfortable with each other. She prayed for healing and to bear loving him without hurting him

Catherine was writing about 1997, when she gave up her house. She finally grieved over it. She hadn't at the time because she was too busy and too exhausted. Now she did, remembering how she had loved that house. After all, she had played a big part in planning the design of it, and all the years she had put into it, raising her boys, the holidays and birthday celebrations, Cecilian meetings, the Gilbert and Sullivan pot-lucks every year; so many memories. Now she had the sad chore of writing about her tour with Aadi which became such a heartrending disappointment. Catherine wondered whether she was healthy. She knew she had emotional scars and that she had not healed. She wished she had someone to help her. Some time ago, she had thought it was Aadi, but of course that was wrong. He could not help her. He didn't even want her.

Jannu called one Saturday and asked her to come for lunch, which she did. They sat in Reception and chatted like old times, then went to the Common Room and had lunch because it was cooler there. Prem and Uma were there also. Prem was five months pregnant and hoping for a son. After lunch, all took naps and then the children made lists of what they wanted Catherine to bring them from the States. Suchana and Jannu told her there would be another reading of the Ramayana and invited her to join them for the closing ceremony. Catherine was so happy and honored. She dressed in a sari and joined them, feeling part of the family. Afterwards they watched some of the World Cup on TV, Cricket being India's great national sport. And then they had dinner together.

Then Catherine got bad news, another letter from Bran. Someone had informed him about Aadi. Who would do such a thing? He knew about her tour with him in September of '97, and that she had purchased a car, for the purpose of taking him on a tour of the U.S, and that he went to Europe with another woman. Catherine felt betrayed. Also, did this someone think they were being kind to Bran? In the first place, the facts were inaccurate and were none of his/her business, but were extremely hurtful. They were meant to hurt her. But they did more damage to Bran. She phoned Robert and then Russell, who got very angry with her. She also talked to Anne. But she decided the culprit was Julie. Robert called her back and reassured her.

Aadi phoned Catherine at the haveli and told her he was leaving for Delhi to see doctors and then on to Europe. He told her the last half of October he would take her to Gujarat. Jannu told Catherine that Aadi was going to the U.S. to meet with his clients. Catherine's heart broke. All the times she had asked him to go with her and he would never agree, and now he was going with someone else. She was devastated. The pain was terrible and she wept. She knew she should be looking at the positive that he had called her and promised to take her to Gujarat in October, but it was killing her just the same. Jannu informed her Aadi would be going to Washington D.C. This was one place Catherine had hoped to share with Aadi because she had never been there herself. Now that dream was destroyed along with the others.

CHAPTER THIRTY FOUR
A TRIP HOME TO THE U.S.

Catherine flew to Delhi on August 1st and arrived in the U.S. on the the 3rd. She stayed at Roland's for a couple of days, and then flew out to Portland to see her mother. Due to the distance between her sister and herself, she stayed in a motel and took taxis to her sister's house. Her sister never offered her a cup of coffee and her mother, bless her heart, never noticed. Catherine spent three and a half days with her mother and then flew to L.A. Joe Angeletti had phoned her before she had left India, inviting her to come to California for a visit. She thought this would be great if she could work it into her busy schedule. Joe met her at LAX and they drove to his home in Mammoth Lakes in the Sierra Mountains. It was her first trip there and she found it delightful. Catherine liked his wife, Janine, very much and they got along very well. She even attended one of their AA meetings and enjoyed it, finding it interesting. Joe had been sober for many years now and had many crazy stories to relate. He had met Janine at an AA meeting some years back and they never missed a day without attending a meeting, even when they were traveling. Joe and Janine took Catherine around, showing her the beautiful area where they lived, and then on the last day they drove to Reno where Catherine was to take her flight to Minneapolis. She requested a special favor since they were close to Lake Tahoe. She wanted to see the office of Toni Neubauer; Myths and Mountains. Joe found it and parked just out of sight of the house/office building. Catherine walked into the driveway and into the office. It was not large. There were three girls working there.

"May I help you?" asked one of them.

"I'd like one of your brochures," Catherine said.

"Yes, of course." The girl handed one to her, and must have noticed that Catherine was wearing Indian dress. "Would you like to see Toni?" she asked.

"No," Catherine replied.

"But she is just upstairs. I can call her."

"No thank you. I'm going now." And Catherine left. She had no desire to see Toni. She didn't know if Toni would recognize her and she didn't want her to either, so she took her brochure and walked away, her curiousity satified.

When she got back to Minneapolis, she went to Fargo to be with Robert and his family and to consult with Dr. Abdullah, a plastic surgeon, regarding a face lift. He was well known in Fargo, according to Robert, and Catherine liked him. He did the surgery on her face on August 24th in his clinic. She recuperated quickly and drove to Duluth on the 28th, against the doctor's wishes, but her time was short and critical. She had other appointments with dentist and other doctors.

During this time, she saw Helga for a Regression. This was quite an interesting experience. Helga put her into an altered state as she lay covered with a light blanket on a recliner. At first she felt like she was in a womb and told Helga so. Helga said, "Come out." And she felt a sudden gush, like a going out by the feet. It was strange.

Then she saw herself as a young girl, kneeling on one knee, holding out her arms to a little boy, whom she knew was her baby brother. Another time, she saw the same little girl holding this little boy's hand and another boy's hand. The three of them were facing away and walking barefoot; although she couldn't see their feet because they were walking in a field of tall grass.

Helga asked about their family and all she could tell her was that there was one, but they were dark shadows in a room.

Somehow, Catherine knew that the little boy was Aadi and the older boy, also her brother, was Jannu. Helga told her later that she had also been Aadi's mother in a former life, and that the depth of feeling in her encompassed her whole body. Helga had seen Aadi running with many boys also; she saw him as a homosexual in a former life.

Catherine was concerned about her back and had contacted Dr. Donaly. Bran thought very highly of him. He was a neurosurgeon at the Duluth Clinic. When she saw him, however, he seemed more interested in how Brandon was faring than in her problem. However, he did order an MRI at St. Mary's Hospital and she had that done on the 2nd of September. The follow-up however was a great disappointment. When she phoned Dr. Donaly on the 15th, his answer was, "Well, amputation isn't warranted." What kind of a diagnosis was that? She was furious and was again left with no answers to her continuing back problem.

It was back to the Twin Cities again for her 50th reunion from St. Joseph's Academy. She was staying at Roland's for a few days. They had asked to read her book and although she had misgivings, she gave it to them. It was a grave mistake. Roland didn't say anything, but Anne was furious.

"I never want my girls to read any of this," she told Catherine.

"Why not?"

"The way you depict their grandfather and their great grandmother! I don't want them to have that kind of an impression of them."

"Well, Anne, this is my life. I'm not going to sugar-coat it for posterity. This book is not being written for children. It's being written for adults. You had a happy childhood and a happy marriage but I didn't."

"I'm not going to apologize for that."

"I'm not asking you to, Anne. But I'm writing my story as I lived it, and someday, my grandchildren will be interested in my story."

"Well, I won't allow my children to read this."

Catherine knew that Anne was also upset with the sex in the book, but Anne did not mention that, at least not to her. She mentioned it at some later date to Randall and also to Mary Ann as something which was 'entirely inappropriate' for the book. But the situation of their reading her book made it difficult for Catherine to live side by side in the same house with them.

Luckily the reunion took place over two days and then Catherine was to fly to Chicago to renew her visa. From there she was to fly to visit her friends in Boston, so she packed her bags and was ready to move out.

Her reunion took place at the Sheraton Midway Hotel. It was lovely to see old friends and acquaintances again. Many she didn't recognize and had to check their name tags. The following day there was a 10:00 AM Mass for their class at St. Thomas University. This also was very beautiful.

Catherine spent a day in Chicago and then flew out for Providence, RI. It was easier for Marie and Paul to pick her up there than drive all the way into Boston and getting her at Logan Airport. She spent four wonderful days with them and saw their family also. Upon her return to Minneapolis, she went to stay with Carmel and Al rather than with Roland and Anne. It didn't feel good there anymore. And on October 5th, she flew out for India and home.

Toward the end of the month she started hearing from Aadi, although she missed some of his calls. She wondered if he still planned on taking her to Gujarat. Finally, they were able to get together on the 22nd and she gave him his birthday present, a lovely silver message box, which she had engraved with his name in Duluth. Before opening it, he guessed it was an umbrella or a lampshade. They laughed a lot over that. And he liked his gift very much. He surprised her by telling her to stop by his house any time she was at the haveli. Her heart swelled with love for him.

She waited and waited to hear when they would be going to Gujarat, but he didn't call. In the meantime Catherine had made friends with Neeta Young, the woman who lived in the house in front of hers near the street. That house belonged to Dr. Nanavati's brother. Neeta's husband was Sheel and they had two daughters. All of them spoke English very well, but Neeta asked Catherine to give her further lessons, so Catherine was tutoring her and enjoying it. Their friendship had also developed after they had met and decided to walk together every morning. Catherine enjoyed the early morning exercise and getting to know this young woman, who she found was Christian. Her daughters attended St. Mary's Catholic School, but the Youngs were Protestant and belonged to the Church of North India in Chetak Circle.

Then, on Sunday, October 24th Catherine was at the haveli when Aadi called her there to tell her they would not be going to Gujarat in the near future. He was leaving for Mt. Abu for four days. Catherine was terribly upset and hurt and had to hide her feelings at the haveli. But that night she couldn't sleep and wept most of the night and the following day. She was devastated. Once again she had trusted him, believed him, and once again he had backed away. Finally on November 2nd Aadi came to her and told her he was sorry that he was unable to take her to Gujarat, but promised they would go before Christmas. Another promise? But they spent a lovely day together talking and watching TV.

Catherine called Brandon and learned that Randall was bleeding from the rectum. Both were concerned he may have cancer. He was to have a colonoscopy on November 15th and both Bran and Catherine wished it could be sooner. She went to the haveli to ask for prayers for her son. She called Randall in the wee hours of her night on the 16th and learned that the test was negative. He had bleeding hemorrhoids. Thank you God. Her sweet Randall was all right.

Internet was still in its infancy and a technician was coming to her house often to work on her computer. She would send messages, but not receive any in return, so she didn't know if she was doing it correctly or not. Sometimes it worked, other times it would not connect and she would be frustrated. The internet seemed to have a mind of its own. Then suddenly a message would come through and how excited she'd be to hear from a friend from across the world.

One evening in November Aadi came to Catherine. He didn't want water, or tea, nor dinner. She showed him the internet, which he was interested in. Then when he was leaving, he held her in his arms and began kissing her, deep, open- mouth kisses, which went on for a long period. She felt his erection as he rubbed against her. But he broke away, and still holding her, smiled. She told him once again that she loved him, and he left.

Catherine wondered. Was it loneliness that brought him to her? Did he need her and was he afraid to ask? She was afraid to go further than kissing for fear that he didn't want anything more. Their relationship was so easy and comfortable and she didn't want anything to change.

CHAPTER THIRTY FIVE
GUJARAT

For most of the month of November Catherine wept in loneliness for Aadi. He was 'out-of-station' as they called it, and she didn't know where he was or with whom. Her heart was broken and she constantly wondered when he would be back and if he would still take her to Gujarat as he had promised. Finally, he called on December 7th and told her he was going out on tour until the 12th and then they would go to Gujarat on the 13th. She ached to see him, but felt better knowing they would be going together in a few days time.

Catherine thought back over those days when he was gone. He had been so loving just before he left, so she surmised he had been with Honey for twenty days or so after that. Jannu had told her that Aadi had called him and asked him to call her to tell her he'd take her to Gujarat on Monday. Jannu told him to call her himself! Good for Jannu! She started to pack, hoping she was doing the right thing.

Chain was not to be their driver, and Catherine was to ask Jannu to hire a car and driver for their tour to Gujarat. She felt a bit strange about this, but good also because she knew Aadi was too close to Chain and she didn't want a repeat of their tour of Rajasthan. Aadi showed up at her house the evening before they were to leave, to get his injection. He was tired and seemed very remote. Catherine asked him if he really wanted to go to Gujarat and he assured her he did, but she felt sad and wept after he left. She was determined to make this a good trip for him as well as for herself. If he did not enjoy it, then certainly she would not. She didn't expect intimacy either because they hadn't had any for so very long. But she looked forward to the intimacy of sharing a room and being together. She also knew she'd feel the need to touch and be touched by him.

Jannu wanted to know how many days she would be out in order to tell the driver. She had asked Aadi, but he left that decision to her. Catherine decided she wanted to be home for Christmas, so she told Jannu ten days or less. Aadi arrived around 3 PM on the 13th with the car and driver, whose name was Manji. Catherine immediately set her mind to having a joyful, positive experience. The drive to Ahmedabad was long, but she and Aadi talked amiably along the way, although she did most of the talking. There was a hold up near their destination of a terrible accident. A truck had hit a minibus and seven people were killed.

It was dark when they arrived in Ahmedabad. Aadi decided they should have a nice dinner before going to their hotel, so they stopped at the Sofetiel Hotel for food.

The hotel Aadi found for them to stay at was modest, but clean. Catherine noticed Aadi falling against the wall as they walked to their room.

"You shower first," she said. "You are exhausted." He did and when she was finished with hers, he was already asleep. They slept long the next morning, both needing the rest, especially Aadi. Then after prayers and a light breakfast in their room, they went to the Calico Museum. It was fabulous! Catherine had never seen such beautiful fabrics, some 400 years old, the colors vibrant, and the work so intricate. They had an excellent dosan, who showed them around the estate, which contained more buildings. And the grounds were full of trees, flowers, and ponds; so beautiful!

They took time out for lunch at a restaurant serving Gujarati thalis. It was excellent. The three of them, Aadi, Catherine and Manji, ate their fill for only Rs 165. At these restaurants, the waiters were smiling as they kept refilling the thalis. They were so happy they were enjoying the food.

Then Aadi and Catherine went back to the museum to see the other buildings where there were samples of technical work. It was interesting for Catherine to see all the embroidery stitches they had used because she had done needleart all her life. As they were walking along, they overheard two Frenchmen speaking, evidently with questions. Aadi immediately stopped and answered them, explaining in their language. Catherine's heart almost burst with love for him, she was so proud of him. He was so intelligent and so knowledgeable. At the museum store she chose a lovely fabric wall hanging for Rs. 2000, which Aadi particularly liked and insisted on paying half of it, saying it was her Christmas present.

After the museum, which took up most of the day, they walked through the old part of the city and visited a market, which was very interesting. They also went to a mosque and saw many Muslim men praying, this being the month of Ramadan.

That evening in the hotel, they received a phone call, that is, Aadi did, from a friend he knew in Udaipur. The man wanted Aadi to meet with him, but Aadi declined. Catherine told Aadi to go, but Aadi said no, and she felt so grateful to him. They looked at maps until there was nothing else to discuss and Catherine knew he didn't want to get intimate, so they said, 'good-night'. She cried herself to sleep, but was careful not to let him know. Her nose binders were not sticking, so she was afraid her snoring would bother him.

The following morning they woke early to pray and shower. Aadi noticed that Catherine was breathing deeply, which she was unaware of. But it was due to her holding in her emotions. She was feeling battered and bruised, being close to the man she loved, but having not even the slightest physical contact with him. She wept through her prayers, but again she was careful that he didn't notice.

After tea and a light breakfast, they left the hotel and were on the road. It was a beautiful day. Their first stop was only a short distance away to Adolaja, which looked like nothing as they approached it. But there in the ground was this magnificent, the most beautiful in all India, a 10th century stepwell; and going deeply into the ground, there were many, many pillars, friezes, arches; the details of the carvings so impressive, so beautiful. Aadi had a slight altercation with a 'guard' who kept insisting no flash photos could be taken there. She didn't even take her flash attachment with her, but Aadi was incensed and argued with the stupid man.

Their second stop was much farther along and northwest to Modhera. The setting was serene and peaceful with trees, lawns and flowers. As they approached the Sun Temple, first was the immense stepwell, not covered, but deep, and very beautifully arranged steps and many small temples inside and along the sides. This also was a 10th century structure. There were two buildings; one, a kind of pavilion, the second, a temple. The entire complex was of sandstone, intricately carved. Some outer figures had become worn away because of the closeness to the sea. Aadi pointed out many facets of this beautiful place that she never would have noticed or understood on her own. This was known as SATYIA MANDIR or SUN TEMPLE, dedicated to the Sun God – Satya

From there they followed a bumpy road a long distance, or so it seemed, to Zainabad, where on the edge of the Little Rann of Kutch and nature sanctuary was a lovely camp belonging to the Nawab Dhanraj Malik.

There were seven huts, very rustic and basic, but comforable and clean. However, after meeting the prince, a young, engaging man who knew Aadi and who was very welcoming and hospitable to them, they learned that the compound was completely filled with students from an exclusive school in Ahmedabad. However, the Nawab said they were welcome to stay in a room in his house. They had tea, then joined a New Zealand girl and went to the sanctuary in a jeep driven by a man from the camp.

The Rann is a wasteland and was as Catherine had pictured it. They did see wild ass, the only place on earth where they exist. They are of the horse family and are beautifully marked; cream and tan. One male takes care of 30 to 40 females. There is a herd of many males who do not mate. They also saw Nilgai, or blue bulls, wild of course. As they drove close to the animals, they would move away. Aadi and Catherine did get out of the jeep and followed on foot to take photos, but when they got closer, the animals moved off. Aadi used his telephoto lens and got good shots. She was afraid hers would be distant, but she shot many just the same. She also shot one of the sunset over the bleak, cracked surface of the Rann.

Then back to camp in the dark where they were taken to the Nawab's house. They quickly showered and dressed, then were driven back to the camp to have supper; a vegetarian buffet. They sat a while afterwards talking to another guest, a travel agent and the Nawab. The sky was full of stars and because of being out in the wilderness, they were a magnificent sight. Catherine tried to interest Aadi, but he wasn't.

Back in their room, they undressed quickly and got into bed, Aadi first. This was the first place where the beds were together, but Catherine was under no illusion that there would be any intimacy. The mattresses were comfortable and big with feather quilts.

"Aadi, please wake me if I snore." But she knew he would never do so. Again she felt desolate and alone as there was no bodily contact whatsoever. She cried herself to sleep, but kept waking up and weeping all over again. Catherine got up a couple of times and went into the bathroom to relieve her plugged nose from all her crying. She sat on the toilet seat cover and wrote in her journal, not knowing what time it was, but it was dark outside. Then she lay in bed next to the man she loved who was sleeping soundly. She knew she couldn't compete with the German girl, who had youth and history on her side. Nor could she compete with Toni who was the source of his income.

"I am nothing," she thought. "Because of me, he wants nothing and needs nothing. I am less than nothing. I am non-existent. The pain is great and by sheer force and strength of will I must not allow him to see this, nor realize what is happening with me. At all cost to myself, I want to protect him. Dear God, help me not to hurt him."

Dhanraj Malik, the Nawab, was a very sweet, kind man. He was regarded as a father to the villagers around the area because of all he had done for the people. As they rode through them, Aadi and Catherine noticed the smiles on the faces of the people and how joyously they waved at him, showing great love and respect. Aadi told her Dhanraj had a lovely wife and one daughter. His father still lived and was an ornithologist.

Their morning began somewhat emotionally. Catherine prayed while Aadi showered. She wept a lot and couldn't hide it, but went into the bathroom after Aadi and slipped on the wet floor and fell. She didn't hurt herself, but when she was dressing, she was holding her head.

"Are you all right?" Aadi asked her.

"Yes, I'm fine."

"You are holding your head."

"Aadi, I'm FINE. Stop reading something into every little gesture. My blood pressure is fine. My blood sugar is normal."

"Do you have a cold, because you seem to have the sniffles?"

"No I don't have a cold."

"How many times do you get up in the night?"

"Why do you want to know?"

"I'm just curious."

"Was I disturbing you?"

"No, no."

"I told you, Aadi that I am in perfect health physically. You know that I am very strong mentally. But I am emotionally very fragile. I'm having a hard time. Please understand I am so grateful to you for bringing me here. I am so happy to be here. When I pray, I become emotional because I ask God to help me through this. Now, today is another day. It is going to be beautiful, so let us go and enjoy it."

They ate a late breakfast in camp, and then Dhanraj took them in the jeep to the sanctuary to view birds. There was a lake, and they parked at some distance, walking in. However, the ground became muddy and soon they were sinking into very thick muck. Aadi got closest, but Catherine saw pelicans, spoon bills, flamingos and other birds, but at such a great distance, she was sure her photos would show very little. Besides her lens was getting very dirty.

Back at the camp, they drove to the house and packed their things and then had lunch with Dhanraj. They paid him Rs. 2000 for the one night, the food and two safaris. He refused to tell Aadi what the bill was, but Aadi decided it was a fair price. Then Dhanraj gave them directions to the roads leading to Bhuj and they were off.

The drive was long and hot, but the roads were good most of the way. Catherine and Aadi talked and laughed and really enjoyed a good time. They stopped for chai and then continued on. Still, Aadi talked and talked and also snoozed for a short while prior to their stop. It was truly a beautiful day, Catherine thought. Aadi decided on the Prince Hotel in Bhuj. It was very nice with good beds, and a clean bath and shower. They showered and dressed, talked and laughed, then went downstairs to walk to a Gujarati restaurant for a typical thali. This is when the entire evening went berserk for Catherine.

Manji met them outside and he and Aadi immediately started up a conversation in Hindi and walked along with them. Catherine couldn't believe Aadi was doing this AGAIN! She had told him after the Rajasthan tour two years ago with Chain that she wanted their dinners ALONE, with no drivers. Catherine was hurt this night and churlish. She barely spoke, only answering briefly to Aadi's questions. She wanted to run back to the hotel and let them go on. She knew this was not the thing to do, but her mind was in turmoil.

After a really excellent thali dinner, Aadi decided they should walk around for awhile. They found the lake, and then walked along finding old and new houses, some with beautiful architecture. They passed the museum, whose façade showed British influence. They walked past the City gates and the palace, also a particular temple, very ornate, for a special sect of Gujarati Hindus. Then Aadi realized he was lost and began asking questions on how to get back to the Prince Hotel. He found someone to lead them, but Manji and Catherine couldn't keep up. They lost Aadi.

Catherine became very upset, not because she was afraid, but because Aadi did not check to see they were following. So, she and Manji walked many streets, alleyways, and deserted, dark areas, looking for a way out. The smell of dung and garbage was heavy and Catherine was near tears before they finally found their way to the main street of the hotel. When she got to their room, Aadi was not there, so she showered, washed her hair and waited for his return. She was furious. Very soon afterwards Aadi arrived.

"Where were you?" he asked. "I went back for you and couldn't find you."

Catherine could hardly speak, she was so upset, hurt and angry. Then she opened up. Aadi tried to apologize, but she spoke over him and in a loud strident voice.

"You left us! You didn't look back once. We couldn't see where you went. We walked through dark streets, back streets, alleyways filled with cow dung and garbage, deserted streets. Where were you? Did you once think to look back to see where we were? You just abandaned us. You abandaned ME. You never would abandon Honey, would you? You never would abandon Toni, would you? Or any of your precious clients, oh no. But me, that was OK. Who am I anyway? A Nobody! And what was all that about asking Manji to have dinner with us?"

"He worked so hard all day, I felt he deserved a good dinner tonight."

"Really! Well, Aadi, we went all through this once before with Chain. I told you I didn't care how much money you gave the driver to have a good meal and where he went to eat it. But I want to have dinner ALONE with you. It is the only private time we have together all day. But if you prefer not to have my company, please say so and I'll take the first convenience back to Udaipur in the morning."

"I'm sorry, I'm sorry, I'm sorry, I'm sorry."

Catherine just thought he was mouthing the words, and when she tried to get him to explain, he started screaming at her.

"I said I was sorry, so leave it. Good night." At that he went into the bathroom. She sat, stunned. It was the first time he had ever spoken to her like that, and under her breath she called him a 'bastard'. She was still sitting on her bed when he came out of the bathroom, his whole demeanor changed.

"Would you like some water?" he asked kindly.

"Yes," she answered. He poured her a glass.

"I wasn't really angry with you, but terribly hurt," she told him. "And that's the first time you ever yelled at me."

He nodded and it seemed it was all over. He put out the light and she wept. After a while, she called his name. She wanted to apologize for her behavior because she felt it was also her fault that a perfect day had been spoiled. She wanted to tell him, but he didn't answer. Perhaps he was awake and afraid that she wanted intimacy. Whatever! She wanted to apologize for her churlishness, selfishness, and oversensitivity and over reaction. She decided she had to tell him in the morning.

When Aadi woke up, Catherine took his hand, but she could tell he gave it to her reluctantly. She apologized, just as she had planned the night before.

"I should not have gotten so angry," Aadi said.

"I over reacted, Aadi. I'm so sorry."

The day went well, but Catherine was still heavy of heart. They spoke very little and the joy and laughter were not present. After breakfast in their room, they gave their clothes to be laundered, and then set out for the Gahal Safari Lodge. It was an absolutely lovely spot, quiet and serene, with white, cone-shaped cottages overlooking a dam reservoir. The woman who owned it was a cousin of Prem Ranawat, Jannu's sister-in-law (Vibu's wife). She told them she had another cousin who was the owner of Travel Plan in Udaipur. Jannu used to work for Travel Plan. They got the names of nine villages they were to visit the following day, which was their reason for being there.

With this list, they drove back to Bhuj and went to the government office to get permission to visit the villages. Aadi took Catherine's passport and got photo copies of it and her Indian visa while she filled out forms in the office. They were given permission for only seven villages, but Aadi said that was enough and probably the other two were too close to the border.

They visited the Gujarat Museum, which Catherine enjoyed very much because she saw textiles and beautiful embroidery work once again. Then she and Aadi enjoyed a quick South Indian lunch of dosas and ice cream. Aadi had told Manji to go elsewhere. Catherine told Aadi that wasn't necessary, that she was only concerned about dinner and their evenings together.

"Aadi, are we OK? My heart is still heavy," she told him.

"Yes, my head is fine," he assured her, but he seemed very quiet.

The Palace Museum was interesting for its jewelry, textiles again, glass, and many European and Chinese articles. There were many photos of Maharajas as well as royalty of Britain. From there they drove to see the palace garden, but it wasn't open that day. Perhaps they could see it the next morning. So they went to visit the royal chhatris. Aadi and Catherine walked in and she took some photos, after which they went back to the hotel and had chai, took showers and relaxed, talking about where they would go on the following day.

They left in the morning for Gahal Safari Lodge, where they were to pick up a jeep. They were late coming from Bhuj so the jeep had already left. They waited, having chai and choosing one of the 'huts'. Catherine decided she liked the new ones better because they were more spacious and the bathrooms were better.

She did like the old ones for their colorful interiors however, but the new ones were pretty too. When she first checked on the rooms, she noticed the beds were together, but later when they arrived, they had been separated. She supposed at some time Aadi had requested this, but he had never seen them. When the jeep arrived, Catherine sat in front with the driver and Aadi sat in back with Manji.

They drove a long way to the village of the Meghawali people. Catherine bought a few lovely handicrafts and took photos of the people and inside their beautiful, spotlessly clean houses. Then they drove off to another village where Catherine bought two small carved wooden trays. Aadi bargained for a lovely piece of mirror and embroidery work which she liked, but the villagers refused to come down in price. Aadi said they could find the same piece elsewhere and they drove off. Catherine was disappointed and they never did find that same piece again. They ate their packed lunch from the lodge, sitting in one of the houses. One of the headmen told them that he came to Shilpgram in Udaipur with his wares every year.

Again they were off to another village, this time to see Rogain painting on fabric. This artist's family was the only one in India doing this work, the only one in the world. He gave them a demonstration and Catherine was very impressed. A glue-like substance was made from castor (castor oil) and colored with vegetable dyes – all natural. He used a tool and pulled the paint substance over the fabric, painting the designs outright. The paintings were expensive, but Catherine chose one of the most expensive and bought it; that of a peacock on black background. She thought it was exquisite, and paid Rs.10,500. Aadi thought she was crazy and thought she should choose a less expensive one, but this was the one she wanted and she bought it. They visited another village where an American woman had set up a business helping the villagers to profit from their handicrafts. Catherine didn't buy anything there. After that, they drove back to the Lodge, finding the weather had turned cold.

They showered in cold water, got dressed and made their way to the dining hall for dinner. Afterwards Catherine wanted to stay awake and talk, but Aadi was tired and was coughing. Their blankets were not sufficient, so Catherine took a heavy one from the settee and put it over Aadi. He insisted that he would go down and ask for one for her, but she told him to get back in bed. In her suitcase, she took out her heavy 'trundlebundle' and slipped into that. She convinced Aadi she was very warm in that and she was.

But Catherine was sobbing into her pillow and had to get up to blow her nose into the sink and wash her face. She got back into bed, but slept only for a short while before waking and sobbing again. She needed him desperately. Her nerves were on edge wanting to touch him, needing to be held. She was ready to jump out of her skin. It was very, very difficult being so close and not being able to be with him.

It was Sunday, the 19th. The boy came to the door with chai, which they drank and then Aadi went to shower. Catherine started her prayers, but Aadi came running and called her outside to see the sunrise, which was beautiful. He went back in to shower again and she to her prayers. She was still praying when he came out to chant his prayers and Catherine found the moment so sacred and beautiful that she couldn't help but weep. Just at that moment the boy from the kitchen came with their breakfast. It didn't seem they were given one moment of privacy; it was either chai or breakfast! When Aadi finished his prayers, Catherine broke down and sobbed.

"What happened?" he asked

"I am so close to the man I love more than my life. He is a part of my soul." She told him. "But I can't touch him. I can't enfold him." Catherine sobbed uncontrollably.

Aadi came up to her. She was sitting on her bed. He was clothed only with a towel about his waist. He took her face between his hands and said,

"But I'm here. We are together."

"But I need contact, Aadi."

He pulled her to him, her face to his chest and her arm about him. She sobbed and he held her.

"I don't need to be fucked, I just need to be held." And he held her as she sobbed all over him and occasionally kissed him gently on his chest. Then they broke apart and started talking about the good things they were going to do.

That day they drove south to the ocean, to Mandvi, to see the palace, which was fairly new, early 20th century and very British. Catherine didn't care for it. Besides, they had to remove their shoes and then walk through a lot of bird shit on the terraces and the top floor. The mogul garden lay-out was lovely in the back, but there were no flowers. There were many trees of various kinds, and different shades of green were very pleasant. From there they drove to the private beach area of the maharaja and walked in the sand. Manji was with them, but stayed back most of the time, giving them privacy, which Catherine appreciated. She walked in the water, probably ruining her shoes, which she finally removed. It was so beautiful and reminded her of Goa. She thought, "I didn't have Aadi with me there, and I was weeping for his company. Now I have his company, but that is all I have, no intimacy, and it's killing me."

From the beach they drove to the town of Mundra Bandar and walked into the old section and found OSHO Restaurant. Manji came along and that was OK with Catherine. They had to walk up a ladder of sorts in the restaurant to get to the tables. They were the only ones there until suddenly a big group of Indian tourists arrived and filled the entire room with a lot of noisy talk. The food was Gujarati thali and very plentiful. The waiters kept trying to get them to eat more and more. Catherine was stuffed to the gills. After the lunch, she and Aadi walked about the town for a while and then went back to the car. They drove next to a beautiful Jain temple, which wasn't finished yet, but all the statues were in place and it was a working temple. Aadi and Catherine walked completely around it, but were not allowed to take photos. Afterwards they were served chai in a cafeteria.

A fairly long drive took them to Mundra, a walled city known for it's tie-dying, but it was Sunday and all the shops were closed because of Ramadan. Much of the work was done by Muslims. But Aadi and Catherine walked around in the crowded, dusty and really dirty streets. They stopped at a telephone exchange, where Aadi called his home and called Jannu also. Catherine spoke briefly to Jannu, who asked her if she was enjoying her tour.

From Mundra, they drove back to Bhuj and then into Gahal. After their showers, they went for dinner but ate on the veranda instead of in the dining hall. The owner joined them for a little while. Catherine noticed that everyone who knew Aadi seemed to love him. They greeted him so warmly and were so very happy to see him. He gave instructions for them to be awakened the next morning at seven with chai because they had a long trip ahead of them.

They left Gahal Safari Lodge, but not as early as they had wanted. They had their chai, but no breakfast as there were no bananas and the boy couldn't make parathas. They drove east of Bhuj, then over some of the same ground as they had coming from Zainabad, but not as far. They needed to travel NE in order to go SE to Morvi and then south to Rajkot, and again south to by-pass Gondal. Aadi said that there was nothing of interest there. They skirted Wankaner earlier, where there was only a palace, with a collection of cars belonging to the Maharaja. They stopped somewhere along the way for a quick Gujarati thali lunch, but it was not as good and not served with love as the one at OSHO the day before. They pushed on hard to Junagadh, and didn't stop. Finally, at sunset, around 7 PM, they arrived at Sasan Gir.

They pulled into the Taj Hotel, but they stayed in the small guest house in the back, which was part of the hotel but not as expensive. It had everything but a TV and Aadi checked it out first because when he had been there before there had been rat droppings in his room. This time the floors were dirty, but there was no sign of rats. Both Catherine and Aadi hated rats!! They ate at a buffet in the hotel, which Catherine didn't particularly like, and they asked for a hot drink of honey, lime and water for Aadi. He had one before dinner, then carried one back to the room so he could drink it before sleeping. He was acting rather silly, drunk-like, which of course he wasn't. But it made them laugh a lot and they kidded each other. Catherine finally got Aadi to lie in her bed with her and she held him close and kissed him. He held her and submitted, albeit somewhat reluctantly. She knew he was tired and let him go to his own bed.

Catherine slept better that night than all the other nights. That was the first time she didn't weep before going to sleep and not waking to weep again. They were to have a 5:30 wake-up call, but didn't check the clock when they were awakened. Aadi made chai and then noticed it was 6:20. They were supposed to be at the hotel at 6:30, so they raced to get ready and ran for their jeep.

Off they went to the Gir Sanctuary. They drove a long way and saw spotted deer (Chital), one blue bull (Nilgai), many peacocks, and finally a lion,–a lioness! She was quite close so Catherine got a photo of her. She had her binoculars with her too, and watched her as she moved away. They heard growls of lion in other sections, but didn't see another. It was a beautiful morning in nature. However, it was quite cold and Catherine was worried about Aadi catching cold. She insisted that he wear her shawl, but he only wrapped it around his neck, and she wanted him to cover his head so his cough wouldn't get worse. They had scalding hot chai in the village, and then back at the hotel they ate brunch of parathas, toast, juice and more chai.

They left soon again for a drive back to Junagadh to see the 273 BC Ashoka inscription on a huge rock. It was housed in a building and the translations were printed in Hindi and English.

Catherine found this absolutely fantastic! Then they drove into the fort, visiting first an old 17th century mosque. From there they walked downhill a way to caves dating from the second century AD. There was first an area to collect water and then two floors below, beautifully carved pillars still in very good condition. They sat there while a group of children ran noisily through, then they walked back up to the surface. This was truly the highlight of the day for Catherine. It had been dug at the time of Ashoka.

After that they saw an extremely deep stepwell, and then another deep well that Aadi said had rooms facing it. They didn't walk down either one. Then they proceeded to a lovely garden. It was once absolutely gorgeous because it was all there but in bad condition. They walked up to the walls and saw the canon and looked at the city below. Then they stopped for a snack and went on to the museum, which was most interesting – the Durbar hall was filled with so many chandeliers of every description, gilded chairs and sofas, mirrors and then photos of the various maharajas and nawabs. They saw lots of silver and many photos. The last nawab wanted the state of Jungadh to become part of Pakistan. When it was ruled against, he left with his family in 1947 for Pakistan, leaving his history and heritage behind.

They were still at the Taj Hotel and were going to leave very early the next morning because of the long drive ahead. Aadi came out of the toilet room, Catherine noticed, with his white Brahmin string over his ears.

"Aadi, what is the significance of the string over your ears?"

"It is very holy," he replied, not explaining further.

"Oh, I'm sorry, I shouldn't have asked."

"It is all right." But again he said nothing more.

Suddenly Catherine remembered an incident during their trip in Rajasthan. She had been lying in bed and he had come to her with his string over his ears, and had asked her if he could come to her and make love to her. She made the connection and it saddened her deeply because Catherine believed he had been in the toilet masturbating. Also, he was not feeling well. His throat was sore and he was coughing more. It was a long drive to Porbander, Gandhi's birthplace, and Aadi snoozed part of the way. He felt better when he woke up.

Porbander was a lovely town on the sea. They saw the square and then Gandhi's house. They walked through it, all three floors. Gandhi was born on the ground floor. The house was very well maintained, of course, and photos were not allowed, so Catherine took them outside and from the windows. They visited the small museum, which was filled mostly with books and then she and Aadi walked about the town. They noted the pretty houses that were no longer kept up, and saw 'Ba's' house not far from Gandhiji's, where she was born and grew up.

Then they took off back down the same road, but driving east. They came to a small ashram which Aadi liked very much. It was founded by a French woman who came to India and became a 'satyana' (holy one). There was a small shrine dedicated to Hanuman, the monkey god, and the setting among the trees and flowers was lovely and peaceful. They sat there, Aadi, Catherine, and Manji, and Aadi told them about the woman and the ashram. At that time, the woman was in Switzerland, but the ashram was constantly maintained. As they sat under the trees on a small mat over a rock, a young woman brought them each a small dish of coconut ice cream. They walked around the grounds, but photos were not allowed. However, memories were all in place. A group of young boys were seated in a meeting area, and it seemed they were there for an outing and were telling each other stories and jokes. Catherine told Aadi to leave money there, so he took out bills and she chose a Rs.500 note and placed it inside the little shrine.

Somnath was their next destination, a very long drive down the coast of Gujarat. There was a new shrine there dedicated to Shiva, built after Independence by Patel. It had been destroyed centuries back by Muslims. It was now right on the seashore, a very beautiful, natural site. The lingam was an original, never having been carved. Catherine and Aadi walked inside; one side was for men, the other for women, with a small dissection down the middle. There were more men than women, so Catherine held back and came to the altar at the same time as Aadi. He chanted prayers aloud and as he did so, her heart filled with love and so much else she couldn't readily decipher. Aadi told her this was a very important shrine for Brahmins because they prayed and lost lives in its defense. They came out together and he bought 'prasad' to be shared also with Manji.

They crossed the sand and sat on a retaining wall looking out at the sea and the people below them on the beach. It was not clean and they watched as two dogs took after and caught a baby pig. Later Aadi saw that it was killed and he wanted to leave the place then. But before that, Catherine was choked with emotion. They had talked for a while about religion and beliefs. Yes, she had said, she was a Christian, but she believed that God was in that temple and to see the people worship and have such faith, she could feel the love and especially to see and hear Aadi praise God, touched her heart deeply. Aadi told her he knew and understood what she was feeling. After talking a long while, they waited by the car so Manji could visit the temple. He wouldn't leave the car unattended. Then they left and stopped for chai and shared the Prasad (blessed sweets).

Back at the hotel they had dinner and ordered Aadi's honey and lemon hot drink once again. He wasn't acting as silly as the two previous nights, but after his shower, Catherine was shocked to see him coming out of the toilet room again with his string over his ears. After turning out the light, she lay on his bed with him although she knew he was ready for sleep.

They arose at 6:45, showered, dressed and packed, then went for breakfast. Catherine was surprised when they checked out at how small their bill was. It came to only Rs.175 for three nights including all their food, laundry and phone as well. But Aadi had lost his binoculars. He had called Gahal Lodge and

Zainabad, but no one had found them. Catherine had been praying to St. Anthony, and she told Aadi to call Dhanraj again and have him search the backs of the jeeps thoroughly.

They drove south again toward the sea, arriving shortly at Diu, the once Portuguese state, which was now a government province of Delhi. It was a delightful visit. The first thing Catherine noticed was how clean and neat the streets were. They went to the Fort first and Aadi and Catherine walked all about taking photos. Then they drove to the beach, stopping occasionally to take photos. It was not a large beach, but lonely; some parts sandy, other parts very rocky and black. Then they drove into the old city and parked. They walked and walked, taking many pictures of beautiful houses, sadly now all in decay. Aadi had been coughing a lot and at times getting breathless and almost choking. Catherine became so worried about him and started looking for a pharmacy. All the shops were closed for siesta. They went to a small hotel restaurant and had lunch, but the food was not very good. Aadi laughingly asked Catherine if she wanted a beer. Gujarat is a dry state and Gujaratis came to Diu to drink, so the restaurant had a small bar.

Aadi took Catherine to two Catholic churches. One was no longer in use and had many statues set up with saints names printed on cards. What really turned her off was a huge glass case containing a life-sized figure of Christ lying in his tomb. She wanted to scream, "Don't you know He is RISEN? He no longer lies in a tomb!!" Then they went to a 'working' church, but it didn't seem to be 'working'. Painting was in progress, although no painter was in sight. On the ceiling were many decorations in blue. Aadi took her to the cloister area and they listened to children singing the National Anthem from the attached school.

Having left Diu, they drove into Una, where they finally found a decent pharmacy. Catherine went in with Aadi and chose a cough syrup with codeine, some Vicks Vaporub and some lozenges, which seemed to be good. Instead of waiting for Catherine to buy a spoon, Aadi swigged down some cough medicine right from the bottle. His cough lessened, but not entirely and he became sleepy. Catherine couldn't get him to put his head on her lap however. Finally, she took Manji's big towel from the front seat and put it behind Aadi's head. He changed positions often and finally curled up with his head in her lap, but not for long. They stopped for chai, and then were off again. It was getting late and they had a long way to go.

Their destination was Palitana in Bhavnagar. Manji said he heard from someone where they had stopped for tea, that if they turned off at a certain point, they could go straight into Palitana, so they took the turn. However, the road was not good, but it was a real piece of luck. It saved them going all the way to Bhavnagar, saving them time in the morning when they wanted an early start for Palitana. The hotel was decent, very basic, but had a lizard in the toilet. Catherine wouldn't use it until the staff came and removed it.

They went down for dinner and Catherine gave Aadi his medicine and a lozenge. She also rubbed his neck and chest with the Vaporub. She didn't bother him this night lying next to him because he desperately needed his sleep and they had to rise very early in the morning.

It was December 24th, Christmas Eve morning. They arose at 4 AM, got ready, packed and checked out. Breakfast for Catherine was a couple slices of toast and after one sip of chai, which smelled like fish, they left for the place where they were to begin the climb for the Jain temples on the mountain. Many pilgrims were there already. Aadi said later that they started climbing about 6:30 AM. There were many 'bearers' who carried people to the top on a seat held by a heavy pole. Some have two poles for one seat, for a heavier load. It was very dark and hard to see at first, but Catherine followed Aadi.

The bearers were hemming in around Catherine wanting to be hired to carry her. She kept refusing and Aadi told them, "No" many times, but they kept insisting. Catherine got very upset.

"Aadi, they are spoiling this experience for me," she complained.

He took her aside and kindly told her to relax, that the men just wanted to make money and they would give up after they went a little further. They finally did, and Catherine felt comfortable climbing at her own speed and resting when she needed to do so. There were short expanses of no steps where they could walk up to the next flight, and the steps were low and not difficult, some deep, requiring two steps to a step. Some people, she noticed, walked one step up, then cross-walked for a short space, and then took another step up. Aadi and Catherine didn't do that. They watched the moon in the West, which was silver instead of the golden 'harvest' moon they had seen the night before. Then, through the branches of a near-by bush, they watched the sunrise in the East.

It was surprising to watch the bearers carrying up so many young women, also children, but very few old people, who preferred to walk, many carrying bundles on their heads. Catherine noted many were barefoot, others wore special sandals on their feet, made of cotton and very flimsy. The climb was 2 km (2,500 steps). There were a couple of stretches with no steps and that was a relief. Catherine could see something like a wall or some temple and wondered if they were arriving. Once she pointed to the top and of one of these and asked Aadi, "Is that the summit?"

"No."

"How far have we come?"

"Just over half way, but you are doing very well."

The climb really wasn't that bad, and Catherine was more worried about the descent, and she was right to worry. She made it to the top! Aadi had done it many times previously. Catherine watched the many beautiful saris – women dressed in their most beautiful clothes on their pilgrimage. Also, there were Jain nuns, who were dressed all in white. One was carried up by four women dressed not in white, but in many colors. Catherine took a photo of them. That was all they carried up, their cameras, no food or drink. But at points there were water stops, not for them however since it wasn't mineral water. Aadi told her many Jains boiled the water, which was good, but they couldn't chance it. Besides, no one drank water going up, only going down.

Before gaining the summit, they saw the main 'block' of temples. There were many blocks built later by wealthy people. But they arrived, after climbing 2¾ hours, and Aadi told her she did very well. Catherine thought he had worried at the beginning that she wouldn't be able to do it, and he was ready to hire a bearer for her.

"Aadi, you have to know me well enough by now to realize that I have a stubborn streak and an iron will, and I was determined to climb all the way to the top."

The main temple was dedicated to Adinath, very beautiful, but the temples were not as old, nor as finely carved as those at Mt. Abu and Ranakpur. There were the prophet statues all around the main temple, each in his own nook with symbols and readings to know which one he was. They went in and Aadi made obeisance. Then they walked around and around once again and sat in an appropriate place for a short time. Aadi took a photo of her in front of a temple, and then they walked around some of the 'blocks'. Each was somewhat different. Of course they removed their shoes often, and Aadi had to get permission for her camera. He asked her if her imagination of the site was different from the reality.

"Yes, because I had thought all the temples were on level ground. And now I find they are on hills and all connected to each other; that is, one complex to another."

Catherine saw stained glass in one temple. They finally left the temple site by a different door or entryway, and there by the door, was an old man serving salt or sugar curd. Aadi got each of them one, and then they began their descent.

Her legs started to bother her almost immediately; first the right knee pained her as she came down on that leg. The left knee hurt also, but the worst was the left thigh, which went numb and then gave her excruciating stabbing pain. Aadi asked if she wanted to be carried, but she refused. He could see the pain in her face. They sat and rested at one point and Catherine was able to express some of her feelings to him.

"I feel good about being in this holy place, Aadi, on Christmas Eve Day, a holy season for me. And watching the devotion of these pilgrims is an extra special experience for me, knowing we all are worshiping God in our own way. I feel so grateful to be here with you on this holy day. Aadi, you are the person I most want to be with, because I love no other person on earth the way I love you."

"I feel that," he said, in response.

They continued on, each step becoming more and more difficult for Catherine. Again Aadi wanted to hire a bearer for her.

"Aadi, do not mention it again. This is all part of my pilgrimage and I am offering up my pain to God for His Blessings, and in my thanksgiving. Also I am offering up my pain in reparation for any hurt I have done to anyone." She meant that with all of her heart and it was a very emotional time for her.

It had gotten warm; the sun was beating down on their heads and the sweat was pouring down Catherine's neck and face and streaming into her eyes. She had to stop often to wipe her eyes of the salty perspiration with her dupatta. Finally, they were able to see the bottom, but it was still a long way off and took them probably another hour to get there. They were very thirsty by then also, and Aadi gave her his arm and shoulder to help her. She was so grateful for the support.

At long last they were walking in sand, no more steps. They had made it to the ground or street level. Catherine spied a coconut stand and asked Aadi to buy them some, which he did. They stood and drank the refreshing nectar, then found Manji and went to a small shop for a drink of water, lemon, spices, salt and sugar. Then they drank mineral water until they felt they were sloshing in it. Aadi said there was a Jain lunchroom where they could eat and Catherine agreed, remembering the delicious food they'd had at Ranakpur.

First however, after coming down the mountain, they were met by Jains who honored them with a tiki and a brand new shiny Rs.1 coin. Then they went to the lunchroom for food, but Catherine found she could not eat, she was too exhausted and shaky, probably due to low blood sugar. She realized this, so forced herself to eat something, but could not finish. Also, she had not urinated since early morning at the hotel and had no desire even after all the liquid she had taken.

"Catherine," Aadi said, "We'll be in Ahmedabad for dinner and then get to Udaipur later tonight."

"Aadi, I don't want to rush home. Let's stay in a nice hotel in Ahmedabad tonight. It's been a long, hard day today. We are hot, sweaty, dusty and tired."

"All right."

Sometime later in the afternoon, Manji turned off the main road. They were on the way to Lothal – the ancient 4000 year old remains and archeological site. Catherine was so surprised and absolutely delighted. The museum was closed because it was Friday, but she enjoyed the canal, the Customs House and the streets where houses once stood.

"Aadi, wouldn't it be fun if we could go back in time for just a day and experience the life here?"

After they had left the site, Aadi brought up going on to Udaipur.

"Why, Aadi? Do you need to be back?"

"No, it doesn't matter to me. I'm just concerned that you get home for Christmas."

"Aadi, I am exactly where I want to be on Christmas – with you. But I would like to find a Catholic Church and go to Mass tonight."

"Should we stay in the same hotel we stayed in earlier?"

"That was OK, but why not splurge and stay in a 5-star hotel tonight?"

"That is a waste of money.

"But it's Christmas, and it's for us."

So they drove into Ahmedabad and Aadi directed Manji to the Fortune Hotel, a Welcome Group Hotel, which was lovely, but Catherine didn't think it was 5-star. They signed in and when asked, she told them they wanted a 'no smoking' room. They were taken to a lovely room on the second floor, but it had a double bed. Catherine immediately asked for twin beds. The bell hop came back and took them to another room, but when he opened the door, she smelled smoke and told him that room would not do. Another room had to be found for them, which it was, and then Aadi made tea for them because the room service tea was cold and not good.

Aadi went to Reception and got the address and hours of Mass at a Catholic Church. There was a Midnight Mass and an 8:30 AM. Catherine said she'd like to attend the Midnight Mass, so they decided to go. Aadi went to shower first and when she finished and came out, he was all dolled up in his Jodhpur black suit. She was so touched by this. She had no idea he had it with him. Catherine had washed her hair, so except for that, she looked OK. They ordered room service and enjoyed a lovely dinner. Then they turned on TV and learned of the Indian Airlines hijacking. It put a damper on the evening. They had wanted to just sit and relax. Instead they were worried about the passengers on the plane, and kept their eyes glued to the TV. Aadi guessed correctly they would take the plane to Afghanistan or some other Arab country. They landed at Amritsar, then Dubai, then flew to Afghanistan

At 11 PM they took a rikshaw to the church, St. Ignatius Loyola, which was a huge complex. The grounds were lit up with small red and green lights. They followed the people to the back where there was a grandstand facing an altar. At 11:45 the priests processed in – eleven of them. The main celebrant proceeded to talk for a good 15 minutes regarding the 2000 anniversary of the Pope opening the door of St. Peter's Basilica in Rome. Finally, Mass began and the choir sang, but none of the traditional Christmas hymns which Catherine was familiar with and sorely missed. They were singing in Gujarati and Aadi told her they were spiritual songs.

The readings began in English and finished in Gujarati. The homily started in English, and then began again in Gujarati. Catherine fell asleep. The length and tedium drove her crazy and she worried about Aadi. At the beginning there was candle-lighting, just like, or similar to Easter.

"Aadi, we will leave immediately after communion," she told him, and they did. Catherine made sure she was the first to receive before the crowds came up behind her. She took their snuffed candles as a remembrance and reached out to take his arm. Only he pulled away. Indian women do not hold a man's arm or hand. But Catherine couldn't help but think that when he walked with Honey, she held his hand and arm all the time. But of course their relationship was an intimate, sexual one, and had been for years. Catherine couldn't stop thinking about it.

She and Aadi hardly spoke on the way back to the hotel. He was exhausted and had gone through that long tedious Mass for her sake. She told him she knew it had been difficult for him and she was very grateful that he had taken her. She put Vicks on his chest and they went to sleep.

25 December 1999 – Christmas Day! They slept until 8 AM and then had their tea, and packed. They went down for breakfast and found that it was 'complimentary'. They had quite a nice spread of various foods. Catherine chose several things. Aadi chose a Southern dish – Uppam, a flat pancake with herbs. He gave her half of it and she found it delicious. In their room again, Catherine looked in the Yellow Pages for 'Stained Glass'. Aadi took the book from her and took down addresses.

After checking out of the hotel, they looked for the places in the phone book. A rikshaw driver took them to one studio, but there they only sold pieces, and all Catherine saw was a beveled glass door. She asked a woman, who wanted to know what color glass Catherine wanted. Catherine was dismayed. What color??? Then the woman sent a man with them to a house where there was glass piled up, all dusty and in no kind of order. Catherine realized if and when she was to start stained glass in earnest, she would have to come to Bombay and research the glass. This day it was hopeless.

They got back to their car and set off for Udaipur. Aadi was very tired and slept much of the way. Catherine also slept. They stopped for lunch at a very dirty place and Aadi told them to wash the table. He refused the salad, but ordered hot vegetables and chapatis. The food was good. Then out in the car, a boy came with ice cream which Aadi had ordered – for Christmas. 'Merry Christmas! Merry Christmas!!' Aadi shouted.

Finally they came into Udaipur and to Catherine's house. Dr. Nanavati wasn't home, but Mrs. Nanavati was there to open the security door for her. Aadi and Manji carried her bag upstairs and she tried to get Aadi's things separated from hers so he could take them. She knew he was anxious to get home. He gave her the money that was left from the trip, which was Rs.1000 and told her to give that plus 300 more to Manji for a tip. She did, and then decided she would ask Jannu what she owed Manji for the car and driving. Catherine gave Aadi a big bag of candy for his family as a Christmas gift. He shook her hand, than leaned forward and placed his head and cheek next to hers.

CHAPTER THIRTY SIX

A NEW CENTURY BEGINS

After returning, Catherine called Jannu and went immediately to Kankarwa for the opening ceremony of the reading of the Ramayana. She enjoyed dinner with the family and told them briefly of her tour of Gujarat and then returned home. Before leaving however, she gave Jannu her Christmas letter, which was everything she had expressed in her heart for him.

HAPPY HOLIDAYS MERRY CHRISTMAS

My dear Jannu,

Christmas is a season of love. It is a celebration of the birth of Christ, who all Christians or followers of Christ, believe is the Son of God. Not a separate God, but only one of three persons in the ONE godhead. We believe God is all Love, and Christ the personification of that Love.

To find a card to wish you the love of Christmas is impossible. There is no card that could possibly convey the depth of my feelings for you. It is a filial love and the deepest love one can have for a friend.

You literally saved my life. By telling me the truth, you indeed set me free. I told you that I didn't want to live. I don't think I told you that I had been looking for a place to hang myself, and I knew then that I was in deep trouble and needed help desperately. Even though I worried so about hurting you, the Grace of God led me to confide in you. He used you to bring me out of the darkness and into the light.

For a long time now I mistrusted the spiritual message I received in Kovalam Beach. It was like a distant memory that I thought perhaps was only wishful thinking. But I believe once again that God truly 'spoke' to me, telling me to come, live in India, and be happy. I've gone through what we Christians call 'the dark night of the soul', and thanks to God and YOU, I came through it. I have a lot of healing to go through yet. It may take the rest of my life.

You see, it wasn't only the hurt of the past year, but all the years of my childhood and years of my marriage. For fifty years, my self-image was systematically destroyed, first by my parents but most effectively by my husband. Knowing Aadi was the first and only time I felt good about myself. When I realized that he had lied to me, I felt not only rejection, but that I was nothing but garbage, flotsam on the river of life. I even felt that God had turned His Face from me. It seemed to me that He decided to show me and give me a taste of what it was that I had always needed and wanted, then pulled it out from under me, and laughing, told me that I didn't deserve it.

I guess I'll never know why God put me through all that pain. And I could wish that I had never met Aadi, except that then I would never have come to Kankarwa and met you and the family. I have never felt so loved and accepted anywhere. My sons love me, but I don't really feel a part of their lives anymore. It is a totally different culture there, and my heart, my spirit is not in the States. That is no longer my place. Perhaps it never was. You told me that we probably had a connection in a former life and that is why we are close now. I believe that also, because I can't explain nor understand why I am so at home and comfortable here in Udaipur, Kankarwa to be more specific. In fact, I always think of 13-A Saheli Marg as my house, but Kankarwa as my home.

She gives me everything that my spirit needs. Sundays are my favorite days because I get to spend the whole day there. My heart pours out in love for you and the family. I am very emotional right now because I've been *through a very difficult time. But now the tears are of love and gratitude and not of sadness and despair.*

Christmas is a time of giving and bestowing one's love on another. There is nothing that I wouldn't give you or do for you. You need only to ask. I know that you might feel uncomfortable doing that, but it would give me the greatest joy to help you in any way should you ever be in any need. Thank you over and over for being my friend, my confidant, my savior, for being the magnificent, honorable man that you are. May God's Light shine On you, Before you, Behind you, Beside you, and In you during this Holy Season and all the days of your life. Auntie

When she returned home, she called her boys and Lisa, also her mother, whom she found at Monica's. Her sister refused to talk to her. She phoned Mary Ann and Carmel too. She read all her letters and became very weepy, although she chided herself for feeling sad. Catherine had just returned from twelve wonderful days with the man she loved and she was grateful to God for those days. No, there had been no intimacy, but Aadi had been kind and good to her and had allowed her to kiss him each night. She ached for this man, not so much physically as emotionally. She needed his love. She needed his heart, but he wasn't capable of giving her either one. He knows and feels her love, but cannot respond in kind, but he is so good, such a wonderful person and human being. She felt her love was not misplaced.

December 27th was Divyarishi's birthday. Jannu called Catherine early in the day to make sure she would be there. She wondered if Aadi would be there or would he be out of Udaipur. Already she missed him. She went to Kankarwa for the birthday party, and dressed in sari. She talked to guests of the haveli and found that Aadi had indeed shown up for the festivities. Catherine asked him if he could come to her house to pick up his things from their trip. He said he would, but he didn't come and left the following morning for Delhi. He was starting another tour.

Great plans were afoot for New Years Eve. Catherine shopped for and bought a beautiful red silk jiri sari to wear for the occasion. Jannu was busy ordering and arranging everything for the evening. Aadi's clients were expected to arrive. They were staying across the lake at the Trident Hotel and were coming across via boat. Jannu had canopies placed over the roof for privacy as well as for warmth. White covered mattresses with cushions were placed on the floor of the roof and placed about were small low tables for dining. A bar had been set up and candles were lit all over the haveli. A special group of cooks were busy in the kitchen making many different Indian dishes, which was to be served on silver thalis. Champaign was also to be served in crystal flutes. Aadi's clients were Americans, a group from Toni Neubauer's 'Myths and Mountains'. Originally, the group had been over 40 people, but had dwindled to half that size before leaving the United States. Evidently some people were afraid of strange happenings when the new century began.

The New Year was ushered in with great fire works from the Lake Palace Hotel, from the City Palace, and just as great from Kankarwa Haveli and from other hotels around the lake in a smaller way. The canopies had holes in them from the fireworks, but that didn't matter. The spectacle was fabulous. Jannu had also hired musicians from Delhi to dance and sing, so it was very festive. Guests from the haveli had been invited to join as well as Aadi's 'uncle and aunt and cousins' and his sister and brother-in-law. Even so, there was too much food, and much went to waste. Catherine waited until everyone left before she ate, then Jannu's cousin, Kidu, took her home. She had had many compliments on her beautiful sari, which pleased her.

****

It was January 2nd and Aadi called Catherine to wish her a happy birthday. It was a day early, but it made her very happy. She couldn't hear him very well, so she went to turn down the TV, but when she got back, the connection had been cut. On the 13th he came for his injection. He told her he had called three times on her birthday, but no one answered. Catherine couldn't figure that out because she was at home the whole day and the phone never rang. He had just gotten home from a tour the night before and had brought her a plant.

He came over and they watched THE FAR PAVILIONS on TV. She felt bad. She could have cooked something, and didn't. On Suchana's birthday Catherine dressed in a sari and Aadi took her to Kankarwa for the celebration. He didn't care to stay for the dinner because he said it was for family only.

"But, Aadi, you are always included in family functions. Why don't you stay?" Catherine asked him

On the 18th, Catherine called Aadi and invited him to lunch. He called her at 2:30 and told her he was running late, but arrived at 3:00. She got the food served and he kept telling her how 'delicious' everything was. She had made rice, palak paneer (spinach cheese), peas and carrots, aloo (potato), a few hot chilis and some chutney. Afterwards he asked if he could lie down and she pulled off the bedspread and told him to lie down and be comfortable, that she wouldn't disturb him. He fell asleep immediately.

Later she wished she had covered him, but she didn't want to disturb him by doing so afterwards and awakening him. He did awaken at 5:30. She was standing on her terrace and tears were coming because she wanted his arms around her. She needed him emotionally. He was still sleepy-eyed when he called to her from the bedroom. She turned and gave him a big smile and asked if he had slept well. He said he had. They went to watch more FAR PAVILIONS and she gave him water to drink, since he didn't want chai. She also wrapped a blanket around him because it was chilly in the room. They watched the video and Catherine cried when Ash and Juli made love. At 7 PM Aadi said it was late and left for home.

It was the 26th and Catherine was just having her lunch when Aadi arrived unexpectedly. He came with a plant for her, an Ashapallav. She offered him food, but he wanted nothing, not even chai. He did have pani (water), however. Then he asked to watch the Cricket match, but kept changing channels. Finally, he wanted to watch THE FAR PAVILIONS. At a break in the video, Catherine went into the kitchen and made up a large tray of fruit and nuts, including oranges, pineapple, banana, cashews, almonds and peanuts. Aadi really enjoyed that. He talked for a while and then gave her the loveliest hug and kiss 'good-bye', and she could feel his erection.

Catherine laughed and said, "You know, Aadi, I was wishing you would lie on my pillow again. It smelled of you and I enjoyed that for two nights. We all have a particular smell and I like yours."

Aadi came the following day for lunch also, but it was very late due to the fact that he had travel agents he had to show about town. Catherine didn't mind. She was happy he was coming. She had made Gujarati dal, aloo methi, and cauliflower with peas and rice. They sat on the floor in front of the TV and watched FOREST GUMP, since Aadi wanted to watch an American movie. But Catherine had to explain much of the humor of it to him, and she had to explain Watergate. After the video, he used the toilet, then hugged and kissed her before he left. He had come by rickshaw, so he had to find one to get home.

A day in February Catherine got word from Mumbai that her shipment of medication was being held in Customs due to no Dr's prescription. She called Jannu, who told her to call Chain to take her to a Dr. in Hiren Magri. She was so angry, she didn't call immediately. Jannu called back to make sure she had done what he had told her, but then she couldn't contact Chain. About that time Aadi showed up and when he saw the address, he said he'd take her to the doctor.

Aadi's friend, Atul Srivastava, lived in Hiren Magri, so Aadi took Catherine on his scooter to Atul's house and introduced her to Atul, who then took Catherine on Aadi's scooter to the Dr's office. The doctor imported vaccines and didn't care to get involved because he was afraid Customs would give him problems. He gave Catherine an address in Delhi where she could write.

Back at Atul's house, Catherine found Aadi very much 'at home'. He was calling Atul's wife 'Bhabhi'. Her name was Anu. They had no children. When Catherine asked Aadi, he shook his head and frowned in a way so that she knew not to ask further. They asked her if she'd like to stay for dinner and she said it was up to Aadi, who immediately agreed. Catherine learned that Anu worked only a block from where she lived in a government building on Saheli Marg, across from Sahelion ki Bari. She was a chemist and did research there. Atul drove her there every morning. He wasn't working, but owned granite mines, which were closed down at the present time.

Catherine invited both of them to stop by whenever they could and Atul came the very next morning after dropping Anu at work. Catherine made chai and they talked for a long time. He came a few days later with Anu and then they invited Catherine for lunch the following Sunday. Atul came to get her and first drove to Hiren Magri section 14 where he had property. He told Catherine he thought she should build a house in that area, but she noted the lots were only 30 feet wide by 64 deep. She didn't like that. At Atul's, she met Anu's brother, his wife and daughter from Dungapur. They enjoyed lunch, then drove to another relative and then to the Monsoon Palace, which was situated on the highest hill in Udaipur. Then they had dinner at the in-laws house.

On the 13th of February, Catherine was just leaving for the market with Chain, when Atul arrived. He had great news. They had just adopted a baby girl – two days old. They got her in Jodhpur. The father had died earlier in a car accident and the mother had died in childbirth. The family was not able to care for the child, and Atul and Anu knew the family to be a good one and knew the doctor as well. Catherine was thrilled for them, and told Atul that she had an adopted son.

Atul then told Catherine Anu had had many pregnancies and miscarriages and they had given up trying. No wonder Aadi had given her a 'sign' not to ask anything. Atul wanted her to come as soon as possible to see the baby, but she gave them a few days and then went to see the baby.

The baby was extremely tiny and weak. Atul's nephew, a little boy, was there. He was hovering over the baby and Catherine noticed immediately that he had a cold and was snuffling and coughing. She gently pointed this out to Atul and Anu that this was not good for the baby to be so exposed and they agreed.

"Catherine," Atul said, "when we build our house, we will insist that you live with us."

"What? Atul, you've only known me for two weeks. You can't be serious," she laughed.

"Of all the people Aadi has brought to this house, you are the only one I feel I would ask to live with us."

"I am honored, Atul." And Catherine started to cry, because she was deeply touched. Earlier as she watched Anu cook, Anu asked Catherine if she liked chilis. "Of course," Catherine replied. Anu told her when Aadi had brought his German girl friend, she didn't want food so hot, so Anu had to cook without chilis. Anu couldn't remember her name, and Catherine said she had never met her.

It was almost time for Catherine to leave India again on her six month exodus. She asked Jannu if he would like to go to the U.S. with her. He came to her house one day with Kiddu and told her his mama would not allow him to go. Catherine was devastated, and felt she had once again been 'broad-sided' by Mama, who obviously didn't trust her, and saw her as a threat. Catherine was very hurt, and no longer felt a part of the family.

Now she started looking for places to stay in Nepal because it was highly unlikely that Aadi would agree to go with her to the States. She went to Atul and Anu's and held the baby for a long while, and they told her that Aadi had been there a few days earlier. Catherine had told him to go, but had not told him the reason and he wanted to know, but she wanted him to be surprised. That was the first he had heard of the new baby.

The next time Catherine saw Aadi she asked him to think about going with her to the U.S. He said he'd let her know, and he gave her great hugs and kisses. Then they talked politics. Aadi loved Clinton, and Catherine didn't, so they had many laughs and were comfortable with each other. Even so, she decided to contact Sunil and have him make reservations for a trip to Nepal early in April.

She went to visit Atul and Anu and spent time holding the baby, which gave her much comfort. On March 11th Atul and Anu celebrated the birth of their baby with a special puja. This was usually done on the sixth day after birth for both mother and baby, but due to the special circumstances, the Srivastavas did this one month later. Both sides of the family were in attendance and Catherine felt honored to be invited. At a particular moment, Anu gave each woman rupee notes, but to Catherine she handed a very old rupee coin. Catherine was deeply touched and honored. There was great food in abundance and everyone enjoyed a wonderful day. Atul brought Catherine home at 11 PM.

Catherine discovered a growth in her neck. The pain had been there, in the same spot for several weeks. She decided to see a doctor in Nepal. There was an International Clinic in Kathmandu. Aadi finally came back to Udaipur the end of March and called her, but only stayed for half an hour at her house. Then, the day before she left for Delhi, he came, had lunch with her and watched videos and spent five hours with her. It was April 2nd. It had been a busy day because she had been to the haveli to say 'good-bye' and had had to cook, and pack and wash her hair. Atul had wanted her to come for lunch, but she had begged off because she had expected Aadi and rightly so.

She left early the following morning for the airport and was met in Delhi by Sunil, who later hired a car for her. Catherine needed to go to a shop in Chandni Chowk in Old Delhi with Aadi's camera to be fixed. She had told the driver to wait for her by the Red Fort while she took a rikshaw to Chandni Chowk. She had no problem finding the shop that Aadi had directed her to and she was only there for ten minutes. When she returned, she couldn't find her car and driver. There were so many cars parked and her driver was nowhere in sight. Catherine spent over an hour looking for her car, walking back and forth among all the cars in the parking lot, until finally a kindly Sikh driver took pity on her and asked her who she was looking for. She told him she didn't have the number of her car, but her driver was a Sikh and her car was an Ambassador. He found her car for her. Her driver was lying down in the car asleeep!! It was no wonder she couldn't find him. He was negligent at his duty. He should have been on the look out for her. She was very angry and upset. She thanked the other Sikh for finding her car and driver.

Catherine then told him to take her to the Khan market, which he missed by two blocks and she wandered around and found only lighting shops. She was looking for a pharmacy, and when she got back to the car, he was across the street having chai. He finally came back after asking directions and found the Khan market. She did not find Calcium Citrate after going to two shops, and then saw the shop where she had purchased the hot water electric pot. There she found a lovely pottery tea set which she bought to bring home. It was 17 pieces and British. Then she wanted to go to the Ashan supermarket. It was a huge plaza and mall and very posh, but she found she didn't have the time to explore when she got there, and she only had the car until 5 PM. When she got back to Sunil's, the driver charged her Rs.370. She gave him Rs.400. He said he had no change. Sunil said to give him only Rs.250, but the driver said he was charging for mileage. Catherine told Sunil about how the driver had acted with her and he immediately called the company and complained.

The home situation was not good in Delhi. Mita told Catherine that Tapa had intimidated Mama to the point where she was afraid to talk to Sunil and Mita. Piku went to another house after school until Mita's servant went to get him and bring him home. He was not included in any gathering with Tapa, Mama and Sonu. Sujeet, Sunil's brother was begging Sunil for money to get him out of debt, promising to pay him back each month, but he hadn't done so. He was drinking heavily. Mita had given up on the family and kept to herself. Sunil planned to build on to the house, a full two storeys. They really needed more room for themselves, since Piku was growing up. He was too old to be sleeping in the same room with his parents. When Catherine was there, she slept with Mita in the one bed and Piku slept on the floor with Sunil.

On April 4th she flew into Kathmandu and spent a long time in the Arrival Hall in queue to get her visa, then was met by a young Dutch girl who took her to the CWIE Clinic. She was seen by a Dr. Pandey and sent to an ENT specialist regarding the pain in her throat. He thought it was an infection on the left salivary gland and gave her a prescription for an antibiotic. After that she found a lovely café, Chez Caroline, and treated herself to iced tea and chocolate cake.

Then she was on to Dhulikhel, by car, where she was warmly welcomed and found a lovely room. There were five bungalows at this resort called 'High View', and high it certainly was. The owner was Mr. Luitel Keshab, who seemed very nice and friendly and informed her that he had built the resort just over a year before. He had good ideas, which he told Catherine he had picked up traveling in Europe.

Some things she would have changed, such as the bathrooms, although very beautiful in white ceramic tile, were too large and had a large picture window overlooking the valley and mountains, which was very nice, but unnecessary. The room sported a lovely fireplace and a large picture window also facing the valley and mountains. On each side of this window were small screened doors opening to a wide balcony, on which were a small white wicker round table and two matching chairs. Inside the room were a large double bed and a single bed, two bedside tables, a wardrobe, which couldn't be opened due to the single bed beside it, and a dressing table with a mirror, two comfortable chairs and a table. There was a nice tiled floor in front of the fireplace, but the room was carpeted in a green commercial rug, which Catherine didn't like. The draperies matched the upholstered chairs. She didn't care for their selection either.

Her balcony was tiled the same as the floor by the fireplace. As she looked out, she noticed a great abundance of flowers and trees. The steps were brick, but walkways were loose stone, and not small, making it difficult to walk upon.

On April 6th there was some kind of strike going on. It was Communist instigated, so all the shops in Kathmandu were closed and no cars were allowed to be driven. It was called an 'armed' strike because people had been threatened with harm if they had not complied. Kishab had been in Kathmandu, but came back the night before with her passport and airline ticket. Catherine couldn't leave in the morning, but had to wait until evening to fly out. Therefore, she would not be able to pick up Aadi's camera in Delhi as she had planned. Sunil would have to do that for her.

Catherine had been on her balcony enjoying the view when she spied Kishab, who waved to her. She waved back, and he came walking up and asked if he could join her. It was chilly outside, so she invited him into her room. He ordered double drinks for himself and chai for her. Then he ordered snacks and asked her if she'd like to have dinner there in the room. He ordered food and a bottle of wine. She finally agreed to share some with him. At some point he began to read her palms and then put his arm around her. Catherine pulled away and he backed up. Three times more he made moves toward her and each time she laughed and pulled away. He was in his cups and being silly, but this did not go over well with Catherine. She did not get angry, but she was disappointed. A one night stand of sex disgusted her. It was not in her nature to give herself like that.

In the morning she paid her bill in rupees. It came to Rs.7,711 and she felt that was very cheap. Her car came for her around 1:30 and she took off for the airport, stopping first to get the remainder of her antibiotics. Her throat wasn't hurting anymore, but she had been taking heavy doses of aspirin as well as Ibuprofin.

When Catherine got to Sunil's, she phoned Aadi and told him she was unable to get his camera. It was not fixed yet and they wanted more money, so he was going to have to pick it up himself. She saw him on Sunday, the 9th, when he came to watch videos.

It was exceptionally hot already, this April. Catherine's power was off and there was also no water. She sat by her shrine in the nude, praying because it was so hot. She didn't go for a walk and her throat was hurting again. Aadi had come for his injection and brought a huge papaya. Catherine had made lunch for them, which he enjoyed and then they watched a video again. She was writing many letters to family on Brandon's side asking for names and dates and information for the family tree. She hoped they would respond favorably. Her thumb was hurting her badly, as she had caught it in the gate a few days earlier and now an infection had set in near the cuticle.

Easter came and went. Aadi called and wished her a Happy Easter, which gave her heart so much comfort. He came often, but never often enough for her.

Catherine called Sunil regarding Aadi's camera and he said he'd pick it up that day or the next and send it to Udaipur with a client or hold it until Aadi could get there to pick it up himself.

Suchana had been very ill with asthma. She was ordered to bed rest for a month. Catherine went to the haveli for lunch many times however and saw the kids, whom she loved so much.

Then it was Tapasya's birthday on May 4th, and Suchana was somewhat better. It was so good to be all together. Aadi joined them for dinner, and it was great for Catherine to see him there. Chain took her home and told her that Aadi had told him to bring her to his house the next day. Chain said the best time would be between 4 and 5. She decided to wear a sari in respect for Aadi's parents.

Chain first took her to Atul's and they were so happy to see her, that she had just dropped by without calling first. Then she went to Aadi's by 7 PM. He was still busy with his pump, working on digging his well. She was graciously received by Aadi's sister, Shashi and her three children, then Aadi's mother, Jiji. Shashi showed Catherine the house, and it was a wonderful house; so beautiful, with the great old neem tree in the courtyard dominating the scene and all the plants and other trees around it. Shashi and Catherine talked well with each other and then Aadi joined them. He was reluctant for her to leave, but she finally did around 9 PM. She had spoken briefly to his father, who liked her sari. Catherine felt she had been greatly blessed by God that day.

Catherine filled her terrace and sunroom with plants with the help of Aadi. He took her to the nursery and helped her to choose the plants. Also, if it hadn't been for him, she would have paid much too much for them, since the nurseryman was about to overcharge her a great deal. Her pots had been painted by the man who painted the walls at the haveli and they had been filled with soil that had been delivered to the house and then carried up to her apartment. Aadi worked hard to plant each of the flowers they had purchased and then watered them. He then showered and left. By June 1st her terrace and sunroom were in order and looked lovely.

Her sunroom had many windows, but no screens. She left them open and one day Catherine noticed bulbuls had nested in one of her light fixtures. They were very sweet birds, smaller than robins, black, with a cock on top of their heads and a red rump. They seemed to trust Catherine and didn't fly away when she used the sunroom to read. In early June, Mama Bulbul had three baby chicks. Chain climbed up and saw them. Catherine told him not to disturb them because maybe mama bird would not feed them then, if she smelled a human on them. But everyday, both mama and papa were busy feeding them until they were bigger than the parents. One day, all three flew out of the nest and landed in different places in the sunroom. Papa tried to get them to fly out of the window and succeeded with two of them. Catherine tried to watch closely, but this was not wanted. She was being flown at by the parents to keep away, so she watched at a distance. The last baby sat on the window sill at dusk and didn't move. Catherine felt badly for it and went with a towel to pick it up and bring it in, but in doing so, lost it. The next morning, Papa bird came into the sunroom looking for the lost birdie and didn't find him. But Catherine didn't find him outside on the sidewalk or on the grass, so he must have flown away. The bulbuls nested one more time there when Catherine went to the U.S. Then pigeons got in and broke the glass fixture and that ended the nesting.

Jannu called to warn her that the police were watchin Chain's brother-in-law and that she should not allow that man into her house. She had a few times before and had even been to his home for dinner one time. He had a jewelry shop in the name of his wife however and Catherine had had her nose pierced there by him. She had gotten a terrible infection and had had to get antibiotics. Anyway, she also worried that her phone might be tapped. She told Neeta about Jannu's warning and gave her Jannu's phone number in the event the police came to take her away. Jannu said if this happened, there would be nothing he could do to help her. Catherine gave Neeta one of the keys to her house also and then called Robert to alert him to the possibility. This man had been in prison for dealing drugs and the police were watching him again. Whether or not he was dealing again was unsure, but she was not about to go near him. He now had a hotel in Lal Ghat, near Kankarwa, and she had been there once and gone through it, for he had wanted her to see it.

Aadi took off for Delhi in June to get his visa for Europe. Catherine was sure he'd be back, but he didn't return. She was devastated. She wondered if he really loved his German girl but she didn't think so. Jannu came to her house and told her that Aadi had planned to come back to Udaipur, but couldn't get a flight out to Europe for 20 days, so left immediately with only the clothes on his back and had to send for luggage. This information made her feel better. Also, Jannu gave her more warnings regarding Baba Singh, but said it was OK for her to come to the haveli. The family had gone to Sikar and Mama had gone to visit her brother in Alwar, so Jannu was alone.

Catherine phoned the U.S. on Father's Day and spoke to her sons and to Brandon, who sounded weaker to her, and promised to write to him. She started a letter that night. She also finished Chapter Twenty-Seven of her book. She took Chain and Neeta to the Shiv Nivas for lunch one day and stopped at Atul's so Neeta could meet Atul and the baby. Then Chain drove them to the nursery where Catherine bought more plants and one for Jannu. Then they stopped at Kankarwa and Catherine introduced Neeta to Jannu and showed her the haveli.

It was Robert's 38th birthday and he called the evening before. He had just spoken to Jannu, asking him what the problem was concerning the police and thanking him for all he was doing for his mother. They evidently had had a nice chat.

In the middle of July Catherine was at Atul's when he brought up the subject once again that when he built his house he was going to insist she live with them. Then later in the day he spoke of Aadi having a big problem, that he couldn't live in Europe because he was the only son and responsible for his parents and his German girlfriend refused to live in India. His parents wanted Aadi to marry. Oh God! This hit Catherine very hard, and she wanted to run home and cry. She couldn't do that. Anu's brother and wife were there and she had to stay for lunch. She wondered, did Aadi want to marry Hannie? This somehow didn't seem to add up. Catherine took a rikshaw home and continued to pray because she was in terrible pain. She was beginning to think of ending her days in an ashram.

Anu came one day with her sister-in-law for chai. And Chain dropped by, talked and asked her about when she had met Aadi. She was getting tired of having Chain drop in whenever he pleased and stay for hours. Neeta asked her if she'd like to share a house with them and she agreed. She started making reservations for leaving India for the U.S. and had a date for the 25th of September. Catherine hoped however that Aadi would be back before then and that she would feel his arms around her before she left.

She phoned Bran and realized he had some form of speech aphasia due to what? Age? Disease? Medication? Or a combination of two or all? She pitied him and told him she'd write him again as he said how much he enjoyed her letters. Catherine prayed that God would spare him to see his new grandchild, who was due in September. Russell emailed that Julie didn't want to use our Christening dress; she wanted to use her own. Roland invited Catherine to stay at their house when she came back and she was pleased at the invitation.

It was Oshima, Neeta's older daughter's birthday. Catherine was upset because some months ago she had given Neeta money to buy Oshima a bicycle. She had noticed the two girls trying to ride one small bike in the driveway and felt sorry for them, so had given Neeta the money to buy another for Oshima. Instead, Neeta used the money to buy video tapes and basketball stuff and a few other frivolous gifts. Catherine felt 'used' by Neeta and very disappointed in her.

Early in August Catherine experienced chest pain as well as pain in her right arm. Sheel and Neeta took her for an EKG and she saw a cardiologist. The test was negative. What was going on with her? She was weeping and scared.

Then she heard from her sons. They were scared and crying. Bran was very bad, very weak. She talked to him and to each of her sons. She could barely hear Bran. He was so weak. Catherine felt very, very sad. She decided to leave immediately for the States.

Nanavati was not happy with her decision to give Neeta her key to water her plants. He didn't like the Youngs at all, principally because they rented from his brother, whom he didn't get along with. Also, when they ran out of water, Catherine allowed the children to take baths at her house and Nanavati was furious about that and shut off the power. Catherine had had words with him about that and told him it was her business if she wanted to share her water with them; that she never complained when his family came to visit. He said her family was welcome any time and she laughed at him and said that was highly unlikely. He also was very sly and she often saw him standing next to Young's window eavesdropping on their conversations.

Catherine went to the airport on August 17th, but couldn't get a flight out and had to go home. She called Jannu, who got her a flight out that evening on Indian Airlines. Then there was no flight out of Delhi, according to Sunil. But he took her to the KLM office with Robert's fax requesting she return ASAP due to his father's deteriorating health. KLM worked hard and found her a seat for that night and she was so grateful. Sunil emailed Robert of her arrival, and in the meantime she had a lovely lunch at Sunil and Mita's.

CHAPTER THIRTY SEVEN

A BIRTH AND A DEATH

After a three hour delay, Catherine flew from Delhi, then a short wait in Amsterdam and on into Minneapolis. Roland and Anne met her at the airport and took her to Randall's, where they had brought in a bed for her and placed it in the basement.

Bran was sleeping when she arrived and looking ghastly. He was extremely gaunt, his facial skin dark. When he awoke, he was very happy to see her.

Catherine spent most of the following day with Bran. Randall worked 8 – 4 and then was too exhausted to take her to the store for groceries which they needed. Bran was very weak, but spoke coherently most of the time. However, it was difficult to hear him because his voice was so weak. Roland and Anne arrived with the girls, who were wonderful and delightful. They got used to Catherine very quickly and then made too much noise, irritating Brandon, so they left. Russell and Julie arrived, and then Randall cooked meatless spaghetti. Catherine tried to watch TV, but kept falling asleep. She was jet lagged and would be for a couple of days yet.

Bran fell asleep often and complained of 'stomach' distress. He ate no lunch or dinner. He asked Catherine to check on him during the night, which she did, because she thought this was a sign the end was coming. Finally Catherine talked Randall into taking her to Cub Foods where she spent $183. Bran had been sleeping when they left, but Roland called later and gave Catherine Hell for leaving him alone. She made meat loaf and macaroni and cheese for dinner, which they all enjoyed. Even Bran ate a little and liked it. She washed towels and some clothes also, and the Hospice worker arrived to give Bran a bath in the morning.

Bran was talking about going into a hospital and seeing a doctor for help. Catherine found him very unaccepting of his fate and very grumpy. A case manager came and morphine liquid was ordered and delivered. It was easy to dispense in a small syringe and put under the tongue. Bran said it tasted awful, but it took his pain away almost immediately.

She took Randall shopping for more bedding and kitchen stuff and then called Jannu. Suchana was very ill and Jannu was extremely troubled and not himself. Catherine was having trouble with Randall, who was upset with her messing his kitchen and his bathroom. She felt she couldn't stay there anymore. Anne came with lunch for her. Bran was sleeping more and more and not leaving his bed. The care person came to give him his bath. He started having pain, so Catherine gave him .50 MS by mouth in the morning and he was free of pain for the rest of the day.

It was the end of August and Robert came with her car. Roland, Anne and the kids arrived. Julie stopped for a short visit and Kerry came with their kids to pick up Robert. They saw Brandon, who had just gone to bed. It would be the last time. Randall apologized to Catherine for his behavior to her, so things got better between them. Catherine read her email at Roland's and sent one to Jannu and one to Aadi.

Bran was becoming obstinate and Catherine yelled at him. She had gotten a commode, which he wouldn't use, nor would he use the new, easier urine bag, which would be so much better for him and for her to empty. She ordered a hospital bed and it was to be delivered the following day. It was early September and Catherine called India. Jannu told her Suchana was improving, thank God. She spoke to Atul and Anu, also Neeta, who told her her plants were doing well. She learned Aadi was 'out-of-station' until the 22nd of September.

Catherine found Brandon difficult to deal with now, since he was having a lot of dementia. Randall was reluctant to take him on alone. Mary Ann and Harold sent flowers to brighten her day, and they called every day as well. Catherine was wondering how long this would go on. Bran was weak, but hanging on with all his available strength. He couldn't walk anymore, but stood with much help. Dementia continued, and it was very difficult at times.

Bran's family, that is his sister and her kids, never came to see him. Evelyn called several times and hung up when Catherine answered the phone. She knew who it was by the caller ID and just shook her head. Finally one day, Evelyn did talk to her. Evelyn had called Russell at work and he had chewed her out, telling her to talk to his mother. She was mad at Catherine for divorcing Bran, but said she gave her credit for coming back when he needed her. Catherine didn't respond to this at all. She told Evelyn Bran was extremely weak and he was nearing the end. But none of the family came to see him.

Brandon lived to see his 78th birthday, but Catherine was not sure he was aware of it. Roland and Anne came with the girls and brought an ice cream cake. They fed a little bit to him and he ate it. Russell and Julie also came and Robert called. Catherine wondered how long he could hold on. September 11th Catherine's new granddaughter was born. She arrived at 11:58AM, weighing 8# 12oz, 20-1/2 in. long. She was fat and healthy and Russell was thrilled. They prayed that Bran would not die that day!

Bran was still hanging on the next day and Catherine told Randall they should spell each other every night, taking turns sitting with him. She sat the first half of the night, and Randall the second half. He didn't swallow water anymore. At one point, she started to read aloud psalms, but he became irritated, so she stopped. She prayed silently for God to take him to eternal life. But he seemed to be fighting the inevitable. It was so sad to watch.

He died alone at 11AM on September 13th. Randall was home alone. Catherine had just left for the Picket Fence, and when she got back, she found that Roland was there, so she knew it was over. She called her cousins, the Klecatskys, who came to pick up the body. The boys watched as the car drove off down the street with their daddy. It was sad. She phoned people who had to know of his death, such as his brother and his sister.

The next couple of days were taken up cleaning the room of his clothes and bagging them for Goodwill, calling Allina to remove hospital equipment, and then Roland came and moved the computer and furniture to make the home more livable and pleasant. Roland and his family spent a whole day with them. Cindy and Catherine's mom sent a snow crab tree, in remembrance, which was planted in the front yard. Catherine went with her sons to West Funeral Home to choose an urn for Bran's ashes and learned the many options. Tom Klecatsky took care of them. Many flowers arrived at the house.

It was the end of September and Catherine drove to Fargo. It was her time to spend with Robert and his family, also to see Dr. Abdullah. Robert's basement was finished and lovely. She had a nice, comfortable room and bathroom. The kids were great and Allison looked so much like Robert. At her appointment with Abdullah, he told her she had an abdominal hernia, which surprised her. She planned to have an abdominalplasty, removing all the fatty tissue that had accumulated over the years. Because of her high blood sugar, he insisted on doing the surgery in the hospital and having her there overnight. He told her if the hernia was large, he would call in his wife, who was a general surgeon.

Catherine phoned Aadi early the next morning, but didn't find him home. Then she called Jannu to tell him she was having surgery and that she was at risk. The next voice she heard was Aadi's, and she started to cry. Both Aadi and Jannu assured her she would be all right. She was not afraid of the surgery, or of the pain, or of dying, but she anguished that she may never see Aadi again. Surgery was at noon.

The following day, Catherine found herself in the hospital on oxygen and not breathing well. The doctors and nurses were very attentive. Robert and Kerry arrived with long stemmed red roses. The next day, she was still not breathing well and still on oxygen and respiratory therapists were coming in regularly to check on her. She was in no pain, but had many tubes coming out of her abdomen. She suddenly realized that she might die, but she wasn't scared. She asked for a priest, but he didn't come. They did many pokes in her radial artery for blood gases and she could tell by the color of the blood, that it was not good.

A priest finally came and gave Catherine the sacrament of Extreme Unction. First, he looked at her and tried talking with her.

"Wouldn't you rather have your own parish priest?" he asked her.

She just looked at him. Her oxygen mask was over her face and she couldn't answer him. If she could, she would have told him she lived in India. She just shook her head. So he administered the sacrament, but did not give her Holy Eucharist. He never returned either, and the church was just across the street.

Robert arrived and stood in the doorway.

"Mom, you've got to fight to live," he told her. "You are very ill."

Russell phoned and she tried to talk to him, but with the oxygen attached, she had difficulty. Then the evening nurse told her she was going to 'special' her during the night. Catherine looked at her.

"Am I that bad?"

"Yes, you are. We are holding a bed for you upstairs in ICU," she said.

Catherine suddenly decided she had better start working on getting better, not for herself, but for her sons. It wouldn't do for her to die right after their father. From that moment, her breathing seemed to get better, and finally after being in the hospital five days, she was able to leave. This cost her dearly because none of it was covered by her insurance.

As soon as she got to Robert's, he asked her to see a psychiatrist for her depression. He was so concerned, she agreed, although she knew that it was not going to work because she wasn't going to be in Fargo very long for any kind of treatment. In the meantime, she felt that God had been working a miracle in her, taking care of her, healing her, either for her son's sake, or for her own. Perhaps He had more work in store for her in her future. She had been released from the hospital on the feast of the Guardian Angels and Catherine felt that was very significant, that hers had been watching over her.

The psychiatrist Robert took her to told her there was nothing he could do for her, since she would not be there for counseling and he could not give her drugs, all of which took six months to work and went through the liver. And with her liver history, it was not advisable to medicate her with those drugs. She agreed and asked him to please explain this to her son, which he did.

Catherine soon left for Duluth, stayed with Lisa and then drove to visit Ellie in Eau Claire, Wisconsin. After that, she went back to Blaine and stayed the rest of her time with Randall. Her new grandbaby was baptized Lesley Elizabeth at St. Timothy's Church in Blaine and it was a happy occasion. Julie was not very friendly with Catherine, but that did not bother her too much, except the day before she was to fly out, she called Julie and asked if she could come and see the baby.

"You want to see the baby?" she asked Catherine.

"Yes, Julie, I'm leaving tomorrow. I'd like to see her once more."

"Well, Russell will be home at 9 tonight. You can come then."

"All right. Thank you. I'll be there." She had to wait until nine in the evening? Catherine thought that was crazy, but she waited and went at that time. Julie put the baby in Catherine's arms and gave her a bottle so she could feed her. Russell came home at that time, so she was able to say 'good-bye' to all of them.

By the end of November Randall lost his job at Dayton's. They closed their warehouse in St. Paul and moved it to Chicago. Catherine needed a new printer and her VCR had to go to the shop to be fixed. A few days later she printed all her Christmas letters, and then addressed all the envelopes. She had to go to the bank to pay for her new printer and the scanner she had purchased. It had been six months since she had seen Aadi and her heart was broken. She missed him terribly and she wept often. And then it was December. Atul and Anu were transferred to Chulu near Bikaner, so far away. She missed them, such good friends. And Catherine was rememembering that a year ago she and Aadi had gone to Gujarat. She had to stop weeping. It was bad for her. She started decorating her house to keep herself busy.

Catherine received a terrible email from Cindy and sent back an equally bad one, 'Fuck you, Bitch!' She felt sorry about that, but felt she deserved it. Aadi finally came to her house after she made a call to him. They discussed politics and also going to the U.S., but he changed the subject. He hugged her and kissed her and she felt better, but she was regretting her email to her sister. The following day Chain took her and the silver elephant, which was her birthday gift for Aadi to his house. He wanted her to come to see a CD hookup so she might decide whether or not to purchase one. They had tea, and each time she stood up to leave, he told her to sit and stay.

It was almost Christmas and Catherine had decided to write a proposal for Aadi to visit her country, not with her, but with Hannie. She felt he would only do this with the woman he loved, and it would not be with her, so Catherine planned for him to do this after her death with a substantial amount of money and her car. All this she put in writing and gave it to him. However, he did not respond to her proposal.

Chain was to have picked her up and taken her to Mass on Christmas Eve. She was dressed in sari and waited and waited, but he never came. Aadi had come earlier and given her a beautiful pink pashmina shawl and they had listened to The Three Tenors on TV. She had also made a lovely dinner for them, and Aadi had lit her candles on the terrace.

Catherine did not get to Mass because the stupid Chain could not understand she wanted him to come on Christmas Eve, not Christmas night. She called her mother at Monica's and spoke also to Karl, who seemed somewhat distant, which was probably due to his mother's influence. Jannu, Subhash, Tapasya and Kiddu came to her house Christmas night. Then Chain brought his wife and younger daughter and they invited Catherine to their house the following night for dinner.

Divyu called and invited her to his birthday party on December 27th. That was always a wonderful gathering of family and friends and haveli guests. Aadi was there also. Catherine saw him for only moments, and then he went with the men. Aadi's two nieces and his nephew were also there.

Catherine was being introspective, wondering why her sister hated her. Catherine didn't hate her. She didn't hate anyone. She loved too many and too much. She loved Aadi so much and she ached all the time with wanting him and needing him. She decided to phone him to invite him to come on New Year's Eve. When he answered, he told her he would have dinner with her. She felt comforted knowing they would be spending the last evening of the year together.

However, on New Year's Eve day, Jannu called telling her to come to the haveli for dinner. She told him she had invited Aadi for dinner and he said not to worry that Aadi would be there. She called Aadi and he had already heard from Jannu, so why did all that make her so sad? She had expected to be alone with the man she loved, but that was not to be. She dressed in her rani pink poshak and the pink pashmina shawl Aadi had given her for Christmas and went to the haveli for the last night of the year.

CHAPTER THIRTY EIGHT

A NEW HOUSE

It was a new year and Catherine was thanking God for all His blessing upon her. He had been good to her in so many ways, especially giving her wonderful sons and friends in India. What would she do without her loving family Ranawat at Kankawa? They had taken her in and made her one of their own. And there were the Youngs, her neighbors; Neeta, who walked almost daily with her and with whom she enjoyed her company.

Sheel Young was using Catherine's computer to write a computer workbook for St. Mary's School. Neeta came and watched TV with Catherine waiting for Sheel to finish. Then it was Suchana's birthday again and the family invited her to join them for dinner at the Trident Hotel. The kids loved going there, especially for the pizza. Catherine sat with the men and had a wonderful and fun time. She talked a lot and they all laughed and enjoyed the evening. The women were dressed beautifully and Catherine too wore a sari.

Aadi finally came to her house and she asked him once again if he'd go with her to the U.S. or if he wanted to go with his German friend. He told her he would go with her, not the German, but could not give her a time frame. Again he felt pressured and left soon afterward, asking Catherine not to 'hit' him, meaning pressure him. He came one evening in early February with a papaya and gajuk, an Indian winter sweet. He was very loving, kissing and hugging her and telling her that he would be out of Udaipur for 14 days on tour. He told her when he came back he would take her to Gujarat to see a doctor for her sore ankle. This filled her with so much love for him that after he left, she cried and cried with joy.

In the meantime, Catherine went to an orthopedic surgeon, Dr. Kumar. He sent her for x-rays and then a CT scan. She told him she would not consider surgery in Udaipur. But he said surgery was not warranted. He gave her prescriptions for medications and said perhaps a shot of cortisone would be needed.

Jannu called and asked if Yogi could come and stay at her house. She agreed immediately. There was a big problem with Yogi's mother and uncles. They were against him inheriting the hotel, which was just up the street from the haveli. Yogi's father was dead and his mother wanted her brothers to take over the hotel in favor of her own sons. Yogi was of age and wanted to take charge, but his uncles had him beaten up in the streets and his mother gave him no protection. She sided with her brothers against her own son. So Jannu, thinking to protect Yogi, asked if he might stay for a while at Catherine's, but Yogi did not come. She even thought he could come after dark dressed in woman's clothes, but he did not come. The Kankarwa family loved him and was afraid for him.

After many days Aadi came to her to have an injection. It was the 1st of March. He had just finished a tour and his clients had left. He was exhausted and had come immediately to her. He kissed her deeply and lay on her rug. She decided to give him a back rub, which he seemed to really enjoy. Aadi came again in another few days with papayas and mangoes and lay on her rug and fell asleep. Then they talked, but not about a trip to the States and she was getting scared. She gave him another backrub and when he was leaving he held her tightly, giving her a long, deep kiss. She felt his arousal and wished that it meant that he wanted her.

Aadi came the following day and lay on her bed and asked for a backrub. She gave very good backrubs and used Amway glycerin lotion to facilitate the rubbing. Suddenly she realized he was becoming very uncomfortable and she wondered why, and then he grabbed her and pulled her down under him and started to make love to her. He pulled off some of her clothes and then she helped him. Catherine was so surprised. It had been two years since they had been intimate, but she knew this was a terrible need on his part due to the backrub and for nothing else. She didn't care. She loved him and would give him everything she could possibly give him. He left the next day for Delhi.

The following week Krishna, Papa's sister from England came to Udaipur. She brought a friend, Brenda Hill, and asked Catherine if she would escort her around the city and environs. Catherine was pleased to do that. She found Brenda to be a lovely woman and excellent company. They took in the City Palace, the Lake Palace, the Jag Mandir and this brought many poignant memories to Catherine, since it was her first trip back since Aadi and she had been there together. They drove to Ranapur one day and toured Kumbhalgarh Fort as well. Another day they shopped, visited the lovely gardens at Saheli ki Badi, had a leisurely lunch at Shilpi, and went to the Trident Hotel to freshen up. There they met some people from Texas. Then they went on to the haveli. From there it was a short walk to the Shiv Nivas Palace for dinner by the pool, a fitting ending for Brenda's stay in Udaipur.

On March 17 Catherine took the family to the Lake Palace for dinner to celebrate the children leaving for Mayo, the boarding school in Ajmer. She dressed in a sari and went to the haveli in a rikshaw. They sat at a corner table and Jannu and Catherine decided on the food. After dinner they walked around the lily pond and the swimming pool and saw the oldest suite, the 'Sanjjan Suite'. Afterwards, Jannu drove Catherine home.

The next day at the haveli, Suchana asked Catherine, "Auntie, why didn't you ask Aadi to join us last night?"

"He is out-of-station, Suchana. I believe he is with his German girl. Besides, this was a family occasion – just for us."

Catherine was not satisfied with the service at the Lake Palace, but thought the food was very good. She told the kids, “Next time we’ll go to the Shiv Nivas.”

Tapasya replied, “I’ll be home next month.” She was very unhappy to be leaving.

Aadi came back after being with his German friend, Hannie. He came to Catherine, watched Cricket on TV and then had sex with her on the rug. He told her he would come the next day and they would talk. He did come, but Catherine had to drag it out of him to get an answer regarding his going to the States with her. Aadi told her he would only go if he could pay his own way, flying separately from her. He also finally admitted to Catherine that Hannelore had been to India and that he had been with her. He suggested that instead of going to the U.S. they go to Malaysia or Indonesia. He left the next day for Delhi to pick up another group for another 14 days. Catherine was devastated and weeping once again. He saw her disappointment and tears when he left, but obviously that made no difference to him.

She talked at length with Lisa who gave her a few insights. Lisa didn’t think Aadi was married, nor did she think Hannie prodded him as Catherine did. And she didn’t think Aadi shared himself with her anymore than he did with Catherine. These thoughts, although not a certainty, gave her comfort.

On March 27th Catherine went with the Youngs to see another house. She liked it immediately. The Youngs decided to live on the ground floor and the second floor was available to Catherine. It was spacious and all white marble, very airy with a terrace, although the kitchen was small. She wanted Jannu to see it, but he had hurt his back and he couldn’t come. The landlord, Talesra, lived on the first floor with his wife and one adult daughter. He owned a paint shop with his brother who lived in the adjoining apartment building. This building was on a quiet street, but not far from markets. Catherine decided to take it for Rs.8000 per month. It was less than she was paying at Nanavatie's. Jannu's back was still 'out' two days later and he couldn't walk, so he didn't go to see the new apartment.

In the meantime, Catherine had Robert draw up a codicil to her Will which included Aadi's having her car and enough money to travel around the U.S. with Hannie, after her death.

The First of April found Catherine busy with packing the last of her things and moving boxes and boxes over to her new house with help from Chain and his son, Mahendra. They worked very hard, and after three loads, she took them to the Laxmi Villas Hotel for lunch. Pankaj came to work on the computer, disconnected it, then had it taken by car to the new house to be installed there. The second day Catherine made five trips and paid workers Rs.1500. She and Chain had lunch at Shilpi and that night she slept in her new house, but woke often because of the heat.

Ishwar, Chain's son-in-law, who was an electrician, was very helpful to Catherine, going to her old house and removing all her light fixtures and bringing them to her new house. It was a big job, after which they went out for food, then came back and Ishwar connected everything in the new house.

The house was extremely hot, so Catherine had an A/C put in her bedroom so she was finally able to get some sleep. She was also waiting for a screen door to her bedroom and one for her parlor or sitting room. The screen doors were finally put in, but the workmen took three hours and the work was very poor. She wondered where these men were found! Catherine was anxious to see and talk to Aadi, but he was still out-of-station and she was getting nervous. She needed to talk to him regarding going to the States and she worried about it constantly. Then from Chain she knew he was home, but he didn't come. Her time was getting short, and she was feeling desolate.

Aadi finally came after she phoned him one Sunday morning, using the landlord's telephone. They talked about the house and he told her he preferred the old one and left when she approached the subject of leaving the country.

Then many things started happening. Atul and Anu came to see her and her new house. Atul didn't like the fact that there were so many steps to climb. Catherine thought this was crazy, that it was good exercise for her. Atul said he wanted her to see his uncle's house in Hiren Magri Sector Three. It was near Aadi's bagaji. Well, Catherine didn't like Hiren Magri, but she didn't tell Atul that. She told him she would be happy to look at his uncle's house. Then Aadi came to her house and offered to give her his bagaji to build a house on. She was flabbergasted. He said he would help her with the plans. He also told her to give him a day to think about going to the U.S. with her. Catherine was losing hope that he would ever go with her, but she kept praying for a miracle just the same. Then Jannu arrived with the codicil for her Will, which Robert had sent her.

It was Easter. Catherine went to the Vigil Service which was mostly in Hindi and consisted of nine priests and the bishop. It lasted until 2 AM. She was praying for an Easter miracle, but was not very hopeful. The following day, April 15, was the anniversary of Catherine's father's death. She remembered him with love and prayers.

Sheel Young was helping her to get a mobile phone and also connect her cable so she could get TV. She had to get the mobile in Sheel's name and was waiting for Talesra to put in a land line for her also in his name.

Aadi finally came to her, cooked lunch for her and they enjoyed it very much.

"Aadi, have you given our trip to the U.S. enough thought? Are you ready to give me an answer?"

"No, Catherine, I am not going with you. It would not make me happy. But I will go with you another time and when you come back I'll take you to the mountains."

"I see, well, I think you will be happier going there with Hannie, so I've made arrangements for you to do that after my death."

"What do you mean? What are you talking about?"

Catherine went to get the codicil and showed it to him. He got angry.

"I don't want this."

"It's an insurance policy, Aadi. When I die, you will be able to take Hannie and see my country and have the money with which to do it."

"I don't want this," he told her, and got up and left.

The following day Catherine went to see Atul's uncle's house in Hiren Magri. They sat outside in a lovely garden in front of the house and then proceeded inside. Catherine was appalled by the interior. She knew she could never live there. It consisted of one huge room. A tiny kitchen was off to one side and in the back were a bedroom and a bathroom, both very dark. Atul took her upstairs to the roof and showed her where Aadi's bagaji was just across the way, but she knew she could not live there. The house was totally impossible. Catherine also looked at Aadi's property and wondered about building there. It was a possibility, but something she needed to think about.

Catherine took some time deliberating whether or not to build on Aadi's property. Jannu drew up a plan which looked very inviting to her, but she still didn't like the location of Hiren Magri. Also she wasn't sure she should build on Aadi's bagaji. Finally, she decided not to build and stay where she was at Talesra's apartment.

In the meantime, Sheel was continuing to use Catherine's printer and she became concerned to the point where she asked Pankaj regarding this. He told her that so much usage would burn out the printer and she would need to buy a new one. She knew she had to put a stop to this because she couldn't afford to buy a new printer.

She was increasingly upset with Aadi because he would tell her he was coming and then not show up. She wondered if he planned to go to the States with Hannelore, but she was afraid to ask him.

Neeta came on April 26th and asked to work on her computer, but Catherine couldn't believe it when she awoke at 4 AM the following day to find her still there.

"Neeta, this is too much," Catherine told her. "You cannot use my printer like this. My engineer told me it would burn out and I simply cannot afford to buy a new one. This is not a professional printer. It's just a home model. You cannot use it anymore."

"Catherine, this is the same kind we used last year and nothing happened to it. It will be all right."

"I'm sorry, Neeta. But you cannot use my printer any more. Enough is enough. Now, turn it off and go home."

On April 27th Aadi came for his injection and invited Catherine to lunch at his home the following day. His parents were not there, but his sister, her husband and children and Jannu came. Catherine wanted to ask him if he was going with Hannie to the States, but there was no chance to talk privately to him. His brother-in-law took her to Kankarwa. She wondered, "Why him?"

The following day Aadi came to hang her curtains. She could have asked him about Hannie then, but she was afraid. Instead she asked him,

"Will we still be going to the mountains when I get back?" He took a very long time answering, "Yes."

"When are you leaving for Europe?"

"I don't know."

Aadi came the following day. They had lunch and then had sex. Catherine knew he didn't love her. The power was off and it was terribly hot and uncomfortable. When would he come again? She was so devastated and weeping the next day, knowing he would be leaving soon for Europe and possibly for her country with HER.

She spent May 4th at the haveli celebrating Tapasya's birthday and the next day celebrating Shiva with Aadi's family at his home. She wore a beautiful Rani pink silk hand loomed

Calcutta sari, which was admired by everyone. Aadi insisted she stay for dinner, but he didn't eat with her as the family was invited out.

Sunil met Catherine in Delhi at the Domestic airport. She left that night on Sri Lankan Airways. It was a nice flight and a beautiful plane. No visa was required. On arrival help was available to change money and a Taj representative called the hotel verifying her reservation. An agent got her a taxi for the long ride into Columbo. She noticed there was strict security in and round the city. When she arrived at the hotel, she was shown a room which had a terrible smell of cigarettes. Catherine immediately requested another and one that faced the sea. By the time she was settled, it was past 4:30 AM.

Catherine watched a wild sea as storm clouds passed over. She was thinking of and missing Aadi. She had eaten too much that day and also slept a lot, being so exhausted due to travel and little sleep. Her room was lovely and she enjoyed watching the sea and pounding waves. There was a thunder storm later that night. She had gone to bed early after a good dinner in an Indian restaurant there in the hotel. Catherine ate lobster tonight, about $25 market price. But it had been a very long time since she had tasted lobster thermador. This day she also splurged, buying four pairs of earrings, spending about $400, and buying a few gifts as well. The next day was her last and she wished she had taken more photos because it was raining and blustering and very dreary again. She spent some of her time having her palm read. On May 10 she left Sri Lanka early in the AM and arrived at Sunil's.

Catherine was home on May 11th. She spent the day at the haveli and then went to her own home and called Aadi. He did not come until the following day for lunch.

"When are we going to the mountains, Aadi?" she asked.

"Wait for some time," he answered her.

She was desolate. He didn't want intimacy and she felt bereft and very, very sad when he left. "Aadi has pulled back from me," she thought and wept that night. She knew she was on an emotional roller coaster and knew it was her own fault. She loved him and realized he could never respond in kind.

Catherine went to the haveli to say 'good-bye' to the family. They were going to the mountains for a holiday in a few days. When would she be going with Aadi? She continued to wait, only to be disappointed over and over again. Jannu called her and asked to use her camera on their journey to the mountains. She felt such sadness because she could not say she would be using it for her own trip to the mountains. She called Aadi and he already knew that Jannu wanted her camera.

"Give him yours," he said.

"So we are not going?"

"The camera doesn't matter. We can use mine."

Aadi visited her the next day and asked her where she wanted to go in the mountains, so she guessed he actually meant to take her, and hopefully soon. Then she realized she didn't want Chain to drive them and that she would have to explain this to him. It was selfish, she supposed, but when the three of them were together, she felt like an outsider. And this trip was meant for her and Aadi. She didn't want to share it with Chain.

Lisa sent her an email that she was looking for a fare to India in July. What a great joy and blessing if she could come! Chain took Catherine and Aadi to a nursery, where Aadi helped her choose plants. He said he'd come and transplant them for her.

Another week went by and Catherine felt no closer to going to the mountains. He kept saying, "I'll let you know", and it seemed hopeless to her. He had also put off working on her plants. In the meantime, Sunil Biswas and his family arrived in Udaipur. They came to Catherine's house and had chai with her and Neeta. Then they took Catherine with them to the Shiv Nivas where they were staying and had dinner. The following day Sunil never came by again or called to say 'good-bye'. She wondered why.

On May 23rd Chain took Catherine to the P.O. to pick up a package, but they would not give it to her without her passport. She went home for it and came back, but they wanted her signature as well. She became very angry and grabbed the package from the postman and took it from him. He fell off his chair unto the floor and she walked away with her package and out the door. Chain did not follow her. Catherine sat in the car waiting for him and four or five postmen came after her and rapped at her window asking her to come back. She ignored them and finally they went back into the P.O. Chain did not come out, so she left the car with her package and took a rickshaw home. She was furious.

Later her doorbell rang and it was Aadi's brother-in-law and his daughter to interpret for him. Evidently the P.O. wouldn't allow Chain to leave until she came back and signed a paper, so Chain had phoned Aadi. She told them she would NOT go back there, and they had no right to keep Chain a prisoner. They left and Aadi showed up, very angry with her. She got angry at him for not taking her side in this whole debacle. It was totally ridiculous! Finally someone from the P.O. came and asked for her signature and she signed.

As days passed she felt rejection from Aadi and decided she wanted to leave Udaipur if he did not want to take her to the mountains. She was not angry, just resigned. She was also thinking, during her prayer time, of asking Randall to visit her because he was out of a job and this would be a good time for him to come. When Aadi finally did show up Catherine was so upset she could barely speak to him and he left. Chain had shown up at about the same time and she gave him 10,000 rupees to buy a much needed refrigerator for his family. Jannu called that night to inform her that they were home. She was happy to hear from him, but otherwise she was still upset and weeping.

Catherine took Chain and his family to dinner at Ashwarya, an all vegetarian restaurant. Hemlata, Chain's wife, now had her refrigerator and was very happy. Chain told Catherine he took Aadi to his Ranakpur property where he planted thirty mango trees and had three partners now. They would open their restaurant at Divali. Her depression continued to grow, but she went to the haveli to see the family and to check her email.

She phoned Aadi the next day and he said he thought she was mad at him. Then he came to see her and had lunch. They laughed a lot and joked and just enjoyed being together, but had no sex. Catherine was just happy they were together, but he gave her no answer regarding when they could go to the mountains.

At the haveli she viewed photos of the family on their holiday in the mountains. They looked so happy and she felt so sad that she couldn't have been with them or have gone with her beloved Aadi.

Then a problem arose in her fourth bathroom which she used as a storeroom. Rats! They were coming up in the drain under the sink. Her landlord, Mr. Talesra, brought a plumber and he poured acid down the drain and then the bathroom was cleaned out for her and all the storage put back. Then Talesra called a cable man and Catherine paid 500 rupees to have a connection made to have a TV. Little by little she was getting settled in her new home.

It was early June and Aadi was still too busy to take her to the mountains and Catherine was weeping and distraught. On the 9th Aadi, his father and mother and Jannu went to the site at Ranakpur to do puja on the property. She didn't understand why this made her sad; except that perhaps she felt 'left out' and Aadi didn't tell her they were going to do this. Another rejection.

Catherine found another rat in her bathroom; a dead one, and a great stink. She called Talesra, who called the plumber again and he again treated the drain and once again they cleaned out her bathroom. Hopefully that was the last of the rats!

On June 12th Aadi invited her to come to Ranakpur with Chain on the next day to pick him up at the temples. They were to have lunch together at the site on his property. It was a totally beautiful day and the site was magnificent, set high in the mountains, overlooking a river and surrounded by lovely orchards and more mountains. The next day Aadi was to return with Brahmin priests for another puja. Catherine went to the haveli and learned from Suchana that Jannu also went to Ranakpur. This hurt Catherine very deeply. Why all the secrecy?

Aadi showed up at her house a week later with mangos from his property at Nagda. They talked only for a short while, and then he fell asleep on her bed. She lay next to him and watched him, but did not touch him. He slept a long time then rushed off to meet someone at his house. She had no chance to tell him her thoughts, or tell him how she needed him, but she was so grateful for the time he had spent with her.

On the 22nd of June she was thanking God for the wonderful gift of her Robert. It was his 39th birthday, and she was writing him, thinking that God gave her this beautiful young man whom He gave her in trust to nurture and love into adulthood. What a gift she was given! Thank You, God.

A couple days later Aadi came and talked to her regarding some property near Hiren Magri Sector 14. It was selling for $10,000. She would have to decide by that evening. He came later and talked about his garden plot and said she could build there, but he would pay her back for the cost of the house. She wanted to talk to Jannu about this, but his phone was out of order so she had to go to the haveli to see him the following day.

When she saw Jannu he told her that the property for $10,000 would not be developed for another five years, so she decided against that immediately. She was too old for that kind of speculation. Then Jannu drew up some plans for a house for Aadi's garden and she got more interested in building there. Aadi also drew some plans, and a couple days later told her that his father had no objection to her building on his property if she kept it simple and small because they insisted on paying her back.

On July 4th Aadi came for five minutes to kiss her 'good-bye'. He was leaving for Delhi that night and on to Germany. Catherine was devastated and weeping.

CHAPTER THIRTY NINE

DEATH OF A DEAR FRIEND AND NINE/ELEVEN

Catherine took the family to Shiv Nivas for dinner on July 15th the evening before Tapasya and Divyu were to leave for Mayo in Ajmer. Yogi joined them and it was a lovely evening. She kissed and hugged Divyu and Tapasya 'good-bye', but Tapasya was extremely unhappy to be leaving. She held on to Catherine, who let her love flow into her.

Catherine got a phone number, but as yet, no phone! Her cell phone was not working either. Catherine asked Jannu to help her with this, but he was unable to do so. Finally on July 26th she got her phone and Internet. She called Roland, Robert, Randall, her mom and Lisa, and was sure she wracked up a huge bill, but was so happy to connect with her family at long last.

Catherine's cell phone was in Sheel Young's name. It was the only way she was able to get one. Consequently, most of the calls were coming for the Young's. Early in the morning she had to get out of bed and run down two flights of stairs to give them the phone, or late at night. It was getting very annoying. When the bill came, Neeta gave it to her and she crossed off all but what was hers and paid them only what she owed. They didn't like that very much. They began sending their daughters upstairs for the phone whenever they wanted to use it and she refused. Catherine tried to have a private conversation with Neeta and Sheel, but they avoided her, so she sent them a letter. Sheel sent her a nasty note in return, so Catherine sent the phone chip back to him. That ended their so-called friendship. Perhaps there never was a friendship, only her feeling of being used. Two days later Sheel sent Catherine a long ugly letter, which she could have ignored, but decided not to allow him to think she agreed with him. She could not get to sleep after writing a response, and she was also upset that Neeta had broken her confidence by telling Sheel about her and Aadi's relationship.

On August 10th Randall emailed that he was thinking of coming to India. This was indeed a great blessing from God and Catherine was thrilled. She called him because her email refused to SEND. She now 'walked' him through the steps he had to take to get to India. The following day she heard from Randall again that he had his passport application.

Some weeks before Jannu drove to Jodhpur and ordered bookcases for Catherine. She needed them for her living room and wanted to go with him, but it was very hot and Jannu felt he could shop for them without her. Jannu had excellent taste and Catherine knew she could trust him to choose something she would like. Finally the bookcases arrived and she was so happy with them, although originally she had wanted three of them, she found two to be sufficient.

Catherine heard from Jim Galvin that his mother, Ellie was to have three by-pass surgeries on August 13th. Ellie was Catherine's best friend of many years.

She prayed for her safe recovery. On August 15th, the Assumption of Our Lady, Catherine was still praying for Ellie. She hadn't heard yet from Jim about his mom. Then she got word that Ellie had had a CVA, a stroke, the night before. The prognosis was not good.

In the meantime Catherine heard from Randall. He was getting nervous about coming to India. She felt this was her fault because she had been pushing him to come sooner. Catherine thought she had better back off. She had her chair and footstool reupholstered, and she put up curtains in her guest room.

Ellie was in a coma and on a ventilator since her surgery a week before. Catherine was praying that God would take her soon because the CVA affected her entire brain severely. She wouldn't want to live like this, Catherine knew. Ellie was stable and would be placed in chronic care because of her coma. Catherine's prayers and thoughts were with her and Jim especially. She believed Ellie would enter eternity that day, August 23rd because there was no hope for her and she had a living will. Catherine wept for her and for her family, especially Jim, and for herself, because she knew her time was also limited.

She spoke almost an hour to Randall that morning. He was reluctant to spend more than two weeks with her. It was difficult getting him to take her advice also in what he should pack and travel with. Then Jill, Ellie's niece, emailed and told her Jim probably would remove Ellie's life support on Monday afternoon. Catherine was weepy and silently saying 'good-bye' to her dear friend of 50 years. May the God of Love embrace and welcome her.

On August 28th her sons took Bran's ashes to Duluth and placed them in Lake Superior according to his last wishes. His brother Everett was with them. The following day she was still awaiting word from the States that Ellie had died. She prayed God would take her soon for the sake of Jim and her family. Catherine heard from Jim! Ellie passed into eternity on Tuesday evening, August 28th. Jill's email was so beautiful. Catherine felt she must respond with gratitude and appreciation. Her heart was sad and she wept that her friend was gone.

Randall received his passport on August 30th and Catherine emailed Wendy at Portown Travel in Duluth to ticket him for his travel to India. Randall didn't want to leave until the 12th or later. She was hoping to get him to India earlier, but she knew she must not push him. Robert called in the middle of the night. He'd lost the phone number of the florist for Ellie. He also told her Randall was getting things done for his travel to India, and she was looking forward to seeing him in two weeks.

Catherine received an absolutely beautiful email from Jill recounting the memorial service and burial of Ellie. She was so touched and grateful to her and wept again in memory of her friend. The next day she received another email. This one from Randall telling her he would not be leaving for India on the 12th as planned. Catherine was beside herself, after having ticketed him and now losing all that money. The following day Robert talked to Randall and changed his mind. Catherine also talked to Randall. She found him so afraid, so overwhelmed. He was so like his father. She ached for him to take charge of his life, to empower himself. Otherwise he would never know happiness, never live a full and complete life. Catherine felt she must pray for him. And she needed to be in Delhi on the 13th to meet him. On September 7th Randall had his ticket and his visa was on its way. Catherine talked to him and found him as relaxed as possible.

September 11th dawned in the United States and Catherine was watching TV in India. Suddenly there was a break in the news. Terrorists had struck in New York. The World Trade Center was hit by two airliners. She watched as smoke and fire arose from both towers and then both fell. In Washington DC the Pentagon was hit by another airliner and more people were dead. A fourth airliner on its way to California was hijacked midair by terrorists, but courageous passengers overtook them and the plane crashed into a field in Pennsylvania. It was learned that the terrorists were Muslims under the direction of Osama Bin Laden. Over 3000 people lost their lives that day, including fire fighters on their way up the stairs of the World Trade Center to rescue people trapped on upper floors. Many people jumped from higher floors rather than burn to death.

Catherine knew that Randall had to reschedule his flights because all airports had been closed and flights had been cancelled. She talked to Randall and he seemed to be taking this setback well; her brave, wonderful son. However, the following day she heard from Robert, who told her Randall was not coming.

He, Robert, was predicting WWIII happening very soon, like that very weekend. Catherine's heart was desolate, heavy and sad. She was in great pain with loss and disappointment. Catherine called Lisa, who affirmed the feelings of hostility in America over the terrorist attacks.

Friday, September 14, America's Day of Remembrance. This day was to have been a joyous day, sharing with Randall her India. Instead Catherine sat alone in her apartment weeping and weeping and weeping in sadness, grief, disappointment, and pain. She watched TV most of the day and night; London – St. Paul's Cathedral, Washington, DC – National Cathedral. America stood strong in her grief, sorrow, and determination.

The following day was the feast of Our Lady of Sorrows.

"Oh, Blessed Mother of Sorrows, hear the pain and suffering of Americans today", Catherine prayed. "And hear my pain too", which seemed so selfish in the wake of all the terrorists' attacks on her country. But she was filled with sorrow for herself and for her country.

On the 16th she was still totally desolate and weepy and could not even say all her prayers. She offered up her sufferings and asked God to help her. Then she heard from Jannu who asked her to come to the haveli. An American was there.

"Auntie, he's an American from San Francisco. I think you need each other. Please come."

"All right, Jannu."

He was a young man who was equally as distressed as she was and talking with him helped them both. However when she returned home she was again depressed.

Russell called on September 18th and told her Lesley was walking. She could hear her in the background. Mostly they discussed the attacks and the state of the world. The next day she was crying over the hopelessness of loving a man who loved another woman. Her heart was broken and her spirit was in the dust and her soul in shreds. However, that night, Aadi came to her and stayed for three hours. He had come home two days before.

At the end of the month Aadi called and told her to be ready by 8 AM. They were going to Ranakpur. Aadi, Nerpat, his little daughter, Himanshu and an architect picked her up and they drove to the site. It was a wonderful day, full of joy and happiness. There was very little time alone with Aadi, yet it was beautiful. The restaurant was coming along well. It was very big with views great from all the many windows. The sign was ready to be placed; ARANYAVAS, meaning 'Jungle House'. They had a hearty lunch and she and Aadi walked all over and took photos.

The next day Catherine planned to look at Nerpat's house in Hiren Magri Sector Three for a possible move. Chain drove her to Nerpat's house, but Nerpat was not there. His wife showed her the house, which she did not like. Chain had come in with her and they stayed for only a few minutes. She did not discuss her reaction to the house with Chain. They just went on their way. Later Aadi called her and was angry that she hadn't stopped at his garden before going to Nerpat's. He told her she should have 'used common sense'. Then she heard from Jannu that Chain had told Nerpat that 'Auntie didn't like his house. It wasn't good'. How cheeky of him! He was getting too bold and too outspoken for his own good. He had no right to speak for her. And she was angry.

Catherine was getting ready for her trip back to the States and Aadi took her for xrays and MRI of her back. She knew she had to have surgery because she was having a great a deal of pain. After the MRIs Aadi took her to Lodhas, who lived a short distance away and they had dinner with them. The MRI was very bad and she realized the surgery would not be easy.

Jannu called Catherine on October 7th to tell her the US and Britain attacked Afghanistan. She was deeply saddened and awoke to watch TV for a while. Jannu had been hearing talk about her in the market so it was obvious Chain had been gossiping. She asked Jannu to instill in Chain to stop talking about her, that he was possibly endangering her by doing so. Robert called to tell her he made an appointment with a Dr. Dulebohn for her to be seen on the 19th of November. That seemed to rule out Thanksgiving with the family if she would have surgery soon after that date. Then Russell called worrying about her and wanting her to see his baby.

Catherine received a surprise phone call from Aadi. He was on tour with a group and in Dharmsala and 'thinking' of her, he said. She was thrilled and when she hung up, she wept. The following day she went to Lodhas, had lunch with them and bought a lovely painting of Sonu's of two girls, reminding her of sisters.

Time was getting short and she wanted to see the kids before she left for the States. Early Sunday morning, October 21st, Jannu called her.

"Auntie, get ready. We're coming."

"What do you mean?"

"We're going to Ajmer."

"Oh, wonderful! I'll get ready right away."

Jannu and Subhash picked her up and off they went on the five hour drive to Ajmer. They stopped once for tea on the way, but since it was the Hindu festival of Navatri, Jannu and Subhash were fasting and could not have anything to eat. When they arrived in Ajmer they stopped at a shop and bought some treats for Tapasya and Divyarishi, then went to their respective schools to see them. The kids were so surprised and delighted. Because of the long drive they could not stay long, but Catherine was so thankful to Jannu and Subhash for taking her to see the children before she had to leave for the US. When they got back to Udaipur they drove to the haveli and had dinner. Then Jannu drove Catherine home.

Aadi arrived home and came to her the evening of October 25th. She was so happy to see him. They had chai, talked, and kissed many times. She loved him so much and enjoyed having his arms about her again after so long a time.

After many, many hours spent traveling to the US and long, tiresome flights, Catherine finally arrived safely in Minneapolis-St.Paul. Randall was at the airport to greet her and she was so happy to see him. They drove to his house and she talked to all her sons that night.

Robert called from Fargo and she spoke to Allison as well. Russell came to see her and told her she wouldn't be able to see Lesley until Tuesday. This was Sunday! Catherine was hurt by this, seeing this as a rebuff from Julie. But Russell had good news for her.

"You are to be a grandma again, Mom, in June" he told her. She slept intermittently that night, then the terrible fatigue left her, but she was aware the jet lag was still with her. It was good to be with Randall and she was hoping to see Roland, Anne, Kim and Bailey soon. She also wanted to email Jannu that she had arrived safely. Aadi was also constantly in her thoughts and she wanted to email him as well. After seeing her sweet granddaughters, Kimberly and Bailey, Catherine took Randall to Udupi, a lovely Indian Restaurant not far from his home. Randall loved Indian food, and they both enjoyed it.

Catherine's hands and feet were terribly swollen and her blood sugar level was a high 271. She found her clothes very tight as well. She emailed Aadi and Jannu and heard from both of them via email the following day. Aadi said he was wearing the gold chain she had given him for his birthday October 15th. Finally it was Tuesday, the 30th and they went to Russell's to carve pumpkins. Catherine was able to see her darling Lesley at last! Why did they make her wait until then?

The following day she went to St. Paul and ordered frames for the miniature paintings she had bought for her sons in Udaipur. Then she met Jim Galvin for dinner at Udupi, where they reminisced over dinner, sharing memories of Ellie. Jim showed her photographs and they talked long after the restaurant closed.

Another day she had lunch with Pat and Henry Gillis, then saw Al and Carmel Wawra. Al was failing in health and life was becoming difficult for Carmel. She felt the need to email Jannu and Aadi again as she missed both of them so much. Aadi sent her a loving email in return and her heart melted.

Catherine went to Mass at St. Timothy's. The celebrant was Father George, an Indian priest from Kerala. She spoke briefly to him after Mass. Then she decided to see her Aunt Ethelyn that day. Aunt Ethelyn was 91, very fragile, but still of sound mind. Tom, her son, and Cynthia, his wife met Catherine at her house and took her to dinner afterward with their daughter, Beth. They enjoyed a lovely evening. When she got back to Randall's, Russell was there to see her.

"Mom", he said, "I will bring Lesley to see you on Tuesday morning before you leave for Duluth."

Catherine thought it very strange that there were no other invitations to his house. She left for Duluth, staying with her dear Lisa. She had appointments with Dr. Huska for many tests prior to surgery, then took Lisa for dinner to the Scenic Café on the North Shore. It was one of their favorite places. Lisa made her think that her relationship with Aadi was truly beautiful and also thought he had no higher level of relationship with Hannelore than he had with her. Could that be true?

The following day was spent seeing and talking to old friends and packing for her trip to Oregon. On November 10th Lisa took her to the airport very early. She had to change planes in Minneapolis and arrived in Portland, taking a shuttle/van to Tigard Howard Johnson Motel for $30. Catherine visited her mom and then Cindy took her to dinner with her friend Arlene.

Catherine found her mother her usual feisty self.

"Have you combed your hair today? You haven't lost a pound since I last saw you! Where is your wedding ring? Have you gone to church?" Catherine found her very trying and noticed Cindy was showing great stress.

Joe and Janine Angeletti showed up late in the afternoon and stayed in the connecting motel room with her, but strangely kept mostly to themselves. Cindy invited all of them for dinner and later Joe made the observation that Cindy was 'a bomb ready to explode.'

It was Mother's 98th birthday and Catherine dressed in a sari for her party, after which Joe, Janine and Catherine took her out for dinner. When they brought her home she refused to be put to bed. Joe and Janine went back to the motel and Catherine stayed for some time waiting for Cindy who was not home. A male friend of Cindy's arrived, so Catherine felt she could leave. Later she received a screaming phone call from Cindy that she had 'dumped' Mother. Cindy was totally out of control. In the morning Catherine walked over to Cindy's and said a short 'good-bye' to her mother before leaving for the airport in the shuttle/van.

Back in Duluth Catherine visited and saw more friends and had doctor and dental appointments as well. Lisa took her to see Dr Dulebohn on November 19th as per Robert's appointment for her. It was almost an instant dislike on both their parts. He looked at her MRIs and told her they were 'old'. He was reading the dates backwards and refused her explanation. Then he noticed her swollen feet, which she explained were due to the amount of flying she had been through and that she had had a clean bill of health from Dr. Huska for surgery. Dr. Dulebohn told her his office had called Huska's office and Huska had never heard of her. At this point, Catherine got up, grabbed her MRIs and walked out.

After Christmas Catherine saw Dr. Huska again and reported her exchange with Dr. Dulebohn. Dr. Huska laughed and said many records had gotten lost over in Dulebohn's office. He then set up an appointment at St. Luke's Hospital for her to have a spinal injection of cortisone for temporary relief of her back pain. It was then time for her to return to India.

CHAPTER FORTY

I'M HOME! I'M HOME! I'M HOME!

Upon returning to India, Catherine and Suchana wept in each other's arms. They were so happy to see each other. Jannu was very bright-eyed and smiling.

"You were greatly missed, Auntie," he said.

Aadi came to her house, but only hugged and kissed her. Then he left for South India on tour.

The following month Catherine went to the haveli to talk to Jannu with a specific proposition in mind.

"Jannu, I need to talk to you about something very serious."

"Of course, Auntie. What is it? Tell me."

"I'm wondering, if in my last days, if I can rent a room here and have the servants look after me under the family's supervision?"

Without hesitation, he answered, "Of course, Auntie. The family will always be here for you."

"Don't you need to ask them first?"

"No, Auntie. I don't need to ask them."

She was deeply touched by his response, tears came to her eyes. There was so much love emanating between them.

Aadi returned from his tour but came to her only after she called him. He hugged and kissed her, but she could tell by his body language he wanted nothing more. A couple days later he came again and gave her great kisses. He was on his way once more to Mumbai for another South India tour. She wept again after he left, knowing and believing the man she loved would never love her. She reasoned that she was now too old to expect a meaningful relationship with anyone. She wrote in her journal.

> *'Help me, Jesus to turn away from sin. Forgive my sinfulness. Help me to live a life of holiness for Your sake. My life is nearly over and I look forward to eternity in Your Presence. Help me to keep my eyes always on this Prize.'*

Also in her journal on February 4th there was a quotation from Mark 5:19 *'Go back home to your family and tell them how much the Lord has done for you and how kind He has been to you'*

Once again Catherine was sad and weeping. She was aware that Aadi was home from his tour and he hadn't called her. Finally she called him and he sounded happy to hear from her. He told her he had been busy, but he would come to see her the next day. Aadi showed her yoga exercises, but she felt a distance between them and after he left, she wept.

Catherine reminisced in prayer that her sons had their own lives and didn't want her in them, except on the periphery. This made her sad. Living in India she hadn't given them up. They had given her up. This is how she felt when she had been living with them in the States.

Aadi came to Catherine's with a Mexican woman who showed her yoga exercises. Catherine was deeply troubled. Was this woman staying at Aadi's house? Was she traveling with him? He was due to leave the following day as was she. He was going to Gujarat. Was she also? Was he coming for his injection? Catherine was weeping again.

She went to the haveli and found Jannu at home. They had a long and intimate talk. He spoke about spirit and mind, believing that when they connect, they are truly great. Catherine found Jannu to be a most beautiful human being. She admired him, respected him and loved him dearly. Jannu was renovating the temple in the village and Catherine offered to help by giving him Rs. 10,000. However he told her he had to check with the family and pray about this to find out if it was possible to accept this gift from her.

In her prayers Catherine found herself confessing her great dislike of Muslims. She thought they created such violence and hatred in the world by their ignorance and fanaticism, which was all in the name of God (Allah). "How truly evil," she thought. "And I am supposed to love them." Catherine found this very difficult.

Sometime in March Jannu accepted the 10,000 rupees she had gifted him for the renovation of the temple. She was so happy to be of help because she knew it was a very holy place and very special for the family. And now she was part of it.

Catherine started going to Shilpi where there was a pool. She never learned to swim, but now she found the water so refreshing and cool in the hot summer. She had difficulty at first, but eventually swam across the pool, but never down the length. Chain brought her there every day and she thoroughly enjoyed it. Her back was giving her much pain and the water seemed to help.

Just before Easter Aadi invited her to Aranyavas with a couple of his friends. She hadn't been there for some time and found there was another building which was to become a bath house with toilets. There was a change to the façade of the restaurant. It was now elegant and had the stamp of the architect, but Catherine regretted that it no longer had the simple, common stone façade which made it so much a part of the land itself. She told this to Aadi, but realized he had little to say in the matter since he now had four partners. When she talked to Jannu, he shared some unsettling thoughts with her regarding Aadi's property and his partners.

Holy Week arrived and Catherine remembered all the past years of singing in choir at St. Michael's; the beautiful liturgies and all her solo work. It was so rewarding. Now, here in India this year it was the Hindu festival of Holi and everyone was celebrating the feast of color. Aadi came and 'painted' her very erotically. Easter Vigil was at the Cathedral of Our Lady of Fatima. Catherine went there and found it much better than the year before. Even so, the music was all in Hindi, but she received the Eucharist and got home at 2 AM, the liturgy having begun at 11 PM.

It was getting very hot now and she was using her A/C. Her back was paining her a lot and she was missing Aadi who was in Delhi. She was getting many emails and thinking of going to the U.S. in July so she would be gone when Aadi was in Europe. It was Randall's birthday – April 2nd – and Catherine was thinking of him and praying that he would change his mind and visit her in India. He was without a job and could easily come, but he was adamant.

April 10th arrived – her sister, Cindy's birthday. Catherine prayed, asking God's forgiveness and that someday they could at least respect each other. The Lodha girls came for lunch making it a fun day.

Srikant brought some of his first crop of American sweet corn and it was so delicious. Srikant Srimali was a new friend, introduced to her by Aadi. He lived only two blocks from her house on a large piece of property. It was his family home, but he had lived away until his father became ill. He then moved back with his wife and daughter to care for him. After his father died, he stayed to care for his mother. There were two houses on the property. Srikant lived in the larger one with Vimla, his wife. His mother lived in the smaller house. Bitu, Srikant and Vimal's daughter, had married an airforce captain and followed him wherever he was transferred. The property had gardens surrounding the houses where Srikant planted many vegetables. The last time Catherine had been in the States, she brought him many seeds including those of American sweet corn because Indian corn was a totally different species and very difficult to eat. The Srimalis were Brahmins and had two beautiful

Alsatian dogs, named Danny and Stephie. They were very fond of Catherine and ran to meet her whenever she came to visit. Stephie always tried to get into her lap, which was impossible due to her size, but she often stood by her and cried.

A few days later Aadi asked her and Srikant to go with him to Aranyavas. She was up early to say her puja and then was ready to go.

It was a beautiful day. She planted a Neem tree, but had no private time with Aadi. Last year she had been hoping he would take her to the mountains as he had promised, but it never came to fruition. Would it happen this year? Probably not and her heart was in shreds. Aadi, Shrikant and she went to Nagda and enjoyed a lovely brunch. Aadi was very distant and Catherine was desolate, becoming emotional and weeping when she returned home. She longed to spend time alone with him, and in front of others, she had to be very reserved. That day she experienced no fun.

Catherine was spending a great deal of time with the Lodhas. The girls were coming to her home often for lunch. She would put away all her photos of Aadi. Then she would be invited to the Lodhas for lunch and dinner, at which time they showed her albums of Aadi and his German friend, Hannelor. She saw the two of them in Hannelor's home and garden. She was very blond, buxom and short. Catherine was afraid to look too long or closely in front of the girls. She also saw a photo of Hannelor's mother. Thinking of these photos, Catherine couldn't sleep that night and just cried and cried.

She was invited again with Srikant to Aranyavas, but didn't have fun. She heard Srikant mention Hannelor. And then more sad news; she heard that her cousin Al Wawra had died. She felt very sad for his family. He was a very good and kind man and had been close to her family for years.

It was May and the temperatures were 110 degrees every day. Catherine bought another A/C. Her landlord had a paint shop but strangely he was unaware of a certain paint which when used on the roof deflected the sun and kept the floor below cool. She had heard this from Srikant and told her landlord about it. Catherine found this very humorous, but her landlord looked into it and immediately painted the roof and was amazed that it worked.

A five day puja began at Kankarwa Village. There were 15 Brahmin priests, among them Aadi's father and uncle. Catherine was so happy to be part of it. But she did not overnight with the family. Instead she left from home early every morning. She dressed in sari every day despite the terrible heat. Catherine felt truly blessed to be sharing in the worship of God in this holy place with such deeply spiritual people. She was exhausted and got little sleep each night, but was so happy to have had the privilege of sharing this with her family. They felt many good things would come to them after this and they included her in this also. After the puja, the family fed the entire village of five to six thousand people. She was so thankful to God for the honor of being a part of that very spiritual experience.

It was possible that India would go to war with Pakistan over the continuous border territories. The American Embassy was advising Americans to leave India and for Americans not to come to India. Catherine was saddened by this news and wanted to remain in India if there was a war, but she had to leave by the 10th of July and had plans to go on the 9th.

In the meantime she knew Aadi was entertaining his Mexican woman in Ranakpur. Srikant told Catherine he went with them to Aranyavas and then left them there. She was devastated, weeping and not sleeping. Had their relationship deteriorated so much? Would he visit her before leaving for Europe? She was filled with pain, sorrow and despair.

As war became more imminent, Catherine was getting calls and emails from her family and friends who were worried about her safety. She became sick with diarrhea, but was visited by the Kankarwa kids and that was such a joy to her. She stayed in bed and they just ran around and played. Srikant and Vimal came for a visit bringing their beautiful dogs, Danny and Stephie. From Srikant she learned Aadi was still in Aranyavas with the Mexican. Now Catherine felt Aadi had destroyed Aranyavas for her and she vowed she would never go there again.

She went to visit her family at the haveli and her heart was warmed and lightened being with them. They talked and laughed together and she spoke only to Suchana about Aadi.

Once again she had many emails from home worried about her safety, but she was not worried about herself. She was longing to receive Christ. It was Sunday, but she stayed at the haveli and didn't go to church. She was looking forward to Mass in the U.S. A couple days later, Suchana, Jannu, Tapasya and Diksha came for a visit and were all dressed up. Catherine felt so honored.

Srikant came for a visit and told her he had gone to Jodhpur with Nerpat, Aadi and the Mexican. They had chosen and ordered furniture for Aranyavas and had stayed over night. She had another sleepless night and more pain. How could she continue loving with all this pain? A few days later Srikant called her and invited her to dinner at his home, telling her that their friends, the Bhatnagars would also be there.

Catherine was so afraid that Aadi would come with his Mexican and she would have to leave because she could not bear the thought of being in the same room with them. However Aadi was still at Aranyavas.

Jannu brought two British clients to her home to watch the World Cup on her TV because the haveli didn't have that channel. She was so happy to entertain them and that Jannu felt free to bring his clients to her home. A few days later the kids called and asked her to come, wear a red sari and go to lunch. So she dressed up and took the family for lunch and had a good time. It was always wonderful being with them.

Russell called the night of June 11th. His baby was born – Matthew Joseph, weighing 10# 2oz and 23 inches long. He was a big baby. Catherine was so happy for him. She called her mom to tell her the news. She had tried to make peace with Cindy, but she refused, so Catherine prayed for forgiveness for both of them. Jannu and she were going to go out for dinner and watch the World Cup, but his stomach was upset, so they didn't go out. She gave him black tea and some antacids to chew while watching TV.

The Mexican left Udaipur on June 17 and the next day Aadi showed up at Catherine's house with Jannu to watch the World Cup match on her TV. It felt very strange to her. The following evening she went to the Srimali's for dinner. Srikant spoke of his disillusionment with Aadi, so Catherine opened up and told them of her love for Aadi and their history. Srikant told her Aadi had gone to Jaipur with the Mexican for tests on his leg and that he planned to go to Germany and Greece and then to Mexico. He was sending his medical records to Mexico. WHAT??? Such insanity! Who goes to Mexico for expert medical attention? Catherine felt the woman was pulling him there by his penis. She was sick at heart worrying about him.

One evening toward the end of June Jannu called her and told her they would all go out for a lovely dinner that night. She loved Jannu. He was such a good man; a man with integrity. If Aadi ever had integrity, he lost it somewhere along the way and she was sad and sick to the core of her being.

Catherine took the family to The Trident for dinner and only Suchana was absent. Catherine's stomach was upset because she had been taking codeine for her constant back pain.

It was July and time was closing in on her. Before the week was out, she would need to spend a day at the haveli, have dinner with the Lodha's, and another at the Srimali's. The Lodha girls would also spend a day at her house. And no Aadi! Had he totally erased her? When she had dinner at the Srimali's, Srikant told her Aadi was leaving for Europe in two weeks. The Lodha girls came for lunch and shared many of their sorrows. Finally Aadi arrived for his injection and stayed more than an hour. He took Catherine in his arms and kissed her when he left. He told her once again that he would go to America with her. Aadi's niece, Ninu phoned her and invited her for lunch on July 6, but Catherine was going to Kankarwa, so Ninu invited her instead for dinner. She was very touched. She spent the entire day at the haveli, went home, showered and then went to Aadi's for dinner. They had no time to be alone as he had asked Ninu to be in the room with them. He showed her pictures of the furniture he had bought for Aranyavas. It hurt her. Jannu called her before she left Aadi's, telling her to stop. She did and he gave her four jars of achar (pickle) to take with her to America to remind her always of India.

Catherine was so emotional leaving her home. She so needed to be held one last time by Aadi, but of course that wasn't possible. Her plane was leaving at 1:00 PM and she was going to Srikant's for breakfast.

It was a nice flight with a good lunch and then she slept until landing in Delhi. Sunil met her and took her to his home. It was a very beautiful new home. She was so happy now for him and all of his family. Deepa and her family lived on the ground floor in front; Tapa on the ground floor in the back. Sunil and his family lived on the entire first floor and his brother, Sujeet with his family on the entire second floor. Hopefully now everyone would live happily.

Her travel to the US was uneventful, but arriving in Minneapolis, she had to wait. Randall was late picking her up. However they stopped at their favorite Chinese restaurant and picked up some wonderful food to bring home to share with Russell, Anne, Roland and kids. Catherine held her new grandson for the first time and rejoiced, finding this to be a great day. She ate some of Jannu's achar and loved it, but no one else liked it. She spent most of the day resting and sleeping, trying to get over the jet lag. Then she went to Russell's to hold her two beautiful youngest grandbabies.

Catherine felt her days speeding by. She knew better than to ask Randall again to come to India. He was adamant, refusing to go, which made her sad. She did take Randall, Russell and Julie to Udipi for an Indian dinner, but only Randall really enjoyed it the way she did. Roland and Anne invited her for dinner and she wanted so much to see the little girls, but Randall wanted her to stay with him. However she needed to spend time at Roland's and see Kimberley and Bailey. Catherine was shocked and saddened to hear from Roland that he no longer believed in Christ. He told her that he was more attuned to believing that aliens had begun our life here on earth. Later she shopped with Randall and cooked supper for them, then watched a movie. She also phoned her cousin Antoinette and learned the sad news that her husband, Albert was dying of cancer.

It was time for her to spend time in Duluth. She stayed with Lisa and started making her round of appointments and seeing friends, but worrying all the time about Roland and his loss of faith. Lisa and she had a lovely lunch at the beautiful Scenic Café on the North Shore. She saw her friend Kay Reardon and visited Harriet Schwenk, who used to work for her. Harriet had suffered a heart attack, but was recovering well. Catherine had a dental appointment and then needed to see Dr. Austen regarding her eyes. During this trip she had had a cataract removed from her right eye, but her sight was not good with her new glasses. Dr. Austin sent her to a retinal clinic where she learned she had a very strange disorder; Juxtafoveal Talangietasia, swelling on the retina. There seemed to be no cause for it and no cure. Gradually her sight would worsen. They thought both eyes had it, so they didn't want her to have her left cataract removed until it was absolutely necessary, because this condition didn't appear until the right cataract was removed. They gave her laser surgery, but she didn't find any difference in her sight.

Catherine went to Mass at the Monastery, but missed seeing Sr. Mary Charles. The following day she spent two hours with Meridith, her spiritual advisor, who gently told her that God wanted her to be happy, and for her to ask God to help Aadi make better choices for himself. Hopefully she and Meridith would meet once again. She had moles removed from her back, but got no advice regarding her hair loss. She then visited her old neighborhood and saw old friends Bonnie, Bev, and Marsha. That same night she took Connie and Mike Kylmala out for dinner.

Back in Blaine, Catherine attended Matthew Joseph's baptism at St. Timothy's Church on Sunday, July 28. From there, she drove to Fargo to spend time with Robert and Kerry and her two oldest grandchildren, after which she drove to Duluth. A few days later she flew out to Oregon and saw her mom for another couple of days, staying at a near-by motel, her relationship with her sister in no better shape than before.

Catherine had about two more weeks before having to go back to India. She spent time with Robert again in Fargo and with her other sons and grandchildren. On September 23rd she was once again air-born for India. Flying into Delhi, she watched the lights below her and her heart sang. 'I'm Home! I'm Home! I'm Home!'

CPSIA information can be obtained
at www.ICGtesting.com
Printed in the USA
FFOW02n0245080317
33167FF